THE IVP NEW TESTAMENT COMMENTARY SERIES

Luke

Darrell L. Bock

Grant R. Osborne
series editor

D. Stuart Briscoe
Haddon Robinson
consulting editors

INTERVARSITY PRESS
DOWNERS GROVE, ILLINOIS, USA
LEICESTER, ENGLAND

InterVarsity Press
P.O. Box 1400, Downers Grove, Illinois 60515, U.S.A.
38 De Montfort Street, Leicester LE1 7GP, England

InterVarsity Press®, U.S.A., is the book-publishing division of InterVarsity Christian Fellowship®, a student movement active on campus at hundreds of universities, colleges and schools of nursing in the United States of America, and a member movement of the International Fellowship of Evangelical Students. For information about local and regional activities, write Public Relations Dept., InterVarsity Christian Fellowship, 6400 Schroeder Rd., P.O. Box 7895, Madison, WI 53707-7895.

Inter-Varsity Press, England, is the book-publishing division of the Universities and Colleges Christian Fellowship (formerly the Inter-Varsity Fellowship), a student movement linking Christian Unions in universities and colleges throughout the United Kingdom and the Republic of Ireland, and a member movement of the International Fellowship of Evangelical Students. For information about local and national activities write to UCCF, 38 De Montfort Street, Leicester LE1 7GP.

USA ISBN 0-8308-1803-0
UK ISBN 0-85111-678-7

Printed in the United States of America ∞

Library of Congress Cataloging-in-Publication Data

Bock, Darrell L.
    Luke/Darrell L. Bock.
        p.   cm.—(The IVP New Testament commentary series)
    ISBN 0-8308-1803-0
    1. Bible. N.T. Luke—Commentaries. I. Title. II. Series.
BS2595.3.B57   1994
226.4'07—dc20   *94-31572*
                                                                      CIP

British Library Cataloguing in Publication Data

A catalogue record for this book is available from the British Library.

17	16	15	14	13	12	11	10	9	8	7	6	5	4	3	2	1
08	07	06	05	04	03	02	01	00	99	98	97	96	95	94		

To the saints of Trinity Fellowship Church,
Richardson, Texas,
and most especially to the elders,
past and present,
for your prayers, friendship and discipleship:
thanks for modeling our Lord's love.

General Preface

In an age of proliferating commentary series, one might easily ask why add yet another to the seeming glut. The simplest answer is that no other series has yet achieved what we had in mind—a series to and from the church, that seeks to move from the text to its contemporary relevance and application.

No other series offers the unique combination of solid, biblical exposition and helpful explanatory notes in the same user-friendly format. No other series has tapped the unique blend of scholars and pastors who share both a passion for faithful exegesis and a deep concern for the church. Based on the New International Version of the Bible, one of the most widely used modern translations, the IVP New Testament Commentary Series builds on the NIV's reputation for clarity and accuracy. Individual commentators indicate clearly whenever they depart from the standard translation as required by their understanding of the original Greek text.

The series contributors represent a wide range of theological traditions, united by a common commitment to the authority of Scripture for

Christian faith and practice. Their efforts here are directed toward applying the unchanging message of the New Testament to the ever-changing
world in which we live.

Readers will find in each volume not only traditional discussions of
authorship and backgrounds but useful summaries of principal themes
and approaches to contemporary application. To bridge the gap between
commentaries that stress the flow of an author's argument but skip over
exegetical nettles and those that simply jump from one difficulty to
another, we have developed our unique format that expounds the text
in uninterrupted form on the upper portion of each page while dealing
with other issues underneath in verse-keyed notes. To avoid clutter we
have also adopted a social studies note system that keys references to
the bibliography.

We offer the series in hope that pastors, students, Bible teachers and
small group leaders of all sorts will find it a valuable aid—one that
stretches the mind and moves the heart to ever-growing faithfulness and
obedience to our Lord Jesus Christ.

Author's Preface

This commentary reflects over thirteen years of sojourn in the Gospel of Luke. I do not remember when I first became intrigued with Luke, but I do know that once I started to mine its riches I began a labor of love that has never stopped and that will never end. Both my doctoral work at Aberdeen and my teaching labors at Dallas Seminary have focused on this Gospel—so much so that my colleagues tease me by asking if there is another Gospel in the canon as far as I am concerned!

In another way this commentary is a natural extension of my journey of love. I had already spent seven years producing a two-volume technical commentary on Luke. Those who are familiar with that volume will quickly see the difference in focus between that work and the current one. When I was asked to join this series and produce a relevant, more accessible effort, I immediately accepted the opportunity to extend my labor in a new and fruitful direction. Having served in both the seminary and the church, I have learned to appreciate both the scholar's detailed, often-lonely labor and the pastor's relational work. The church needs both accuracy and relevance.

My earlier work on the technical commentary concentrated on accuracy and on addressing the discussion that currently swirls around Luke. Building on that foundation, this work focuses on relevancy. My notes and comments in this current volume draw on works that update the earlier commentary, especially focusing on the recent commentaries by Robert H. Stein and Luke T. Johnson. One never makes such a journey alone; one takes companions to talk with along the way. My companions, both technical and semitechnical studies, have been the voices of others who have made the journey through Luke before me and to whom I owe much. I have not always agreed with them, nor they with me; but they have helped me appreciate even more how deep the message of this Gospel is.

Technical commentaries are important. They aim for accuracy concerning the text's message, as well as trying to explain the rationale for that understanding. But sadly, the reality is that they are both underutilized and underappreciated in the church today. In the rush of pastoral duties and thus in the need to reach a bottom-line conclusion quickly, few pastors or serious Bible students take or have the time to make full use of a comprehensive, encyclopedic commentary. There is often just too much material to wade through as they seek the specific things they are interested in considering.

For Luke this is especially unfortunate, for the treatments by I. Howard Marshall, Heinz Schürmann, François Bovon, C. F. Evans, Joseph A. Fitzmyer, John Nolland and Luke T. Johnson are full of details that illumine the text. For the careful reader, there is much to reflect on in these works. One would hope that some of these volumes are consulted as resources and used judiciously for the wealth they provide.

Yet technical commentaries often lack one thing: a concern to develop faith's relational side. Technical works build a foundation for understanding a book, along with the "whys," but as we read them we don't readily grasp the way life should be altered as a result of our new understanding. This is not the commentaries' fault, since it is not their goal.

Semipopular technical commentaries have the value of editing down the details of a full technical treatment. Here one can see the options and parallel passages quickly and thus gain understanding more easily.

Still, they also tend to underplay application, concentrating on the book's message. Luke is also well represented in this genre—the works of Frederick W. Danker, David L. Tiede, Robert H. Stein and Craig A. Evans leap to mind. Each of these treatments has its strengths, with Danker being strong on Hellenistic backgrounds, Evans on Jewish and Old Testament backgrounds, Tiede in Lukan theology, and Stein in a solid survey of both the message and the scholarly discussion on the book. These volumes are also worth having, studying and reading.

Deep appreciation needs to be expressed to my editors: Grant Osborne, Haddon Robinson, Stuart Briscoe, Jim Hoover and Ruth Goring. They kept probing me to make my remarks clear and relevant and saved me from many an infelicitous sentence. They performed their roles above and beyond the call of duty.

A heartfelt dedication comes with this study. It is to the people of Trinity Fellowship Church in Richardson, Texas. I have now served there almost fifteen years on the pastoral staff and more recently as an elder. These believers have modeled what a Christian community should be like. I have treasured my friendship and weekly prayer meetings with the elders and my somewhat raucous Sunday-school classes with the *hoi polloi* (better known as the multitude). An example of their support is Herb Bateman, who read through parts of the initial draft with care and comment. If this commentary comes close to describing what this community models, it will have been well worth the effort.

Having lived with such resources and friends for more than a decade, I am thrilled at the opportunity to share my journey with others who desire to experience what God has for them in Jesus Christ through the Gospel of Luke. My journey, which began with deep anticipation, now reaches fresh heights of satisfaction, since I can share the tour with others and treat issues that influence how one sees and lives life as a Christian. I hope that our trip is an enjoyable one, and that as we see the sights we'll occasionally pause to thank those who have toured before us.

In doing so, I realize that yet another Companion was always with me. I cannot say that I have always heard his voice, nor that I always followed his lead, but I have known that I was never alone, even when my back was turned. A commentary has no merit unless it serves and honors him, for of all the companions along the way, he is the most faithful.

So whether your journey in Luke is a new or a renewed one, I hope that this commentary will serve you well as together we seek the voice of the One whom this Gospel reveals. May he lead us through this study on that even greater sojourn, the journey of life with him.

Introduction

A Gospel is a theological narrative about Jesus Christ; it teaches its theology while recounting the events surrounding this most famous of lives. It is told from the perspective of an observer of the events, who guides us through the actions and thoughts of those who occupy this history. It often makes its points through dialogue, speeches, characterization, plot and narrative comment. Such teaching often emerges implicitly, within the story and through the interaction of its characters, rather than through simple, reasoned arguments or clearly articulated propositional summaries (more common in epistles). This means that keeping track of the story's movement and its characters is crucial. Nevertheless, the theology of the Gospels is not less valuable than that of the Epistles, even if mining out its truth is a little more difficult. The Gospels are theology revealed in the context of life, clothed in flesh and blood. In the Gospels are found all the drama and tension of life. They are to be read and reread, each one on its own terms, since Matthew, Mark, John and Luke tell their story in very individualized ways.

This study of Luke will concentrate on his portrayal of Jesus and how it reveals Jesus' person, mission, values and ethics. Occasionally I will compare Luke's painting with those of his canonical companions, but for the most part we will keep our eyes focused on the gentle, rich brush strokes of his portrayal. Too often the beauty of the individualized pictures of Jesus in each of the Gospels is lost when elements from the four paintings are mixed together too quickly.

For a long time Luke was the most neglected of the Gospels. Matthew was the most popular Gospel in the early church, because of its apostolic roots. John was always highly regarded because of its explicit presentation of Jesus. Mark came to be an important Gospel in the nineteenth century, when many scholars began to argue that it was the earliest; its association with Peter also did not hurt its reputation. Luke was often the odd man out.

But one could make a case that Luke is the most pluralistic of the Gospels, so that it is tailor-made for the modern world. After all, it is Luke that discusses in detail how the promise of God expanded to encompass the Gentiles. This Gospel also contains numerous unique parables. Only this Gospel writer produced a sequel to explain how Jesus' ministry relates to the development of the new community that became the church. Luke also offers much teaching that deals with the ethics of relationships and with wealth and materialism.

Most important, Luke attempts to develop how God's plan met, meets and will meet its fulfillment in Jesus. The gospel is universal in perspective and cosmic in scope, and Luke's story explains how an originally small Jewish movement grew into a community that spans all nationalities. As we look at our multicultural world with its sometimes bitter ethnic divisions, certainly there is relevance in a Gospel that highlights how men and women of different ethnic origins can be transformed into a unified community and how humanity can come together in a relationship with its Creator.

So who was Luke, and why did he write this account of Jesus' life? Answering these two questions sets the stage for the commentary that will follow.

Notes: Introduction   This essay is an adaptation of Bock 1992. A brief overview of Luke's theology also appears in that article. This introduction limits itself to matters of

Authorship

Neither Luke nor Acts names the author of these two volumes, but information from these books and some external historical evidence help us determine the author and his background.

Within Luke-Acts, two major observations are helpful. First, the author is not an eyewitness of all the events he describes. In Luke 1:1-4 he indicates that he is at best a second-generation Christian, for he says that he has gone back to eyewitnesses for his description of Jesus' ministry. Second, he *is* an eyewitness of some of the events in Acts. The author is a companion of Paul in the famous "we sections" of Acts (16:10-17; 20:5-15; 21:1-18; 27:1; 28:16). Though some scholars have questioned whether the "we sections" indicate authorship, reflect traditional material or use a purely literary rhetorical device, it is best to regard them as places where the author speaks for himself (Ellis 1974:43-44).

Perhaps the major reason for challenging the authenticity of the "we sections" is the argument that the Paul of Acts is not the same Paul as is reflected in the Epistles (Vielhauer 1966:33-50). But this case is overdrawn and neglects the fact that how a person portrays himself and how another person sees him will not always be identical (Bruce 1975-1976:282-305). These internal considerations are important because they show that the author is a sometime companion of Paul.

Early church tradition has consistently named Luke as the author of these volumes. Justin (*Dialogues* 103.19), the Muratorian Canon, Irenaeus (*Against Heresies* 3.1.1; 3.14.1), the so-called Anti-Marcionite Canon and Tertullian (*Against Marcion* 4.2.2; 4.5.3) name Luke as the author. Such unanimity, when numerous Pauline companion candidates exist, argues for the veracity of this identification.

What is less certain is Luke's ethnic origin. Was Luke a Gentile (so most), or was he more particularly a non-Jewish Semite (Fitzmyer 1981:41-47) or even a Hellenistic Jew (Ellis 1974:51-53)? Important evidence is Colossians 4:10-11, which fails to list Luke among "the only Jews among [Paul's] fellow workers." But beyond this it is hard to be certain. Church tradition places Luke in Antioch of Syria, while Acts 1:19

the setting and the purpose for Luke's writing, as well as briefly covering some of his major themes.

describes a Semitic name for a field as a name rendered in "their" language. These factors suggest a Gentile but do not rule out the possibility of a non-Jewish Semite.

This racial background is significant because it makes Luke the only non-Jewish author of the New Testament. His presence gives a pluralistic perspective to the ministry of Jesus and explains why Gentile issues are so central for him.

Luke's Audience

Both volumes are addressed to Theophilus (Lk 1:1-4; Acts 1:1-4). We know nothing else about this individual. To determine Theophilus's concerns we must look carefully at the text. We do know he needed reassurance. The amount of material about persevering in the Christian life suggests that he is already a Christian rather than a person considering coming to Christ. In fact, the whole emphasis on Gentile inclusion, which continues through Acts, suggests that Theophilus is a Gentile who finds himself in an originally Jewish movement. But curiously and disturbingly, that Jewish movement is under intense pressure from Jews. He may be asking a very basic question, Do I really belong here? He is probably wondering whether this new community really is of God. Luke offers assurance by outlining God's plan and explaining why this community suffers. For Luke, Jesus is God's agent, and Gentiles *are* included in God's work. The result is a Gospel that highlights the beauty of racial diversity in God's plan, a theme not unlike that of Ephesians.

Date

The date of the Gospel of Luke is not entirely clear. Many argue that its emphasis on Jerusalem and the judgment associated with the city indicates a date after A.D. 70—sometime between A.D. 70 and 90. Two major passages cited for the view are Luke 19:41-44 and 21:20-24. The first text describes the siege of the city in detail and is unique to Luke's Gospel, while the second text highlights the city's fall while relating the Olivet Discourse in ways the parallel accounts of the discourse do not. This view also argues that Mark needed time to circulate and to be used by Luke. Since most date Mark in the mid to late sixties, Luke must be later. It is also argued that time was needed for Paul to have risen to a hero status, while others argue that the theology of Luke reflects a later, more "catholic" theology, with a more structured church than in the earliest period.

Several of these premises, however, are faulty. It is not at all clear that Paul had to have been an established hero figure before he could be a major character of Acts. Nor is it clear that Mark needed a long circulation time to reach Luke's hands. Bo Reicke (1986) has argued that the two Gospel writers may have been in direct contact. The debate about the catholic character of Luke's theology is also questionable (Marshall 1970:81-83, 212-20).

The one argument of potential merit is the focus on Jerusalem, but even it is suspect. Many of the descriptions of what would happen to Jerusalem have Old Testament roots. Like a number of passages in the Prophets, they picture what happens to the nation when it is engaged in covenant unfaithfulness (see Lk 19:41-44; 20:20-24 for details). Jesus' prediction of the fall of Jerusalem has exilic precedent. So there is no need to argue that a past event is in view.

Other factors suggest a date in the sixties. First, the portrait of the Jews' knowledge about the church in Rome suggests an earlier period. Second, the failure to discuss either the death of James (A.D. 62) or especially of Paul (c. A.D. 67) is surprising, if the book is late. In fact, Acts lacks any note about the outcome of Paul's initial Roman visit. Third, there is total silence about any fulfillment of the promise of Jerusalem's destruction—a surprising lack in two volumes that highlight fulfillment. Fourth, the mixed makeup of the church and the amount of attention given to Gentile inclusion suggest an earlier, not a later, date. The book fits a period when Gentile inclusion was still a live issue. This topic is central to the two volumes as a whole. However, it is hard to be more specific than "sometime in the sixties," since there is so little direct data to evaluate.

Though Luke's date is largely related to factors associated with the date of Acts, the literary linkage between the two volumes suggests that Luke and Acts were thought of as a pair in Luke's mind and were composed with each other in mind. They are tied together by the ascension, a crucial event that concludes Luke and begins Acts. The many parallelisms between the characters in the two volumes argue for a literary linkage as well. Thus it is likely that Luke's date is linked to that of Acts. As the first volume of the series, Luke should precede Acts only slightly in time of writing.

Purposes

Scholars propose many different purposes for Luke. Given the complexity of the volumes, it is unlikely that any one purpose adequately covers the entire Gospel.

The themes of God's plan, salvation's arrival and the triumph of God's Word about Jesus are certainly central. They permeate the entire Gospel, from the note in the infancy material that God is bringing his promise to pass to the Great Commission setting forth the church's mission as a fulfillment of promises centered in the Christ.

Others argue that Luke desires to defend God's faithfulness to his promise, offering a kind of theodicy to explain what has happened to Israel while defending the inclusion of Gentiles and the rise of the new Christian community. The Gospel goes into great detail to explain Jewish opposition and hardheartedness. Luke compares the Jewish nation's condition to the hardheartedness their ancestors displayed to the prophets of old. Such concerns, alluding to the pattern of national unfaithfulness first set forth in Deuteronomy, indicate that this purpose was also in Luke's mind (Moessner 1989). It also shows that Luke's view of history was informed by the ancient history of God's people.

Still another purpose was simply to defend theologically the social inclusion of Gentiles in the community. Though this theme emerges much more clearly in Acts, the groundwork for it appears in Luke.

Of course Luke's own reason for writing is to reassure Theophilus (Lk 1:1-4). But what concern needs Luke's explanation and encouragement? God's plan, God's faithfulness and Gentile inclusion are all worthy candidates for inclusion. And then assuming Theophilus will receive reassurance, Luke goes on to urge faithfulness and perseverance as the appropriate response to God's grace in Jesus. So there is a strong ethical note in Luke. The Gospel explains what a vibrant disciple looks like and how a believer lives in the larger, often hostile world. This Gospel is the most pluralistic of them all. We see how Jesus lived in the midst of a world that does not understand God. Jesus models how disciples are to live, since disciples are called to follow after him.

Major Theological Themes

The plan of God is a major Lukan theme. Numerous texts unique to Luke discuss this concept (1:14-17, 31-35, 46-55, 68-79; 2:9-14, 30-32, 34-35; 4:16-30; 13:31-35; 24:44-49). The clustering of such texts in Luke's infancy section shows how the theme is a major introductory note in the Gospel, a fact that highlights its importance.

The basic temporal structure behind this theme is the pattern of promise and fulfillment. The era of promise lasted from the Old Testament era until John the Baptist (7:28; 16:16-17). The era of fulfillment starts with Jesus' ministry and continues through his return (17:21-37; 21:5-38; 24:43-49; Acts 2:14-39; 3:14-26). Though Jesus brings the era of fulfillment, Gentiles are more open to the message than Jews, though there are those in the nation who do respond, a faithful remnant (Lk 2:34; 3:4-6; 4:25-27; 7:1-10; 10:25-37; 11:49-51; 13:7-9, 23-35; 14:16-24; 17:12-19; 19:41-44). Luke's emphasis on fulfillment explains why so many texts highlight what is happening "today" in announcing the arrival of God's salvation (2:11; 4:21; 5:26; 13:32-33; 19:5, 9, 42; 23:42-43). John the Baptist is the bridge between the eras. He announces that he is not the Christ, but the one who brings the Spirit will be the Christ, since the Spirit is the sign of fulfillment (3:15-18).

So the plan has a mission. Jesus will preach good news to the poor (4:16-30). He has come to heal "the sick" by calling sinners to repentance (5:30-32). He has commissioned representatives to take the message abroad (9:1-6; 10:1-24; 24:43-49). He has come to seek and save the lost (19:10). Even his betrayal and the offer of himself on the cross are no surprise (9:21-27; 18:31-34; Acts 2:22-24). "It is necessary" that certain things occur. Jesus must be in his Father's house (Lk 2:41-52). He must preach the kingdom (4:43). He must be numbered among the transgressors (23:37). There are no surprises in the events surrounding Jesus; they are a part of God's plan and Jesus' mission.

At the center of the plan stands the Christ. Luke builds his Christology from the earth up. Starting with a miraculous birth, Luke's portrait of Jesus shows he is special from the beginning. Jesus is seen as a teacher (6:20-48), a prophet (4:21-30), the Christ (9:18-20), the Son of Man (5:17-26; 9:21-27) and the Lord (20:41-44; 22:69; Acts 2:30-36).

Notice the progression of emphasis. The Gospel starts its portrait of Jesus in categories that are familiar to Luke's readers and then moves into deeper and more elevated aspects as the story unfolds, much as a person experiences Jesus. This allows readers to grow in their understanding of who Jesus is. Luke makes his case for Jesus a step at a time.

Christ comes to set up the kingdom. God's rule and promise are manifested on earth in fulfillment of earlier promise (Lk 4:18, 43; 7:22; 8:1; 9:6; 10:11). Some texts associate the kingdom as already present in Jesus' activity with his authority pictured in the power he exercises (10:9, 18-19; 11:14-23; 17:21). Jesus' miraculous activity underlines the totality of this authority. Other aspects of kingdom promise have not yet come and await fulfillment in the future (17:22-39; 21:5-38; Acts 3:20-21). As Acts 3 argues, what is yet to come in kingdom promise will fulfill the rest of what the Old Testament promised would come to pass in the Messiah.

The key indicator of the promise's arrival is the Spirit (Lk 3:15-18; 24:49; Acts 1:8; 2:1-39). The key event that allows the distribution of the Spirit is Jesus' resurrection-ascension. This event represents a key fulfillment of Psalm 110:1 (Lk 20:41-44; 22:69; Acts 2:30-36). As that text indicates, Jesus rules from the side of the Father in fulfillment of Old Testament messianic promise. His rule is indicated by his authority to distribute the promised benefits of the New Covenant.

So Jesus brings promise and salvation. Salvation involves sharing in the hope, experiencing the blessing of Jesus' rule from the side of the Father and sharing in the forgiveness of sins and the gift of the indwelling Spirit. It also looks forward to the glorious completion of what Jesus started by coming to earth. The Spirit empowers us for the mission of proclaiming Jesus and also for living an ethical, God-honoring life. Though Luke does not emphasize it, the ground for such blessing is the cross, which enables the New Covenant to be activated (22:20; Acts 20:28). To describe receiving blessing, Luke uses three terms for the same basic action: "repent" (Lk 11:32), "turn" (1:17; 22:32) and "faith" (5:20; 7:47-50). To trust Christ is to rest in his spiritual care and begin a journey that is to last until the promise of salvation is fully realized. Those who share this faith have formed a new community, not because they sought to be separate from Israel and the Jews but because they were forced to become a new community.

The nature of new community life is seen in various emphases including the call to love (6:20-48), prayer (11:1-13; 18:1-14), the call to be persistent (8:13-15; 9:23; 18:8; 21:19) and the need to avoid obstacles to discipleship, like excessive attachment to wealth (8:14; 12:13-21; 16:1-15, 19-31; 18:18-25). Luke writes not just to reassure Theophilus but also to encourage him to reflect those characteristics by the Spirit's enablement, to live in faithfulness before God.

Why Preach Luke?

There are manifold reasons to preach Luke. When we consider Luke's portrait of God, we see a God who controls history and yet is full of surprises. Who could imagine that the Savior of the world would so identify with humanity that he would make his grand appearance on earth in a stable for animals? Who could imagine a plan in which deliverance comes through the deliverer's death? God's ways are beyond figuring out; they must be revealed to us, and we must listen.

When we consider Luke's portrait of Jesus, we see a figure in whom are wrapped up all the promises of God. He is the second Adam, a prophet, wisdom incarnate, a leader-prophet like Moses, the Son of Man, the Christ and above all Lord. The book of Acts will tell us that because he is Lord of all, the gospel can go to all. Luke lays the foundation for such a message of redemption. More than that, Luke tells the story in a "seeker-friendly" way. He starts with descriptions of Jesus that reveal him to be a teacher, prophet and king—all categories we understand. Only as the story progresses and deepens does it become obvious that Jesus is more than any of these categories. Hearing or reading the story one step at a time, just as it was written, allows a person to grow gradually in his or her understanding and appreciation of Jesus. Too often we try to tell the story all at once and thereby overwhelm some who are just getting to know Jesus. Luke gently takes us on the journey one step at a time. There are hints of the finish, but he reveals them in such a way that the joy of discovering Jesus resembles that of finding a lost treasure.

When we consider Jesus' work, we get a fresh perspective on Jesus' death. Luke does not emphasize Jesus' death for sin as a substitutionary atonement—he leaves that for Paul. Rather, he highlights the victorious, exalted Lord who emerged from that death, along with the opportunity for forgiveness he provides. Here is the victorious Servant, the Lord who sits at God's right hand, ready to pour out God's Spirit on those who turn to him.

When we consider Jesus' miracles, we see the victor in a cosmic struggle. If Jesus casts out demons by the finger of God, then the kingdom of God has come in its initial form as evidence that Satan is and can be overrun. The power of God is greater than the forces of the underworld or the presence of sin. The believer shares and rejoices in that victory. Anyone struggling to live without being self-destructive in practice or in relationships can appreciate the power Jesus makes available to those who draw on him. Greater is he who died and indwells us than he who roams in the world to destroy us.

When we consider Jesus' teaching, we see Jesus at his most ethical and concrete. Luke shows how to love God through trust, patience and perseverance and how disciples love their neighbors through compassion and service. More than any other gospel writer, Luke puts working gloves on disciples as he paints a portrait of the call of God. In fact, Luke has more parabolic material from Jesus than any other Gospel. Luke is the Gospel that reveals the heart and mind of Jesus. It is here that we see how God cares for the sinner, the poor and the despised, the ones the text calls "tax collectors and sinners." Luke reveals how God cares for people who normally despise one another. Here Luke sets the table for the message of reconciliation and the possibility of healthy relationships, even across ethnic lines, that should be the result of a response to the gospel. Here we see Jesus relating in a healthy way with those of a different gender, valuing their contribution to the work of God. If believers wish to know what God would have us do in forming relationships and values, Luke is a beautiful port for reflective pause.

When we consider the Spirit of God in Luke, we see how the Spirit reveals, leads in praise, gives insight and produces boldness for ministry. The Spirit is a gift God provides to enable effective ministry to occur, especially in the face of opposition, which is inevitable for the faithful.

When we consider how persons can come to know God and the gospel, we can see how Jesus is the key figure in the plan. Luke spends less time telling the how of salvation than introducing the One who brings it. Coming to God in faith means knowing about the strength of the One who is trusted. The saving response of belief is described variously to underline its multidimensional quality. So whether somebody repents, turns or trusts, the picture is of a change of direction brought by that person's coming to God. That possibility of life change motivates disciples to pursue sinners and show compassion.

When we consider what God will do in the end, Luke gives brief hints of what is to come. He highlights an event, the destruction of Jerusalem in A.D. 70, that served as a sneak preview of the judgment that will come at the end. He mentions in a few texts the judgment Jesus will exercise before humanity as well as he evaluation of the stewardship of those who seek to serve him. Jesus is coming again. All people are accountable to God, and disciples are accountable for their stewardship. There is a kingdom to come where Jesus reigns with full authority, and those who know him will rejoice at the banquet table of his glorious presence. In the interim, those who have responded to the gospel seek faithfully to serve the Lord in thought, word and deed. The preaching of Luke explains how God wishes that to be done, assuring believers of their experience of God's grace and urging them to pursue the lost so that others can share in the eternal joy.

Conclusion

What I have told in a summarized, organized way here, Luke tells in a narrative account. His work is pastoral, theological and historical. God's plan removes old barriers of race and removes the obstacle of sin. The destroyer of the barrier is Jesus. Both Jew and Gentile—that is, anyone!—can belong to the new community. One need only respond to him. The promised Messiah-Lord, Jesus, sits at God's right hand and exercises decisive authority over the benefits of salvation. Those who call on him will be saved. Persecution and opposition are not a judgment against Jesus and his new community but reflect a hardhearted rejection of the salvation God has offered. Yet God's plan marches on. Being a disciple is not easy, but the blessings of Jesus far outweigh the fear of facing Jesus in judgment one day in the future. For he will sit as Judge of the living and the dead. Being a disciple means access to the Spirit and to rich blessing, both now and in the age to come. Such reassurance Luke gives to Theophilus and to the generations of readers who have followed him. God's gift of this Gospel reveals his desire to encourage his children and call them to deeper faithfulness. It is our calling to hear his voice.

Outline of Luke

COMMENTARY

☐ Preface: An Invitation to Be Reassured (1:1-4)

Things are not always as they seem. Sometimes what most hinders our perception of what God is doing is our own expectation of what God should do or would do. For example, we might assume that God's saving plan, sovereignly introduced into the world by an omnipotent God, would be carried out quite straightforwardly, like a championship team steaming through the playoffs to a triumphant Super Bowl or World Cup victory. Surely God would vanquish all foes and would be embraced by all people, especially when he reveals his messenger with wondrous displays of power. Some groups within Judaism had always hoped for such a day (*Psalms of Solomon* 17—18; *Testament of Levi* 18; *Testament of Judah* 24). They expected that once God came to deliver, he would do so by mightily overthrowing all opposition. Then God would grant salvation to his people and rule in glorious power. Surely this is how God would save a world desperate for rescue.

But the message of the gospel has never been popular. Despite the wondrous works associated with Jesus' ministry, the world did not embrace him with open arms. Jesus' honesty about the human condition met with rejection and resistance. Many fled from the mirror held up in his words. Others fought his teaching and sought to crush his message. Those who did recognize the image Jesus described and realized their deep need for God were going against the grain. They became reminders that life is not defined by independence but by dependence. The question became on whom or what did one depend to define and find life.

The Gospel of Luke is about life and God's plan. It is a story written to a man, Theophilus, who in all likelihood was a believer who needed reassurance (1:4). A Gentile in the midst of what had originally been a Jewish movement, he seems to have been asking whether he really should be a Christian. Had God really called all nations to enter into life with God? Was a crucified Messiah the beacon of hope for both Jews and Gentiles? Would God really save through a ministry that ended with crucifixion? What about the endless obstacles the church was suffering in getting its message out into the world? Might the obstacles not be a sign of God's judgment on a message gone awry, rather than evidence of blessing? Questions like these probably haunted Theophilus. They are not unlike questions we might raise as we contemplate what God has done and imagine how we might have done it differently.

This is why Luke wrote his Gospel: to explain how the God of design and grace works out his will through Jesus, the ascended Messiah-Lord. Luke wishes to make clear how Jesus is Lord of all, so the gospel can go to all. He also wishes to explain the journey that is salvation. To be saved involves coming to Jesus in faith, but the act of faith is only a first step in a journey that many others do not understand. How does the salvation-traveler face life in the midst of great opposition? In sum, Luke's Gospel, as his preface makes clear, is a reassurance that through Jesus one *can* know God and experience life as God designed it.

Luke introduces his topic with a formal literary preface that explains why he writes a Gospel though others have already presented the life of Jesus (1:1-4). Luke seeks to build carefully on precedent. By doing so he hopes to strengthen Theophilus's faith. As we read Luke's account, we realize that Theophilus is not alone in his need to be reassured. In each generation there are many like him.

The Precedents (1:1-2) Luke's preface fits the ancient pattern in which a writer explains the rationale for his work (2 Maccabees 2:19-31; Josephus *Antiquities* 1. *proem.* 1-4, and *Against Apion* 1.1 §§1-5; *Epistle to Aristeas* 1-8; Lucian *How to Write History* 9, 39-40, 53-55). Luke con-

Notes: 1:1-4 In light of verse 4, it is quite likely that Theophilus is a Christian. What is uncertain is his ethnic origin. Is he a Gentile (Stein 1992:26) or a Semite who is not a Jew (Fitzmyer 1981:57-59, 300)? It is even possible that he was a God-fearer before becoming a believer, since Luke's story seems to assume a clear knowledge of many Jewish practices and of numerous details of the history of the ancient people of God. It is unlikely that he is a Roman government official, though he may well be of high social status, given the

sciously introduces his work to show where it fits in ancient literary terms. Some speak of Luke as "apologetic historiography" (Sterling 1991), but Luke is writing more for internal exhortation, so that any apologetic has a pastoral purpose.

Luke describes his work as a narrative, *an account (diēgēsis)*. Such narratives came in both oral (8:39; 9:10) and written forms (Heb 11:32). The ambiguity of the term means that Luke may be referring to more than the sources biblical scholars mention today when they discuss the Synoptic problem (Mark, Q, L, M or Matthew). However, the remark that *many have undertaken to draw up* (literally, "many have set their hand to"; *epecheirēsan*) such an account suggests mostly written sources. It is important to remember that the ancient world did not have the printed page, and written texts were not in wide circulation. The fact that *many* had undertaken to prepare an account shows Jesus' importance.

What these accounts discussed were *the things that have been fulfilled among us*. This detail raises an important Lukan theme right at the start. The events surrounding Jesus fulfilled the plan of God. Numerous passages make this point (1:20, 57; 2:6, 21-22; 4:21; 9:31; 21:22, 24; 24:44-47). The *us* in v. 2 includes all those who experienced the effects of Jesus' presence up to the time of Luke's writing. All those who shared in the realization of what God brought in Jesus share in the experience of fulfillment.

Now these accounts had sources who *handed down (paredosan)* the story of Jesus, *eyewitnesses* who became ministers of the Word. Luke's stress here is the credibility of the sources, since they saw firsthand what has been described in the tradition. Luke makes a key point—the tradition about Jesus had roots in the experience of those who preached about him. These witnesses were with Jesus from the beginning. Thus these first two verses mention at least two generations: those who preached Jesus and those who recorded what was preached. There was precedent for what Luke was doing, both in terms of larger ancient

courtesy with which he is addressed in verse 3. For an early church tradition regarding his origin, see Pseudo-Clementine *Recognitions* 10.71. For the phrase "O *most excellent,"* see Acts 23:26; 24:3; 26:25.

1:2 *Handed down* is a technical term for the communication of tradition (Mk 7:13; 1 Cor 11:2, 23; 15:3; Jude 3).

history and in terms of the story of Jesus.

Luke's Approach (1:3-4) There is debate whether Luke's choice to write after his predecessors was a critique of their effort. Some suggest that the writing must mean he was unhappy with previous efforts (L. T. Johnson 1991:29-30). But the words *it seemed good also to me (edoxe kamoi)* show Luke joining himself with his predecessors. It is likely that he engages in the effort because he knows he can add to the portrait of Jesus currently in circulation, but Luke is not unappreciative of the previous efforts. His predecessors blazed a difficult trail ahead of him. Luke's contribution will add a unique sequel to the portrait, Acts, and will bring in much new detail about Jesus, since virtually half of the material in Luke's Gospel does not appear in the other Gospels we possess. The other Synoptics help us to see what Luke's alternatives were like; he includes much more teaching material, especially parabolic material.

Four characteristics mark Luke's approach to his task. First, he *investigated (parēkolouthēkoti)* the story. This appears to refer to the fact he studied his topic. Luke was not himself an eyewitness to the events of Jesus' life. So only his study could produce such a work. But we should not think of Luke in a library here. He would have traveled through the community gathering information, both from recorded texts and from conversations with others who had seen Jesus.

Second, Luke went back to *the beginning (anōthen)*. This is why the story starts with John the Baptist. This Jewish prophet was the starting point of the renewal of God's activity, as Luke 1—2 will make clear.

Third, his study was thorough: he says he studied *everything (pasin)*. Though what we have in Luke is surely a select collection of material, the Gospel writer wants it known that he did his homework. Luke was very concerned to get the story right, to be accurate in his portrayal of Jesus.

Fourth, Luke did his work *carefully (akribōs)*. As the Gospel itself reveals, Luke's work is thought out and precise in its development of the story.

Luke calls his account an *orderly* one *(kathexēs)*. For some this means

1:4 On the term *know the certainty* or "assurance" *(asphaleia)*, see Acts 2:36, 21:34, 22:30

he wrote in chronological sequence. But such a meaning is unlikely here. He has done some rearranging of the order of events for thematic or literary reasons (for example, 4:16-30; the order of the temptations in 4:1-13; the placement of John's arrest in 3:19-20).

There is a geographic flow to the order: Galilee through Samaria to Jerusalem. But above all, the order seems to be redemptive-historical. Luke is concerned to trace the progress of God's redeeming work in Jesus, especially by highlighting his teaching and the rise of opposition to him. The emphasis on promise-fulfillment also suggests this sort of order. The Gospel is roughly chronological, but not precisely so. More important to Luke is revealing how God worked through Jesus. This is "sacred history" revealing the order of God's plan.

All the care Luke gives to the task, as noted in his preface, is designed to reassure Theophilus, who has been *taught (katēchēthēs)* on such matters previously. Whatever pressure this believer is under, he should be confident that God has moved to fulfill his plan through Jesus. Luke is carefully building on precedent to tell anew the story of Jesus. Like a pastor comforting a believer under siege by the world, so Luke wishes to encourage his readers. Theophilus may well be asking, "Is Christianity what I believed it to be, a religion sent from God?" Whether it is internal doubt, persecution or racial tension with Jews that has caused this question to be raised, Luke invites his reader to consider the story of Jesus again and know that these indeed were events *that have been fulfilled among us.*

□ Infancy Narrative (1:5—2:52)

How does one extract theology from a narrative? The infancy material in Luke 1:5—2:52 is an example of a narrative text that is full of theology. It (1) reviews and previews events, (2) uses scriptural quotations and allusions to reveal God's purpose, (3) reveals that purpose through dialogue from God's commissioned agents, and (4) gives testimony through reliable characters within the account (Tannehill 1986:21). In fact, these first two chapters serve as an overture to the Gospel, revealing the major themes that Luke will develop throughout his portrayal of

---

and 25:26. It refers to being emotionally assured of or determining the facts with accuracy.

Jesus. Even the style in these chapters differs from the rest of the book, as it mimics the style of the Greek Old Testament. This is a neat literary touch, for it signals the recounting of sacred events. By explaining the relationship of John the Baptist to Jesus, Luke notes how the torch of God's plan is relit and moves ahead.

John is the major focus of Luke 1:5-25, 46-80, while Jesus is the subject in Luke 1:26-38 and 2:1-40. Technically the infancy material ends at 2:40, since the scene of 2:41-52 involves Jesus' actions as a young adolescent. However, in literary terms the section extends through this passage, since the note about Jesus' growth in 2:52 parallels the note about John's growth in 1:80. As we shall see, the section is rich in theology, but three points stand out: (1) Jesus is superior to John, (2) God is bringing to pass what he promised long ago, and (3) what God promises now through his Word will come to pass. Even the amount of time spent on Jesus versus John reveals the first point, while the second and third points emerge in how the infancy story is told.

Announcing the Forerunner, John the Baptist (1:5-25) The announcement of John the Baptist's birth signals God's renewed activity on behalf of his people in light of promises made long ago. Many of the details of this event and those that follow in the infancy section recall events of the Old Testament. God is again at work to bring his promise to pass.

A Tragic Situation (1:5-7) When God acts to fulfill his promises, he meets a wide array of needs. After a long period of silence, here God acts in the time of Herod the Great to begin realizing key aspects of his plan. Though he is concerned to fulfill his promises to Israel, God is also meeting the personal needs of a righteous couple.

Notes: 1:5 For an ancient's description of the rule of Herod the Great, 37-4 B.C., see Josephus *Jewish Wars* 1 §§203-669. Though sects like those at Qumran were an exception, many in Judaism believed that God, though still addressing and caring for the nation, was not revealing himself to them by revelation (2 Baruch 85:1-3; 1 Maccabees 4:46; 9:27; 14:41). Luke's description of events in this section and his style mimicking the Old Testament would indicate that God is renewing his activity on behalf of the nation.

1:6 Luke's description of the parents highlights their righteousness by using terms common of significant saints: *upright* (Deut 6:25; 24:13; Ps 106:31; Susanna 3 LXX; Sirach 44:17) and *observing all the Lord's commandments and regulations* (Gen 26:5; Deut 28:3; 1 Sam 1:3, 5; 1 Kings 3:14; 1 Maccabees 2:21; *Testament of Levi* 14:4). This does not mean that

Luke introduces the parents of John as pious, law-abiding saints. Thus from its very beginning the new movement of God is steeped in righteousness. Yet despite their righteousness, they have suffered the disappointment of barrenness, a condition Elizabeth will later refer to as a *disgrace* (v. 25). Elizabeth's feelings are perfectly understandable, but to be barren is not an indication of the presence of sin or of condemnation; it may be an opportunity for blessing, whether God grants a child late in life or allows a couple to pursue other opportunities of service. In Scripture, when God allows a woman to be barren, he often has something special in mind for her (Sarah, Gen 18:11; Rebekah, Gen 25:21; Rachel, Gen 29:31; Samson's mother, Judg 13:2, 5; Hannah, 1 Sam 1—2). Aware of this pattern, the rabbis of Judaism argued that when Scripture says, "She has not," God gave a child (*Genesis Rabbah* 38). So in the case of Elizabeth and Zechariah, God's action parallels the way he often worked among the fathers and mothers of Jewish faith. His word and plan are coming to pass again.

The Announcement of John's Birth (1:8-23) The announcement of John's birth comes at a high moment in Zechariah's career. As one of about eighteen thousand priests, Zechariah serves in the temple twice a year, but only once in his life does he get to assist in the daily offering by going into the holy place. This honor had fallen to him by *lot* (*m. Tamid* 5:2—6:3). His job was to offer *incense,* a picture of intercession rising to God (Ps 141:2; Rev 5:8; 8:3-4). Everything about the announcement's timing points to a moment of high piety. Zechariah goes in while the people are praying. A later prayer from the Targum of Canticles 4:6 may well express their thoughts: "May the merciful God enter the Holy Place and accept with favor the offering of his people."

As Zechariah offers up the incense and prayer, *an angel* appears.

---

they were sinless, but it does mean that they faithfully looked to God to deal with their lives, including their shortcomings.

1:8 The number 18,000 emerges from information in the *Letter to Aristeas* 95, which notes that about 750 priests were a part of each of the 24 divisions of the priesthood. So 24 times 750 is 18,000. On the 24 divisions in the priesthood, see 1 Chronicles 24:7-18. Zechariah belongs to the eighth division of Abijah (Lk 1:5). Details of how the daily offering proceeded are in *m. Yoma* 2:2-4 and *m. Tamid* 6—7. This offering took place at 9:00 a.m. and 3:00 p.m. each day. Given the nature of the crowd, most scholars believe an evening offering is in view here (Josephus *Antiquities* 14.4.3 §65; *m. Pesaḥim* 5:1).

Angelic visitations to announce births of major figures are common in the Old Testament (Gen 16:10-11; 17:15-19; 18:10-15; 25:23; Judg 13:3-21). This announcement is unusual, however, in that the father rather than the mother receives the message. The angel's arrival produces fear in the priest. He senses the presence of God's agent (Lk 1:29-30; 1:65; 2:9; 5:8-10, 26; 7:16; 8:37; 9:34) and is taken back by this surprising development.

The angelic announcement proceeds in stages: the child's name (v. 13), the response to the child (v. 14), the position and character of the child (v. 15) and the mission of the child (vv. 16-17). Zechariah's *prayer* is being answered. Since he had given up believing that God would give him a child (v. 18), his prayer has probably been focused on the nation's hope, especially since much of the angel's message focuses on this point. Nonetheless, the child will also fulfill the personal desire of Zechariah and Elizabeth, being a cause of *joy and delight* for them and for many in the nation. So God is tackling two requests at once, one national and the other personal, a prayer that had long since been abandoned and all but forgotten. Sometimes God's answers to prayer come in surprising ways after a long time.

The child will be named *John.* When God names a child, that child is especially significant in God's plan (Gen 16:8, 11; 17:19; 1 Kings 13:2; Is 7:14; 49:1; Mt 1:21; Lk 1:31). This child will be *great* before God. In Luke 7:28 Jesus says that no one greater had been born of woman before John. His greatness emerges from his prophetic role and from his function as a forerunner to Jesus, as the rest of Luke 1 makes clear.

John is to live an ascetic life of discipline. This will stand in contrast to Jesus (7:31-35). The refusal to drink shows a special consecration, and the language recalls the description of the prophet Samuel, Israel's first prophet (1 Sam 1:11). Since the angel does not say that John should not cut his hair, however, he is probably not being called on to take a Nazirite vow (Num 6:1-21; Judg 13:4-5).

More important, the child will be empowered by the Spirit *even from birth* (that is, from his mother's womb). The Spirit is very active in these opening chapters (see 1:35, 41, 67; 2:25-27). This promise has an initial

---

1:11 The Greek verb *ōphthē (appeared)* is often used by Luke for supernatural appearances

fulfillment in the events of Luke 1:39-45, especially verse 44. But the Spirit's abiding with John is an intensification of the Spirit's presence among Old Testament prophets (contrast with 1 Sam 10:10; 2 Kings 2:9-16; see Is 61:1; Ezek 11:5; Joel 2:28). Everything about these events shows that they hark back to the great era of old, but reveal an escalation of God's work and thus the approach of a new era.

John will be a prophet. His call to the people to repent will be detailed in 3:1-20. Here the angel describes his ministry as preparing a remnant for God: *Many of the people of Israel will he bring back to the Lord.* In other words, he will turn Israel to the Lord their God. The expression "to turn" has Old Testament roots (Deut 30:2; Hos 3:5; 7:10). John will redirect those who respond to his message toward a walk with God. In fact, he will be like Elijah in his ministry (1 Kings 17—18; Mal 4:5; Sirach 48:10). In speaking of turning the hearts of parents to their children, Luke is indicating that reconciliation with God will produce reconciliation elsewhere. When God touches a life, relationships with others on this earth are also touched. So John will *make ready a people prepared for the Lord.* This language recalls Isaiah 43:7 and 2 Samuel 7:24. This will be a nation of people God has called to himself, a faithful remnant sharing in the realization of God's promise because they have turned to him.

Zechariah's response, though coming from a pious man, is very human. He does not take the miraculous as a matter of course. He has a natural objection to the promise that they will receive a child: their old age. Zechariah understands the basics of biology and aging. He and his wife are "past their prime."

In response, the angel announces his name, Gabriel, and indicates that God will bring his promise to pass. The angel's giving his name and position communicates that his message is to be accepted as coming from the throne room of heaven. Zechariah, righteous as he is, needs to learn that God will fulfill his promises when he sovereignly chooses to act. The God of heaven may even do things out of the ordinary. The major lesson in this announcement for the priest, as well as for Luke's readers, is that God will do what he promises in his own way.

(Lk 24:34; Acts 2:3; 7:2, 30, 35; 9:17; 13:31; 16:9; 26:16).

To drive the point home, Zechariah becomes temporarily deaf and dumb. This short-term judgment from God allows the priest to reflect on what he must learn. As Luke 1:56-79 shows, Zechariah will learn from his time of silence. The angel is explicit that the reason for the imposition of muteness is that Zechariah *did not believe* the angel's words. Sometimes we experience trial so that we can learn to trust God more.

The crowd becomes nervous because of Zechariah's delay in emerging from the holy place; they deduce that something unusual is slowing down the ceremony. According to Jewish tradition, the high priest was to recite a short prayer when he was in the Holy of Holies ministering on the day of Atonement, lest the people worry (*m. Yoma* 5:1). It was assumed that God's holiness made it difficult to stay in his presence for very long. Such an attitude seems to fuel the people's concern here.

When Zechariah emerges, he is unable to give the benediction, which probably consisted of the Aaronic blessing from Numbers 6:24-26 (*m. Tamid* 7:2). So he signs a message. The people conclude that Zechariah has experienced a very direct encounter with heaven, *a vision.* Zechariah heads home, reflecting in his silence on what God is going to do.

The Beginning of Realization (1:24-25) God's word will be realized. So Elizabeth becomes the next one to encounter his work. The text simply notes this fulfillment by mentioning that she *became pregnant.* There is no fanfare, just a simple declaration that what the angel had promised in verses 13-17 comes to pass. For some time Elizabeth *remained in seclusion.* Her withdrawal has no stated motive, though many have speculated on her reasons. What we do know is that she praised God for what he was doing through her. Her *disgrace,* the reproach of barrenness, was gone. Such thankfulness for the arrival of a child was common (as in Gen 21:6; 30:23). Joy and relief are mixed together in Elizabeth. She appears to be preparing herself for what is ahead. God is powerfully at work again for Israel and for this righteous couple, who are learning anew what it is to trust God. When God speaks and acts, people are supposed to listen. His word will come to pass.

Notes: 1:27 It is debated how much influence Isaiah 7:14 had on Luke's description of Mary. Some who doubt the historicity of the passage see it or Psalm 2:7 as influencing the presence of a "virgin birth" motif (C. F. Evans 1990:156-57). Others see the text as historical and alluding to the fulfillment of this passage (Marshall 1978:72-77; Nolland 1990:46-48).

The Announcement of the Birth of Jesus to Mary (1:26-38) It often is said that good things come in small packages. This passage adds a twist to that theme. For the announcement of Jesus' birth shows that wonderful things come in surprising packages. God does not always do things the way we would do them.

The announcement to Mary sets up a parallel to John's birth and mirrors a number of birth announcements in the Old Testament. But this passage's mood is very different from the Zechariah account. A simple calmness rules the exchange between Mary and Gabriel. Where Zechariah was in the midst of activity before the whole nation in its religious center, this announcement comes to the future childbearer privately, in the country. Had we designed these events, pomp and circumstance probably would have attended the announcement and birth of Jesus, but God chose to use an average young woman and to announce his intentions in quiet obscurity. The fulfillment of God's promise came to earth in an unadorned package of human innocence, without any pomp, far away from any palace. The promised one entered human life as he still seeks to meet it: at the level of everyday experience with everyday people.

Mary and the Angel's Arrival (1:26-28) God again takes the initiative when he sends Gabriel to Galilee, a region some forty-five to eighty-five miles north of Jerusalem. God's announcement comes to a betrothed virgin, Mary. God will bring an unexpected addition into her family. Betrothal in the ancient world was part of a two-stage marriage process. The initial phase, the betrothal, involved a formal, witnessed agreement to marry and the giving of a bridal price (Mal 2:14; *m. Ketubot* 4:4-5). At this point the bride legally became the groom's and could be called his wife. About a year later the actual marriage followed, and the husband took his wife home. In the first century betrothal could take place starting at the age of twelve. Mary's age is unstated. It is during this betrothal stage that Gabriel breaks the news.

Mary's chaste character is highlighted by the description of her as a

---

Others see the event as historical but do not see a conscious, explicit use of Isaiah 7:14 in Luke (Bock 1987:61-62). Others are agnostic (Barclay 1975:12-13). At best, Luke's appeal to Isaiah is implicit; Matthew 1:23 is much more explicit. As to historicity, one's evaluation of this question is determined largely by worldview questions. As Marshall has noted, if one

virgin. It is clear that the account attributes Jesus' origins to the Holy
Spirit (vv. 34-35). But the human Davidic connection, the tie to the royal
line, is also noted in verse 27. The point is important, for it seems that
this connection is attributed to Joseph and comes to Jesus through him.
Joseph need not be the biological father in order to pass such lineage
on to Jesus (Schweizer 1984:27-28). The virgin birth is one mark of
superiority for Jesus over John the prophet. It makes Jesus totally unique.
The only other person to have had such a direct divine intervention in
his birth was Adam—a point Luke will note in 3:38.

The portrait Luke paints of Mary is significant. She is a model believer,
taking God at his word, in contrast to Zechariah (vv. 37-38). She is
favored of God (v. 30), thoughtful (v. 29; 2:19, 51), obedient (v. 38),
believing (v. 45), worshipful (v. 46) and a faithful follower of God's law
(2:22-51; Craddock 1990:27-28). It must be emphasized, however, that
despite all these qualities, God's choice of Mary to bear this child springs
from his grace, not from any inherent merit that she possesses. She is
the object of God's unmerited, graciously provided goodness. Her description as one who has found *favor with God* (*kecharitōmenē,* v. 30)
makes it clear that God has acted on her behalf and not because of her.
In fact, Mary is totally perplexed by the sudden announcement. She did
not ask for or seek this role in God's plans; God has simply stepped into
her life and brought her into his service. Her asset is that she is faithful.
She should be honored for her model of faithfulness and openness to
serve God, but that does not mean she is to be worshiped. Luke wants
us to identify with Mary's example, not to unduly exalt her person.

The Announcement About Jesus (1:29-38) The announcement of
Jesus' birth, which is formulated like Old Testament announcements

believes in the Incarnation, then accepting a virgin birth is not a problem (Marshall 1978:72-
77). The strongest defense of the virgin birth is still Machen's *The Virgin Birth* (1930).

Those who question the virgin birth raise two issues beyond those tied to a supernatural
worldview: the differences in the genealogies of Matthew and Luke and the absence of any
explicit mention of the virgin birth in the New Testament outside of Matthew and Luke. But
neither of these objections should override the impression of the text; in any case, the
absence of such mention in Mark is quite understandable, since that Gospel starts with John
the Baptist and omits any mention of Jesus' origins. On the genealogical question, see Luke
3:23-38. Barclay's attempt to relate the tradition to the general Jewish view that God is
involved in all births fails to take seriously enough the uniqueness of what is said about
Jesus here. In addition, Paul's speaking of Jesus' being "born of a woman" (Gal 4:4) may

(Gen 16:11; Is 7:14), stresses three things about Jesus: his position (*Son of God, Son of the Most High,* ruler), his authority (seated on Israel's throne forever; ruler of a kingdom that will never end) and his divine ties *(the Holy Spirit will come . . . and . . . overshadow you).* In short, Jesus is the promised king of the Davidic line. Old Testament roots for this promise come from 2 Samuel 7:8-17 and Psalm 89 and 132, along with Isaiah 9:5-6; 11:1-5, 10; and Jeremiah 23:5-6 (C. A. Evans 1990:25). The kingdom in view here was the promised messianic kingdom, and Luke will develop and expand the Old Testament understanding of that kingdom through Jesus' teaching, the hymnic material of Luke 1—2, the ministry of John the Baptist and the miracles of Jesus. The expansion will not be at the expense of what the Old Testament promised, but comes in to complement it. God will complete promises made to Israel, the original recipients of his promise, even as he expands that promise later in the New Testament period to involve the Gentiles. In Christ both Jew and Gentile—that is, all humanity—have access by faith to God (Gal 3; Eph 2:11-22; 3:1-7).

So Jesus is not only *great,* as John was, but *Son of the Most High, Son of God* (vv. 32, 35). To Jewish ears this would be the same as calling him king (2 Sam 7:8-17; Ps 2:7). The Jews did not expect a "divine" Messiah, as the Gospels themselves make clear. God had promised David that the king would be God's son, since Yahweh would be the son's Father. This birth would be the first step in bringing the promise to David to its permanent, ultimate fulfillment. This long-held Father-son relationship was to reach unique heights in Jesus. It is clear from Mary's reactions to Jesus in his early years that she did not understand the angel's promise to be a declaration of Jesus' ontological deity (2:41-52; see also Mk 3:31-

---

well imply a virgin-birth understanding, since the normally prominent human father is not mentioned.

By the way, Mary's name probably means "excellence." The pattern of the birth announcement in this passage follows the pattern of the announcement to Zechariah: fear, fear calmed, announcement made and then a sign given.

1:32, 35 The terms *Son of the Most High* and *Son of God* were used in a variety of ways in Judaism (de Jonge 1965-1966:132-48; Bock 1987:63-67). The two titles, which are synonyms, have turned up in a fragment at Qumran, 4QPsDan A² 2:1 (also known as 4Q243 or the Rule Annex). Unfortunately, the text is incomplete, so the exact force of reference in these expressions is unclear. However, it seems clear that a regal figure is in view (Fitzmyer 1973-1974:382-407).

33). Her hymn and those that follow it in the infancy section stress Jesus' regal and delivering role. Jesus is *the holy one;* he is begotten of God; but the full implications of these statements will not be realized for some time. Luke chooses to present Jesus from the "earth up"—that is, showing how, one step at a time, people came to see who Jesus really was. He starts with Jesus as the promised king and teacher who reveals himself as Lord in the context of his ministry. Only slowly do people grasp all of what is promised.

This approach matches how most people today come to see who Jesus is. Drawing on two thousand years of theological reflection about Jesus, the church often tells the story from heaven down, but there is merit in Luke's path. It is the path of people's experience. Luke's approach is different from that of the Gospel of John, which presents Jesus as sent from heaven to earth. At the start of John's story there is no doubt that Jesus was with God in the beginning. Both approaches are true; they are just different ways to consider the person of Christ. The church has tended to emphasize John's approach, because it is the full story, but there also is value in unfolding the story gradually as Luke does.

Mary has difficulty comprehending the announcement. She asks, *"How will this be?"* She knows she cannot yet have conceived a child, since she is a *virgin.* The answer comes in terms of God's creative overshadowing power. Mary's faith is put on the line at the start. Will she believe that God has the capacity to create life within her? God does not leave her alone in the decision. The angel notes the life that is stirring within the womb of an elderly woman, Elizabeth, Mary's relative. Thus John serves as a pointer to Jesus not only in his preaching but also in his birth.

The angel states the basic premise *"Nothing is impossible with God."* Mary simply responds in humble acceptance, *"I am the Lord's servant. May it be to me as you have said."*

We can only imagine what this announcement required of Mary, especially as her condition became obvious. A hint of the issue is raised

---

Notes: 1:41 The motif of unborn children is rare but interesting. Genesis 25 is the one Old Testament example, while this passage is the New Testament example. In later Judaism there is a tradition that the unborn babies of the exodus sang in their mother's wombs at the parting of the sea (*y. Soṭa* 5, 20ᶜ; Strack and Billerbeck 1926:2:101). The text implies the presence of a person in the womb, much as Psalm 139 suggests more explicitly. It is

in the story of Joseph's dilemma in Matthew 1:18-25. Is God's power such that he can create life and exercise sovereignty over it? This is a question Jesus' birth should raise. Would people believe the claims surrounding Jesus? The questions are profound. Wonderful things come in surprising packages, but they *can* come, because God has the power to deliver them.

Mary's Meeting with Elizabeth (1:39-45) In terms of Luke's plot, this meeting expands Luke's characterization and serves as a crucial pivot in the infancy narrative. Though the mothers of John and Jesus meet, the account is portrayed as a meeting of the two children, since John reacts to the meeting as Elizabeth makes clear. In fact, John's reaction anticipates and mirrors the forerunner role that he will have in Luke 3. Much in the passage parallels Genesis 25:22-26, though there are some major differences. In Genesis there is internal tension as Jacob and Esau struggle for supremacy in the womb. Here there is a total absence of tension: John *leaped for joy* (vv. 41, 44) at the presence of Jesus' mother, who bears Jesus in her womb.

John's ministry starts very early; he is a forerunner even as he responds in Elizabeth's womb (vv. 14-15). This next note of fulfillment of the angelic promise comes from one filled with the Holy Spirit from the womb. The fact that Elizabeth is *filled with the Holy Spirit* as she reports the response indicates how Luke views her response: she expresses the mind of God. This sign sets the mood for the passage. The basic response to the arrival of Jesus onto the scene of history should be *joy*.

Elizabeth is exemplary in her response. She is the "amazed saint." Her attitude is summarized in the question *"Why am I so favored?"* Here is humble amazement at being able to participate directly in God's plan and see him at work (2 Sam 6:9; 24:21). All who have a role in God's plan should share this wonder.

Elizabeth recognizes the unique blessedness of Mary *(blessed are you*

---

clear that life exists in a person long before birth.

The filling of the Spirit is frequent in Luke and is noted again in this chapter (1:67). For Luke the Spirit is often the instigator of praise and the source of revelation. But the Spirit appears intermittently in Luke, while in Acts he indwells, showing one difference between the precross and postresurrection periods (Lk 24:49; Acts 2:16-20).

among women) because of the child she bears *(blessed is the child you will bear)*. The remark is rhetorical and should not be read as if Mary is the most blessed of all women. It means she is "very pleased" (compare Judg 5:24; Song 1:8). The attitude of Elizabeth is representative of what Luke desires in any believer. What a joy to share in the events associated with Jesus. What a joy to share life with him.

Elizabeth also reveals a second exemplary attribute, one that also is found in Mary. While reporting the leaping of John in her womb, she expresses a beatitude for Mary's faith: *"Blessed is she who has believed."* Here is the essence of response to God, to trust his word to be true and live in light of that belief. To be blessed is to be happy because God has touched one's life. Such divine benefit rains down on those who trust him and his promises. Blessing emerges from God's ability to bring his promises to completion, but to share the benefits, we must be confident that God does what he says. The first sign of such faith in Mary was her willingness to let God use her (v. 38). The second was her immediate *(hurried)* visit to Elizabeth, who herself served as a sign that God keeps his word and can give life (vv. 36, 39).

Theophilus and readers like him should not doubt, but rejoice and be assured that God keeps his promises. Trust and joy are two vital aspects of a successful walk with God. Elizabeth's joy is shared by Mary, who will utter a hymn of praise to God for his gracious work on her behalf. Mary's psalm also comes from the heart of a grateful believer.

Mary's Hymn of Praise: Magnificat (1:46-56) Mary's hymn is one of three major hymnic pieces in the infancy material (the others are known as the Benedictus, Lk 1:67-79, and Nunc Dimittis, Lk 2:28-32). The Latin names come from the phrases that begin the hymns. Mary's hymn expresses praise to God for his treatment of her, but then extends her praise to how God has treated the righteous throughout the ages and how he will vindicate them fully in the future. Understanding what God

---

Notes: 1:46-47 There is an important shift in tense in the verbs of these verses. The praise of verse 46 is expressed in a present tense, while the rejoicing of verse 47 uses an aorist. Numerous suggestions have been made to explain the aorist, including (1) it is a timeless aorist and can be translated as a present (Fitzmyer 1981:366) and (2) it is an ingressive aorist, so it speaks of the beginning of rejoicing (Nolland 1990:69). This latter option seems

is doing, Mary possesses a mood of joy. She speaks for herself and for her community, the people of God throughout time. God is worthy of praise for what he will do in taking care of his own. Understanding God's blessing moves the believer to joy and appreciation, since the Almighty cares personally for us and acts on our behalf.

Mary is exemplary of the humble, faithful disciple. That a woman provides such an example is significant, since first-century culture often relegated women to a secondary status. Such examples exist in the Old Testament as well (Miriam in Ex 15:21; Hannah in 1 Sam 2:1-10; Deborah in Judg 5). One of the beauties of Luke's infancy material is that different sorts of people all experience joy at the arrival of Jesus. This reveals Jesus' universal appeal.

Praise for God's Word to Mary (1:46-49) Mary's poetic outburst echoes Old Testament language with a perspective that sees the present in light of God's consistent activity throughout time. Her praise is personal—her *soul* and *spirit* offer praise. She *glorifies the Lord,* which means her words acknowledge his goodness and bring attention to him like a huge neon light shining out from a building (Ps 34:3; 69:30). She makes his name great. She approaches him recognizing her *humble state* as his *servant* and thus acknowledging him as sovereign Master (see also v. 38; 2 Kings 14:26; Ps 9:11-14; 25:16-18). Yet though she addresses God as *the Mighty One* (Deut 10:21; 34:11; Ps 44:4-8; 89:8-10; 111:2, 9; Zeph 3:17), she knows that she has nothing to fear from his power, because he also is her *Savior* (Ps 25:5-6; Is 12:2; Mic 7:7). All these titles serve to show Mary's humble spirit. Her humble perspective forms the basis of her gratitude. The exemplary character of Mary grows out of her understanding of God's character. God owes her nothing; she owes God everything. All the good things that come from his hand are acts of grace.

Despite her humble position, she will be honored by *all generations.* Here is the reason for both her honor and her praise—God the Almighty has done great things on her behalf. Generations will see her as an

---

slightly better, since a present tense would have reflected a simple parallelism more clearly. The ingressive idea suggests that it is God's recent actions on Mary's behalf that have moved her to respond.

1:48 The phrase *from now on* is used frequently in Luke to indicate that things from this moment on are quite different (5:10; 12:52; 22:18, 69; Acts 18:6).

example of a simple human touched by divine power and presence. But it is God who is unique, as her declaration of his holiness makes clear. He is the one "set apart" who is worthy of praise. For her, his name is wonderful because his character is true.

Praise for God's Acts to All (1:50-53) Mary generalizes her praise: God's *mercy extends to those who fear him.* This description is important in setting the context of the hymn's statements. It is the righteous, those who look and turn to God, who are the objects of his blessing. Though the blessings of verses 50-53 come to those in need, they are not a carte blanche offer to all the poor and hungry, but only to those who look to God for care. God's mercy shows his "loyal love" or *hesed.* Such love is faithful as well as gracious (Ps 103:2-6, 8-11, 13, 17). Loyal love is the hymn's basic theme, and God's treatment of Mary is but one example. His divine loyalty requires his action on behalf of the beloved. Those who stand in opposition will face God's power and authority to bring down.

So God will deal with the proud. His *arm* will be raised against them (Deut 4:34; Ps 44:3; 89:13; 118:15). The promise of God's judgment here recalls the exodus, when God exercised his power in total judgment (Ex 6:1, 6; Deut 3:24; 7:19). Whatever earthly authority exists, it is nothing before the mighty, decisive exercise of divine authority. *He has brought down rulers* (Ps 68:1; 89:10) *but has lifted up the humble* (1 Sam 2:7; Ps 147:6). *He has filled the hungry with good things* (1 Sam 2:5; Ps 107:9; 146:7) *but has sent the rich away empty* (1 Sam 2:5; Job 15:29; Jer 17:11). Here is God working on behalf of the pious downtrodden, a group the Old Testament called the *'ănāwîm* (Ps 9:11-12, 17-20; 10:1-4; 12:1-5; 18:25-29).

These verses express the traditional Jewish hope of vindication in the face of oppression at the hands of foreign, pagan rulers (1:71-75 is similar; in Judaism, see *Psalms of Solomon* 17—18). Mary's remarks are often misinterpreted in two directions. Some see them solely as a ref-

---

1:51-53 The verbs of these verses are also aorist, but the tense's force is disputed. Some see them as "gnomic," describing what God has done throughout time (Hendriksen 1978:108-12). But others argue for a prophetic aorist here, since the praise reflects what God is and what he will do in light of his current activity in Jesus (Ellis 1966:76; see v. 48b, which sets the temporal tone of the hymn). Even though verse 50 mentions that God's mercy

erence to God's defense of all the poor, all the hungry. A whole theology of liberation is built around such a reading of these verses and others like them. This ignores the spiritual dimension present throughout the hymn, not to mention the national character of the hope expressed in verses 54-55. On the other hand, some want to dilute the references to the poor and hungry altogether and speak only of the poor and hungry in spirit. This also undercuts the passage's force. The spirit of this text is reflected in other New Testament texts (1 Cor 1:25-31; Jas 2:5). Often it is those in need who are the most spiritually sensitive to God and who are gifted with faith by him. God promises them that despite their current deprivation, they will experience great reward in the future.

Luke raises a theme here that he will return to again and again: God's desire to minister to the poor. Luke will stress a ministry of social concern for those in need and warn those who are wealthy not to hoard what God has given to them (6:20-26; 7:22-23; 12:13-21; 14:12-14; 16:14-29). He warns about a reversal of roles in the judgment for those who do not hear this admonition.

Praise for God's Acts for His People, Israel (1:54-56) God is acting for his people, Israel. God's actions reflect his mercy. He committed himself to such loyalty and compassion when he made promises to Abraham (Gen 12:1-3). One of the lessons of the infancy section is that God keeps his word, including the promises made to the nation of Israel. Mary knows that the promises of God abide, and this is evident in her praise. God's loyal love is central to the hope and assurance of those to whom God has made himself known.

Israel is called *his servant*. This reference recalls a major motif from Isaiah (Is 41:8-9; 42:1, 2, 21; 45:4; 48:20; 49:3). Later Luke will describe Jesus in terms that picture the Servant (Lk 22:37; Acts 8:32-33). Even later in Acts, Paul and Barnabas recall this calling to serve as "light for the Gentiles" (Acts 13:47). The various points of connection to the Servant concept mark this as a pattern prophecy: the role God had designed for

---

extends *from generation to generation,* making the statements in verses 51-53 look timeless, the vindication that is described in verses 51-53 comes in the future, so Mary looks ahead to what God will eventually do. The future is so certain it can be expressed as past.

1:55 Abraham is a major figure for Luke, who mentions him twenty-two times in Luke-Acts. The most detailed description appears in Acts 7:2-8 (Dahl 1966:139-58).

Israel is fulfilled in the regal representative of the nation and in those who are identified with him.

Though Luke will develop the concept of God's constant care for Israel according to covenant promise, his portrayal of Mary here shows a woman confident that God will care for a remnant in his nation. They, like she, will see the Lord's powerful hand move on their behalf. God's loyal love and the truthfulness of his holy character make such assurance and hope possible. Even more amazing is what the progress of Luke's story reveals. Others who were not originally included in the promise, namely Gentiles, will come to share in this hope and will benefit from the vindication described here. In fact, it is quite likely that Theophilus himself is one of these additional beneficiaries, along with many others after him who have come to fear the Lord.

In fact, the two points of assurance are linked. Since God remembers the loyal love promised in covenant to Israel, Theophilus can rest assured that God will remember his promises to this Gentile believer. God's care for one promise reinforces the other. The basic teaching implied here is very similar to Paul's argument for the hope of Israel in Romans 9—11.

The Birth and Naming of John (1:57-66) With the birth of John, God continues to fulfill what he promised in Luke 1:5-25. As the promise of God moves ahead, God shows he will bring his word to pass and teaches some personal lessons as well. The most important lesson is that even the pious must learn to wait on God's timing and ways.

As in Luke 1:39-56, where there was a meeting (1:39-45) and then a hymn (1:46-56), John's birth is followed by a hymn. In each case the hymn details the significance of the previous event. The difference is that Mary's hymn focused on how God deals with his people, while Zechariah's hymn will highlight the main players who bring such blessing on humanity.

John's Birth (1:57-58) When Elizabeth bears a son, all those around her hear that *the Lord had shown her great mercy*. Though these events

---

Notes: 1:59 A late Jewish text speaks of a tradition that had Moses named at his circumcision (*Pirqe Rabbi Eliezer* 48, 27c). Others suggest that Genesis 21:4-6 reflects this timing, but it is hard to be sure. Greek children were often named seven to ten days after birth (Ellis

are cosmic in their reach, they involve the divinity's personal touch. God has shown his mercy and magnified it to Elizabeth (compare Gen 19:19; 24:12; 40:14; 47:29; Ruth 1:8; 4:13). Those who had shared her pain now rejoice with her. God's mercy expresses itself in concrete, loving action.

The Surprise in the Naming of John (1:59-66) According to custom, the circumcision and naming of the child follow. Though children were often named at birth in the Old Testament (Gen 25:25-26; 29:32-35), it appears that sometimes such naming was associated with circumcision. The presence of the parents at circumcision shows them as pious, law-abiding Jews (Gen 21:4; Lev 12:3).

Many features of the naming of John are surprising. The crowd fully expects custom to be followed. They wish the child to be named Zechariah. Children were often named after fathers or grandfathers (1 Maccabees 1:1-2; Josephus *Life* 15; *Antiquities* 14.1.3 §10; 20.9.1 §197; *Jubilees* 11:15; Fitzmyer 1981:380). Elizabeth rejects the crowd's desire and goes her own way. The name she chooses is the one the angel gave Zechariah in verse 13. The text is silent on how she knew this name, but that detail is unimportant. The choice of the surprising name indicates that a major lesson of obedience has been learned. And as noted above, when God names a child, that child is significant in his plan.

The protest of the crowd shows that they are unaware of what God is doing. Surely the father of the house will not sanction this breaking of custom. So they motion to Zechariah to find out what the name of the child should be. Their signing to Zechariah indicates that he is both deaf and mute. The reply comes on a wooden tablet covered with wax. By repeating the name his wife gave, Zechariah echoes the instructions of the angel, not the crowd and custom. He goes the way of God and amazes his neighbors.

His obedience yields additional reward: his tongue is loosed *immediately* and judgment ends. Just as the angel promised in Luke 1:20, the temporary situation of silence ends with the fulfillment of God's word. The point of the linkage is not to be missed: believe and know that God fulfills his promises.

1966:78).
1:64 It is often the case that miracles or healings occur rapidly in Luke (4:39; 5:25; 8:44, 47; 13:13; 18:43; 19:11; 22:60).

The event has three unusual features: (1) the old have given birth, (2) the child has a strange name, and (3) Zechariah's handicap is taken away, whereupon he launches into praise about what God is doing. Such remarkable events cause the crowd to fear and reflect. Something different and surprising is happening, things worth remembering and considering. So they wonder, *"What then is this child going to be?"* Luke wants his readers to consider the same question. The story's close indicates that *the Lord's hand was with him.* Luke is saying, in effect, "Be assured, Theophilus or any other reader of my account, that God was in these most unusual events." When God's *hand* is mentioned, usually an opportunity for deliverance is around the corner (Ex 13:3; 15:6; Is 5:12; 26:11; 66:14; Ps 28:5; 80:17; 1 Kings 18:46; 1 Chron 28:19; Ezek 1:3, 3:14, 22; Marshall 1978:90; Stein 1992:98). And Zechariah, in his silence, has learned to believe God.

With John, God has prepared the way for his promise. God's ways were not traditional or what had been culturally expected, but they were his ways nonetheless. Sometimes going God's way means going against the grain of our culture.

Zechariah's Hymn: Benedictus (1:67-80) This hymn surveys God's plan through the forerunner and the anointed Davidic heir. *The Lord, the God of Israel,* is blessed for how he works through these two major agents. Where Mary's hymn was cosmic and personal, Zechariah's is cosmic and universal. Zechariah rejoices that God has raised up the Davidic horn to do his work of deliverance, as well as sending a prophet to prepare the way for him. That deliverance possesses both political and spiritual dimensions, as verses 71-75 and 78-79 show.

Luke describes the hymn as Spirit-inspired. In other Lukan accounts, often the Spirit's presence leads to a prophetic declaration or to praise (Acts 2:17-18; 11:27; 13:1; 19:6; 21:9). This hymn offers a divine commentary on God's plan. John is the *prophet of the Most High* pointing to Jesus, the bright Morning Star. So Zechariah highlights Jesus just as his son John will.

Notes: 1:68-75 The verbs in this hymn are aorist and are clear examples of prophetic aorists. Verse 69 makes it clear that God is to be praised for sending the promised Davidic

Praise for Messianic Redemption (1:68-75) John's birth means that God is once again working actively to redeem his promise (vv. 72-73). Zechariah praises God, for *he has come and has redeemed his people*. What the NIV refers to as God's coming heralds an important Lukan concept, God's visitation (1:78; 7:16; 19:44; Acts 15:14). This introduction makes the hymn a praise psalm. The theme of the praise occurs in verses 68-70, while the explanation of the theme involves the rest of the hymn. God's visitation comes in Messiah's visitation (Lk 2:26-32). God *has raised up a horn of salvation for us in the house of his servant David.* God often acted in history to "raise up" a prophet (Deut 18:15, 18), a judge (Judg 3:9, 15), a priest (1 Sam 2:35) or a king (2 Sam 3:10). Luke likes the idea as well (Acts 3:22, 26; 13:22), showing how God directs the events of his plan.

This Messiah is a picture of strength, which is why Zechariah mentions the *horn*. The horns of an ox are used for protection and for defeating opponents (Deut 33:17). The same image is used for a warrior (2 Sam 22:3; Ps 75:4-5, 10; 148:14) or a king who saves (1 Sam 2:10; Ps 132:17). Luke's starting point for thinking about Jesus is that he is a king.

God is doing what he promised. His word will come to pass. These events are *as he said through his holy prophets of long ago*. The promise involves rescue: God will save his people from their *enemies* and *from all who hate* them. Such salvation reflects the *mercy* of God and the recollection of the *covenant* made with Abraham. In this way the hymn actually combines two sets of divine promises—those about David's son and those made to Abraham. What God will do for his people he does through Messiah. The fresh fulfillment of both covenants begins with Jesus' arrival.

But what is the goal of this salvation? Here is perhaps the most insightful part of the hymn. Zechariah is not retreating from life or looking only to a future reward in heaven. His heart's desire is *to serve [God] without fear in holiness and righteousness before him all our days.* This is the expression of an exemplary soul. The meaning of life comes in faithful service to a holy God. By saying *our days,* Zechariah represents many

ruler, whose work as the Son of David involves both political deliverance and the giving of spiritual benefits, as the rest of the hymn shows.

who share this desire. Salvation enables the child of God to serve God.

Who are the enemies referred to in the hymn? In the context it seems clear that Zechariah anticipates freedom from the opposition of enemies (v. 74). Possibly he hopes for rescue from Rome, much as John the Baptist seemed to anticipate when he asked Jesus whether he really was "the one who was to come" (7:18-23). Such a political deliverance for the people of God is also anticipated by John in Revelation 19.

But this is only a partial answer. Zechariah's hymn is an introduction to Luke's entire book. To ask what the hymn means for Luke, we need only to see how he develops the theme of enemies within his Gospel (Bock 1993:443-48). Such an examination shows that the enemy consists of supernatural opposition (11:14-23). Jesus is the "someone stronger" who overruns the strong man Beelzebub. To provide real victory Jesus will need to vanquish not only human opponents but the spiritual ones that stand behind them as well (Eph 6:10-18). Jesus' activity shows his goal to be the reversal of the effect of demonic presence (Lk 13:10-17). As the Davidic Son, he heals and shows his authority (18:35-42). The power of his *horn* extends even into these dimensions of reality. The miracles are not only events of deliverance but pictures of a deeper reality. To know Jesus is to have access to authority that can overcome the presence of evil. We are able, as a result, to serve God in holiness and righteousness.

Prophecy About John and Jesus (1:76-80) Two agents are responsible for this work. John the Baptist, as prophet, *will go on before the Lord to prepare the way for him.* In the context of the hymn, it is best to see *the Lord* as a reference to God the Father, since he is the source of all the activity the hymn describes (as also in 1:17). Luke 1:76-77 speaks of his *way* and his *people,* a reference that looks back to 1:68, where the people are God's. For Luke, God is the producer-planner and Jesus is the plan's directing agent. John's preparation involves giving *knowledge of salvation through the forgiveness of their sins.* Forgiveness

---

1:76 It is debated whether before his public ministry John was a member of the sectarian Jewish Qumran community. However, there are serious problems with this view. (1) That community strongly opposed the priesthood, which would mean John rejected his father's vocation. (2) John had only one washing, while several existed at Qumran. (3) John's message was not that of a separatist but of one building a remnant for the nation. (4) John's

is a major Lukan theme (Lk 24:47; Acts 2:38; 5:31; 10:43; 13:38; 26:18).

Forgiveness is also a principal component of the expression of God's *tender mercy*. He is the one who makes the dayspring dawn upon us from on high, or in the NIV rendition, *the rising sun . . . come to us from heaven*. This is a reference to the sun's dawning in the morning. The Davidic horn (v. 69) is an image of light (Num 24:17; Is 11:1-10). The image of light will be important in Acts (13:47; 26:17-20) as well as in Luke (2:32). The picture is of a world cloaked in darkness and death, desperate for someone to lead it into light and life. For Zechariah, this rescue is Messiah's mission. The Christ is the bearer of forgiveness as his day dawns. Once his day dawns, the light of the "Sun" never sets. He is the one who guides *our feet into the path of peace*. Even the righteous Zechariah recognizes the need to be totally dependent on the one God will send. Those who are righteous know that the only true journey in life is the one taken in the hands of God. In Luke 1, Zechariah has grown from a figure of doubt to an example of dependence.

So John and Jesus come by God's mercy to prepare and lead God's people. John will proclaim salvation, but Jesus will take them to it.

For this reason Luke notes John's growth briefly and ends the chapter by placing John in the desert, where he will minister to the nation. Then Luke turns the story's spotlight from John and his birth and shines it on the star of his narrative, Jesus, the Davidic horn and king who delivers his people into the light.

The Birth of Jesus (2:1-21) If ever there was an opportunity for God to enact his plan with a majestic flourish, it was at Jesus' birth. But God did not presume upon humanity when he stepped in to redeem it. There was no pretense in this arrival. Rather, God chose to identify in the humblest way with those made in his image. The story of Jesus' birth in Luke mixes praise with simplicity. Its contrast to the birth of John the Baptist is remarkable. John's birth was announced in the capital, at the

---

preaching lacked the legalism of Qumran. Apparently people could submit to his baptism with a change of heart; they did not need to wait to undergo cleansing as at Qumran. Though it is conceivable that John knew about this community, it is unlikely that he was a member of it (Schürmann 1969:94-95).

temple, in the center of the Jewish nation. But Jesus arrives in rural anonymity. John is the child of a priest and his righteous wife; Jesus belongs to Jews of average social status.

Yet it is Jesus' birth that draws an angelic host. Once again, appearances are deceiving. As humble as the setting is, his birth is accompanied by the attention of the heavenly host. The shepherds who are privileged to share in the moment become bearers of a story full of wonder. Jesus' birth is more than a cosmic event; it is the arrival of divine activity that should provoke joy, reflection and attentiveness. That is why Mary ponders these events and the shepherds return glorifying God.

The Birth (2:1-7) A regional *census* leads Joseph and his betrothed, Mary, to the city of David, better known as the hamlet of Bethlehem. The decree comes from Caesar Augustus, better known as Octavian, who ruled alone from 27 B.C. to A.D. 14. The administrator of the census was Quirinius (Tacitus *Annals* 2.30; 3.22, 33, 48; Strabo *Geography* 12.6.5). This census probably sought to produce a registration list for taxes. A journey to the ancestral home would have fit Jewish practice, so that the custom was done in a culturally inoffensive manner (2 Sam 24). This was important, since the tax itself would have been a painful reminder of Israel's position before Rome. Nazareth to Bethlehem was about a ninety mile trip, assuming that Samaria was bypassed. Such a journey would have taken around three days.

That Bethlehem is *the town of David* indicates the birth's connection to promise (Mic 5:1-2; the Greek is literally "city of David"). Luke makes the connection less directly than Matthew 2:6 does, but the association of David with the birth sounds a regal note, even if the allusion is made

Notes: 2:1-3 Perhaps the historicity of no event in Luke's Gospel is more challenged than that of this census under Quirinius in about 4 B.C. Extrabiblical sources record a census under Quirinius in A.D. 6, which is too late for this event (Josephus *Antiquities* 17.3-5 §§342-54; 18.1.1-10). Discussion of why many doubt the connection is summarized well in the revised edition of Schürer, *The History of the Jewish People in the Age of Jesus Christ* (1973:1:162-71). But various efforts to explain Luke's statement also exist. Some take a lexical approach, arguing that certain terms carry less than common but possible meanings. Others are historical, arguing that we do not have complete records of governorship for this period and then positing Quirinius in the gap, or else suggesting that Quirinius had "governorlike" authority during the census, so the title here is descriptive, not a technical title. Others argue that the text's syntax has been misread in associating Quirinius directly with this census. For a discussion of the options, see Hoehner 1977:14-27 and Bock 1994b: excursus on the

subtlely. As the couple arrives in the city, the time comes for the child's arrival.

Many of the details supplied in Christmas tellings of this story do not come from Luke. There is no indication of a long search for a place to stay or of an insensitive innkeeper who made Mary and Joseph stay outdoors. The text merely describes the arrival in simple terms: *She gave birth to her firstborn, a son. She wrapped him in cloths and placed him in a manger, because there was no room for them in the inn.*

In all likelihood, the manger is an animal's feeding trough, which means the family is in a stable or in a cave where animals are housed (Hengel 1974:53-54). Swaddling clothes were cloth wrapped around the baby's arms and legs (see Ezek 16:4); they kept the limbs covered and protected. The contrast between the birth's commonness and the child's greatness could not be greater. The promised one of God enters creation among the creation. The profane decree of a census has put the child in the promised city of messianic origin. God is quietly at work, and a stable is Messiah's first throne room.

Response to the Birth (2:8-21) Jesus' birth sparks joy, surprise and wonder. All these emotions flow from the experience of the shepherds, who observe with amazement as heaven confesses the child's identity (vv. 10-11). The major offices of Jesus are confessed in one sentence: he is *Savior, Lord* and *Christ*—that is, deliverer, master and anointed king. As unbelievable as it may seem, the one with authority over salvation spends his first nights not in a palace but in the open air among simple people like the shepherds. Born in the ancient equivalent of a tent village, Jesus arrives to fulfill God's promise. All the imagery shows

census. Though no solution totally commends itself, the assumption that Luke has erred here is the least satisfactory, given the gaps in our knowledge of the region and other possible explanations for his statement.

2:1 For details on the career of Octavian, see Fitzmyer 1981:394, 399 and Stein 1992:105.

2:7 The December 25 date for Jesus' birth is a product of tradition, since the text does not give us an exact date. In our historical sources, a general winter date was in place by the time of Constantine (A.D. 306-37). The celebration appears to have coincided with the pagan feast of Saturnalia as a Christian alternative to it. But the tradition may be older, since it might be mentioned by Hippolytus (A.D. 165-235) in his *Commentary on Daniel* 4.23.3. The Eastern Church celebrates Jesus' birth on January 6, but a December date was firm in the West by the time of Augustine (*On the Trinity* 4.5).

God's concern for people regardless of their social status or vocation. He cares for all and identifies with all.

Joy comes with an angelic proclamation of good news *(euangelizo-mai)*. The message is for *all the people.* Though in the original context such a messianic announcement would have been understood as being for the people of Israel, the development of Jesus' ministry shows that Jesus' work reaches beyond such national boundaries. The two volumes of Luke-Acts tell the story of how Jesus, the Savior, Lord and Christ, brought salvation to all people regardless of nationality. They need only turn to him (Acts 10:34-43).

As with other incidents in the infancy material, the angel describes a sign: the shepherds will know this announcement is true when they see the child in a manger. The angelic announcement does not come in mystical isolation; it connects to concrete events.

The praise of the heavenly host offers honor to God and peace to *men on whom his favor rests.* This last phrase is not a declaration of universal salvation but refers to those who are the special objects of God's grace. They are like the God-fearers Mary mentioned in Luke 1:50-53, whom God will exalt with his blessing. They are the "saved" or the "elect," those on whom God has bestowed the favor of his grace.

In this account each set of characters plays a major role. The angels present the commentary of heaven on the events of Luke 2:1-7. They identify the child and reflect the heavens' excitement that this child has come to do God's work. The shepherds have the type of response any of us should have as we contemplate these events. Their curiosity leads them to *go to Bethlehem and see this thing that has happened.* As they see God's word honored in the presence of the sign, they come to testify to God's work and tell the story of the child. Mary depicts the wonder of experiencing the inbreaking of God in her life. She *pondered* these things *in her heart.* The audience to the shepherds' report *were amazed.* Their response exemplifies the awe that should fill anyone who hears

---

2:8 Some have argued that the presence of shepherds here shows God identifying with the despised. But the evidence for such a negative view of shepherds within Judaism is later than the first century and must be questioned. In addition, the shepherd image in the New Testament is mostly positive (Mt 18:12; Mk 6:34; Lk 15:4; Jn 10; Eph 4:11; Heb 13:20; 1 Pet 2:25; not to mention the Old Testament figures of Abraham, Moses and David, who were

Jesus' story.

In addition, there is the shepherds' *glorifying and praising God for all the things they had heard and seen.* This birth is no mere arrival of a new life, as poignant as each such event is. The story is not told so that hearers can identify with the new mother and father or enjoy a story of hope, of a touching birth in humble surroundings. This birth has value because of whose birth it is. The shepherds have found that the angel's words were true, that events have transpired *just as they had been told.* God's word is coming to pass; his plan is again strategically at work. They break out in praise to God because he has sent Jesus, the Savior, Lord and Christ.

Reflecting the piety of obedient Jewish parents, Joseph and Mary undertake to circumcise the child on the eighth day and give him the name the angel said he should possess, Jesus. In every action this couple is showing faithfulness. They are examples of faith. As devout Jewish parents, they follow the Mosaic law. Jesus has been born into a good family.

The Witness of a Man and Woman at the Temple (2:22-40) The testimony to Jesus continues as both a prophet and a prophetess reveal God's plan. By showing how each gender among the people of God testifies to what God is doing through this child, Luke is saying that all should rejoice at his coming. And culturally it is no accident that both Simeon and Anna are advanced in years. Here is the testimony of two with a full résumé of life experience.

Anna's and Simeon's prophecies share a note of hope and expectation, along with declarations that in this child God's promise is moving into realization. Luke also reveals Jesus' superiority to John in this passage, for the testimony about John stops with his circumcision but the praise of Jesus extends long past the eighth day of life. Here two old and wise prophets of Jewish piety speak not only for the nation but for all humankind, as Simeon's prophecy mentions Jesus' relationship to the Gentiles

---

all shepherds at one time). What they do represent is the humble.

2:14 For this technical meaning of "men of his good pleasure" (Greek) or *men on whom his favor rests* (NIV), see 1QH 4:32-33, 11:9, and benediction 17 in the ancient Jewish prayer of the Eighteen Benedictions (Jeremias 1964a:364; Schrenk 1964b:745-50).

(for the first time in the book). This passage also provides the first hint that all will not go well. Mary will experience the pain of seeing her son rejected by a divided Israel.

The Purification of Jesus (2:22-24) Jesus' parents are law-abiding Jews. They show up at the temple to perform sacrifices associated with the wife's purification after birth (Lev 12:2-4, 6). Such a ceremony occurs forty days after the child's arrival. At the same time the firstborn child is to be set aside to the Lord (Ex 13:2, 12, 16; 34:19; Num 18:15-16). Jesus' parents bring the child along, though that is not necessary. They offer *a pair of doves or two young pigeons.* This offering recalls Leviticus 12:8, though the wording is closer to the Greek Old Testament version of Leviticus 5:11. Since this offering is the one usually made by the poor, Jesus is identified with the very people he reached out to save (1:52; 4:18-19; 6:20; 7:22-23; Greeven 1968:69). But Joseph and Mary do not live in abject poverty, since Joseph is a carpenter by trade (Mk 6:3; Plummer 1922:65). This could be the offering of someone from a "middle-class" background as well. Regardless of their precise social status, Luke is making it clear that Jesus' parents are not spiritual renegades, but Jews who are sensitive and faithful to the Mosaic law—a point reinforced in Luke 2:40-52, when they will make their customary annual pilgrimage to Jerusalem. All the persons surrounding Jesus at his birth have a heritage of devotion to God. The testimony to Jesus stands on the shoulders of a series of highly respectable figures.

Simeon's Prophecy (2:25-35) The Spirit leads an old man to the temple to greet Jesus. He is *righteous and devout* (compare Mt 10:41; 19:17; 23:29, 35; 2 Pet 2:7-8), yet another witness to Jesus who possesses a vibrant walk with God. Such piety includes having an eye on the hope of God's redemption. Luke expresses this hope in national terms appropriate for this first-century saint: Simeon has been *waiting for the con-*

Notes: 2:22-24 The offering of a sacrifice for *purification* of both parents *(tou katharismou autōn)* has raised a historical problem for some, since only the wife needed to be purified. Luke seems to have compressed his description here. Either Joseph, because he shared in the birth process, had also become unclean and needed ritual purification, or Luke recognizes that both participated in the child's dedication and so shared in the various temple sacrifices.

2:25 There are extrabiblical traditions surrounding Simeon. Protoevangelium James 24:3-4 calls Simeon a priest, while Pseudo-Matthew 15:2 puts his age at 112. We cannot determine

solation of Israel. He longs for the nation's deliverance, just as Zechariah had (1:68-75; Is 40:1; 49:13; 51:3; 57:18; 61:2; 2 Baruch 44:7). In fact, later rabbis will call the Messiah *Menahem,* or Comforter (Schmitz and Stählin 1967:793; *y. Berakot* 2:3). It was such deliverance that Simeon expected.

The Spirit of God directs this scene, because he had revealed to Simeon that death would not come until he *had seen the Lord's Christ.* Promise, fulfillment and God's direction stand behind the prophecy of this old saint.

Simeon's remarks are set within a hymn known as the Nunc Dimittis, from the Latin of the hymn's opening phrase. The prophecy itself is a statement of mature faith. Simeon can die in peace *as you have promised* and be taken by God, his *Sovereign Lord (despota* or Master), because *my eyes have seen your salvation.* There is a significant equation in this remark. To see Jesus is to see God's salvation. They are inseparable. There is joy, even in the face of death, when one has seen the source of life. Simeon's job as a sentinel for Messiah is done. The Lord can take him home. Simeon pictures a faithful servant who is at home in God's purpose and plan, even when his time is up.

God's work is for *all people (laōn).* As in 2:10, the reference to the people ultimately is broad, encompassing both Jew and Gentile, as verse 32 makes clear. In fact, Jesus is *light (phōs),* an image that recalls the description of the Davidic son as the dayspring or bright morning star in 1:78-79. But Jesus serves as light in two distinct ways. For Gentiles he is a *revelation.* This term refers to his opening up the way of salvation to the nations in a way unknown before his coming. But for Israel, God's people, Jesus is *glory*—that is, his activity represents the realization of promises made by God and thus shows Israel's special place in his heart (Is 46:13). The remarks in this verse recall Isaiah 60:1-3, which in turn

---

the truthfulness of either of these traditions. What Luke stresses is the man's spiritual condition.

2:31-32 I have opted for a syntax in which *light* functions as a summary of the entire work of Jesus, while *revelation* and *glory* are in parallelism to one another. Another view of the verse's syntax interprets *light for revelation* as tied to Jesus' work for Gentiles and *glory* as tied to his work for Israel. The difference between the two views is very slight. I would argue that Luke 1:78-79 and Acts 26:22-23 associate light with Jesus' work for all persons and thus favor our reading.

recall imagery surrounding the promised Servant of the Lord. Though the church today associates the Servant figure with the suffering of Jesus, Luke prefers here to highlight those aspects of the Servant's work that mean hope and vindication.

Once again, the parents *marveled* at the prophecy. Luke's reader is to identify with their response and sense of wonder.

But Simeon is not done. There is a note of foreboding he must leave with Mary. Jesus will be the cause of division: *This child is destined to cause the falling and rising of many in Israel.* The imagery of this verse comes from Isaiah 8:14-15 and 28:13-16. These Old Testament texts are frequently alluded to in the New Testament (Rom 9:33; 1 Pet 2:6-8; Lk 20:17-18, also at Qumran, 1QH 2:8-10; 14:11). Jesus will divide the nation in two. Some will respond and others will oppose. That means that he will be *a sign that will be spoken against.* People will contend against and about Jesus. The road to promise-fulfillment is not smooth. To identify with Jesus will bring pain, because many will reject him.

This rejection explains Simeon's reference to *a sword* piercing through Mary's soul. She will feel a mother's pain as she watches her son go his own way and suffer rejection, but the *sword* also reflects the pain anyone who identifies with Jesus feels as the world rejects what Jesus has to offer. Simeon's remark to Mary is an aside, but an important one, since it shows that identifying with Jesus has painful personal consequences.

The division Jesus brings reveals *the thoughts of many hearts.* Jesus is God's litmus test for where a person is. Do I sense a need to depend on God and come to him to walk in light, or do I not? My response to Jesus is the test, and the answer comes from my heart. Each person's response to him reveals where he or she is before God, just as one day Jesus will reveal where everyone's heart is (Acts 10:42-43).

Anna's Prophecy (2:36-38) Though no details of Anna's prophecy are given, this section completes the cycle of male and female witnesses.

2:34 Commentators debate the syntactic force of the imagery of *falling and rising.* Is there one group that falls only to rise again as a group—a reference to believers who fall in suffering and rise in vindication (Prov 24:16; Is 24:20; Amos 5:2; 8:14; Mic 7:8)? Or are the people divided into two groups, rejecters and believers, as the New Testament portrait suggests (Lk 4:29; 6:20-26; 12:51; 13:28-29, 33-35; 16:25; 18:9-14; 19:44, 47-48; 20:14-17)?

Again, Anna's piety is underlined by references to her old age, her faithful widowhood and her regular ministry at the temple. She is full of thanksgiving at the arrival of the child who will complete God's promise, and she speaks *about the child to all who were looking forward to the redemption of Jerusalem.* Her teaching would have been heard by all who frequented the temple. Her hope, like Simeon's, looks to the completion of what God is starting.

Jesus' Growth (2:39-40) Having obeyed the Mosaic law, Jesus' parents return with him to Nazareth in Galilee. There Jesus grows in strength and wisdom, receiving the favor of God. There he awaits the ministry that will fulfill what Mary, Zechariah, the angels, the shepherds, Simeon and Anna have proclaimed. God will fulfill his word and perform his plan.

The Twelve-Year-Old Jesus Goes to the Temple (2:41-52) As Luke's infancy overture comes to a close, he makes a transition to John and Jesus' ministry through a single incident from Jesus' adolescence (L. T. Johnson 1991:60). This is the only such incident in the Gospels, though the extrabiblical gospels do include such accounts (*Infancy Gospel of Thomas* 19:1-5). After the host of witnesses to Jesus in Luke 1:5—2:40, Jesus now speaks for himself for the first time. This is the literary climax of Luke's initial section and shows the sense of mission and self-awareness Jesus possesses. Jesus has a unique relationship to God and a clear sense of his calling, one that transcends his relationship to his earthly parents. That this event, though strictly speaking not an infancy account, belongs in this initial literary division of Luke is indicated by the fact that it takes place in the temple, which is where the section started in Luke 1:5. In addition, the note on Jesus' growth parallels the close of the discussion of John the Baptist in Luke 1:80.

The Problem: Jesus Is Missing (2:41-45) The events leading to Jesus' exchange with his parents begin with their annual pilgrimage to Jerusalem. The parents of Jesus were devout Jews. The Old Testament

The suggestion of Mary's pain and the thrust of the New Testament imagery suggests the two-group view.

2:36 Anna's age is debated. Is she eighty-four (NIV)? Or is she in her early hundreds, having been a widow for eighty-four years (NIV margin)? The grammar of the Greek is not entirely clear, though I prefer the latter as a slightly more natural reading of the Greek.

commanded such a trip for three festivals a year (Passover, Pentecost and Tabernacles; Ex 23:14-17; 34:22-23; Deut 16:16). But by the first century, God-fearing Jews made only one journey a year because of the distances involved (Josephus on Passover—*Life* 345-54; *Antiquities* 17.9.3 §§213-14; *Jewish Wars* 2.1.3 §§10-12; 2.14.3 §280; Brown 1977:472). The Passover was the major feast celebrated at the beginning of the Jewish year, Nisan 15, which falls in our month of March or April (Fitzmyer 1981:339-40). Only men were required to make the journey, so Mary's presence shows her commitment (Preisker 1964:373). Jerusalem was eighty miles from Nazareth, so the trip would take three days. Though some have argued that women and children traveled separately from the men as a way to explain how Jesus got lost, there is no ancient text that describes this practice.

Jesus is twelve years old. If the Mishna is relevant to the first-century Jewish practice, which is likely in this case, then religious instruction would have become more intense for Jesus upon his reaching twelve (*m. Niddah* 5:6; *m. Megilla* 4:6; *m. 'Abot* 5:12). The custom of bar mitzvah for a thirteen-year-old Jewish boy was not in place at this time (Fitzmyer 1981:440).

After the seven days of celebration, Jesus' family returns home. The text does not say why his parents fail to make sure that he was present in the caravan. Perhaps, as verse 44 suggests, they assume he is with friends or relatives. In any case, on the first evening of their homeward journey they notice that he is missing. Jesus has *stayed behind in Jerusalem,* so Joseph and Mary turn back to find him.

The Resolution: Jesus Explains His Call (2:46-52) Apparently after one day's journey back to Jerusalem and a day looking for Jesus, it is on the third day that Joseph and Mary discover him at the temple, listening to and asking questions of the teachers. The exact location of the incident within the temple is unstated, but Jesus' discussion with the officials leaves those who listen *amazed at his understanding and his answers.* At the tender age of twelve, Jesus already shows signs of possessing great wisdom. Clearly Luke wants the reader to develop a sense

Notes: 2:49 The idiom *en* plus the neuter plural pronoun plus a genitive refers to being in someone's house (Gen 41:51 LXX; Esther 7:9 LXX; Job 18:19 LXX; Josephus *Against*

of respect for this amazing, blessed child.

When the parents finally find him, Mary steps forward to address the young Jesus in a way that both parents and children can appreciate. She expresses concern about the anxiety Jesus has caused by remaining at the temple.

The mild parental complaint leads to Jesus' self-declaration of mission. With the reply appears the first of many *dei* ("it is necessary") statements in Luke (4:43; 9:22; 13:33; 17:25; 19:5; 22:37; 24:7, 26, 44). The key phrase in verse 49 is elliptical, making its meaning disputed. The statement reads, "I must be in the . . . of my Father" (the NIV renders this *I had to be . . .*). Two views are popular: (1) I must be about my Father's affairs (L. T. Johnson 1991:61); (2) I must be in the house of my Father (Stein 1992:123; NIV). The second view also means that Jesus must be engaged in teaching God's ways, since for Luke the temple is a place where Jesus instructs (20:1—21:4). Greek idiom supports this second view.

Jesus' parents—and Luke's readers—need to appreciate that Jesus understood his mission. From the very beginning he is reflecting on the will of God. He starts revealing himself right in the center of Judaism's religious capital.

But there is a second key detail. Jesus refers to God as his *Father.* This alludes to the sense of family relationship and intimacy Jesus has with his heavenly Father (10:21-22). Such closeness to God not only is something Jesus' parents need to appreciate but also is a point the disciples will struggle to grasp (9:59-62; 14:26; Mk 10:29-30). In fact, Luke makes this the first note in a series of revelations that will build the case for who Jesus is. The infancy material stresses Jesus as Messiah, but this text is one of two hints early in Luke's Gospel that he is also much more. Luke reveals Jesus' identity gradually, bringing the reader along in an understanding of who Jesus is. So this first clue comes from Jesus himself. The other major clue comes in the infancy section, where Jesus' divine origin is tied to the Spirit (1:31-35).

Jesus is breaking new ground with his parents here, and they need to

---

Apion 1.118; *Antiquities* 16.10.1 §302). The point is that Jesus must be instructing others on God's way.

understand who he is, just as Luke's readers do. The text makes it clear that at the time they still *did not understand what he was saying to them.* But Mary *treasured* (or pondered) *all these things in her heart,* an appropriate response to Jesus' somewhat enigmatic remarks. Mary does what Luke wants his readers to do as well. It is good to pause and contemplate who Jesus is and the mission he performs. Even two thousand years of history does not do away with the need for such reflection.

Obedient to his parents, Jesus goes home with them to Nazareth. While there he grows *in wisdom and stature, and in favor with God and men* (Lk 1:80; 2:40). There he awaits God's timing to begin the ministry associated with God's house. In the meantime he shows respect for his parents through his obedience, a model for us in a world where teenage rebellion is all too common.

□ John's Preaching and Jesus' Qualifications for Ministry (3:1— 4:13)

A good hunt dog is special, able to sniff out a quarry's location. A good hunt dog can point the way to the goal and indicate where we should be headed. John the Baptist was rather like that. He could point the way for those who wanted to know where God's plan was going. He was "the one who goes before," while Jesus is the stronger One to come.

The second section of Luke sets the scene for Jesus' ministry. After overviewing the ministry of John the Baptist, including a unique summary of his preaching and the reaction to it in 3:1-20, Luke goes on to detail Jesus' baptism, genealogy and temptations. These elements indicate a divine endorsement of Jesus, as well as presenting his moral and historical credentials to be the representative not only of the nation of Israel but also of all people as Son of Adam, Son of God.

Notes: 3:1 The issues of chronology here are complex. Luke may be using any of several calendars for reckoning, and there are several possibilities for the date of the start of Tiberius's reign. Does one use a Roman or Jewish calendar? Does one count from when Tiberius came to the throne or from the first of January in his first full year of reign? For a full discussion of these issues, see Hoehner 1977:95-111. Since a Roman ruler is in view, a Roman reckoning seems likely. On the date of Jesus' crucifixion, see discussion in Luke 23:13-25.

For ancient discussions of Herod, see Josephus *Jewish Wars* 1.33.8 §§668-69; 2.9.1 §§167-68; and much of *Antiquities* 17—18. For treatments of Pilate, see Josephus *Jewish Wars*

John the Baptist, the One Who Goes Before (3:1-20) Luke's presentation of John the Baptist combines material like that in Matthew 3:1-12 and Mark 1:2-8 with material unique to Luke (Lk 3:10-14). John is a preacher of the coming arrival of God's salvation, just as Isaiah 40:3-5 promised. The preparation for that salvation involves repentance, a heart open and turned to the living God. Forgiveness of sins paves the way for a life lived in honor of God with eyes looking for the One to come. There is a concrete ethical element in John's preaching in 3:10-14. That ethical note is also present in Jesus' teaching about how a disciple is to live with a unique kind of love (6:20-49). So John points both to Jesus and to the kind of heart that will recognize him and respond to him when he comes by honoring him with a life that is fruitful before God.

John the Baptist's Ministry (3:1-6) Like a painting placed inside a beautiful frame, John the Baptist's ministry (3:2b-3) is bracketed between the historical context (3:1-2a) and the context of Old Testament hope (3:4-6). Among the Gospel writers, only Luke takes the time to mention leaders in power at various political levels when John appeared. Luke is also unique in emphasizing the extent to which John's coming represents a renewed realization of the promise of Isaiah 40:3-5. For Isaiah, the initial fulfillment of seeing God's hand had been in the deliverance from exile during the period of Cyrus the Great, as later chapters of Isaiah note. Now the pattern of God's working to deliver his people is renewed in the word of *a voice of one calling in the desert.* God approaches, and creation is to level all geographical obstacles to prepare for his coming, as if rolling out a great red carpet. This leveling includes seeking contriteness of heart (Is 57:14-17).

In listing Tiberius Caesar, Pontius Pilate, Herod, Philip, Lysanias, Annas and Caiaphas, Luke surveys the political and religious leadership from

2.9.2 §§169-77; *Antiquities* 18.2.5 §§53-59. John the Baptist also is mentioned in Josephus *Antiquities* 18.1.2 §§116-19.

3:3 John's baptism is prophetic in character and is unlike its proposed cultural parallels (Schürmann 1969:154-57). It is unlike baptism at Qumran, since John baptized once while the Qumranian baptisms were constant. It is also not like the "proselyte baptism" that a Gentile underwent to enter into Judaism. We do not know if such a practice existed in the first century (Fitzmyer 1981:460); furthermore, John calls those in the Jewish nation for this washing, whereas proselyte baptism was for outsiders. What these cultural parallels do show, however, is that such ritual washing existed, and they all shared the association with cleansing. John's actions would have been understood culturally.

the most distant to the more directly involved authorities. The note about Tiberius's fifteenth year allows us to date the start of John's ministry. Assuming the calendar being used is a Roman one, John's ministry began somewhere during A.D. 28-29. The dating of this starting point is related to the dating of Jesus' ministry, which probably ended in A.D. 33 (though many date the end of his ministry in A.D. 30). Annas and Caiaphas are both called high priests, although only one high priest existed at a time. This description appears to be a case of a person of high office keeping his title even after leaving office, much like an ex-president or ex-governor today. Pilate and Herod reappear only briefly in 9:7-9 and 23:1-25, but both rulers are much discussed in ancient Jewish sources. Philip and Lysanias were the other regional tetrarchs of the period. They, like Herod, were descendants of Herod the Great, who ruled the entire area when Jesus was born.

John's ministry begins during this period. He ministers in the wilderness, brings *the word of God* and preaches *a baptism of repentance for the forgiveness of sins.* The concept of repentance is central to Luke. Not only is its concrete character elaborated in 3:10-14, but Jesus, in his Great Commission in 24:43-47, makes it clear that the roots of the concept come from the Old Testament. Though the Greek term for repentance means "a change of mind," the Semitic concept involves a "turning," an attitude that brings a change of direction (1 Kings 8:47; 13:33; Ps 78:34; Is 6:10; Ezek 3:19; Amos 4:6). Other texts in Luke emphasize this term (5:32; 10:13; 11:32; 13:3, 5; 15:7, 10). On this point Jesus and John echo one another. It is a contrite heart that comes to God for forgiveness, one who knows the need of a spiritual physician (5:31-32). A walk with God means submission to him and a change of direction.

John's baptism is a one-time rite in preparation of God's approaching salvation. Its roots may well go back to the Old Testament association of the Spirit's presence and washing (Ezek 36:25-27). Though John makes clear that Jesus is the one who brings the Spirit (Lk 3:15-17), John's baptism pictures a preparation for what God will do in Jesus.

Still, John's baptism differs from Christian baptism. John's baptism looks forward, while Christian baptism assumes Jesus' provision of the Spirit. John's baptism anticipates the Spirit's coming, while Christian baptism reflects the Spirit's arrival through Jesus. The washing aspect of

John's baptism allows it to be associated with forgiveness of sins, as its connection to the Ezekiel 36 imagery suggests. Here are people of contrite heart, looking to God expectantly for what he will do in the days to come. Acts 19:1-10 reinforces the picture that John's baptism is anticipatory and not an end in itself: when some disciples appear in Ephesus who only knew John's baptism, they are led by Paul to experience what John's washing anticipated—the experience of being indwelt by the Holy Spirit (Lk 3:15-17; Acts 10:37-38; 13:23-24). When an Israelite takes John's baptism, he or she is declaring openness to God and his ways. The nation is put on notice to await the rest of God's promise.

This message is why Luke cites Isaiah 40:3-5, with its promise of the coming of God's salvation. As already noted, this Isaiah text is a "pattern" prophecy, speaking to many periods of history at the same time. In Isaiah these verses introduce the entire second section of the book, which overviews God's saving program for Israel, starting with deliverance from exile and ending in the utopian existence described in Isaiah 65—66. Thus a range of events is in view.

Luke shows how the pattern begins yet again with John the Baptist in the wilderness. John is like Elijah, as Mark 1:2-3 and Luke 1:16-17 note (Mal 3:1). The passage itself compares preparing for the events of salvation to preparing a red-carpet reception for a king. The creation is called to level the path so God can enter. With his entry God makes salvation manifest for all to see. There is nowhere else to look for God's saving work except to Jesus. The appeal to the leveling of creation is best seen as including the removing of moral obstacles to God's arrival. John is the sentry who issues the moral call to clear the way for his coming. The other Gospels make it clear that John also announces that the kingdom of God has "come near," something Jesus also declares (Mt 3:2; Mk 1:14-15). This announcement indicates that some aspect of God's rule approaches that had not been present previously. For the promised kingdom to be "near" means that it is not yet present when John speaks. So John is not speaking of the kingdom of God in its broadest sense of God's rule from the beginning of the creation. Rather, he is discussing the promised, long-awaited rule of God in which the promised Messiah and God's Spirit become evident in a fresh and startling way. John is saying that finally God is fulfilling the long-awaited hope of Old Testament promise.

John's later remarks about the Spirit (3:15-17; Mt 3:11-12) make it clear that one of the signs of the kingdom's arrival will be the Messiah's distribution of the Spirit, an event Peter declares as initially fulfilled in Acts 2:30-36 and in which all believers today share. When the Spirit comes, Messiah is at work, kingdom blessings begin to be realized, and Old Testament promise is coming to pass (Rom 16:25-27; Heb 1:1-13).

John the Baptist's Preaching (3:7-14) Encountering a prophet can be a challenge, as when you hear a preacher who can read your heart. God calls prophets to declare his will to sinful humanity. Often God's prophets use direct, explicit, even shocking images. Often they offend.

John the Baptist is no exception to this pattern. To listen to John is to be called to account. God wishes us to stop and reflect on where we are with God and to take fresh action, if necessary. For Luke, John the Baptist plays a twofold role. He prepares people for the Messiah, and he informs them concerning God's standard of righteousness (1:17). In this representative sample of his preaching, Luke shows how John accomplished the second concern. What does righteousness of the heart look like? What is the product of repentance? John's warning is direct. People need to be prepared to be open to God, to see and experience his grace.

A lesson on the differing responses to God's teaching appears in Herod's response to the criticism John gives in verses 19-20 and the crowd's response in verses 10-14. Where the people ask what they must do to honor God, Herod seeks to remove the prophet from the scene. We always face a choice when God's will is revealed. We may seek to accomplish God's desire, or we may reject it out of hand and try to remove the message (or messenger) from sight.

John's message is simple: (1) judgment is near (vv. 7-9), and (2) repentance means treating others well (vv. 10-14).

John is not at all soft-spoken as he addresses the crowd. His warnings are sharp, even severe. Those who come out to hear him are compared

---

3:7 Luke's reference to the *crowds (ochlos)* compares interestingly to Matthew 3:7, where the Sadducees and Pharisees are explicitly presented as the audience. What seems to be happening is that Luke notes that John spoke to all, while Matthew focuses on pointing out his words were particularly appropriate for the leadership. Luke tends to identify a speaker's

to snakes that slither out of their holes and *flee* across the desert as a fire approaches. God's enemies are often called snakes (Is 14:29; 59:5; Jer 46:22). Who wants to be near a snake? John calls the people snakes to warn them that their heart is not right and that his words must be heeded. No casual response will do; eternal realities are at stake. The snakes need transformation, since the fire of God's wrath draws near.

The reference to *coming wrath* alludes to the Day of the Lord (Is 13:9; 30:23; Zeph 2:2-3; Mal 3:2; 4:1, 5). John scares people into considering the fearful fate that may await them if they do not know and respond to God. The New Testament makes it clear that a person's position in relationship to Jesus is the key determinant of one's fate on Judgment Day (Rom 5:9; 1 Thess 1:9-10). Since John preaches before Jesus comes, he makes the point in terms of a person's self-perception. What might indicate that I am sensitive to God? John's answer is simple: a life that shows the *fruit* of caring about God by caring about others. Submit to God and serve others.

John asks for genuine *fruit.* In Greek the word for fruit is clearly plural, so John is asking for multiple produce. *Repent* is a slippery word in theological circles today. For some it merely means to feel remorse about something done, or maybe even just to attend confession with no real hope to stop the sin. But in biblical terms, to repent means to alter one's direction and perspective on something, to change sides or points of view. (For more on the centrality of repentance for Luke, see discussions on 3:1-6 and the introduction to Luke.) First Thessalonians 1:9-10 illustrates this meaning. The Thessalonians changed their allegiance from idols to serve the living God.

Jesus' call does not differ from that of John or of Paul to the Thessalonians (Lk 6:43-45; 13:6-9). In fact, for Luke *repent* is a key term that typifies what should be the response to the gospel's message (24:47). God wants us to come to him in repentance, but he calls us to him so he may grace us with a changed heart and a changed life. God honors a changed heart.

---

audience in general terms (Marshall 1978:138).

3:8 The verb *poiēsate (produce)* is aorist and suggests an urgent command in this context. They are urged to *produce fruit* worthy of repentance.

As John prepares the crowd to meet Jesus, he asks them to consider their identity. John is clear: religious heritage is not good enough. A good heritage can be an advantage, but it is no guarantee of blessing. The Jews of John's day thought that mere ancestral ties to Abraham would be good enough to guarantee them blessing (2 Esd 6:56-58). Some today think similarly, that one can be born a Christian or that attendance at church makes one a saved child of God. John warns that such thoughts of inherited salvation should not even cross their minds. Inherited salvation is no salvation at all. To come to Jesus we must come on his terms, not through a pedigree or by association with a certain organization. Though a good environment and roots can be of benefit, they do not yield salvation. Blessing is not a matter of physical heirship but of God's creative power. That God *can raise up children* out of *stones* pictures the reality that God's power is what produces new life. To get new life, we must come to him.

So John preaches that the one who pleases God seeks to serve others. Such a new outlook on life was imperative because *the ax is already at the root of the trees*. The poised ax makes it clear that any unfruitful tree will be removed and burned. The many allusions to fire in verses 7-9 show how warning dominates the section. The flame of judgment will consume. It is better not to get burned. John urges his audience to flee the threat of judgment just as they would run from a fire.

Judgment and accountability to God are not politically correct concepts in today's society. Nonetheless, they are present throughout Scripture. God as Creator has the right to hold our feet to the fire. We cannot be saved unless we are saved *from* something. God is neither a baby sitter nor a spectator; he is our Savior. Once the ax is wielded and the flames are kindled, it is too late. John is saying, "Watch out. Don't get

---

3:9 Hendriksen (1978:204-5) raises an important problem here: how can John speak of the day of the Lord as near when it did not come quickly? Such a question may be asked from the wrong perspective. The fact is that with the coming of John and Jesus, a person's relationship to the day of the Lord and judgment is determined. The day is near, because the decision one makes now is key. Since the decision is so crucial, it should not be taken lightly or put off till the future; as the well-known parable of Jesus suggests, the Lord may say, "This very night your life will be demanded from you" (Lk 12:20). In the plan of God, the day of the Lord and Jesus' coming are intimately linked, and thus with Jesus' coming the day is near.

burned!" Unless we come to him, we are at risk.

John obviously scored with some in his audience. Three different groups ask, *"What should we do then?"* John does not simply say, "Be baptized." Rather, he points them to their jobs and personal relationships. True repentance is a matter of the heart and results in change in everyday behavior. That is why the word *do* is repeated several times in verses 10-14. Each group wants to know the appropriate response to John's call; each reply points to how others are treated. The answer is in the spirit of the Old Testament and the Ten Commandments, which deal with how one relates to God and how one relates to others as a result. John makes it clear that he is not interested in their being baptized merely to participate in a sacred rite, but that the act represents and should point to a new way of responding to God.

The people should be ready to share their clothes, if they have more than they need: if someone is without clothes, clothe him. (The *tunics* were actually undershirts that were worn beneath the first-century tunic [Bauer 1979:882, χιτών].) The same response goes for food. Luke reports John's ethical and social concern, the call to give willingly to others and meet their needs (negatively, 12:13-21; positively, 14:12-14). Luke possesses a sensitive, compassionate theology of the poor.

The tax man is simply to collect the appropriate taxed amount, not extort additional monies. In the first century, tax collection was loaded with middlemen, who each added their own surcharge, so the potential for abuse was great (Donahue 1971:39-61). The soldier is not to take advantage of his authority; he is not to oppress the citizens with threats or violence.

The teaching of this text is not an ethical given. Little did I realize this passage's revolutionary power until I traveled in Latin America and

---

3:12 The tax situation in the first century was complex (Michel 1972:94-105; Safrai and Stern 1974:328-34). The tax was collected for the government by the person who submitted the best bid. He would then hire out additional men to collect it. With the addition of middlemen came the potential for extra surcharges to be passed on to the taxed citizen. So the citizen would be taxed by the system of collection as well as by the state. There were generally three types of taxes: a citizen's (or poll) tax, a land tax and a type of sales tax on items purchased or leased in a region. Tax collectors fell into public disfavor because of this system. The biblical phrase "tax collectors and sinners" shows just how far this disfavor went.

realized the history of abuse of military authority and that of guerrillas who challenge the government. Guns and intimidation have played a large part in their history as well as in the present activities of many nations. Of course, twentieth-century history has shown that such abuse is not limited to Latin America. Power corrupts, because sinful human beings use it to take advantage of those who are powerless. But service in the name of the state is not a license to abuse authority. So soldiers should exercise restraint in dealing with the citizenry and should be content with their wages.

In ancient times a soldier was paid only enough to maintain a basic standard of living (Caragounis 1974:35-57). Contentment with salary was key, because discontent might lead to the temptation to extort additional funds from others. Service to an institution does not mean one has the right to rob the till or take advantage of others' powerlessness.

John's answers are stated directly and concretely. The penitent is committed to fairness to neighbors, sensitivity and responsiveness to others' needs, and willingness to accept a "no-frills" standard of living (Barclay 1975:34). If Paul had food and clothing, he was content (1 Tim 6:8). John does not tell the hated tax collector to seek a new job, but to perform his job faithfully and compassionately. How we treat others is a litmus test for how we are responding to God. As Jesus says later, "Be merciful, just as your Father is merciful" (Lk 6:36).

John asks, "Where do we stand as the day of God's evaluation draws near?" Since John comes before the period of the cross, he cannot tell the people to place their trust in the work accomplished there. Rather, he calls them to live as children of God.

If such a life was pleasing to God before Jesus' coming, surely it pleases the Lord to see it in his children today. Heritage and words by themselves count for nothing. They may point us in the right direction, but they do not lead automatically to blessing. What pleases God is responding to him and showing concrete kindness to others. Such kindness involves compassion and concern for those in need, an ethical value that has corporate and individual dimensions. Authority should mean not the wielding of power but faithful service. Such is to be the life of God's saint still, as James 1:26-27 makes clear.

A Promise of the One to Come and Other Warnings (3:15-

20) John the Baptist's ministry is a two-sided coin: a plea for repentance
in preparation for the Lord's coming on one side, and looking to Christ
on the other. Like a good pathfinder, John points to Christ. But Christ
is no mystery for John; he is the bearer of the Spirit. John serves humanity
and the Messiah by showing humanity what the anointed one of God
will do. This section explains why John is a pointer, not the center of
God's plan. The theme is clearest in verses 15-17 (v. 18 simply notes that
much more could be said about John, while vv. 19-20 reveal Herod's
reaction to and rejection of John). By mentioning John's arrest here, Luke
places all the events of the Baptist's ministry in one passage. This arrangement enables Luke to concentrate on Jesus from this point on. The
picture of John as the servant who points the way to Jesus illuminates
what servants of God are like: they magnify the God they serve (Jn 3:25-
30).

The power in John's message leads some to speculate that perhaps
John is the Christ. The question is logical, since John has spoken of the
coming Day of the Lord, God's wrath and the approach of God's deliverance. Many Jews at the time expected that God would crush his enemies decisively during the time of Messiah (*Psalms of Solomon* 17—18).
So maybe John is this figure. Luke states the popular expectation with
the Greek particle *mēpote* ("perhaps"; NIV *if*), indicating that the answer
to the question is negative. If this grammatical hint is not enough, John's
reply settles the matter.

But then a question remains: if not John, then who is the Christ? John's
answer expresses Jesus' superiority at three points. First, Jesus has a
higher position than John. John will detail exactly what this means in the
following two points. When he calls Jesus *one more powerful,* he is
thinking more of personal authority than of physical power. So great is
the One to come that a prophet of God is not worthy to untie his sandals.
This illustration carries great power. Among the many tasks that a first-
century slave performed for his master, one of the most demanding and
least liked was removing sandals from the master's feet (Schneider
1977:88; Mekilta Exodus 21:2). John reverses the image to highlight the
gulf between human beings, even great persons, and the One to come.
It is not that untying sandals is too demeaning for the prophet; it is that
he is not worthy to be that close to the Messiah. This is like a CEO saying

he is not worthy to take out Jesus' garbage.

John's humility gives a proper perspective on the relationship of humanity to Jesus. Human beings are not Jesus' advisers or equals; they are greatly honored to know him and serve him. John does not draw attention to himself; instead he points to the superior greatness of the one to come. To direct others to Jesus is the call of God's servant.

The second area of Jesus' superiority is the blessing he brings. John has a baptism of water, but as verse 16 shows, this is a mere preparatory baptism. Jesus baptizes with the Spirit, bringing blessing, discernment, enablement and divine presence. To say that Jesus' baptism is *with the Holy Spirit* and *fire* raises an interesting point, since only one baptism is in view. We know only one baptism is described because (contrary to the NIV) the terms *Holy Spirit* and *fire* are tied together by one preposition, *en* ("with"). John is prophesying of all the Spirit will do as Jesus forms his people. Thus this is not addressing the rite of water baptism, but pictures the Spirit's coming to gather a people to himself. It refers to the promise of the Spirit's coming to those who trust in Jesus, while excluding those who do not respond to him (1 Cor 12:12-13). *Fire* is a key image for purging and judgment (Is 1:25; Zech 13:9; Mal 3:2-3; Dunn 1970a:12-13). A key Old Testament passage mentioning Spirit and fire together is Isaiah 4:4-5, where people are purged so some may dwell in God's presence. *The Holy Spirit* and *fire,* then, represent two integral aspects of Jesus' ministry. He comes to gather and to divide (12:49-53; 17:29-30). The offer of the Spirit must be received. Those who respond are purged and taken in, while those who reject are tossed away like chaff, as verse 17 suggests. Jesus is far superior to John because in the end it is Jesus alone who matters for any person.

The third and final point of superiority marks the ultimate difference.

3:16 There are four interpretive approaches to the image of *fire* as tied to baptism. (1) Some tie the it exclusively to Pentecost, the coming of the Spirit like fire in Acts 2:3 (Ellis 1974:80). But that image has to do with how the gift spread, not the gift's nature. This meaning also cannot explain the imagery of Luke 3:17 and its picture of the burning of *chaff*. (2) Others, relying exclusively on the imagery of verse 17, see only a mention of judgment. For them the Spirit is a mighty wind, while *fire* carries its normal Old Testament force of judgment (Fitzmyer 1981:474 has a full discussion rejecting this view). This approach limits John to making only a warning, a point that seems excluded by the reference to John's preaching good news in verse 18. (3) Others see a reference to two baptisms: one for salvation, the other for judgment (Schürmann 1969:174-77). This approach, though possible,

Jesus is superior because he is the Judge who makes distinctions between people. The wheat retained for storage and chaff that is blown away, gathered and burned evoke a picture of harvest time and are symbols with Old Testament roots (Job 20:26; Prov 20:26; Is 34:8-10; 41:15-16; 64:6; Jer 15:7). The key image is that of sifting, the separation Jesus makes between people. There is no room for universalism in this imagery: *the winnowing fork is in his hand*. Note the juxtaposition of judgment and fire—an echo of verses 7-9. The difference between John and Jesus is ultimately the difference between a prophet and the Judge. Jesus is stronger because he has all authority.

Luke's point is crucial. Jesus is not simply a great teacher, a moral example or a friend to those in need. He is these things, but he is also much more. Jesus' significance is evident in our accountability to him. In his hands God has placed ultimate authority. This picture of Jesus as ultimate Judge is central to Luke and to the preaching of Acts (Acts 4:10-12; 10:42; 17:31; Rom 10:9-13). If we wish to hear the voice and will of God, we must hear Jesus and those who carry his gospel message. This authority is why John pointed so exclusively to Jesus and why he counted it an honor to serve him. We do well to emulate John's respect for Jesus and total commitment to his uniqueness. In fact, doing so is a matter of life and death.

Luke next notes that John *preached the good news to them*. His preaching included a variety of other exhortations. Calling John's message *good news* might seem odd to us, given his direct, challenging, even harsh tone. His words seem more caustic warnings than good news. Our problem is our failure to appreciate what John is offering. Reality, especially spiritual reality, often seems a bitter pill to swallow at first. Healing can involve pain, especially when we are asked to look honestly at ourselves.

---

runs into problems with the verse's unified grammatical structure, though conceptually it is similar to the view I prefer. (4) Others, and I agree with them, see a reference to a baptism that purges and thus divides humanity (Marshall 1978:147; Fitzmyer 1981:474; Dunn 1970a:12-13). Subsumed within this view is the notion of Spirit's distribution to believers, though this image is broader in scope, revealing the Spirit's work among all people.

3:17 The harvest imagery reflects the practice of sifting grain in the first century. A wooden *winnowing fork* would lift the grain into the air so the wind would carry the lighter chaff away while the heavier grain fell to the threshing floor and could be gathered and stored. On the winnowing fork, see *ptyon* (Bauer 1979:727; Moulton and Milligan 1930:558). On the *threshing floor,* see *halōn* (Bauer 1979:41; Moulton and Milligan 1930:24).

Yet healing is good news, and John is calling people to genuine healing of the soul.

Herod's reaction to John's preaching stands in negative contrast to the openness of the crowds in 3:10-14. Like many Old Testament prophets, John holds the political leader accountable for his moral insensitivity and failure. Herod's marriage to Herodias is objectionable on two grounds. First, both have left previous marriages to marry each other. Second, Herodias had previously been married to a near blood relative of Herod; thus her union with Herod is forbidden under Jewish law (Lev 18:16; 20:21). Since Herodias had been married to Herod's half-brother, Herod Philip, in effect she is Herod's wife, sister-in-law and niece all in one (Barclay 1975:36)! John also points to other sins of Herod, but the use of the general term *pornērōn* ("immoral things"; NIV *evil things*) does not allow us to speculate on what these things are specifically.

Herod's response to the exposure of his sin is instructive. He does not face the sin and take responsibility for it; he strikes back, taking advantage of his authority to do so. Such a response is all too familiar. Herod will use all the authority at his disposal to silence the voice of conviction, for eventually he will execute John. Sin confronted but unchecked often becomes sin multiplied and magnified. Defensiveness in the face of sin is inevitably self-destructive. Unfortunately, the damage often extends beyond the one who is sinning.

Also instructive is an evaluation of John's ministry against the modern standard of success. By that standard John's scripturally honest but confrontational style could be seen as the cause of his downfall and failure. A modern PR consultant might have advised him, "Don't say anything that's too upsetting to your hearers, even if it's true. Work especially hard to avoid offending those with influence, because you might lose them." But the call to Jesus is not a call to maintain the status quo; it is an invitation to personal renovation. Our spiritual well-being may require that we recognize and deal with sin. Renovation implies change, and problems need to be exposed if they are to be corrected. Confrontation occurs because of a commitment to the hope of renovation; proper

3:19-20 On the relationships within the Herodian dynasty and the problem of a Herod named Philip, see Hoehner 1972:131-36. Josephus in the *Antiquities* 18.5.2 §§116-19 con-

moral correction means moving closer to God.

John may be in prison, but his ministry has been carried out faithfully and is a success, for he has pointed people to God's will and to God's agent. He has treated the hated tax collectors and Herod the same way, calling them all to walk with God. These two practices still make for an effective life compass today: (1) to honestly appraise one's spiritual condition and (2) to focus on Jesus and the gift of his grace.

Jesus, the One Who Comes (3:21—4:13) John has pointed to Jesus, so Luke turns now to describe Jesus' preparation for ministry. A divine endorsement accompanies Jesus' arrival (3:21-22), while the genealogy (3:23-38) and the temptations (4:1-13) give his historical and spiritual credentials. These latter two passages highlight Jesus' connection to Adam, showing that Jesus, though unique, has come to serve all humanity. Jesus' faithfulness to his ministry, along with God's endorsement of him, is the theme of Luke's opening presentation of Jesus' ministry.

Jesus' Baptism (3:21-22) The closest modern parallel to Jesus' baptism—though of course it is not at all the same—is the selection of a presidential candidate at a political convention. At this ancient "convention," however, there is only one elector who speaks, only one vote that counts. This is the first of two times in Luke's Gospel that a voice from heaven addresses Jesus (the other is in 9:28-36). Both events represent a divine endorsement of him (Acts 10:37-38; 13:23-25). This first endorsement contains two elements—the descent of the Spirit and the word from heaven; the second is marked by a cloud and a divine word.

After almost two thousand years of established theological teaching about Jesus, it is hard to appreciate how revolutionary the baptismal endorsement was, even though in all likelihood Jesus experienced it privately. The description of this miraculous event, unlike accounts of other miraculous events, gives no indication of bystanders' reactions (compare Paul's conversion, Acts 9:7; 22:9). There is simply a word to Jesus. Luke's presentation of the event, like the parallel Synoptic accounts (Mt 3:13-17; Mk 1:9-11), pulls the curtain away from the heavens and lets

---

firms this account of John's arrest while highlighting Herod's fear of the political consequences of John's preaching.

us see how God views Jesus' arrival.

The divine word from heaven explains who Jesus is and uses Old Testament language. As important as this description is, the environment in which the remark appears is also significant. Jesus, by submitting to baptism, identifies with humanity's need for cleansing. Luke will return to the connection between John and Jesus' ministry in 20:1-8; Matthew makes more of this identification by speaking of the need for fulfilling all righteousness (Mt 3:15). But the point here is crucial. The temptations will show that Jesus is different from Adam; he is able to resist the temptation to go his own way selfishly in sin. So Jesus does not accept baptism for the sake of his own sin. His participation in the rite indicates his readiness to take up humanity's cause in salvation. Here begins the realization of what John preached, the opportunity for the forgiveness of sins (Lk 1:76-79). John baptizes in water to picture cleansing, but Jesus brings the Spirit to wash away sin, to bring God's presence into people's lives and to guide them into the way of peace. This hope is why the Spirit descends on Jesus: God both endorses Jesus and pictures the enabling presence that comes in and through him.

A second key element associated with this event is that the Spirit descends after prayer. Luke alone notes this detail. With this unique mention of prayer the theme of devotion and nearness to God emerges. Jesus looks to God during every step of his mission.

The endorsement is clear, direct and filled with Old Testament background. There are three points of Old Testament contact.

First, Jesus is *my Son*. This is an allusion to verse 7 of Psalm 2, a regal psalm that probably has roots in the promise to David that God would be a father to David's descendant (2 Sam 7:14). Hebrews 1:5 explicitly

Notes: **3:22** Scholars debate the significance of the Spirit's dovelike descent. It should be noted that the Spirit is not a dove but is pictured coming down from heaven *like* one. Nonetheless, the Spirit was a visible entity, since he descended "in bodily form" (Greek *sōmatikō;* only in Lk). Whether this means the Spirit looked like a dove or simply descended from heaven in a manner that looked like a dove is unclear. Six views exist for this association of *dove* with *Spirit,* but no one of them is very clearly correct. In fact, some look unlikely. In Greek culture generally, birds were often associated with divine activity (Greeven 1968:64-66). Others mention a connection to the "Bath Qol" of Judaism, where the Spirit speaks as a voice for God (Betz 1974:288-90). But here the voice that speaks is not the Spirit, but God the Father *(my Son).* In addition, there is no clear reason that an association with a dove should emerge from this connection. Thus this suggestion is most unlikely. Others

links these Old Testament texts together.

Second, the quality of this relationship emerges in the description of Jesus as the beloved Son, the one *whom I love*. Here the emphasis may well be on Jesus' elect status (Is 41:8), highlighting that he is uniquely chosen for his task. Others suggest the allusion is to Genesis 22:12, 16 and to Isaac typology, but then *Son* would have both regal and national meaning simultaneously. Since Luke lacks Isaac typology elsewhere, this sense seems less likely.

Third, this Son is one with whom God is *well pleased*. This portion of the statement alludes to Isaiah 42:1 and serves as an initial Lukan description of Jesus as connected to Isaiah's Servant figure (on the evidence for this allusion, see Marshall 1969:336-46). As Servant, Jesus will carry out both prophetic and representative roles.

So in this short event heaven places its endorsing stamp on Jesus. He is the promised regal Son, the chosen one, unique in his call. He reveals the will of God and serves him. This is the one for whom John prepared the people. Anointed with the Spirit, Jesus is truly the Christ, a term that means "anointed one" (4:18). He is ready to minister and carry out his call.

The Genealogy of Jesus (3:23-38) Genealogies are interesting because they show our roots. A glance at a person's ancestors can often reveal much. Such is the case with Luke's genealogy of Jesus. Jesus has connections with David, Abraham and Adam. The latter connection is especially important, since it directly suggests his divine sonship and his relationship to all humankind. The Jews often kept genealogical records for important people, especially priests (Josephus *Life* 3-6; *Against Apion* 1.7 §§30-36). In Greek culture a tracing of such roots would be done to

---

suggest allusions to the imagery of God brooding over creation (Gen 1:2), Noah's dove (Gen 8:8-12), Israel (Hos 11:11) or a call for a new exodus (Deut 32:11, but this is an eagle!). It may be best to view the dove is simply as a way of picturing the descent. If symbolism exists, the connections to Genesis and the association with God's presence are the most likely options.

3:23-38 Some have challenged the notion that an Adamic connection is the major theme (M. D. Johnson 1969:234-52). Instead they emphasize Jesus as the Son of God or as a prophetic figure in the line of Nathan. But the literary character of this genealogy, which ends with Adam where Matthew's does not, is too distinctive to ignore, especially when the reference to Adam is placed before a set of temptations whose function recalls and contrasts so clearly with Adam's failure in Genesis 3.

show Jesus' qualifications for his task (Diogenes Laertius *Life of Plato* 3.1-2; Plutarch *Parallel Lives,* Alexander 2.1; L. T. Johnson 1991:72). The fact Jesus is God's Son would be particularly significant here, even though that sonship in this context is mediated through Adam. What Luke implies here is explicit in Paul, where Jesus is the second representative of humankind, the second Adam (Rom 5:12-21; 1 Cor 15:20-28, 45-49).

Several features of Luke's genealogy distinguish it organizationally from the lineage in Matthew 1:1-17. (1) Luke's placement of the list between the baptism and temptations makes the sonship of Jesus the issue, since that is the point of both the baptism and the temptation accounts. Can he be the Son? (2) Because it goes in reverse order, Luke's list allows Adam's name to be the last human echo before the temptations of Jesus are described. (3) Where Matthew stops with Abraham, highlighting Jewish interest in Israel's founder, Luke goes back to the birth of humanity by God's creative hand. Thus he shows that Jesus' story is humanity's story.

There are also key content differences between the two genealogies, including a significant divergence in the names between Abraham and Jesus, where the genealogies overlap. Matthew has forty-one names in this section, while Luke has fifty-seven. In the period between David and Jesus only two names are common in the lists: Shealtiel and Zerubbabel. Some sixty names in Luke's list are not in Matthew's. The most significant differences are that David's descendant in Matthew's list is Solomon, while Luke mentions Nathan; and Jesus' grandfather in Matthew's list is Jacob, while in Luke it is Heli (Stein 1992:141). The difference after David helps to explain the vast variation in names after that point.

There is no certain explanation for these differences. Some argue that there is no way to bring the two accounts together (L. T. Johnson 1991:72). But various explanations have been proposed. (1) A popular explanation is that Matthew gives Joseph's genealogy while Luke gives Mary's, especially given his concern for Mary in Luke 2 and the remark about Jesus' being *thought* to be Joseph's son in Luke 3:23. The problem

---

3:23-34 The numbers for the descendants between Abraham and Jesus are approximate, depending on how some portions of the list are read in light of text-critical questions. Especially uncertain is the sequence in verse 33, where several variant readings occur. I

with this is that a genealogy based entirely on a female line of descent would be rather unprecedented, especially for establishing a regal claim to promises associated with David. Furthermore, Luke 1:27 appears to tie Jesus' Davidic connection to Joseph. (2) Other variations argue for two ways to trace Joseph's line. Some speculate that Matthew has the natural line and Luke the royal line. Others suggest the reverse: Luke has the physical line while Matthew has the royal line. A third option suggests that Matthew gives the physical line while Luke gives the legal and "physical" line, with the physical contact being a sister who remarries and bears a child after a childless marriage. All these options appeal to levirate marriage (Deut 25:5-10) as the key at some point in the list, in the vicinity of the grandfathers—so one parent would be the physical progenitor, but the other parent, who died childless, had his name and line carried on through the birth after the levirate marriage. (3) Still a final option suggests that Mary, having no brothers, is an heiress to Heli (also spelled *Eli* in some translations). Heli adopted Joseph as son, as in other cases where a man had no biological son (Num 32:41; Ezra 2:61; Neh 7:63). So Luke's list reflects adoption (Nolland 1990:170-72). Luke's line may be the legal one because of the curse of Jeconiah (Jer 22:30), when he was cast out of the promised line (though Matthew does mention him). (A modern illustration of how a regal line can take a detour is the Duke of Windsor, who renounced all claim to the throne for himself and his descendants.)

Every explanation requires a conjecture that we cannot establish, so which approach might be right is uncertain. Regardless of which option is chosen, what is clear is the list's intention. Jesus has a claim to the throne through David and is related to all humankind through Adam. He has the proper roots to be God's promised one. He has the right heritage to inherit this ministry of deliverance. His roots extend to David, Abraham and Adam. God has carefully designed his plan. There are no historical surprises in Jesus. Ultimately all humanity is a unit, and Jesus is concerned with more than deliverance of the tiny, elect nation of Israel. With him comes realization of the Old Testament hope for that nation, but bound up in him also is the fate of all people.

prefer the reading that includes Aram, Admin and Arni (a variation of the NIV margin), but a couple of other options may be correct.

The Temptations of Jesus (4:1-13) Most lives have a moment of truth, a crossroads where one's mettle is tested and one's character emerges. In such moments the ethical options stand out starkly, and the choice that is made reveals on which road a person is traveling.

Satan's temptations of Jesus are such a moment for the recently anointed Son. How is the "beloved Son" going to carry out his task? His choices reveal his commitment and also point to the road of faithfulness and dependence that disciples should travel.

The event can also be compared to a cosmic, heavyweight championship fight. This is but the first round of many battles Jesus will have with Satan and other demonic forces throughout Luke's Gospel. Though at points, like the crucifixion, it looks as if Satan wins, Luke tells us not to be fooled about who is the stronger force.

Finally, Jesus' numerous quotes from Deuteronomy in response to these wilderness temptations recall another time and place where temptation and God's chosen met in the wilderness. During the exodus, the Israelite nation failed this test. Jesus succeeds where Israel failed. What is more, the genealogy immediately preceding this account has named Jesus as Son of Adam and Son of God. The echo of Genesis 3 cannot be missed. What Adam failed to do as representative of all humanity, Jesus succeeds in doing. Jesus' success is the first of many TKOs Jesus will deliver against Satan; the victory serves to reverse a string of defeats humanity has suffered at the hands of this deceptive, elusive enemy. Jesus shows that spirituality does not always take the easiest road; it trusts God's word and remains faithful to his way.

The temptation recorded here is paralleled in Matthew 4:1-11 and Mark 1:12-13. Mark simply mentions Jesus' successful response, while Matthew narrates the same three temptations as Luke but in a different order. Matthew's second temptation is Luke's third (at the temple in Jerusalem), while Luke's second temptation is Matthew's third (the of-

---

4:2 The reference to the wilderness (NIV *desert*, v. 1) raises the question whether the wilderness as a location has any positive or negative symbolic value. The evidence of Luke is mixed, so a symbolic force is not likely. Sometimes the wilderness is where demons are encountered (8:29; 11:24), but other times it is a place of repose to find God (1:80; 3:2; 5:16; 7:24).

Also interesting is the reference to *forty days*. This is a common number in the Bible. Israel wandered for forty years (Num 14:33; 32:13). Forty lashes was the maximum pun-

fering of all the kingdoms on the earth). This is a case where one Gospel writer has rearranged the order, and either writer could be responsible. But it is more likely that Luke has placed the Jerusalem scene last, as the climactic encounter, for literary reasons. Luke will highlight Jesus' journey to Jerusalem (9:51—19:44), the nation's central city, as the place Jesus is fated to go and suffer death. So Satan's offer to circumvent that suffering is a truly sinister effort to thwart God's plan. The placement of this temptation last foreshadows the strategic role Jerusalem will have in Luke's story.

As significant, threatening and testing as this event is, Luke leaves no doubt that Jesus is directed to the desert. He mentions that Jesus is *full of the Holy Spirit* and is *led by the Spirit.* Tests of character are divinely wrought, even when they place us at risk. One need only think of Job. In Jesus' case the tests come after forty days of fasting. The circumstances could not be worse for Jesus to deal with the offer of food in verse 3. Jesus' circumstances could provide him a ready rationalization for giving in. The contrast of this temptation to that of Adam and Eve in the Garden of Eden could not be greater. Adam and Eve had everything they needed to eat, but Jesus meets Satan in the midst of hunger and deprivation.

The first temptation raises questions of God's care and provision. Jesus' reply in terms of Deuteronomy 8:3 makes the issue God's goodness in providing for and protecting those who are his, just as the original setting suggested for Israel. Satan's words *"if you are the Son of God"* are a subtle appeal to Jesus' power, presenting the premise as if it were true. The assumption is that Jesus can act on his own here. But for Jesus to take action independent of God would have represented a lack of faith in God's goodness. Jesus' reply from Deuteronomy, *"man does not live on bread alone,"* reveals that one's well-being is not limited to being well fed. As necessary as food is, it is not as important as being sustained by the Word of God. For Jesus, truth is living in awareness of God's

---

ishment a man could receive (Deut 25:3). Forty days was the period of uncleanliness after birth (Lev 12:1-4). The flood lasted forty days (Gen 7:4, 12). Ezekiel bore Israel's iniquity symbolically for forty days (Ezek 4:6). Reigns of key kings like Saul, David and Solomon lasted forty years (2 Sam 5:5; 1 Kings 11:42; Acts 13:21). Most important for this account, Moses and Elijah fasted for forty days at key points in their ministries (Ex 34:28; Deut 9:9; 1 Kings 19:8). Usually when the number appears, significant events occur.

promise of care and relying on him even when God leads him into the wilderness. If Jesus is God's beloved Son, as was declared at the baptism, God will care for him. Such trust is exemplary.

The second temptation is Satan's invitation to engage in false worship. It represents a challenge to the first commandment to worship God alone (Ex 20:3). Apparently Jesus is given some type of visionary experience of the kingdoms of the earth and is offered total authority by Satan. As Satan makes the offer in verse 6, he places *you (soi)* in the emphatic position as if to say, "Look what can be yours!" This effort to entice recalls James's remarks about how sin emerges when our desires lure and ensnare us into sin (Jas 1:14-15). Satan is trying to lure Jesus through an appeal to power. The Greek reads, "To you I will give all this authority and glory; for it has been delivered to me, and I give it to whom I will. If you, then, will worship me, I will give it to you." The devil's offer is deception at its best, a half-truth. Though he has great power (Jn 12:31; 14:30; 16:11; 2 Cor 4:4; Eph 2:2; Rev 13:2—pictured as a dragon), he does not have authority to offer Jesus everything. The offer itself reflects extreme self-delusion on Satan's part, or else it is a ruse to get Jesus into the same predicament Satan now lives in as a result of his unfaithfulness and rebellion.

Here is an opportunity to grab power, but to do so and renounce God would be to possess destructive power—and ultimately would mean not possessing power at all. Satan is not worthy of worship. So Jesus' reply rejects the offer totally: *"Worship the Lord your God and serve him only."* The quote is from Deuteronomy 6:13, which follows closely on a passage recited daily by Jews, the Shema of Deuteronomy 6:4. Jesus is certain that only One deserves his service. It is not self or Satan, but God. By putting worship and service together in the verse, Jesus makes it clear that both words and life are meant to honor God.

The third temptation is also probably visionary in character. Jesus is placed on a high point of the temple and is urged to jump, to experience the joy of God's certain protection. The exact location at the temple is uncertain; two locales are possible. Some suggest the high temple gate, but more likely is the "royal porch" on the temple's southeast corner, since it loomed over a cliff and the Kidron Valley, some 450 feet below (Josephus *Antiquities* 15.11.5 §§410-12). Satan now quotes Scripture himself (Ps 91:11-12) to make it appear that taking a leap would be perfectly orthodox. And again the request is made in terms of Jesus' being the Son, as it was in verse 3. Satan plans a private test of God's faithfulness: "Jesus, before you venture out on this ministry, you had better be sure God will care for you. The psalm guarantees your protection, so jump. If you are the Son, God will rescue you; if you trust God, you will jump. Just let go and let God care for you!"

We can guess at what Satan really has in mind as we consider the destructive effects of demonic possession described in other texts (8:33; 9:39). But Jesus refuses to test God's provision by insisting on a miracle. He will not presume upon God and put a mask on unbelief by seeking to confirm God's trust. So Jesus cites Deuteronomy 6:16: *"Do not put the Lord your God to the test."* The Old Testament background is significant. Israel had presumed about God's goodness, doubting why he had sent them out into the desert and promised them the Promised Land. They had tested God at Massah (Ex 17:1-7). Jesus refuses to demand God's protection on his own terms. Such a demand is neither faith nor loyalty; it is sin.

Having failed, the devil departs for a time. This does not mean he leaves the story until Luke 22:3, when he reappears to influence Judas. Rather, he works behind the scenes in the various demonic encounters Jesus experiences throughout his ministry (as in 10:18; 11:19-23). The wilderness temptation is only the first round in Jesus' victory, but it is the first of many victorious rounds. Jesus' success reveals that he is qualified for ministry. The key to Jesus' triumph is his faithfulness in walking with God wherever God leads him, even in the midst of testing times. Here is a loyal and beloved Son who requites God's love. To love God is to be faithful to him, worshiping and serving only him.

□ Galilean Ministry: The Revelation of Jesus (4:14—9:50)

Luke introduces the actual activity of Jesus' ministry in this third major section of his Gospel. It is likely that the events of this account follow the events of the Judean ministry that only John records (Carson 1984:116). The section highlights Jesus' activity and includes two major discourses by Jesus. One discourse shows how Jesus presents himself as the fulfillment of God's promises (4:16-30), while the other reveals his ethical teaching (6:20-49). Miracles dominate the section. Luke focuses on who Jesus is in terms of his ministry's aims and the extent of his authority. Jesus and his power gradually awaken faith within the disciples.

Not all the section's news is positive. The contrast between Jesus' power and the growing rejection of him is the major tension in the story. This conflict is at the center of the plot of Luke's Gospel: Jesus has great power, but many still reject him. Blindness is a strange phenomenon; sin yields a potent darkness. Both together mean that people often miss what God is doing. Nonetheless, be assured that God is with Jesus and will fulfill the promises made to and through Jesus.

Overview of Jesus' Ministry (4:14-44) Luke summarizes Jesus' activity by juxtaposing teaching (4:16-30) with miraculous activity (4:31-44). Jesus' teaching evokes both wonder and rejection, two reactions that continue in our contemporary world. This passage's events take place mostly on one day; only the introductory overview, the synagogue speech and the concluding verses move outside this narrow time frame. The section could be summarized by the title "A Few Days in the Life of Jesus." While up to this point the Gospel's events have moved quickly, jumping months and years at a time, now the pace winds down to give us a slow-motion look at Jesus. Those who study narrative tell us that when time decelerates in the presentation of an account, important events are being related. That is certainly the case here.

In the midst of people's rejection, there is also cosmic struggle as Jesus encounters hostile spiritual forces in 4:40-41. Jesus is always dealing with the reality behind the scenes of everyday life. The passage closes with reflection about Jesus' mission in Luke 4:42-44. He must preach God's kingdom. Jesus must explain how his rule and God's promises come in stages and how he overcomes forces hostile to humanity and to God (10:9, 18; 11:14-23; 17:20-21; 24:44-49; Acts 2:16-38; 3:14-26; 10:34-43).

Notes: 4:16-30 This passage is very similar to Mark 6:1-6 and Matthew 13:53-58. The allusion in verse 23 to performing miracles as Jesus did in Capernaum suggests that Luke has moved this event forward in the sequence of his Gospel to highlight it as a programmatic event in Jesus' life, since Capernaum is not otherwise mentioned in Luke until 4:31. Thus this event typifies Jesus' preaching and the people's reaction to it (compare 4:43-44). Such

Jesus' Galilean Ministry (4:14-15) This short summary makes two simple points. First, Jesus is still led by the Spirit *(Jesus returned to Galilee in the power of the Spirit)*. Second, he is drawing attention to himself through his teaching, as *he taught in their synagogues, and everyone praised him.*

Galilee, lying in the northern region of Israel, served as the major ministry center for Jesus. The headquarters of this ministry was Capernaum, the city mentioned in Luke 4:31. It was because of Jesus' teaching that his fame began spreading throughout the region (so also 4:31; 5:3, 17; 6:6; 11:1; 13:10, 22, 26; 19:47; 20:1, 21; 21:37; 23:5). This is the first of several reports about the popular interest, curiosity and excitement being generated by Jesus (4:22, 28, 32, 36-37; 5:15; 7:17). What message could possibly generate so much interest? The next passage reveals the nature of Jesus' claims and provides initial answers to this question.

Jesus Preaches in Nazareth: The Time of Fulfillment Has Come (4:16-30) Have you ever waited a long time for something? As you see it draw near, anticipation rises. Do you remember the turning points as you moved from dating to engagement and then marriage, the anticipation of graduation, a work promotion, the purchase of a house, the arrival of a child? The moment, when it comes, is full of joy and the emotion of the realization of what had been anticipated.

God had promised the decisive demonstration of his salvation for his people for a long time. Now Jesus turns to declare the day has come; opportunity is present. After almost two thousand years of promise, stretching all the way back to Abraham, Jesus claims that the promises of a prophet like Isaiah are now being decisively realized.

But as in many great moments, questions arise. Is this *really* it? Have we moved from the days of promise to the time of the beginning of realization? Is God at work to fulfill his promise? Jesus' synagogue declaration brings a moment of decision for those who hear his claims. A

---

a placement does not raise any historical problem, since Luke is not intending to write a strictly chronological account. We make similar choices of placement in our reporting of events today. Many a sports column opens not with events of the first quarter but with the summary of a key play before it tells the story of the game. The summary encapsulates how the game went. Luke is doing something similar here.

snapshot of his entire ministry flashes in this brief exchange. Jesus offers much, but the crowd questions what is on offer. In the tension of the contrast, Luke's readers are left to choose sides.

The piety of Jesus' parents continues in Jesus, as *on the Sabbath day he went into the synagogue, as was his custom.* Unfortunately this is the first of several sabbath events that will end in controversy (4:31-37; 6:1-5, 6-11; 13:10-17; 14:1-5). Jesus' piety is not like that of the Jewish leadership. The controversies raise the question who represents God and his way—a major thematic concern in Luke's portrayal of Jesus.

Yet despite the tension, Jesus does not attempt to separate himself from Judaism. Rather, he presents his mission as the natural extension and realization of Israel's hope. As Jesus hopes to show, the time of fulfillment has come. The opportunity to share in and experience release according to God's promise has come this very day (v. 21).

To appreciate the account, it helps to understand the order of an ancient synagogue service (*m. Megilla* 3—4; *m. Berakot* 2). To have a synagogue service required the presence of ten adult males. At the service, the Shema was recited (Deut 6:4-9), followed by prayers, including some set prayers like the Tephillah and the Eighteen Benedictions (*m. Berakot* 2:2). After this the Scripture was read, beginning with a portion from the Torah (Gen—Deut) and moving next to a section from the Prophets. Instruction then followed. Often the speaker linked the texts together through appeal to other passages. The service then closed with a benediction.

Jesus appears to speak during the reading of the Prophets. He reads from Isaiah 61:1-2, a passage that promises the coming of God's salvation. His commentary, unlike most sermons, is brief, declaring simply, *"Today this scripture is fulfilled in your hearing."* The claim is so great that we need to work through the elements of the Old Testament passage carefully.

The passage starts with Jesus' claim that *the Spirit of the Lord is on me.* Jesus claims to be directed by God to minister and preach. The details follow, but interestingly, the reader of Luke's Gospel knows more about what this means than Jesus' original synagogue audience would have known at the time. The first hearers would have heard a claim for a divinely directed ministry, but they may not have realized that at his baptism Jesus had been *anointed* not just for a prophetic ministry but as Messiah. Readers of Luke have the memory of the anointing fresh in their recall. Jesus' remark recalls 3:21-22. His statement, along with what follows, shows that he is both an anointed Son and a prophetic figure. He reveals God's will and brings God's promise.

In the synagogue speech, the next line gives the goal of the anointing: *to preach good news to the poor.* This theme has already received attention in Mary's hymnic burst of praise in 1:51-53. Theologians today debate the significance of what Jesus said. Does this verse and those that surround it resonate with themes of political liberation for the oppressed? Is Jesus supporting class struggle? Luke's use of the term *poor* in chapter 1 and beyond makes it clear this is not only a socioeconomic reference. On the other hand, neither is class excluded from Jesus' concerns. In 1:50-53, the reference to "the humble" is surrounded by descriptions that indicate the spiritually sensitive character of the poor. Luke 6:20-23, too, compares the trouble the poor face in this world to the experience the prophets of old faced. So the text Jesus reads is not a carte blanche endorsement of the poor, nor is it a political manifesto. This hope extends only to the spiritually sensitive poor, to the responsive. The passage recognizes that often it is the poor who respond to God's message and embrace it with humility (1 Cor 1:26-29; Jas 2:5). They tend to sense their need and have no delusions of power, control and independence. They are what the Old Testament called the *ʿănāwîm,* "the pious poor," also called "the afflicted" (2 Sam 22:28; Ps 14:6; 22:24; 25:16; 34:6; 40:17; 69:29; Is 3:14-15; Amos 8:4; Bammel 1968:888).

For those looking to God for hope, Jesus was the answer. To respond to God, one must be open to him. For those in need of God, Jesus has a message of good news. Luke loves to emphasize that a potential audience for this message can be found among the poor. His social concern expresses itself fully through the details of what Jesus said at the synagogue—details the other Gospels lack. But this social concern is concerned with spiritual realities, not political ideologies.

So Jesus is sent *to proclaim freedom for the prisoners and recovery of sight for the blind, to release the oppressed.* Luke 4:31-44 makes clear that the oppression in view here is mainly spiritual. Forces stand opposed to humanity that pull down and bring sin, pain and pressure.

Being under demonic oppression is like being trapped in a prison of pain and despair. Jesus offers release from such pain and dark despair. That is what his miracles picture and point to, the reality beyond the act of the miracle (11:14-23).

Jesus' words, then, work at two levels simultaneously. He will heal the blind, but that also pictures the coming of light to those in darkness (1:78-79). The healing of the blind man in 18:35-43 also pictures what Jesus does for Zacchaeus in 19:1-10. Jesus is the physician who comes to heal the sick (5:31-32). Eventually the ministry of Jesus will bring total restoration and release to the creation (Rom 8:18-39; Rev 21—22), but in the meantime, deliverance means release into forgiveness and relationship with God.

Jesus' statement that he liberates the oppressed makes it clear that he is more than a prophet; he effects salvation. The allusion here is to Isaiah 58:6. Isaiah 58 calls on Israel to respond to God by fasting with a life of ethical honor to God (esp. 58:13-14). The prophet rebukes the nation for having failed to live up to the call of its sabbath worship. What Jesus promises here is a release that will result in his providing what the nation had failed to provide. In fact, many of the sabbath controversies in Luke have to do with Jesus' providing such release despite complaints about the sabbath timing of his healings. But Jesus replies that no time is more appropriate than the sabbath for such healings (and what they picture; 13:16).

This is why Jesus has come *to proclaim the year of the Lord's favor*. Here the allusion is to the jubilee, the year of cancellation of debts (Lev 25:8-17; Sloan 1977:39-41). What happened in that year, when debts were canceled and slaves were freed, pictures what Jesus brings for those who respond to his message of hope. Jesus builds on the picture of Isaiah's ministry, which also proclaimed such hope, and notes that what the prophet had proclaimed Jesus is fulfilling.

In sum, Jesus makes three points: (1) Jesus is anointed with the Spirit. (2) He is the prophet of fulfillment who declares good news. This office is what theologians have called "the eschatological prophet" or "the prophet like Moses," because Jesus proclaims the arrival of a new era of salvation, functioning as a prophet-leader. (3) Jesus is the one who brings release as well as the one who proclaims it. He is Messiah. This final idea helps to explain the blind man's insight into what he has been hearing about Jesus when in 18:35-43 he calls out to the Son of David for healing. The Son of David brings not only a future rule but also present release from sin and a reversal of the effects of Satan's presence in the world (11:14-23). In short, this is the beginning of the fulfillment of God's promise, and Jesus is the source of that fulfillment.

Jesus' claim that *"today this scripture is fulfilled in your hearing"* places both listeners and readers in the position of having to make a choice. No fence-sitting is possible. Jesus' teaching is not some ethical instruction detached from his person. He *is* the promise of God. Either he brings God's promise or he does not.

The crowd does reflect on the claim; they are amazed and perplexed simultaneously. They *spoke well of him and were amazed at the gracious words that came from his lips.* They recognized a persuasive speaker in their midst, but his pedigree gave them pause. *Isn't this Joseph's son?* How could he be the promised one of God? Knowing their thoughts, Jesus responds. In the Gospels, when someone thinks and then Jesus speaks, his words usually carry rebuke (7:39, 49-50; 11:38-39).

Jesus replies in three ways. First, he cites a proverb that indicates they want him to prove it. "Show me" is their basic response to his claim. Yet after the evidence is produced, there will still be doubt. Miracles, as powerful a testimony as they are to Jesus, in the end never convince one who does not want to come to God (16:31). People must be willing to hear the Word of God and receive it before they will see anything as God's work.

Second, Jesus quotes the proverb that a prophet is not honored in his home. This remark reveals Jesus' understanding of Old Testament history. He knows how repeatedly God's messengers were rejected. This theme will also surface continually in Luke (11:49-52; 13:32-35; 20:10-12: Acts 7:51-53). God's message is often met with rejection. The proverb also serves as a prediction that for many in Israel Jesus' ministry will fit into this tragic mold.

Third, Jesus recalls the history of Israel in the period of Elijah and Elisha (1 Kings 17—18; 2 Kings 5:1-14). The history lesson is a warning. That period was a low point in the nation's life, when rejection of God was at an all-time high and idolatry and unfaithfulness ran rampant. So

God moved his works of mercy outside the nation into Gentile regions, as only a widow in Sidon and Naaman the Syrian experienced God's healing. The price of rejecting God's message is severe: mercy moves on to other locales. It is quite risky to walk away from God's offer of deliverance. This exchange reveals the basic challenge of Jesus' ministry: the choice he presents carries high stakes.

The crowd does not seize the opportunity. Rather, Jesus' warning angers them. The suggestion that Gentiles might be blessed while Israel reaps nothing leaves them fuming. Such displeasure at the accountability implicit in the gospel message is echoed in Acts (7:51-59; 13:46, 50; 22:20-22). Many respond similarly today when they realize that the gospel is a matter of "take it or you will be responsible to God for the consequences."

Jesus departs, despite the crowd's efforts to seize him and remove him from the scene. People can try to turn their back on Jesus and do away with him, but he always will be sojourning in their midst.

Opportunities for God's work are also opportunities for tragedy. That is what is pictured in Jesus' synagogue visit. The promise's arrival was a great, historic moment, an occasion to enter into God's rich blessing. But blessing refused is tragic. The crowd's response is the first of many moments of opportunity lost in the Gospel. It is another step in a paradise lost. The gospel brings a choice—and choice has consequences.

Examples of Jesus' Ministry (4:31-44) These verses contain several quick snapshots of Jesus' public ministry during one day in the Capernaum region. The sequence highlights his miraculous activity, the most distinctive aspect of his ministry. Since these are the first miracles Jesus performs in Luke's Gospel, here we should stop to look at how miracles function for Jesus.

First, miracles are real events that evidence Jesus' authority. Since the Enlightenment it has been popular to question the possibility of miracles, because nature has been viewed as a closed world of cause and effect. But the most difficult miracle of all was the resurrection, yet its reality is the only way to explain how the disciples who were so dis-

---

4:31 Capernaum was located on the northwest shore of the Sea of Galilee, about 680 feet below sea level. It was a major Jewish center in northern Galilee with an economy built

traught at the cross became bold proclaimers of Jesus' vindication after the third day. In sum, if a resurrection is possible, the other miracles are a piece of cake. Can God actively intervene in his creation? The testimony of the resurrection and the other miracles is that he can and does with sovereign exercise of his power. And Jesus' consistent exercise of such power testifies to his unique access to God. As Jesus will note, if his power is not from Satan, then it must represent the presence of the "finger of God" (11:14-23).

Second, miracles are audiovisuals of deeper realities. In other words, they are not merely events for events' sake, they picture something more important. This point can be seen in two key miracles. In 5:1-11 Jesus leads four fishermen into a great catch of fish. Yet immediately Jesus makes the point that from now on they will be fishers of persons. The miracle *pictures* ministry. Another example comes in 11:20, where Jesus says that if he casts out demons by the finger of God, then the kingdom of God has come upon his audience. Here he is not speaking merely about the miracle of 11:14, but about all of his activity. The miracles picture a deeper reality about Jesus' authority.

In all the debate about whether miracles are real (or even whether they still occur through spiritual gifts within the church today), we in the West have lost their pictorial value, which is their major point. Those of us who live in the industrialized, philosophically sophisticated West might profit from listening to the testimony of many in the Two-Thirds World who appreciate the symbolism that these texts contain. Numerous passages show Jesus discouraging people from focusing too much on his miraculous activity (Mt 12:39; Mk 8:12; Jn 6:26-27). Sometimes he performs a miracle and asks that it not be divulged (Lk 8:56). Why does he do this? Possibly because he knows the *meaning* of the miracle will be lost if people focus on the event itself. In the rush to take and experience what Jesus has to offer, people can easily forget the One all the miracles point to.

Third, miracles unveil the deep cosmic struggle between the forces of evil and Jesus. If we ask what the miracles show, it is Jesus' sweeping

around agriculture and fishing (Josephus *Life* 13.71-72 §403; *Jewish Wars* 3.10.7-8 §§508-21).

authority. These events, especially those involving demonic forces, reveal hand-to-hand combat (Eph 6:10-12). The miracles pull back a curtain, as it were, so we can glimpse the behind-the-scenes battle within creation.

Armed with these three observations about miracles, we can appreciate even more what Luke 4:31-44 represents. Jesus tackles demons and disease to show he possesses the key to life. That authority and exercise of cosmic power is why he can speak of his mission being about the *kingdom of God* in 4:43. Jesus' authority shows the presence and concern of the rule of God on behalf of those who turn to God in a time of need.

This introductory summary of Jesus' ministry begins in verses 31-32 highlighting his teaching in Capernaum—*his message had authority.* As Jesus teaches in a city that will become his headquarters, the masses are aware that rather than citing what the rabbis had said in the past, Jesus speaks directly about God and his will. The following verses make an additional point: there is more to Jesus' authority than his ability to preach the Word; he can show the presence of God's power.

Jesus' first miracle involves *a man possessed by a demon, an evil spirit.* Demons are mentioned twenty-three times in the Gospel of Luke, but most of the references (fourteen) occur between here and 9:50, in the discussion of Jesus' Galilean ministry. It is clear that the man is threatened directly by this possessive force. Some in Judaism believed that demonic control of humans would end on the Day of the Lord (1QM 1:10-14; 14:10-11; Fitzmyer 1981:545-46). Judaism taught that demonic power would be crushed in the messianic age (*Testament of Zebulon* 9:8; *Assumption of Moses* 10:1), and Jesus says as much in 7:22-23. Here is the second face-off in the battle between Jesus and the forces of evil. With Satan already defeated in the first encounter (4:1-11), his underlings are the opponents here. Both the nature of the times and the victor are revealed in the battle.

Given the descriptions of this condition in the Gospels, it seems clear that demon possession, whatever one calls it, is the direct exercise of demonic power from within a person. If something is "exorcised" or

---

4:33 For a Jewish view of demons, see Josephus *Jewish Wars* 7.6.2 §185; *1 Enoch* 19:1;

asked to depart (v. 35), then something was present that needed removal. Mark 5:1-20 indicates how such possession can become very self-destructive. The New Testament suggests that one can distinguish between possession and sickness (Mt 4:24; Lk 4:40-41; 7:21; 9:1; 13:32), yet some overlap in terms of external manifestations can exist (Lk 8:29; 9:39; 11:14; 13:11, 16). By appearances, then, it can be hard to distinguish certain kinds of sickness from possession. Possession tends to manifest itself in very erratic behavior or physical impairment (Mk 5:1-20; Lk 8:29; 9:39, 42; 11:14; 13:10-17). The concept of possession itself (or, better perhaps, having an unclean demonic spirit, as the Greek of v. 33 puts it) indicates that the destructive and hostile force in control of the person lies inside the person and takes control of him or her from within.

Another way the New Testament lifts the veil on spiritual forces is through the dialogue that accompanies miracles. In this first miracle in Luke, the demon asks whether Jesus of Nazareth has come to destroy *us*. Who is meant nere—all demons, or the demon's complete influence over the man so the two are tied together? If it is the former, then the point is Jesus' authority over all evil spirits, a significant admission early in Jesus' ministry. If it is the demon's strong connection to the man, then the demon thinks Jesus cannot destroy him without destroying the human he possesses. In effect, the remark, though it is posed as a question, poses a challenge. Given the note in the next verse about the man emerging from the exorcism unharmed, the latter sense seems slightly better here: the demon does not think he can be challenged without the man's being harmed as well.

But why does the demon name Jesus and call him *the Holy One of God?* Possibly the naming of Jesus is an attempt to gain the advantage by uttering his true name in the midst of the approaching supernatural confrontation. On a literary level, the naming serves to make clear who the combatants are—an interesting recognition by the forces opposed to Jesus that he is on the side of God. The naming makes it obvious that a battle of cosmic proportions is under way. Though it is hard to be certain about the demon's motive in naming Jesus, his remark serves to

Jubilees 10:5; *Testament of Benjamin* 5:2.

identify the significance of the battle. Jesus meets the challenge and removes the presence and power of evil on the man without destroying the man himself. What a picture of Jesus' power!

So the confession by the demon is very important. Jesus is *the Holy One of God.* In the Old Testament, this title or one similar to it was given to Aaron (Ps 106:16), Samson (Judg 13:7) and Elisha (2 Kings 4:9). In the context of Luke's story we know that Jesus is holy because of his regal authority (1:31-35), a point reinforced in 4:41, when the Son is called the Christ. As James 2:19 suggests, demons have knowledge about God but fail to respond to that knowledge. Here is a case of evil having great angst in the presence of active righteousness. Evil cannot stand up to righteousness when righteousness takes a firm stand. Any victory it may appear to have is fleeting.

Jesus rebukes the spirit and prevails. The term used here may well reflect Semitic terms for calling evil into submission (Fitzmyer 1981:546). In addition, Jesus silences the demonic spirit. Why does he do so? Does he want to avoid any suggestion that he is a revolutionary against Rome (Stein 1992:163)? Does he simply want his works to speak for themselves (7:18-23)? Were only certain types of proclamation appropriate for Messiah? So Longenecker (1970:71-74), who notes similar hesitations in the claims of the Qumran Teacher of Righteousness and Simeon ben Kosebah suggesting a Jewish expectation on this question.

Of all the options, the most likely is that Judaism taught that Messiah should only engage in certain types of self-proclamation. Perhaps also there is concern that the title Messiah would be understood with too political a force (Stein's view noted above). More than one reason may lie behind Jesus' command.

Regardless of the exact reason, Jesus' authority prevails, even though the demon tries to injure the man upon departing by throwing him down (Mk 1:26 mentions convulsions).

The story of this healing closes as the crowd asks, *"What is this teaching?"* In their amazement they recognize that something very unusual has occurred. They see that Jesus approaches evil forces *with authority*

4:41 Other demonic confessions include Matthew 8:29, Mark 1:24, 3:11, 5:7, Luke 8:28 and Acts 16:17, 19:15.

4:43 For discussion of the meaning of *kingdom of God,* see Marshall 1970:128-36, Ellis

and power. A hierarchy of power is being displayed—what could it mean, and where does such power come from? Luke leaves the miracle as an event to ponder. The demon's confession suggests the answer, as do subsequent events: this Jesus is the Holy One of God, and his power exceeds that of the forces of evil. Needless to say, news of the event spreads far and wide.

Jesus' power over evil is not limited to spiritual forces. His healing of Peter's mother-in-law shows his authority over disease, and thus by implication his authority over life. The story is told simply. Jesus merely *rebuked the fever*—a verb that almost personifies the illness. Luke's unique use of the phrase *he rebuked (epetimēsen)* parallels verses 35 and 41, linking the events of the day around the theme of Jesus' power (both verses use the same Greek verb). Immediately the woman's health returns. Again, Jesus' actions reveal special authority.

As the sabbath passes, Jesus continues to heal. People with all sorts of maladies show up. Both sick and possessed come. The healings described earlier are not one-time coincidences. Jesus possesses the power to heal consistently. Note that the order in verses 40-41 (healing, then exorcism) reverses the order of verses 31-39. The pairing shows how Luke wishes Jesus' ministry to be seen. It is a ministry of mercy to those in need, fighting to overcome evil with compassion. Jesus' compassion is pictured by his laying on of hands. In his touch are power and presence. People flock to him because they sense that compassionate element in his work. By the way Jesus reaches out to them, they know he cares.

The exorcised demons recognize his authority. They confess Jesus to be the Son of God. Luke explains that this means *they knew he was the Christ.* Only Luke makes this comment. Jesus' regal, anointed authority extends to overcoming the forces of evil.

When at the break of day Jesus departs, the crowd follows and tries to keep him in Capernaum. Yet again Jesus speaks of his mission: *"I must preach the good news of the kingdom of God to the other towns."* This is why Jesus has been sent. The content of this kingdom message is seen

---

1972, and Blaising and Bock 1992:37-67. Ellis's book focuses on this theme in Luke. What we see is a kingdom in two phases—some of it come now (10:9, 18; 11:20; 17:20-21) and more of it to come in the future (17:22-37; 21:25-28).

in what Luke has already supplied (4:16-30): Jesus fulfills the promise. When John the Baptist raises the question again later, Jesus' answer points to such fulfillment (7:18-23). Jesus does not proclaim who he is; he lets events explain who he is. For him, actions speak louder than words. He is more than an ethical instructor or a psychologist; he has power to overcome the forces of evil that plague humanity. His ministry is not designed for a little corner, but it extends far and wide to take the message out to others. So Jesus takes his message and ministry to the other synagogues of Galilee.

The Gathering of Disciples (5:1—6:16) Jesus' gathering of disciples was not unusual in his time and Jewish setting. Many rabbis would gather students around them to teach Torah. But the *kind* of disciples Jesus gathers is unusual—they are not theological professionals. Fishermen, tax collectors, former revolutionaries and just plain old sinners make up this new community. Jesus launches them on a journey with God, a walk in which God begins to work in their lives. The lesson is that we need not be perfect to come to God; rather, we need to trust God and let him do his gracious work in transforming our lives.

The various "call scenes" that appear in this section underline the nature of the new community (5:1-11, 27-39; 6:12-16). It does not shun sinners, but invites them to come and meet God and his healing forgiveness. Even the miracles of this section show how much Jesus identifies with those he gathers to himself. These unusual events underline the authority he has in creating this new band of followers (5:12-16, 17-26; 6:1-5, 6-11).

The gathering of this unorthodox group of followers and the practices they engage in heighten opposition. Jesus' ways are not the ways of the Jewish leadership, nor are they the ways of a self-righteous elitism. He attracts those who know that they need God and that Jesus has the authority to forgive their sin (5:24, 31-32).

Notes: 5:1-11 There is much discussion about how this event fits with Mark 1:16-20 or Matthew 4:18-22. (Others also mention Jn 21:1-4, but as a postresurrection scene, it should not be compared to this account.) It seems most likely that this event is a subsequent confirmation of the call issued in Mark. (1) In Mark 1:19, the fishermen are washing nets, not mending them. (2) The nets alluded to in verse 5 may not be the same kind of nets Mark describes. Luke describes the use of a *diktyon*, an evening deep-sea net, while Mark's

Come Work with Me: The Gathering of Disciples (5:1-11) Besides teaching and miracles, Jesus' ministry centers on his disciples. Luke 5:1-11 details how Jesus confirms the call of four disciples to serve with him. In this passage, miracle, teaching and discipleship form a collage that explains mission and who is qualified for it.

Jesus performs a nature miracle, but the saying in verse 10 turns the entire miracle into a picture of mission. Here event and symbol merge. The event signifies not only what disciples are called to do but who disciples are as they do it. Simon Peter and Jesus represent different sides of the theology that undergirds the community Jesus is forging. Simon, for his part, knows that he is a sinner who is not worthy to experience the benefits of God's power and presence. There is no presumption that God owes him anything. Jesus, exemplifying God's grace, makes it clear that such a humble approach to God is exactly what God will use. Jesus calls these fishermen to fish for people rather than for finned water-dwellers. Luke presents these two truths quite dramatically and vividly.

Jesus' preaching is popular, so he must ask Simon to let him teach from his boat in the Lake of Gennesaret, better known as the Sea of Galilee. If this is an average ancient fishing boat, it would be twenty to thirty feet long (Stein 1992:169; Wachsmann 1988).

Much in this event is ironic. When Jesus tells Simon to put the boat out and cast down his nets, it is a carpenter's son and teacher telling a fisherman how to fish. It is a little like a pastor telling a CEO how to run technical aspects of his business! Not only that, but Simon's response makes it clear that conditions for fishing are not right, since a major effort the night before had totally failed. Yet despite appearances and against his professional judgment, he follows the teacher's command to let down the nets. Simon Peter is responsive to God's messenger and thus an example of faith.

The result is success and near disaster at the same time. The nets are filled to overflowing, and so is the boat! The fisherman is desperate for

---

verb *amphiballō* suggests the use of an *amphiblēstron,* a shallow day net (Marshall 1978:202). (3) Andrew's absence is also peculiar. Though it is possible Mark has simply telescoped Luke's account, it seems more likely that Luke is narrating a confirmation of the earlier Markan event.

5:7 The term *bythizesthai* is ingressive in this context, so the boat *began to sink.*

help to bring in all the fish. The boat is so full it begins to sink. Jesus has guided Simon to a great catch, but that catch is a picture of how he will guide the disciples in other, more spiritual affairs.

Simon Peter realizes he has been brought into more than a successful commercial venture. As nice as it would be to have Jesus as a permanent fishing guide, God's messenger is in their midst, and the fisherman knows enough about God's holiness to know he is at risk. So Simon falls to his knees and confesses his unworthiness, asking Jesus to depart. He understands that sin produces distance between himself and God. Surely God wants nothing to do with a simple, sinful fisherman. It is best that Jesus go. In fact, Jesus is addressed as *"Lord,"* but not because Peter understands that Jesus is God. It will take events in the next few chapters to lead Simon to confess Jesus as Christ (8:22-26; 9:18-20). Rather, Jesus is Lord here because he is God's agent. Nonetheless, Jesus should go, for Simon Peter is not worthy of the agent's presence.

The size of the catch tells Simon and his companions that this event has been no accident. The greatest moment in their fishing career causes them to stop and ponder what God is doing. Jesus has taken Peter's humble faith and scared him to death with God's presence. But in the uncertainty that often surrounds faith comes the divine honoring of its presence and a calm voice that says, *"Don't be afraid."* Grace is active. Simon Peter, James and John learn that God will take the faith of humble fishermen and ask them to join him in catching other people for God.

Simon Peter represents all disciples. His humility and awareness of his sin do not disqualify him from service; they are the prerequisite for service. Simon's response recalls the reaction of earlier great servants of God like Isaiah and Jeremiah, who also bowed low in humility when they caught a glimpse of God's presence (Is 6; Jer 1:1-10). Jesus does not call those who think they can help God do his work. God does not need or want servants who think they are doing God a favor. Jesus calls those who know they need to be humble before his power and presence. *From now on* Simon will be casting his nets in a different sea, the sea of humanity's need for God.

5:12-16 The only other healing of a leper in Luke appears in 17:11-19. But Luke 7:22 and Matthew 10:8 mention such healings. A biblical precedent for such healing comes in the story of Elisha (2 Kings 5:1-14). The parallels to this account are Mark 1:40-45 and Matthew

A genuine meeting with Jesus alters one's perspective. An encounter with God's power is no reason to draw back from him, but an opportunity to approach him on the right basis, in faith and dependence. In catching fish, Jesus has caught Simon Peter.

The mission is to catch persons alive. The figure involves rescue from danger, since those caught are caught alive (on the term "alive," see Num 31:15, 18; Deut 20:16; Josh 2:13; 2 Maccabees 12:35; on the "fisher" and being hooked, Jer 16:16; Ezek 29:4-6; Amos 4:2; Hab 1:14-17). In the Old Testament this kind of symbolism is usually negative, but for Jesus it is clearly positive.

The response is instantaneous and total. When the boats come in, the former fishermen leave everything behind and follow Jesus. The call had gone to Peter in verse 10, but all those who experience the catch follow Jesus. The fishing expedition has brought in its first catch. Sinners are transformed into servants of God. That is how great God's holiness and grace can be.

The Cleansing of the Leper (5:12-16) If the call of the disciples shows Jesus reaching out to sinners, his healing of the leper shows that Jesus is also concerned for the total outcast. For a modern parallel to the leper, we may think of victims of AIDS. Just like the AIDS victim, the leper of the ancient world was ostracized from society and largely forgotten. True, today the victims of AIDS get much publicity, along with a great clamor to fund research to fight the HIV disease, but many people would prefer to forget these victims of disease and shunt them off to the fringes of society. To get close to them or touch them would be to risk too much.

I think of an attempt to launch a cooperative ministry to AIDS patients in my area. Many churches responded that the goal was admirable and they would offer moral support, but what would they do if AIDS patients came to faith and wanted to come into their church? The risk was too great, so they opted out of supporting the effort directly.

I wonder if Jesus would have responded this way. Jesus said he came to minister to those in need, and Luke 5:12-16 shows how that ministry

8:2-4. The sequence of events in Luke is like that in Mark, whereas Matthew appears to have placed the account where he does in his Gospel for topical reasons.

extends to the very bottom rungs of the social ladder. No one is beyond the potential touch of Jesus' love.

Luke narrates this miracle with extreme economy. Jesus is in *one of the towns*. The leper humbly implores Jesus to help him, confident that if Jesus wills it, Jesus can make him clean. Clearly, word about Jesus had spread even to these marginal colonies in the society. *Make me clean*, though literal, suggests a real cleansing of the person (remember, all the miracles in this Gospel have a "picture" element). The leper knows Jesus' capability, but he is uncertain of the extent of his compassion. The extent of Jesus' compassion is revealed here. In the modern world it is perhaps the exact reverse. Today's person on the street does not doubt Jesus' compassion but does question his capability. Accounts like this demonstrate that Jesus opened himself to all.

Jesus' touching the leper is significant, since such contact rendered him ceremonially unclean (Lev 13:42-46; all of *m. Nega'im*). The physical communication of charity meant suffering ceremonial uncleanness that could affect his involvement in corporate worship. Given that Jesus' other miracles have occurred through the mere speaking of his word, it's clear that the act of touching is conscious. The healing is immediate; the compassion is demonstrable. Jesus is able and willing.

Jesus tells the healed leper to *show [himself] to the priest*, which fits with the command of Leviticus 14:1-32 about dealing with healing from leprosy. Beyond this, however, the healed man should keep silence about what has happened. This part of Jesus' instructions is perplexing. We would think Jesus would appreciate the public relations coup such a healing represents. Think of how we broadcast even the claim of such events today. The contrast is significant.

There are various explanations for the silence. One part of the explanation seems to be that Jesus wants to quell excessive excitement about his healing ministry so that the message he brings does not get lost in a flurry of requests for miracles. It may also be that the man is to keep

---

5:12 *Leprosy* in Luke appears to refer to a wide array of skin diseases, not just "Hansen's disease" (Michaelis 1967a; van der Loos 1965:465-68). The disease created either lesions or swollen areas on the skin. Psoriasis, lupus, ringworm and favus may all have been included within what was treated as leprosy in the ancient world. Leviticus 13—14 discuss how the Torah regulated this disease for social reasons. The ostracism it prompted made it a "living death." Clearly the sufferer lost both self-esteem and the ability to live anything

silent only until the priest formally declares him clean. Regardless, it is clear that Jesus approaches his ministry of miracles circumspectly (Mk 8:11-13; Jn 6:26-27). Perhaps because the miracles are pictures of deeper realities, he wants people not to be overcome by their more obvious, surface meaning—a tendency that proves hard to avoid.

The instruction to go to the priests serves as *a testimony to them.* Is *them* a reference to the priests or to all people? The stress on obeying the Torah suggests that those who receive the testimony are the priests. In the next event Luke explains that the Jewish leadership is present, so clearly the testimony gets their attention. As 7:22 makes clear, the cleansing of lepers is a sign that "the time of fulfillment" has come.

Word does spread. Crowds gather (v. 15). Luke 4:44 is being fulfilled. Mark 1:45 notes that the crowd is growing to crushing levels. Nevertheless, Jesus periodically withdraws to collect himself and commune with God (v. 16). Seeking time with God is key to ministering effectively. In fact, numerous conflicts follow in Luke, so the Gospel writer is making it clear that before Jesus meets with trouble, he communes with God.

Sometimes reaching out to outcasts is unpopular. Sometimes conflict for doing so is not a sign of failure.

The Healing of the Paralytic and the Authority to Forgive Sin (5:17-26) Luke narrates yet another miracle, the healing of the paralytic. This miracle is significant for five reasons. First, it shows that Jesus' authority extends even to the forgiveness of sins. Second, the entire affair is witnessed by the Jewish leaders, the Pharisees and the scribes. They make an instant theological assessment and recognize that Jesus is making unique claims—claims that are blasphemous if they are not true. Third, this is the first time God vindicates Jesus' claims during his ministry. Later Judaism would teach that God does not help sinners or liars (*t. Nedarim* 41a), so if Jesus is not who he claims to be, then this man should not walk away healed. The fact that the paralytic walks away healed means that some type of transcendent power operates through

close to a normal life.

5:14 The process of determining that a leper has been cleansed is detailed in m. Nega'im 14.

5:17-26 This miracle has parallels in Mark 2:1-12 and Matthew 9:1-8. Matthew places the event within a thematically oriented section, chapters 8—9. Mark's and Luke's placements are similar. In a chronological scheme I prefer the placement by Mark and Luke; it seems that Matthew's placement is governed by thematic concerns (Carson 1984:221).

Jesus. Later Luke reveals the debate over what or who that power is (11:14-23). Fourth, the miracle pictures what Jesus can do for people. The paralytic is stationary and totally helpless. But after his healing, he can walk through life and praise God. Finally, the text shows the importance of faith. It is the faith of those who bring the paralytic to Jesus that is highlighted. This detail seems to indicate that God honors us as we seek to lead others to the Lord.

Though Mark 2:1 mentions that this event takes place in Capernaum, Luke simply tells the story. The presence of *Pharisees and teachers of the law* shows that word about Jesus has spread to the upper echelons of the Jewish faith. The Pharisees were a nonpriestly, lay separatist movement whose goal was to keep the nation faithful to God. Their name is probably a transcription of an Aramaic term meaning "separated ones" (Fitzmyer 1981:581). To prevent violations of the Mosaic law, they developed an elaborate system of traditions to codify practice (Meyer 1974:11-48; Josephus *Antiquities* 13.5.9 §171; 13.10.5-6 §§288-98; 17.2.4 §§41-45; 18.1.2 §§11; *Jewish Wars* 2.8.14 §§162-63). They desired to "build a fence around the law" to prevent it from being violated (*Pirqe 'Abot* 1:1). The *teachers of the law,* also known as the scribes (v. 21), helped to study legal questions and develop the tradition (Jeremias 1964c:740-42; Rengstorf 1964:159). The word sometimes translated "scribes" has roots in the postexilic period to refer to one learned in matters of the law (Ezra 7:6, 11; Neh 8:1). Luke reveals that these leaders have come from as far away as Jerusalem.

In the midst of such traditional religious authorities, God's power rests on Jesus. He has *the power of the Lord . . . to heal the sick.* Luke is going to great pains to indicate that Jesus did not require official endorsement from the Jewish hierarchy. His commission was unique, coming directly from God, as his baptism had made clear (see 20:1-8).

The paralytic comes on a *mat* (*klinē,* Luke and Matthew) or a pallet (*krabbaton,* Mark). But the crowds prevent access, so the friends must scale the ladder on the side of the house to get up on the roof, where they can cut through the roof and lower the man in front of Jesus.

5:19 The roof *tiles* mentioned here are made of clay *(keramos).* Some have challenged the believability of this story on two grounds: (1) the roofs of Palestinian homes normally did not have tile, and (2) It seems unlikely that someone could get away with the distur-

Needless to say, such activity is highly distracting. The man ends up *right in front of Jesus.* So now the Teacher must act. What will he do?

Jesus pulls a surprise. No doubt the crowd has expected a healing, since Jesus' reputation has spread far and wide already (4:40-44). But instead Jesus talks about sin. And thus again a miracle becomes a parable. This time it pictures the presence of the destructive forces of sin in the world. This man is a painting of the effects of the Fall. Such a linkage is not surprising in a Jewish setting (1 Maccabees 9:54-56; 2 Maccabees 3:22-28; 3 Maccabees 2:21-22; Jn 9:2-3). Jesus claims to have the authority to reverse those effects, so he says, *"Friend, your sins are forgiven."* This theme is frequent in Luke (5:29-32; 7:34, 36-50; 15:3-7, 11-32; 18:10-14; 19:8-10; 23:40-43).

The remark elicits an instant theological critique from the religious experts present. They *began thinking to themselves, "Who is this fellow who speaks blasphemy? Who can forgive sins but God alone?"* The Pharisees get high marks for perceiving the theological significance of Jesus' statement. They see the stakes correctly. They understand how great Jesus' claim is. The issue of blasphemy will become a central concern at Jesus' trial, as Jesus reiterates an authority for himself there that the leadership will question (22:67-71). To blaspheme was to perform an action that violated God's majesty. Claiming a prerogative that was only God's would be such a violation. So the issue raised by the act and its proclamation is authority pure and simple. Jesus has implied the same authority in Luke 4:18. In his own eyes, Jesus is more than a teacher of ethics.

It seems likely that the Pharisees' musings are private, because the text goes on to note that Jesus *knew what they were thinking.* Usually when Jesus is reading someone's thoughts, a rebuke or challenge follows. Such is the case here.

Jesus poses a conundrum: *"Which is easier: to say, 'Your sins are forgiven,' or to say, 'Get up and walk'?"* Now there is irony here. It is easier to say sin is forgiven, since one cannot see it. But actually to forgive sin is the harder thing to do. Still, the healing of a lame man could

---

bance the lowering of the man would have caused. But the term for tiles may just refer to clay (2 Kingdoms 17:28 LXX). As to the believability of the event, as long as Jesus remained calm, others would have followed his lead.

be corroborated visually; one could see its success immediately. Jesus' remarks, however, link the two actions. Healing will reveal the authority to forgive—and in the process raise many questions about who Jesus is. So Jesus says, *"But that you might know that the Son of Man has authority on earth to forgive sins . . . I tell you, get up, take your mat and go home."* This moment in the account calls to mind the modern sports expression "crunch time." Either the man gets up and walks or he continues to lie there. Either Jesus' claim comes through, or he is utterly embarrassed. God does not help sinners, so what will happen? Jesus has put theological stakes on the event. Will God vindicate him?

This text is important for another reason. It is the first time Luke uses the important expression *Son of Man.* Later in this Gospel it is clear that he is using the term as a title. In Aramaic this phrase was an idiom that either meant "someone" or served as a roundabout way to refer to oneself. Be aware that at this point the Old Testament background for this term has not yet been revealed. Jesus will do that later in his ministry when he ties the title to imagery from Daniel 7:13-14. All *son of man* meant to the audience here was "some human being." But of course, the moment Jesus forgives and heals the paralyzed man, *Son of Man* becomes a very specific reference to him, since the authority he is claiming is not generic to all humans but is his alone.

In sum, Jesus' claim to have special authority and so to be a unique human being is the issue of the passage. The beauty of Jesus' use of this idiom alongside his action is that it allows him to raise a question about his identity in terms that honor both his unique authority and his humanity. The claim, however, rides on what the paralytic does in the next few moments.

Immediately he stood up in front of them. The man's walk means God has talked! As the former paralytic praises God, amazement overwhelms the crowd. They have seen *remarkable things.* The Greek term used here is *paradoxa,* a word from which we get our word "paradox." But in

5:24 For many details on the background and Jewish usage of the *Son of Man* title, along with debate about its meaning in Aramaic, see Bock 1991.

5:27-32 This passage has its parallels in Mark 2:13-17 and Matthew 9:9-13. Matthew has chosen to narrate the call in relationship to the timing of the meal, where Mark and Luke appear to have gone the opposite direction, mentioning the meal with the call earlier in

Greek the term simply refers to unusual events. Again Luke ends the passage asking the reader implicitly to ponder what has taken place. What happened? What has been claimed about what happened? Events speak louder than words (7:18-23): the Son of Man has authority to forgive sins.

Jesus has just painted a picture that speaks more than a library full of books on Christology. He has backed up his words with action. God is vindicating Jesus' claims. At crunch time Jesus applies his authority with great skill. As the paralytic walks, the question becomes who will walk with him and share the forgiveness Jesus has pictured. Fence-sitting is no longer possible, given the nature of Jesus' claims.

The Calling of Levi (5:27-32) Again Jesus' attention turns to a so-cial outcast, in this case Levi the tax collector. Luke has already discussed tax collectors when he described the ministry of John the Baptist (see 3:10-14). Jesus initiates relationships with outcasts, even though pious people in Israel challenge such associations (7:36-50; 15:1-2; 19:1-10). As the earlier account with Peter showed (5:1-11), Jesus calls sinners to righteousness and to share in mission with him. Jesus does not merely forgive sinners, he openly associates with them.

But why? Why does Jesus associate with sinners when so many righteous people do not want to have anything to do with them? Many people think one must choose absolute separation if one is to remain pure, but for Jesus this is a false choice. Jesus views people in terms of what God could make them into, rather than pigeonholing them into who they currently are. There is no compromise with holiness in his relationships with sinners, because one of the very characteristics of God's holiness is the way he reaches out in mercy to those in need (1:46-53). God graciously takes the sinner who is responsive to him and begins the work of transformation.

The story in this passage proceeds simply. Jesus observes the tax collector Levi at work and calls him to follow (9:23, 59; 18:22). Levi's response is total—he *got up, left everything and followed him.* The

Jesus' ministry. These are merely literary choices related to arrangement. In all likelihood, Levi and Matthew are the same person. In the ancient world it was common to have two names (for example, Peter, Cephas; Saul, Paul).

5:27 For more on tax collectors and how they functioned, see above note on 3:12. Levi is a toll collector of lesser status than Zacchaeus, who is a chief tax collector.

instantaneous and comprehensive nature of the decision to join Jesus shows both the reputation Jesus has and the quality of an exemplary response to Jesus. Levi has put Jesus first. To follow him is a priority.

In fact, Levi wishes to celebrate by introducing Jesus to his friends. Such is often the case with recent converts to Jesus. Unchurched friends are often the first to hear about the new discovery. So it should be. The tragedy is that after people have been in the church for a time, they find it hard to relate to outsiders. Jesus does not suffer from this problem; he consciously makes an effort to associate with those outside his community. He does not run or hide from the world in need, but engages with it realistically so its real needs can be addressed. Often what wins an outsider to God is a genuine friendship. Despite Levi's low social status, he feels free to associate with Jesus. Jesus' invitation has made that clear.

A contrasting attitude emerges in the grumbling among Jewish leaders. Their commitment to purity, their sense of what God requires of them and their fear of risking exposure to the world cause them to shun outsiders and criticize those who try to relate in a healthy and engaging way to sinners. Table fellowship in the ancient world meant mutual acceptance. So at stake in the Pharisees and scribes' response is a world-view question. Should we really get close to the socially objectionable, to people like tax collectors and sinners? The Greek word used for their complaint, *egongyzon,* is significant because it is the term Numbers 14:26-35 LXX uses to describe the nation's grumbling to God in the wilderness. This word sounds like its meaning; we can almost hear the harsh tone of voice as we read the words (7:34 repeats the complaint).

Jesus' reply makes it clear that recovery, not quarantine, is the message of his ministry. Jesus pictures himself as a doctor who treats the sick, not the strong. The remark takes the Pharisees' perspective, though it does not endorse their righteousness. Jesus' point is that those who know they need help will respond to the Physician. Often the unrighteous are aware of their need, whereas the unrighteous "righteous" are not. The unrighteous need a breath of potential acceptance and a whiff of God's grace

---

5:33-39 The text has parallels in Mark 2:18-22 and Matthew 9:14-17. Matthew ties it temporally to the healing of Jairus's daughter, an event Luke has much later in 8:40-54. Mark

to open up to his work. The appeal to physician imagery is common in Judaism (Is 3:7; Jer 8:22; esp. Sirach 38:1-15; Bovon 1989:259, n. 24).

Jesus' second point is a mission statement that explains why he seeks the outsider. This is one of several such mission statements in Luke (7:34; 12:49, 51; 18:8; 19:10). Jesus has come to minister to those who have need of repentance. He calls to them to repent. Repentance is a major Lukan theme, and only Luke mentions it in this scene (3:3, 8; 13:1-5; 15:7-10; 16:30; 17:3-4; 24:47). Here Jesus offers a picture of true repentance: it is like going to a doctor for help. The "cure," if it is to come, must come from outside of oneself. A repentant heart is open to God and to his administering the necessary medicine for life. God graciously gives this medicine to those who seek forgiveness through him. Jesus sees opportunity for restoration for sinners and works to achieve relationship with them so they can experience the healing they need. When tax collectors and sinners come to the table in the clinic, Jesus, the Great Physician, is not about to turn them away. As in the other events chronicled in Luke 4:31—5:32, Jesus reaches out to all types of needy people. All can benefit from the power of his healing presence.

Some are still uncomfortable with such an open ministry, but this is evangelism in its most authentic form. Jesus' ministry is about compassion and grace. When Jesus proclaims God's love, the outsider knows Jesus means it. Both his words and his actions show it. In his openness Jesus risks criticism and ridicule. But given that Jesus pursues such contacts with gusto, can his disciples do otherwise?

Why Are You Different? Part 1 (5:33-39) People have trouble accepting those who are different. When someone marches to the beat of a different drum, we are forced to ask questions about them and ourselves. Jesus' outreach to sinners was a different way of doing things, and so was his approach to traditional customs of piety.

Finally the Pharisees get up the nerve to ask why Jesus' disciples do things differently. Of course, they are really asking about Jesus. He is their major concern. When it comes to ascetic practices like fasting, Jesus is not like the Pharisees, or even like his forerunner John the Baptist. So

---

and Luke may have placed it earlier in the story of Jesus' ministry to show how different Jesus' ministry is from traditional Jewish practice.

Jesus' meal with sinners is not the only thing that bothers the leadership. He hangs out with outsiders *and* he does not follow the usual practices of piety. Why is that?

Specifically, they ask him about fasting and prayer. The ancient practice of fasting had a rich heritage in Judaism. It was a highly regarded act of worship. The Day of Atonement was celebrated with a fast (Lev 16:29, 31). A four-day fast commemorated the fall of Jerusalem (Zech 7:3, 5; 8:19). Fasts could be acts of penitence (1 Kings 21:27; Joel 1:14; Is 58:1-9) or could be associated with mourning (Esther 4:3). Pharisees fasted twice a week, on Monday and Thursday (8:12; *Didache* 8:1; Behm 1967a:924-35). Fasts are serious expressions of worship.

Jesus' reply not only explains why his community does not engage in such practice but makes an additional point about what his presence represents. Jesus' simple answer is that now is the time not for fasting but for celebration. He compares himself to a bridegroom at the time of his wedding. His presence marks the beginning of a new era. You do not fast at a wedding! The marital imagery pictures God's relationship to his people in the Old Testament and in later Judaism (Is 54:5-6; 62:4-5; Jer 2:2; Ezek 16; Hos 2:14-23; 4 Ezra 2:15-41). But nowhere in Judaism do we have the image of the Messiah as bridegroom. The New Testament uses this imagery often (Mt 22:2, 25:1; Lk 12:35-36; Eph 5:22-33; Rev 19:7; 21:2). Jesus is saying that the present is a special time to celebrate the arrival of a new point in God's plan. Later, when the bridegroom is removed (4 Ezra 10:1-4), there will be time to fast. This reference to removal is Jesus' first hint that rejection will come. Then there will be need for reflection and fasting. People will long for the ultimate redemption that the bridegroom's initial arrival promised (Rom 8:17-30; 1 Cor 15:20-28; Rev). Jesus does not regulate or legislate fasting. He says simply that it will become appropriate again.

But Jesus does not stop there. He drives home the point that his presence represents something new in God's plan, calling for a new way of ordering the spiritual life. Luke 5:36-39 gives three pictures, what Luke calls a *parable (parabolē)*, to make the point.

5:36, 37, 39 Note how each of the three pictures is introduced with *no one*.
5:39 There is some question whether this verse was original in Luke; if not, this text

Jesus is like a new piece of cloth. No seamstress worth her salt would take a new piece of cloth and patch it onto an old garment. Such a match produces two problems. The new cloth will tear the old, and the pieces of material will not match. There is irony here: the patch that is supposed to fix the garment would end up ruining both. This new era Jesus brings simply cannot be wed to the old practices. It is new and requires new ways.

The second picture involves wine and wineskins. In the first century, wineskins would have been made of goatskin or sheepskin taken from the neck area of the animal (Gen 21:14-15; 19; Ps 119:83). Again, the result of putting new wine into old skins would be disaster, a tragic waste of wine. The new wine would ferment and cause the old wineskins to burst—the new wine would then be lost and the wineskin rendered useless.

There can be no syncretism between what Jesus brings and the old tradition of Judaism. If it were tried, both would be destroyed. Jesus brings a new era and a fresh approach to God that cannot be mixed with the old traditions. In many ways the book of Acts is the historical out-working of this point. The gospel is a new way, so the practices of Judaism cannot contain it. This is why Luke will later call Jesus a prophet like Moses (Lk 9:35; Acts 3:12-26; see Deut 18:15). Jesus, like Moses, is the leader-prophet of a freshly formed community of God, revealing the new ways the new movement requires.

So *new wine must be poured into new wineskins.* Jesus' presence requires a new way, new forms and a new spirit. Even when fasting continues after the bridegroom is gone, it will be different. It will always be done in hope of his return.

Next Jesus faces the possibility of rejection. His third picture involves someone satisfied with the old wine: *"No one after drinking old wine wants the new, for he says, 'The old is better.'* "This is probably a warning and an explanation. Jesus knows that some, especially among the Pharisees, will not come to him, because they are satisfied with the wine they have. Nothing will change their mind. Rejection by some is inev-

---

would have been more like the parallels in Matthew 9:17 and Mark 2:22. But the majority of manuscripts from each textual family support its inclusion.

itable. Jesus' presence means a choice between him and the old style of Judaism. With Jesus' presence things are different. To mark the difference, Jesus does not fast. New times require fresh ways.

Jesus does not specify here exactly what makes his way new. The association with practices of eating and fasting suggests that piety motivated by law and tradition may well be in view. The new dynamic Jesus brings will rely on the Spirit of God (Acts 10:34-43; 15:1-21). Things done merely for the sake of tradition will not be persuasive anymore. Jesus' new way brings freshness and a dynamic, responsive quality to our walk with God.

Why Are You Different? Part 2 (6:1-5) The discussion over the disciples' plucking grain on the sabbath is the first of two consecutive sabbath controversies Luke now narrates. The tension about the grain incident comes because of tradition about the sabbath in Judaism, since it was a day of rest on which all labor was prohibited (Ex 20:11; *m. Šabbat* 7:2; *m. Pe'a* 8:7). Jesus' reply escalates the tension by raising an example involving David that was clearly outside the normal limits of Old Testament law. The legal discussion turns into yet another battle over authority, only this time it is the holy day of the sabbath and the right to interpret the law that is disputed. Both of these matters were of deep concern to many Jews, so the debate is very significant.

Jesus is different from other teachers before him. He and his disciples conduct themselves as if certain practices of the law are not matters of major concern. Why is he different? The previous passage made the case that Jesus' presence means the arrival of a new period. Here Jesus begins to explain why a new period is present. He possesses unique authority. He can evaluate the law and is Lord of the sabbath. It seems that Jesus

6:1-5 The parallels to this account are Mark 2:23-28 and Matthew 12:1-8. Again, the sequencing in Luke is like that in Mark. Matthew places this event after the selection of the Twelve, while Luke and Mark have it earlier. Matthew places the gathering event to set up the sending of the Twelve out into mission. Either sequence helps to make it clear that such controversies contributed to Jesus' rejection by the officials. However, the leaders' resolve to remove Jesus after the incident that follows (v. 11; similar to statements in Mt 12:14 and Mk 3:6) provides a clue to the timing of this event. Such a resolve suggests that Jesus' ministry has had some time to develop a strong opposition, especially given the presence of the Herodians. If that is the case, Luke and Mark have placed the event in a more topically oriented section, while Matthew's later placement may be more chronologically determined.

6:1-2 The sabbath tradition of the *Mishna* is known as "the forty save one," because there are thirty-nine specific, different tasks prohibited in this list (Lohse 1971:12-13). According to these rules, the disciples' actions would have been a quadruple violation! They had

is advocating an ethic in which people have more value than rules—at least this is suggested by the example Jesus cites from David's life. What is harder to tell is whether Jesus is arguing that the Torah was always intended to lead to love, relationship and holiness or whether he is bringing a new law marked by new freedoms. Neither of these options makes Jesus an antinomian. Rather, the question is how we should view some aspects of the law. Whichever option one takes here—and it is not clear—it took the disciples years to sort out the theological issues involved in this dispute, as Acts 15 shows.

The event starts innocently enough. The disciples move through a field and pick some of the grain that has been reserved for those in need (Deut 23:25). The taking of the grain is not a problem; the issue is their "labor." The question comes, *"Why are you doing what is unlawful [ouk exestin] on the Sabbath?"* The Pharisees are saying that such labor is not permitted. So their question is really a rebuke and a warning. The fact that the leaders kept such a close eye on the disciples shows where things stood between the two groups.

Jesus replies with Scripture—*"Have you never read . . . ?"* He appeals to the story of 1 Samuel 21:1-7 and 22:9-10. Some of Jesus' points build on implications in this passage. The story records how David entered the tabernacle and procured for his troops consecrated bread that only priests were permitted *(exestin)* to eat. Jesus notes explicitly that this was not legal according to Torah (Ex 25:30; 39:36; 40:22-23; esp. Lev 24:5-9). First Samuel 22:9-10 suggests that the priest inquired of the Lord and then gave the provisions, so the act was appropriate. In sum, David received legally prohibited bread for his troops and was not judged negatively for it.

---

reaped, threshed, winnowed and prepared food. Even some Jews were aware of the burdensomeness of this tradition. In the *Mishna, Ḥagiga* 1:8 reads, "The rules about the Sabbath . . . are as mountains hanging by a hair, for Scripture is scanty and the rules many."

6:4 The shewbread (NIV *consecrated bread*) consisted of twelve loaves placed in the Holy Place. It was changed once a week and was prepared by the Levites. David's taking of this bread bothered later Jewish interpreters enough to receive comment. Some later Jewish texts argued that the bread was the old bread of the previous week that had just been changed (Strack and Billerbeck 1926:1:618-19; *t. Menaḥot* 95b). Other late Jewish traditions placed this event on the sabbath, a point not made in the text (Lohse 1971:22). For the analogy Jesus makes to have merit, he only needs an apparent violation of the law. Jesus' remark about the sabbath appeals to the timing of his disciples' action, not the timing of David's action.

Jesus' analogy is neat, because it raises an example, sanctioned by Scripture, where the letter of the law was not kept. Thus Jesus becomes an interpreter of the law, either by interpreting its real intended scope or by bringing a new law that shows the old law is passing away. Unfortunately, it is not clear from this Lukan text which direction is in view. But the declaration of Jesus' authority is clear, for he explains, *"The Son of Man is Lord of the Sabbath."*

The analogy is neat for another reason. David and his troops were the ones who took the consecrated bread, so the parallel to the disciples' violation is clear. Now Jesus might be saying that just as David, as the national leader, could procure such bread for his troops, so may I. Or he may be making a greater claim: I have authority over the sabbath. The illustration means that if the leadership condemns Jesus, they had better be ready to condemn David and reject the testimony of Scripture. But Jesus' remark raises the stakes and claims that Jesus rules over elements of the law as important as the sabbath, a day that was sanctified in the Ten Commandments (Ex 20:8-11).

In Jesus' reply both the term *Lord (kyrios)* and the title *Son of Man* are important. They focus the entire reply on Jesus. This is unlike the parallel in Mark 2:28, which highlights the issue of the sabbath being designed for human beings as well. The Markan reply suggests that Jesus is arguing about what the real limits of the sabbath law are. There has been no violation here, since the sabbath, designed for humankind and not against them, was never intended to prevent someone from eating.

The battle over the grain becomes yet another discussion of Jesus' authority. He is not just a teacher, a great example or a moral-religious leader like other greats of history. He claims to possess authority over laws and institutions that God has ordained. Again, the event forces a

---

6:5 There is a textual problem in this verse. The Western family manuscript D has a completely different reading here. It reads, "If you know what you are doing, you are blessed; but if not, you are accursed and a transgressor of the law." What is Luke 6:5 in most texts, D has at verse 10. *Gospel of Thomas* 3 and 14 also have sayings possessing a similar form though with different content. But the reading is not widespread enough in the manuscripts of Luke to be regarded as original.

6:6-11 The parallels to this passage are in Matthew 12:9-14 and Mark 3:1-6. For discussion of issues related to its placement in each Gospel, see above note on Luke 6:1-6.

6:7 There is some text-critical debate whether the term for "watching" is in the present

choice. Is Jesus right or wrong about himself? Does he reveal the way of God or pervert it? It is either one or the other. Making a choice is necessary, since even being neutral is choosing.

Jesus Explains Sabbath Activity (6:6-11) This passage completes a sequence of three controversies that started in 5:33. Jesus has explained in the earlier passages that he brings a new way and that he has authority over the sabbath. When Jesus moves to heal a man on the sabbath, he provides an additional and fundamental explanation for his action. In other words, in Luke's thinking the three controversies form a unit that helps to reveal the rationale for Jesus' style of ministry. If Luke's major lesson is "like teacher, like disciple," then what Jesus teaches here about love's function reveals a central attitude that others are called to follow. The "law of love" demands that Jesus heal on the sabbath. Such a law of concern for others may well be behind the expressions "Christ's law" in 1 Corinthians 9:21 and "royal law" in James 2:8. The law about the sabbath was never designed to restrict one's ability to love and meet needs. Compassion is always appropriate.

Luke begins the account by noting that this healing takes place *on another Sabbath.* As Jesus ministers, his every move is watched closely. The term used to describe the observing scribes and Pharisees is extremely significant. They *were looking (pareterounto)* means they were spying on him, watching him out of the corner of their eye. This adds a sinister mood to the story (Riesenfeld 1972:147; Ps 36:12 LXX; Dan 6:12 Q). The text is also clear that the motive for their intense scrutiny is that they are *looking for a reason to accuse Jesus.* They cannot wait to catch him.

Once again Jesus knows the thoughts of his opponents, and again he acts to deal with their thinking by turning their private thoughts into a topic of public reflection. By doing so he again raises the issue of his

---

or future tense. If it is present tense, then the suggestion is they were regularly on the watch. If future, then this particular incident is in view. Either reading is textually possible, given the manuscript distribution of the readings. Contextually it might be slightly more appropriate to see the focus on this one event and read a future verb here. Regardless of the reading selected, the issue is that the leaders keep a skeptical eye on Jesus.

6:8 The term used for thoughts in this verse, *dialogismos,* is often negative in Luke (2:35; 5:22; 6:8; 9:47). The text also notes often when Jesus knows what others are thinking (5:22; 9:47; 11:17; 24:37-38).

authority. If they wish to challenge him secretly, he will turn their challenge and doubt into a public hearing. Jesus' openness contrasts with the leaders' covertness. His question gets right to the point and is loaded with irony: *"I ask you, which is lawful on the Sabbath: to do good or to do evil, to save life or to destroy it?"* Luke has already revealed the leaders' motives by noting that they have been watching Jesus closely; now Jesus exposes their desire. In attempting to defend the truth of sabbath tradition, they plot harm on the sabbath, while Jesus seeks to meet needs. Who *is* violating the sabbath? There is a sting in the question.

Zeal often leads to unrighteousness, as ends are cited to justify questionable means. Sometimes in seeking to prevent murder or unrighteousness, God's people engage and even justify acts that are just as reprehensible. A Christian leader once told me that certain people were out to get him for "doctrinal defection." They were watching his every move and examining his every sentence. In their attempt to get hard evidence they had broken into his office, searched his desk and even tried to open his computer files. Apparently trespassing along with breaking and entering was all right in the name of righteousness! The pursuit of righteousness should never cause us to resort to tactics that reflect unrighteousness.

Jesus seeks to do good on the sabbath, but the Pharisees seek to do harm and destroy. Jesus' reply is in the spirit of Old Testament prophetic rebukes (Is 1:11-17; 58:1-14; Amos 4:1-8). God puts a high priority on how people are treated and how needs are met.

So Jesus acts, asking the man to stretch out his hand. The very act will show that healing is present. There is irony in Jesus' response. Can you sense how hard Jesus has labored here, uttering just one command? Will God vindicate Jesus' effort? The text tells of the command's success ever so briefly—the man *did so, and his hand was completely restored.*

How will such a good act be received? Surely wonder and rejoicing will follow. But instead hard hearts react in fury. Again, the term Luke uses here is crucial. *Anoia* refers to a blinding, irrational rage that is

---

6:12-16 Luke's placement of this event appears to be very conscious. The parallels are Mark 3:13-19 and Matthew 10:1-4. Mark has a summary of Jesus' ministry before mentioning this selection of the Twelve. So Luke places the plot and selection next to one another in a unique way. Matthew's placement reflects his desire to juxtapose the selection of the Twelve to their mission. Luke waits to tell the story of the mission until 9:2-5. Mark 6:7-11

likened to insanity (Behm 1967b:963; Schürmann 1969:309 n. 69). The
religious leaders refuse to consider the evidence and are enraged about
the facts God had laid before them. God is not supposed to help sinners
or heal through a sabbath violator, yet right in front of them a sabbath
violator has healed a sinner on the sabbath against their interpretation
of truth and tradition. Jesus' action has confounded them. What can they
do? They consider *what they might do to Jesus.* He must be stopped.

The stubbornness of the leadership's opposition is highlighted here.
When we are in sin, we resist reconsidering the route we are taking. In
fact, sin that is not repented of often leads into further sin.

Nevertheless, Jesus' action shows that the sabbath, like any day, is an
appropriate time to minister and meet needs. It is perfectly permissible
to do good on the sabbath. Jesus does not merely proclaim his authority;
he lives it. This sabbath healing supports Jesus' claim that he brings
something new, while highlighting what should have always been a
characteristic of the sabbath: the ministering of good to others. The
withered hand's restoration is a vote of confidence for Jesus and a visible
rebuke to the leadership.

But that vote of confidence strengthens the opposition party's resolve.
The opponents begin to discuss with one another *what they might do
to Jesus.* Often the product of rage is more folly. Jesus' ministry has
produced opposition, even though he has tried to do good to others. The
narrative leaves the question for readers to ponder: was Jesus a trouble-
maker, or did the trouble originate elsewhere? Sin often blindly deflects
blame and then compounds its error by seeking harsh means to remove
the reminder of its failure. For Luke there is no doubt where blame lies,
as well as who has authority to point the way to God.

The Choosing of the Twelve (6:12-16) Jesus knew that he was
doing something new. Because opposition was rising, he needed to form
a new community around him. If Jesus were to be taken out of the
picture, something else would need to be in place. New leadership was

---

also reflects a later placement of the mission story. Though it is hard to be sure, Matthew
may have put together events topically, while Luke has a chronological sequence. Other lists
of the Twelve occur in Matthew 10:2-4, Mark 3:16-19 and Acts 1:13. The lists have some
differences and similarities. For comparisons, see Carson 1984:237 and Fitzmyer 1981:613-
16.

required. Thus it is no accident that Luke places the choosing of the Twelve immediately after the remark about the beginnings of a plot against Jesus.

The selection of those who would end up leading the new community after Jesus' departure was no minor affair. It was a matter of prayer—in fact, Luke shows that the choices followed a full night of prayer. The presence of prayer shows the action's importance. No other New Testament passage speaks of all-night prayer. Jesus knew this step was the first of many actions to put something new in place that would outlast his earthly ministry.

This text is one of several where Luke associates an event with prayer (1:13; 2:37; 3:21; 5:16; 6:12, 28; 9:18; 11:1-2; 18:1; 22:41, 45). Dialogue with God is crucial to spiritual well-being for Luke, particularly a humble attitude as one approaches God in prayer (18:9-14). For Luke prayer is a concrete way of expressing our necessary dependence on God.

The twelve men Jesus chose would be specially trained to lead the church. Only Luke among the Gospel writers calls them apostles at this point. He tells the story aware of where Jesus is taking them. Even though only some of them are mentioned later in Luke's writing, the whole list is important for two reasons.

First, there is an instructive variety in the figures named. In the group we have fishermen like Peter, Andrew, James and John. We also have a despised tax collector, Matthew. On the other hand, we have a "Zealot," Simon. The juxtaposition of Simon and Matthew should not go over-

---

6:15 There is debate about the exact force of the term *Zealot*. Josephus describes a fourth Jewish party beyond the Pharisees, Sadducees and Essenes (*Jewish Wars* 2.8.1 §§117-18; *Antiquities* 18.1-2 §§1-11; 18.1.6 §§23-25). They were a nationalist political group that opposed Rome, even to the point of violence. This is the group Josephus blames for the nation's war with Rome. What is debated is whether a formal "Zealot" party existed before A.D. 66. It is difficult to be certain whether a formal party existed during the time of Jesus' ministry. It is likely, though, that Zealot-type attitudes did exist at this time. For the debate see Smith 1971:1-19, who favors a late origin, and Hengel 1961; the latter's entire work argues for a connection between later Zealots and the attitudes of an earlier generation.

6:16 The name Iscariot is much discussed. Four meanings are suggested (for three of these views, see Marshall 1978:240): (1) it alludes to a region (Kerioth) in Judea (Josh 15:25; Jer 48:24, 31); (2) it is an Aramaic term meaning "false one"; (3) it comes from the Latin *sicarius*, which means "dagger man"; (4) it means "dyer" and thus alludes to Judas's occupation. It is not clear what the exact force is, though the genitive references in John 6:71 and 13:26 suggest a familial reference. This favors the first option (Schürmann 1969:318 n. 51).

looked. One would have collected monies for Rome, while the other would have fought to overcome Roman sovereignty. Yet in Jesus they became part of the same community, functioning side by side. These are people from diverse strata and perspectives, woven together by Jesus into a newly formed community. Finally there is Judas, who is named with the note that he would betray Jesus. Even the seeds of discord and rejection were present in the inner circle. So it was after a night in prayer.

Second, the selected group numbers twelve. This appears to be no accident. Jesus is forming a new, specially trained group of disciples, but the number twelve mimics the structure of Israel. The echo could hardly be missed. The point is not that this new group of disciples is intended to replace Israel permanently. An examination of Acts shows that the disciples present their message as the natural extension of promises made to Israel. These promises are now meeting their fulfillment in this new community. The Twelve represent something new *and* something parallel to Israel. The new community is both distinct from and connected to God's promises for the nation. This is why Jesus promises them authority over Israel later in Luke (22:30). Jesus is building a new structure, but one with points of contact to the old. The leaders of what is to become the church reflect the variety that will always be present in the body. That variety does not emerge by accident, but is the result of Jesus' conscious selection.

Jesus' Teaching (6:17-49) Luke's "Sermon on the Plain" is the Gospel

---

6:17-49 There is much discussion about the relationship of this sermon to the "Sermon on the Mount" in Matthew 5—7. Many of the statements from that sermon in Matthew are scattered throughout Luke's Gospel. This has produced many views on the relationship between these two texts. Three options are possible that honor the historical validity of the material, though none can be proved categorically as correct. (1) The texts summarize two distinct sermons. (2) Luke has reduced the Matthean version, removing elements that relate to concerns about the law. (3) Matthew's sermon is an anthology that brings together in one place what Jesus taught throughout his ministry, as Luke's examples illustrate.

The major obstacle to the second view is the difference in setting between Matthew's mountain and Luke's plain. But some have argued that Luke may simply be referring to a level area in the midst of a mountainous region. Though a decision here is difficult, it is the second option that I find most appealing. For details and a full treatment of all aspects of this question, including a critique of options that discount historicity, see Bock 1994b: excursus on the sermon.

equivalent of Paul's chapter on love, 1 Corinthians 13. Here Jesus sets forth his ethic for daily life in detail. The sermon begins with a recognition of the disciples' blessing as a result of God's grace. The rest of the sermon gives the ethical response to being such a beneficiary. Disciples are to live and relate to others in a way that stands out from how people relate to one another in the world. They are to love and pray for their enemies. Righteousness requires that they respond wisely to Jesus' words by building their lives around his teaching. In sum, disciples are to live and look different from the rest of the world, even as they reach out compassionately to that world.

A Summary of Jesus' Ministry (6:17-19) Luke sets up the sermon by summarizing Jesus' ministry activity (4:14-15, 31-32, 40-41). Jesus ministers on a plain. The term *topu pedinou* refers to a level place, but can refer to a plateau area in mountainous terrain (Mt 14:23 compared to 15:29; Is 13:2 LXX; Jer 21:13 LXX). Beyond this no specific locale is given. Jesus' ministry reflects the compassion and love he claims God has for humanity. So he heals people of disease and exorcises demons. The text emphasizes the *power* that proceeds from him. Whether they are apostles, disciples or part of the crowd, all sorts of people receive Jesus' ministry. Jesus' teaching and ministry extends beyond insiders. He attempts to reach those outside his new community.

A Prophetic Call of Blessing and Woe (6:20-26) Jesus' authority was not limited to his healing activity. He also taught with authority. Nothing indicates that more than the blessing and woe section of the Sermon on the Plain. It recalls the Old Testament prophets. Jesus thunders the truth with promises of blessing and judgment. The four blessings are followed by four parallel woes. This balance reflects the theme of reversal that Luke has presented elsewhere (1:50-53; 16:19-31): God does not always see things as we do. He looks at the heart, not at externals. He gives promises for those who enter into grace humbly, while warning of judgment for those who remain callous.

The key to the section is found in the remarks about the Son of Man and the comparison to the faithful and unfaithful of old. When Jesus

---

6:20-21 Guelich (1982:69) has defined *the poor* here as "those in desperate need (socioeconomic element) whose helplessness drove them to a dependent relationship with

speaks of the poor or rich, he is not making carte blanche statements about people with a certain social or economic standing. His remarks assume both Old Testament and spiritual roots. Jesus is not advocating a political or social philosophy, he is calling people into a spiritual relationship that God imparts to those willing to enter his new community (see commentary on 1:50-53).

Thus the beatitudes and woes serve as a call to be responsive to God in light of his promise of faithfulness to those who are his. The call to love unconditionally in verses 27-36 is a hard one to follow if we cannot trust that God will one day exercise justice. The premise of the sacrificial spiritual life is the promise of God's faithful justice. The beatitudes indicate the kind of person God desires as his child. These blessings are not a works salvation but represent an invitation to let God mold his children into who they ought to be. So God assures those who are needy that he will care for them.

Jesus offers promises to the *poor,* the *hungry,* those who *weep* and those who suffer religious persecution. God sees their spiritual commitment, which has cost them in the pocketbook. To people such as these God promises the kingdom now and blessing later, including enough to eat, laughter and heavenly *reward.* Unlike Matthew, Luke includes woes, not just blessings. Jesus divides humankind into two camps (3:15-18—the purging Spirit of fire). In contrast to the blessed stand the *rich,* those who are *well fed,* those who *laugh* and those who receive praise. Their fate is sorrow, hunger, mourning and a life like those who followed the false prophets. The contrast is stark.

The term *blessed* refers to one who is the object of grace and is happy because of it. Those who are blessed do not face an easy life. The mention of poverty and deprivation reflects the reality that many early Christians were poor. In addition, their commitment to Jesus led to their being persecuted like the prophets of old. In Jewish circles the choice to be a disciple would have meant ostracism. The goal of such ostracism was to punish and shame the "defector," or perhaps to persuade the defector to return. Social isolation would bring economic consequences.

God (religious element) for the supplying of their needs and vindication." For a similar two-pronged definition of the hungry, see Goppelt 1968a:18.

But despite such opposition, disciples are blessed, since God promises to care for them. They belong to his kingdom and are under his rule. The *poor* here are like the Old Testament ʿᵃ*nāwîm* mentioned in the commentary on 1:51-54. They are the pious poor. These beatitudes serve to comfort and reassure those who belong to God. They stand in a long line of the faithful, including the prophets of old. It is often the case that standing up for Jesus and the truth brings ostracism, but God has promised blessing to his children.

The woes also reflect prophetic tradition. A woe warns of condemnation. Here Jesus addresses the judgment of God to the callous rich and others who are comfortable with their state in life while being unconcerned about the needs of others. The lack of a genuine spiritual dimension in their life is seen in the comparison Jesus makes between them and the false prophets. For those who do not engage God on the divinity's terms there looms nothing but the terrible expectation of a day of reckoning. One of the dangers of wealth is that it can lead one to believe a life of independence is possible—a view that Jesus teaches is arrogant and misguided (12:13-21). The world's values are not God's values. The reversal portrayed in the beatitudes and woes reflects the idea that "the one with the most toys" often loses. God's blessing can be found in surprising places. It rests on those who rest in him.

The Call to Exceptional Love and Mercy (6:27-36) Love is many things in our culture. For many it can be likened to an electric charge: either the zap of the feeling is there or it is not. For others love is an arrangement, almost like a contract, sometimes voluntary, other times imposed by circumstances. Love for family members is not a given; instead, events have necessitated it. Marriages often proceed with this kind of arranged love. As long as the contract works and the zap is present, the arrangement is on. Often such love is managed by performance. Love is to be demonstrated by what is done for me: "If you really cared, you would do this for me."

This kind of arranged or easy love is the foil for Jesus' description of what love is for the child of God. The love Jesus calls for is none of the things described above. Jesus decries our culture's version of love. What

---

6:31 For a comprehensive survey of these ancient examples, see Bock 1994b: exe-

is required to possess true love is an understanding of what it is to be loved by God and how God wishes one to love. At the center of Jesus' sermon is a unique concept of love. This love cannot be reduced merely to the "golden rule"; it is love that is golden even when everything around is not.

Jesus does not wait to make his point on the unusual character of such love. Although the righteous will be persecuted and rejected and God will judge the persecutors, Jesus issues a call to love the enemy. In fact, Jesus' call is specific: *love your enemies, do good to those who hate you, bless those who curse you, pray for those who mistreat you.* Whether in attitude, action, word or intercession, the enemy is to be loved. Too often many in the church have a "Jimmy Cagney theology" where the message is to those who do not know God: "You dirty rat, you should not have done that." Jesus wants more than condemnation of the outside world. Jesus' call to disciples focuses not on our words to others, though 11:37-54 does issue a stinging challenge regarding our words. Rather, Jesus zeroes in on our actions and attitudes toward others. He offers no platitudes about how outsiders should be viewed. There is no abstract call to divide one's thought by "hating the sin, but loving the sinner." True as this saying is, Jesus is concerned that we follow through on it and show our love in concrete service for the sinner. Our model is God himself: "God so loved the world that he gave . . ." (see also v. 36). So Jesus calls for the performance of love—in action, thought and petition.

How often do we pray for those who hate the church? The very question shows how radically different Jesus' love is from the culture's view of love. This is "tough love" because it is tough on the believer who loves. It is "radical love" because it calls for denying oneself and being continually exposed to abuse. It is a love not of power, manipulation or arrangement but of service and meekness.

The exhortation is underlined by three concrete examples. First, if someone strikes you on the cheek, then offer him the other. Probably, given the context of religious persecution, the slap refers to exclusion from the synagogue (1 Esdras 4:30; *Didache* 1:4; Stählin 1972:263 nn. 23-24; for conceptual examples of such violent actions, Acts 18:17; 21:27-

gesis of 6:31.

28, 31-32; 23:2). Such a slap would be delivered by the back of the hand, though the context here suggests any action that communicates rejection. Jesus' point is that even in the midst of such rejection, we continue to minister to others and expose ourselves to the threat of rejection. The ministry of Paul among the Jews in Acts is a clear example of such love. Love is available and vulnerable, subject to repeated abuse.

Second, Jesus gives the example of someone stealing one's outer garment. He advises letting them have the undershirt too! The point is that one should not seek revenge but remain exposed and be willing to take even more risks. Luke may well be thinking of the danger of missionary travel in the first century or the risk of violence against those who professed Christ. The situation of Sosthenes in Acts 18:17 comes to mind, as does Paul's risk when he was left for dead in Acts 14:19. Despite such danger, he continued to preach to those who rejected him (1 Cor 4:9-13; 2 Cor 11:21—12:10). As the parable of the good Samaritan shows, travel in Jesus' and Luke's day could be dangerous. In the face of such hostility, the call is to keep loving the enemy.

Third, one is to be generous and not keep account. Disciples should be marked by a genuine readiness to meet needs. To the one who begs, give. From the one who takes, do not seek to get it back. Begging here probably refers to almsgiving (Mt 6:1-4; Guelich 1982:223). Resources are not to be hoarded, but generously dispensed. Paul reflects a similar attitude in 1 Timothy 6:8-18. In the case of theft, there is to be no pursuit of retribution. Such self-denial is the essence of love. The consummate example is the cross. Jesus gave to those who had taken.

The sheer difficulty of these commands has led to discussion of how literal they are. Marshall (1978:261) points out correctly that the illustrations are somewhat figurative, since to follow Luke 6:29 literally would lead to nudism! Yet Jesus' life makes it clear that he took these standards seriously. When his opponents took his life, he did not seek retribution but prayed for their forgiveness. He was more interested in giving something that would build than in retrieving what had been taken. The three illustrations picture the kind of action that manifests radical love. The world's standards of love should be surpassed (6:32-34). But we can only accept such a standard if we believe that God will see and reward the faithful. Without a theological view to build on, Jesus' ethics wilt into futility and foolishness.

So Jesus offers what became known in the sixteenth century as the "golden rule": *Do to others as you would have them do to you.* The verse has Old Testament roots (Lev 19:18). In addition, numerous such ethical statements existed in ancient Jewish and Greek culture. Jesus' formulation of the rule, however, is the least self-focused. Jesus is not saying, "Do good deeds for others so they will return the favor." Instead he is calling for actions of love regardless of how the other responds. Nor is he saying, "Think of what you like, then do that for others." Rather, we are to be sensitive to the needs, feelings and concerns of others and seek to meet them. Sensitivity in love means listening and serving. This does not mean ignoring moral limits, as Jesus' own ministry makes clear, but it does mean caring enough to be concerned about how others feel. The old adage "walk a mile in my shoes" may fit here: look at things from another's perspective and then act with concern.

In the modern world, this would mean not just protesting against abortion but being prepared to care for the child that is born to a mother who has chosen not to abort. More than this, we are called to continue to love those who go ahead with their intention to abort. It means not just talking about ethnic oneness in the church but acting out oneness in community, like Paul's crossing ethnic lines to raise funds for believers in need. Even more, this passage calls us to show tangible concern for unbelievers in need, so when someone tells them that God loves them, they will have seen evidence of such love.

Jesus repeats his examples in verses 32-34 but adds one more point: If we love only those who give us love, what is so great about that kind of love? It is like the love sinners give. If we do good only to those who do good to us, what is so special about that? It is like the love sinners give. If we lend money only to those who will respond in kind, what is so honorable about that? It is the ethics sinners have. The clear implication is that the disciples are not to live and love like sinners. The love of believers is to be different from the love displayed by the culture. As children of God, believers have been transformed to live in contrast to the way of sinners, modeling the sacrifice of radical love.

So Jesus summarizes: *love your enemies, do good to them, and lend to them without expecting to get anything back.* When we give, it should not be with strings attached. When we serve, it should be to meet needs, not to give tit for tat. True service involves a giving that does not demand a giving back. The essence of relationship for the child of God is to love and serve.

But Jesus also attaches a theological dimension of promise to the exhortation: *your reward will be great, and you will be sons of the Most High.* God does notice when we reflect who he is to the world. In such faithful, imitative service, promise and identity merge. He will honor us for reflecting our Father's values. God will reward our love, and our love will reflect our identity as God's children. Children of God, Jesus says, are called to imitate their heavenly Father. We are to be an audiovisual of him. For God *is kind to the ungrateful and wicked. Be merciful, just as your Father is merciful.* The call of the disciple to radical love is "like father, like child." As Plummer (1922:189) notes, "Moral likeness proves parentage." Jesus' ethical call to love is nothing more than a call to imitate the Father. And to love is to have mercy.

On Judgment, Righteousness and Jesus' Teaching (6:37-49)
Jesus develops his description of mercy by highlighting its relationship to forgiveness and judgment. Two ideas dominate Jesus' remarks on judgment. First, the measure we use to judge others is the standard that will be applied to us. Jesus suggests that God responds to us similarly to the way we treat others. The attitude expressed here is not unique to Jesus. In the Jewish *Mishna, 'Abot* 1:6 reads, "When you judge, incline the balance in his favor." In the same Jewish work, *Soṭa* 1:7 reads, "With what measure a man metes, it shall be measured to him again." Negatively, Jesus says we should not judge or condemn. Positively, we are to forgive and give generously. Jesus illustrates the last point with the everyday example of measuring out grain for purchase. The seller would take a measuring container and pour the grain in it. After getting it about three-quarters full, he would shake it to level out the grain so more could be put in. The goal was to get as much in the measure as possible. In the same way God promises to give grace abundantly to those who are gracious.

Second, being merciful means being quick to encourage people toward restoration after they fall. Mercy does not gloat over sin or take pleasure in pointing it out; it roots for the sinner to find a way home to spiritual health. Often after someone falls we are anxious simply to cut him or her off to keep the church body from being leavened or to show that we will not associate with deeds of darkness. The church *is* to be concerned about moral purity. But we also should be quick to help set up opportunities for repentance and restoration. We should be discerning about the presence of sin but not judgmental in dealing with it. To be judgmental is to rejoice in pointing out sin and to refuse to reach out to the sinner to restore him or her to spiritual health. Rather than leaving the sinner to wallow in sin and the pain of moral failure, we should encourage the sinner to find the right path. Perhaps no picture of this commitment is clearer than the career of Hosea. He called sin by its name but always stood ready to receive the sinner back, even after gross sin.

It is no accident that Jesus' words against judgmentalism come right after the call to be merciful as God is. An unwillingness to be judgmental is almost a requirement for those who face persecution. Without it, lines of battle would become hardened and the ability to love the enemy would be destroyed. God is interested not in polemics but in offering the hope of restored relationship to the lost.

This exhortation needs to be set in the framework of Jesus' entire teaching. Jesus does not mean that we should close our eyes to sin and wrongdoing. Jesus' rebuke of his opponents in 11:37-54 shows that being merciful does not mean suspending moral judgment and responsibility. But we are not to hold judgment against the person in such a way that ministry and reconciliation become impossible. Disciples are to bear good news, not hold grudges.

The sermon closes with a series of pictures showing us that Jesus' teaching is to be taken seriously. The first image deals with the importance of choosing the right teacher and looking carefully to oneself before offering criticism (vv. 39-42). The second image has to do with producing the right kind of fruit (vv. 43-45), while the third shows the wisdom of holding fast to Jesus' teaching (vv. 46-49).

The question whether a blind man can lead others is rhetorical, and the point is not developed explicitly. Of course when Jesus asks if the blind are able to lead the blind, he expects a negative answer, as the Greek particle *mēti* indicates. He expects the blind man and his followers to fall into a pit, as the particle *ouchi* indicates. In fact, a disciple *will be like his teacher.* Jesus does not explain the remark or develop the picture, but he is warning us to watch which teacher we follow. If we follow someone who takes in no light, we will stumble. So we are to consider carefully who our teacher is. Religious opposition is the setting for Jesus' remarks. Jesus' own offer of authoritative teaching in the sermon suggests that his disciples should not follow the religious leadership but him—a point he will make more explicitly in verses 46-49.

Given the plethora of options available today, we can sense the importance of Jesus' remarks: Choose your instructors wisely, since you will become like them. To build solidly on a firm foundation, follow the teaching of those who teach God's Word, not tradition or feeling (two alternatives often on offer today). Jesus' message commends itself as worthy of being heard and followed. Those who reflect his message also are worth listening to. In a time when reflection and thought are often given low priority, we ought to give high priority to reflecting on Jesus' teaching.

In fact, there is a reason we should be slow to judge and be careful whom we follow: we all have huge faults that we must deal with before we are in a position to help others. A judgmental spirit often reflects a self-righteous, unreflective, insensitive heart.

Jesus continues to work with the imagery of sight, only here he uses humor. Imagine, Jesus says, trying to see with a plank of wood sticking out of your eye. Just try seeing with a two-by-four as bifocals! A plank would prevent clear vision. How could you complain about dust in someone else's eye when a two-by-four was protruding from your own? Jesus' point is clear. It is important to clean up one's own act before offering advice to others. In fact, one way to examine ourselves for self-righteousness is to consider how often we are interested in correcting others rather than correcting our own attitudes and actions.

Jesus does not say we should not examine the lives of others. But we should do so only with a careful eye cast toward ourselves. Galatians 6:1 is similar in tone. Jesus wants disciples to be a moral encouragement to one another, but there is a proper way to go about it. There is a crying need for humility, an awareness that all of us are learning to walk more

---

6:41 A *dokos* (NIV *plank*) is the main beam of a building, so even referring to this as

closely with God. To help another see clearly, we need to wash out our own eyes first.

In the end, disciples are to reflect good character. Our relationship with God is to produce good fruit. The fruit reveals the nature of the root, *for each tree is recognized by its own fruit.* Bad trees do not produce good fruit, nor do good trees produce bad fruit. To judge a tree's fruit, we don't look at one particular moment but at a period of production. The product of the life reflects the heart. The product of our discipleship reflects our inner character, what Jesus calls the treasure of the heart. The value of our speech and actions is determined by the quality of the soul that produces them. In other words, works are a snapshot of the heart.

Often the church avoids talking about "works" because people could begin focusing on externals or putting good deeds in the place of faith. But the tree image can help us steer clear of such problems. Jesus says that works are a product of something deeper. By linking the heart and the fruit, Jesus ties together motive and action. Works are ultimately a matter of the heart: the product can never be entirely divorced from the motive, and the presence of fruit does not mean the absence of faith!

In fact, the major issue in the life of a disciple is faithfulness. So Jesus issues a challenge in verse 46: *"Why do you call me, 'Lord, Lord,' and do not do what I say?"* The rhetorical question raises the issue of faithfulness. A good heart is faithful, while a hypocritical one is not. Obedience is not a matter of rule keeping but of faithfulness. How can one recognize Jesus' authority and call him Lord and then not follow through on the commitment to walk with him?

With this question Jesus turns to the issue of his authority. He is not formulating some ethic that we could follow independent of relationship to him. Having a relationship with him is at the base of faithfulness. This is why the parallel to this verse in Matthew 7:21 makes knowing him the key. Luke does not emphasize the end-time judgment as Matthew does, but for both consistency and faithfulness are central. Jesus says, If you wish to be wise, you will love as I have taught, follow me as Teacher and Lord, and walk in my way with faithfulness. The implication emerges more clearly in light of the parable that follows.

---

a two-by-four may not do justice to Jesus' imagery.

Jesus concludes his sermon with the parable of the two houses. In a subdivision there are two homes. One is built on rock, the other on sand. Luke's imagery is detailed. One builder *dug down deep and laid the foundation on rock*. A secure foundation takes work. The hard work is worth it, because in the storm this house stands strong and secure. Nothing shakes it. Obeying Jesus will mean being able to stand up in the trials of life. In contrast is the man who quickly builds his house on the top of the earth. There is no depth to his building, only a surface structure. Without a strong foundation, the house cannot hold up when the river floods. The use of multiple terms to describe the house's collapse accentuates the note of tragedy in the image. Translated precisely, the end of verse 49 reads, "Immediately it fell, and great was the ruin of that house" (NRSV). Everything this man had is lost. Jesus offers no editorial comment, but lets his sermon end with the echo of the collapsing house.

The parable gives a sober warning: How tragic not to respond to Jesus' teaching. How foolish not to build on the rock that can weather the storms of life. What a tragic waste when we fail to heed Jesus.

So Jesus preaches promise-judgment in the beatitudes and woes. He calls on disciples to love in imitation of their Father in heaven. He warns them to follow him as teacher and watch their step when they criticize others. He calls on disciples to be faithful and obedient, because that is the path of wisdom, endurance and strength. The product of the life reflects the heart's true nature. Spiritual strength grows out of obeying the Lord Jesus. It is like fixing a foundation deep in the earth. Jesus' sermon reveals the ethics of the disciple, but behind the ethics stands the authority of the commissioned agent of God. Jesus preaches not as a philosopher-teacher but as the revealer of God's wisdom. As the voice

---

6:47-49 There is an instructive contrast with a Jewish parable in *'Abot de Rabbi Nathan* 24. There two houses are built, one of rock and one of uncooked brick. In this parable the house made of uncooked brick collapses, while the house built of rock survives, picturing a life built on the law. The difference reflects the different foci Christianity and Judaism have. Disciples build on the *rock* by responding to Jesus. Both of these parables have conceptual roots in Ezekiel 13:10-16.

7:1-10 The parallel to this passage is Matthew 8:5-13. The most obvious difference between these two accounts is that in Matthew the centurion addresses Jesus directly, while in Luke he never appears; messengers speak for him. How is one to explain this difference?

from heaven will say later in this Gospel (9:35), we should "listen to him."

Movements to Faith and Christological Questions (7:1—8:3) So what will be the response to Jesus, and why should we respond to him? At this point Luke zeroes in on this question. This section's dominant theme is faith. The stories of the centurion, the widow of Nain, John the Baptist's perplexity, the sinful woman, the women who minister to the disciples—all have to do with the presence or absence of faith. Faith involves humility, gratitude and service. In the middle of this section, John the Baptist's question about *the one who was to come* brings a significant response from Jesus about how God's plan advances and where Jesus fits in, even though his style is not messianic in the way people expected. Furthermore, the various accounts disclose that faith has no gender or racial gap. Jesus comes for all.

A Centurion's Exemplary Faith (7:1-10) In the Gospels it is rare that someone receives a clear commendation from Jesus. When it happens, it is an occasion for reflection. The powerful and poignant testimony of the centurion provides such an opportunity, showing us that people in very surprising places and with very different backgrounds have heard Jesus' message and appreciate it. The emphasis in this account makes this miracle different from earlier miracle accounts in Luke. Here the miracle itself is not the focus, since it is mentioned only very briefly in verse 10. Rather, the stress is on the attitude of the one seeking the healing. Luke subtly shifts attention from Jesus' miraculous work to his person and the response to it. Jesus is more than a teacher or a healer. What is Jesus commending in the understanding of the centurion?

The account opens by noting that after the sermon Jesus came into

---

It appears likely that Matthew has telescoped and simplified the story by making the centurion's representatives equivalent to the centurion himself. Such representation was not unusual in the ancient world (compare 2 Kings 19:20-34, where to speak against the king as God's representative is to speak against God). Jesus said of his disciples that if anyone rejected them, they rejected him as well. Today we accept the same principle. When the press secretary speaks from the White House, everyone knows the president is speaking.

Another parallel often tied to this passage is John 4:46-54. But the passage in John describes another event, for it is set in a different town (Cana) and has a different tone (Jesus issues a rebuke there).

Capernaum. A centurion there has a slave who is near death. A centurion was a soldier in Herod Antipas's army who commanded about one hundred men. As a mercenary, he might serve as a tax soldier or a policeman. Only Luke notes that he is a Gentile; but he is not a Roman, since the Romans did not enter such military roles until A.D. 44. Is he from the surrounding region, or has he been sent into service here from one of the countries Rome had conquered? We are not told. Some wonder if the man is a proselyte, given his support for the synagogue. That is possible, though not certain, since if he were directly related to the nation, that point would likely have been made clearly. What is clear is that he is supportive of the Jewish nation and he may be a potential proselyte (v. 5). He is probably what Luke calls elsewhere a "God-fearer," a Gentile who does not yet fully identify with Israel but does respect the God of Judaism (Acts 10:2; Tyson 1992:35-39; McKnight 1991:78-117; Cohen 1989:13-33).

The centurion has heard about Jesus and his miracle-working power. So he sends Jewish elders on his behalf. The action is culturally sensitive: not knowing Jesus personally and recognizing that he is of Jewish heritage, the soldier sends representatives of Jesus' own ethnic background to plead his case. There is no demand made of Jesus, only a request. The reference to *elders* probably indicates that civic leaders are involved (Schürmann 1969:391 n. 16; Marshall 1978:280; Bornkamm 1968:660-61). This man had won respect across ethnic lines. The cultural sensitivity of his actions may well suggest why.

This event allows Luke to show that Jews and Gentiles can get along— a message of ethnic cooperation that would be revolutionary in ancient times, just as it is today. We can only imagine the impact if the whole church were able to visibly show how Christ leads us to respect ethnic diversity *and* to work together across ethnic lines.

In addition, Luke's description of the others in this story as *the Jews* may suggest that his own ethnic origin is not Jewish. The narration reflects the perspective of a non-Jew. These interracial elements enhance the passage's emotional tension. Ultimately, are there ethnic distinctions in Jesus' work? The passage answers that question with an emphatic no. Although Jesus initially preached to the lost sheep of Israel, his ministry eventually extended to all after his postresurrection commission to the apostles (24:43-49; Eph 2:14-17). As for Paul, so for Jesus: there is no Jew or Gentile in Christ (Gal 3:28). In our day, we might say, there is no Caucasian or African-American, no Hispanic or Asian, no Latino, African, European, Jew or Palestinian in Christ. All are in need of his redemption; all become part of the same community when they come to him.

With the elders' request comes a character endorsement. They assert that the centurion is worthy to receive the benefits of Jesus' work. This is the one time in the New Testament that the term "worthy" *(axios)* is used to describe a person positively, rather than a group (NIV renders this term in the phrase *deserves to have you do this*). This soldier supports the nation and has built a synagogue. Here is a man of means and generosity. Roman support for synagogues is well known, since they believed it promoted order and morality in the community (Josephus *Antiquities* 16.6.2 §§162-65; 19.6.3 §§299-311).

So Jesus reaches across racial and social boundaries and begins to travel with these elders; but then a second wave of representatives appears. They end up commending Jesus by explaining that the soldier does not feel worthy to have Jesus enter his home. The teacher need not trouble himself with a journey to the soldier's home. Here Luke reveals the depth of the centurion's humility, despite the elders' estimation of the man as worthy. The remark also recalls Peter's humble attitude in 5:8. Others recognize the centurion's character; he does not carry his own banner. Even so, before Jesus, who is worthy? This text, like Jesus' earlier exchange with Peter, shows that God honors such humility.

The centurion also understands authority, so he adds that Jesus can exercise his authority anywhere. The centurion knows what it is to be *under authority* and to issue commands like *"Go," "Come"* and *"Do this."* If such authority works for a soldier, surely it works for Jesus. He knows that Jesus' authority is all that is needed to produce healing.

Jesus reacts emotionally (this is one of the few places where Luke records Jesus' emotion): he is *amazed.* Jesus is said to be amazed only here, in Matthew's parallel account (Mt 8:10) and in Mark 6:6, where he is astonished at unbelief. Jesus turns and issues his commendation: *"I have not found such great faith even in Israel!"* The statement is like a neon light. Here is faith that should be emulated. Here is trust, confidence, rest in the authority of God and awareness of his plan. The Jewish nation, and all others, can learn from this outsider. Aware of Jesus' authority, the centurion has committed the well-being of his beloved slave into Jesus' hands. Jesus commends the centurion's humility and his understanding of Jesus' authority: such faith is exemplary.

Returning home, the messengers find the slave healthy. The request has been granted, the slave restored. Jesus' commendation must resonate even more powerfully as they contemplate the miracle. Surely if such faith is possible outside of Israel, it can happen anywhere. Furthermore, it is clear that Jesus possesses a unique authority: he does not need to be physically present to bring about what he wills.

Jesus' Authority to Raise the Dead (7:11-17) Modern Western culture is marked by opinion polls. What people think about any topic can be closely examined instantly, with precision and a basketful of statistics. We are a society awash in numbers reflecting opinions.

When Jesus travels to the little village of Nain and raises from the dead the only son of a widow, there is a popular reaction. The confession that emerges keeps the question of Jesus' identity before Luke's audience. And other opinions about Jesus follow shortly (9:7-9, 18-20). If George Gallup, George Barna or *Israel Today* had taken a poll at this point in Jesus' ministry, the popular response would have been that Jesus was a prophet. What caused this popular assessment of Jesus? Luke traces its development here, though he saves for later his explanation of why it is not the decisive description of Jesus.

Luke narrates here with extreme economy. Jesus enters the little town of Nain; this is the only time it is mentioned in the Bible, and this is one of the few times Luke notes the locale of an event. The town probably lay six miles southeast of Nazareth, at the foot of Little Hebron over the valley of Jezreel (Fitzmyer 1981:658). Near the city gate a funeral procession is in process. Probably this only son of a widow died earlier this same day, since Jewish tradition encouraged a quick burial in order to avoid ceremonial uncleanliness (Strack and Billerbeck 1926:4:578-92; *m.*

7:11-17 This account is unique to Luke. It is also one of only four resuscitation accounts in Luke-Acts (Luke 8:40-42, 49-56; Acts 9:36-43; 20:7-12). On the theme of resuscitation in the ancient world, see van der Loos 1965:559-66. Such accounts were received with some skepticism in the ancient world (such as in the third-century A.D. Philostratus *Vita Apollonius* 4.45), so the ancients may not have been as uncritically accepting of miracles as is often suggested.

Sanhedrin 6:5; *m. Mo'ed Qatan* 1:6-7, 3:5-9; Ṣemaḥot 1). According to custom, the bereaved family members would rend their clothes and mourn the death. The process did not begin until it was certain that death had occurred. The body was anointed to prevent deterioration. It was buried quickly and was not kept overnight at home. The corpse would be wrapped in a burial cloth and put on a burial plank for all to see.

During the procession of the funeral entourage, after all these actions have been taken, Jesus encounters the mourning widow and the crowd.

The widow weeps for the loss of her only child. She is now all alone in a hostile world; no family to care for her. Recognizing her intense pain, Jesus approaches the corpse on the plank. He touches the plank— an act that would render him ceremonially unclean, but that pictures his compassion (Num 19:11, 16; Sirach 34:30). He tells the corpse to rise up. If there were no authority behind his words, the action would be blackly humorous or tragically misguided. But Jesus reveals the extent of his authority by confronting death. His words are successful: *the dead man sat up.* This was no longer a deceased mass of decaying flesh.

This miracle is reminiscent of the Old Testament resuscitations performed by Elijah (1 Kings 17:17-24) and Elisha (2 Kings 4:32-37). Those healings took a little more effort: Elisha lay on the boy three times and Elisha touched the boy with the staff and then lay on top of him. When Jesus hands the boy back to his mother, the language recalls 3 Kingdoms 17:23 LXX (1 Kings in English). So even as Luke tells the story, he points to prophetic models. Such historical background explains why the crowds come to see Jesus as a *great prophet.* The Old Testament precedents help explain the event. Given such precedents, the reader should not jump to conclusions about what such events prove about Jesus' divinity, especially since Peter and Paul will do similar works. The belief that Jesus is divine has other bases.

Jesus' comment on the significance of this event and others like it

---

7:16 The exact force of the title *great prophet* is disputed. (1) Is Jesus merely seen as one of the greatest of the prophets? Luke 9:7-9 suggests this may be what the crowd means. (2) Are they seeing Jesus as the great, eschatological prophet who comes at the end of time? The absence of a specific article to specify the title and the general answers of the populace presented in other texts suggest that this latter force is not intended (Cullmann 1959:30; Lk 9:19). Of course under the first category Jesus would not be seen as Messiah.

comes in Luke 7:22-23. These events point to a certain era of expectation and thus suggest who Jesus is, though even in chapter 7 the emphasis falls on messianic fulfillment. When the crowd fears and recognizes Jesus as a great prophet, they are not wrong; their view of Jesus is merely incomplete. With his account of this miracle Luke is steadily building his portrait of the many-faceted nature of Jesus. God is visiting his people. God's visitation is a key theme in Luke (1:68, 78; 19:41-44; Acts 15:14). God is active through Jesus. Public opinion about Jesus is spreading and is taking on various forms. God is at work through him. Yet his activity suggests that no one label or title is sufficient to describe and explain who he is.

But the nature of his work speaks as well. Jesus' ministry is about compassion. It is able to overcome a hurdle as significant as death (1 Cor 15). The scope of his authority knows no limits. Surely someone with such power should be the object of great interest. Surely he should be heeded and allowed to speak for himself, rather than being categorized according to the whims of popular opinion. So Luke turns to an exchange between Jesus and John the Baptist to show how the One who performs such wonders views himself.

Jesus and John the Baptist (7:18-35) Many believers have had moments of doubt about Jesus. Is he who he claimed to be? Why does he not manifest his sovereignty more directly? How could such an unassuming ministry be the most significant moment in humanity's history? Is he really there? Such questions are not just products of the modern era. Their roots are as old as Jesus' ministry. Even John the Baptist had such questions.

Often doubt brings reflection and growth. Such is the case with John's inquiries about Jesus. Not only does the Baptist get an answer that calls for his reflection, but Jesus uses the inquiry to help others consider anew the roles John and he have in God's plan. The psychological adversity of doubt carries the seed of real growth, when the answer is sought from God's perspective.

The scene begins with John's question to Jesus, *"Are you the one who*

7:18-35 The parallel to this passage is Matthew 11:2-19.

7:24 There is a little debate whether the imagery of this verse is literal, referring to the wilderness setting of John's ministry, or whether it is figurative, so that *reed* refers to John's

was to come, or should we expect someone else?" The question is brought by two messengers because John is in prison. In referring to Jesus as *the one who was to come,* John recalls his own description of the promised "more powerful" one in 3:15-18. The reason for John's question is much discussed. In fact, some interpreters are so embarrassed by the tradition that they argue that John is asking the question for the benefit of his disciples. But the most natural reading is to recognize the uncertainty as John's. He is in prison. He had proclaimed the approach of the powerful Messiah. As unusual as Jesus' ministry is, it is not what one would expect of God's chosen king. Scripture is quite honest about how people—even leaders like John—respond to God's unusual and surprising ways.

Luke sets the context for Jesus' reply by noting that Jesus *cured many who had diseases, sicknesses and evil spirits, and gave sight to many who were blind.* His ministry was filled with evidence of God's presence. Rather than answer John's question directly, he tells the messengers, *"Go back and report to John what you have seen and heard: The blind receive sight, the lame walk, those who have leprosy are cured, the deaf hear, the dead are raised, and the good news is preached to the poor."* Then he adds, "Blessed is anyone who takes no offense at me" (NRSV). The term for "offense," *skandalon,* is frequently used in this sense of reacting negatively, often with a reference to Isaiah 8:14 (Rom 9:33; 1 Cor 1:23; 1 Pet 2:8; also, Mk 14:29 illustrates the possibility of failing by being offended by Jesus). This term could refer to a trap or a stumbling block in everyday speech (Bauer 1979:753). It refers to something that ensnares or prevents progress. Jesus is saying to John and others that blessing comes to the one who is not offended by the uniqueness of Jesus' way of ministry. The fact that Jesus' style of messianic ministry is unexpected should not trip people up. Though stated negatively, the verse is a call to trust Jesus and recognize that he knows the way he is going.

Jesus' reply relies heavily on the Old Testament, with allusions to Isaiah 35:5-7, 26:19, 29:18-19 and 61:1. All the passages occur in contexts where God's decisive deliverance is awaited. So Jesus answers the question about his person with passages that describe the nature of the times.

---

character. If it is figurative, then Jesus asks if people went out to see a spineless man. Either sense is possible, but the next verse's more literal force suggests a literal force in this verse as well.

The question is, "Are you the coming one?" The answer is, "Discern the times by what God does through me." We are not to be offended by Jesus, not taken aback by the unusual nature of his ministry. It might not be what we expected, but it is what God promised. Do not worry; the time of fulfillment comes with him.

Jesus takes the opportunity to get the crowds to consider who John is and what God has done through the currently incarcerated prophet. Did people journey into the wilderness merely to see the river reeds blow in the wind? Of course they were not merely taking a scenic trip in the Jordanian wilderness. Did they go to check out John's wardrobe? Of course not—kings' palaces could offer much better fashion shows. So why did they make the journey? Jesus' answer is a clear endorsement of John's ministry, a response reinforced later in a key scene in Jerusalem (20:1-8).

John is a prophet, even more than a prophet. If the Associated Press or Reuters News Agency had a "Top Ten Prophets" list, John would be at the top. Why? Malachi 3:1, quoted here, supplies the answer: *"I will send my messenger ahead of you, who will prepare your way before you."* In fact, this reply combines two sets of images: one is that of the prophet who announces God's saving activity, as promised by Malachi; the other, from Exodus 23:20, is the image of the Shekinah going before the people and preparing the way for them. The Exodus imagery may well explain why Jesus says the messenger will go before *you*—that is, the people. Malachi 3:1 speaks of a prophet who goes before "me"— a clear reference to God—but Exodus 23 says the Shekinah will go before "you," the nation of Israel. This language recalls Luke 1:16-17. It says that John has functioned as a guide to produce a "prepared people." So John's greatness comes in getting God's people ready for God's salvation. He has pointed to God as a forerunner, but he has prepared the people as a prophet.

But as great as John is, he is nothing compared to those who share in the blessing of being in God's kingdom. Listen to Jesus: *"Among those born of women there is no one greater than John; yet the one who is least*

7:27 Judaism shared the view that Malachi 3:1 speaks of the prophet who would announce the period of fulfillment (Sirach 48:10; *Exodus Rabbah* on Exodus 32, section 9).

7:31-32 There is some discussion whether one group of children complain or two. In

in the kingdom of God is greater than he." Jesus is indicating how great
the difference is between the old era of the prophets of promise and the
new era of the kingdom tied to Jesus. The greatest of the old era cannot
touch the position of the lowest in the new! How great it is to share in
the blessing Jesus brings. Even prophets sit at the feet of those who share
in the blessing of the kingdom. Jesus' point reinforces the idea that the
time of fulfillment has begun. Humanity has never seen a time like this.
That is why Jesus said earlier that one should not be offended in him
(v. 23). Other New Testament texts argue that the prophets and the
angels longed for these days (Mt 13:17; 1 Pet 1:10-12). The kingdom's
presence elevates everyone who shares in it to a new status. Those who
know Jesus are greater than the prophets.

It is hard not to think that it would have been great, maybe even better,
to have lived in an era when God was mightily at work, to have crossed
the sea with Moses or seen Elijah defeat the prophets of Baal at Mount
Carmel. But Jesus is clear that as great as the former times were, as great
as John the Baptist was, nothing before that time matches what Jesus
offers. If Moses and the prophets could speak, they would say that they
longed for these days. They would gladly have traded places with us.
That is how special it is to share in the salvation Jesus brings.

In a parenthetical remark, Luke notes that *all the people,* including *the
tax collectors,* "justified" (Greek) or *acknowledged* (NIV) God—that is,
showed the wisdom of his plan—by responding to John's call for baptism. But the Pharisees and scribes rejected God's purpose by refusing
his baptism. Not only was the manifestation of God's plan surprising, but
there were also surprises regarding which groups responded to the message. Often we cannot predict who will respond to the gospel.

The popular reaction to John leads Jesus to offer one final picture of
the current generation. In what we might call "the parable of the brats,"
Jesus compares the current generation to children on the sidelines who
will not play street games because others will not play by their rules.
Note how the introduction to the parable is about *the people of this
generation,* so that the two "tunes" played are what the current gener-

all likelihood, there is one group of complaining children who, given the context of verse
30, represent the leadership. Those who should have been most ready for God's arrival end
up complaining about how salvation's messengers looked.

ation does. So the allusions in the parable cannot be about John (the dirge) and Jesus (the piper). Rather, the children of this generation complain that God's plan is not going according to their demands and expectations. Neither the ascetic John nor Jesus with his open association with sinners and his "wanton" lifestyle of eating and drinking fits what this generation wants to see.

Perhaps if Jesus were ministering today as he did in the first century, some of us too would complain that he was getting too close to sin. Legalism often takes neutral issues of style and tries to turn them into substance. The varying styles of Jesus and John show God's flexibility on such issues. No matter which lifestyle God's messengers choose, many will complain. Nevertheless, Jesus assures the crowd that *wisdom is proved right* ("justified" in Greek) *by all her children.* He means that God's wisdom is revealed in those who respond to his ways on his terms.

God often acts in surprising ways. His unusual path is often lined by people's doubt and rejection. Here Jesus points to his ministry as evidence for the nature of the times. In addition, he warns that others are not interested in seeing God work but simply want to control how God does things. But God comes to us in surprising ways on his own terms. The call is not to be offended by the One he sends or by how he brings his plan to pass. Even in the midst of doubt, we are called to see what God has done and trust that his way is the path of wisdom. Wisdom's children see his ways and walk in them. In wisdom's path is the blessing of sharing in God's presence beyond even what the best of God's prophets enjoyed. Even if many of their peers never acknowledge God's work, those who respond to Jesus are highly privileged. Sometimes the most precious gifts of God are the least appreciated.

An Exemplary Sinner (7:36-50) How do you react when a notorious sinner walks into the room? Do you wish to confront them or to leave them to others? Is their sinfulness so much an issue that you cannot see the person?

In an account unique to Luke, a sinful woman visits Jesus and anoints

---

7:36-50 Many have compared this passage to Matthew 26:6-13, Mark 14:3-9 and John 12:1-8. However, there are numerous differences. The other Synoptics indicate that the meal is held in the house of a leper, a place where Pharisees would never dine. Only John has an anointing of feet; Matthew and Mark mention only an anointing of the head. John is clear

him. She says nothing, but her actions speak a thousand words. The problem is that her intimacy with Jesus produces an array of opinion. Her action forces Jesus to explain how he responds to others, especially sinners. In the response he reveals both his philosophy of dealing with people and his authority.

During a meal at the home of a Pharisee, a well-known sinful woman enters to anoint Jesus' feet. We are not told what her sin has been. Traditionally she has been called a prostitute, but the text is not so specific. Nor is she likely to be Mary Magdalene, who is introduced as a new figure in 8:1-3. Whatever her sin, her reputation precedes her.

It may seem odd that she is able to "crash the party" and approach Jesus, but in the ancient world it apparently was common to allow access to a meal in honor of a major teaching figure. An ancient Jewish text, *t. Berakot* 31b, tells of a poor man who waited outside a king's door and eventually entered the palace in hope of receiving leftover food. Here no one expresses shock that the woman is present; the scandal is that she has drawn close to Jesus and he has let her approach him. As long as she sat in the bleachers, everything was fine, but when she steps onto the playing field, people become upset. They don't think a spectator should become a key player.

The woman's actions reflect great cost, care and emotion. The perfume she uses is both precious and expensive. Such anointing was practiced at civic feasts and for the purifying of priests or the tabernacle (Ex 30:25-30; Josephus *Antiquities* 3.8.6 §205; 19.9.1 §358), not to mention for preserving corpses (Lk 23:56). If this perfume is nard, it would have cost three hundred denarii, or about a year's salary, per pound!

Approaching a reclining Jesus, she anoints his feet as tears of joy and appreciation pour out upon him. The undoing of her hair is culturally shocking. Her kissing of Jesus' feet also expresses an intimacy shunned in this culture. Everything about her action is offensive, except for the attitude that fed it, an attitude Jesus exposes in his parable in verses 41-44. Luke narrates the details with imperfect tenses, featuring the ongoing

that the righteous Mary does the anointing in the scene he narrates, so sinfulness is not the issue there. In the other Synoptics, the conflict comes because the disciples complain about the waste of perfume. Luke 7, unlike the other Synoptics, makes no mention of memorializing. So it seems likely that this is a unique event in the life of Jesus.

nature of each action. Imagine the nerve of the woman, who surely realizes how others are viewing her. The strength of her love has caused her to be bold in expressing appreciation to Jesus.

The Pharisee reacts first, and he blames Jesus. The woman's contact with Jesus is outrageous and intolerable. He thinks, *If this man were a prophet, he would know who is touching him and what kind of woman she is—that she is a sinner.* The Greek reveals a nice literary touch here. The construction is a second-class, or contrary-to-fact, condition. The Pharisee is thinking that Jesus is not a prophet. His actions (the fact that he does not rebuke this woman) indicate his lack of status. There is a theological assumption in this evaluation: pious figures like prophets have nothing to do with sinners. Separationism is the name of the game. If spiritual people are to maintain purity and testimony, association with sinners is prohibited. Luke often mentions this view of the Pharisees in contexts that suggest rebuke (5:29-32; 15:1-2; 18:9-14).

Jesus has a decidedly different view. His evaluation of the woman's act comes in a parable, which Luke tells with much irony. The Pharisee doubts that Jesus is a prophet, yet Jesus has read his mind, as his response shows! Jesus' story is simple. There are two debtors. One has a debt ten times that of the other (the difference is between about two months' debt and slightly over one and a half year's debt). The creditor forgives the debt of both, rather like a car dealer wiping out an entire loan obligation on a car. If that ever happened at a dealership, we could imagine the appreciation, not to mention the publicity, it would generate! Now which former debtor will love the creditor more? The emotion of the story is crucial. Jesus is saying, in effect, Imagine the appreciation and love that flow from the one who has been forgiven a great debt. Jesus is comparing the forgiveness of sins to economic forgiveness. The debtor has no bargaining position; only grace allows the debt to be removed. So which debtor has the greater love?

The Pharisee is a good student. He replies, "I would suppose the one whom he forgave the most." The Greek keeps the double entendre between the story and the idea of forgiveness. The NIV renders the intent clearly: *the one who had the bigger debt canceled.*

Jesus commends the reply. His point is obvious: great forgiveness provides the opportunity for great love. When God forgives a notorious sinner for much sin, the realization of such bountiful forgiveness means the potential for great love. Jesus pursues sinners and welcomes association with them because of the possibility that they may realize God's gracious forgiveness. To keep separate from them would be to ignore a potentially rich harvest field.

Jesus applies the story. He notes that the woman has done what the Pharisee has failed to do. It is not clear that the Pharisee has actually failed to do what is culturally expected (Goppelt 1972:323-24, 328, especially nn. 63, 93-95). But what the woman has done goes above and beyond the call of duty. Love often produces such an extraordinary response. The woman's action reflects not only gratitude but also humility. She recognizes who it is who has made her feel welcome. No washing, kiss or greeting had met Jesus at the Pharisee's door, but the woman supplies them all. She appreciates Jesus' offer of grace and seeks to honor it with devotion and love.

Jesus is not done. In a remark that raises the stakes, he proclaims that the woman's sins are forgiven because she has loved much. It is important that this statement and the parable be combined to allow Jesus' theological point to be clear. Jesus is not saying that the woman's works have saved her. Rather, the love and forgiveness that have made her feel accepted by God (the parable's point) have produced her acts of love. Jesus commends the faith that led to her works (v. 50).

If Jesus' reception of the sinner is a problem, his declaration of the forgiveness of sins is a massive problem (compare 5:22)! Only God forgives sin. Again we see how Jesus' ministry combines ethics and theology. His behavior is an example of how to relate to others but also reflects a unique authority that makes Jesus more than a mere instructor of morality. In saying the woman's sins are forgiven, he is clearly even greater than a prophet. Here is raw authority.

The Pharisees again engage in private thoughts and theological assessment; they know the significance behind Jesus' statement. They know no mere man has the right to forgive sin, so they ask, *"Who is this who even forgives sin?"* The question is crucial. If Jesus has the authority to forgive sin, then he has the right to reveal how salvation occurs. Simon was worried about Jesus being a prophet, but Jesus' pronouncement of forgiveness means he is much more.

Jesus closes with a declaration that deepens the message. He reassures the woman by telling her, *"Your faith has saved you; go in peace."* With this he turns her earlier expression of love into evidence of saving faith. Faith has motivated the response of love and humility that was evidenced in the anointing. Her story shows that sinners can know God will respond when they turn to him.

Jesus represents the messenger of God who ministers God's love. As a result, he is open to and conscious of the opportunity that exists when sinners are loved. He does not ignore sin, but he recognizes that sin can be reversed when God's love is received. The Pharisees' separatist attitude stands rebuked as an inappropriate model of holiness. The heavenly Father is ready to forgive debts when we turn humbly to him.

Jesus also raises again the issue of his authority. He possesses the authority to forgive sin. Jesus is more than an example of one who is open to sinners; he wields the gavel. He can discern the presence of faith, and he can pronounce forgiveness of sins. The sinful woman is an example of faith expressing itself in humble love, even to the point of boldness. The Louvre's outstanding portrait may be the famous Mona Lisa, but in the Bible there is no more beautiful portrait of humble, loving faith than this woman's silent but vibrant testimony.

A Surprising Picture of Faith in Ministry (8:1-3) Because of the centuries that have passed since Jesus walked the earth, it is hard for us to appreciate how revolutionary Luke's picture of Jesus' ministry is. Women's involvement in supporting Jesus' ministry is an example. Though some wealthy women supported religious figures in ancient times (Josephus *Antiquities* 17.2.4 §§41-44), it was unusual for them to be as involved as the women in this passage are with Jesus. In fact, this passage is one of several unique to Luke that focus on women (others include 1:5-39, Elizabeth; 2:36-38, Anna the prophetess; 7:36-50, the sinful woman; 10:38-42, Martha and Mary; 13:10-17, the healing of the crippled woman; 15:8-10, the parable of the woman with the lost coin; 18:1-8, the parable of the woman and the judge). Many men of the time believed that women were not even to be seen, much less heard. In a later Jewish text, *t. Berakot* 7:18, one leader rejoiced that he was not a pagan, a woman or unlearned (Fitzmyer 1981:696). In contrast, Luke and the New Testament declare that women have equal access to the blessings of grace and salvation. Whatever distinctions the Bible makes between male and female roles, there is no distinction when it comes to being coheirs in grace (Gal 3:28-29; 1 Pet 3:7).

This small summary paragraph is important not only because women are included but also because of the variety of women mentioned. Mary called Magdalene ministered in response to Jesus' healing ministry. His exorcism of demons from her had drawn her to him. Though from the time of Gregory the Great she has had the reputation of a sinful woman, this text gives no indication that she was immoral. Joanna was the wife of a major political figure, Chuza, who served as Herod's steward. Thus Luke shows that Jesus' message had reached the highest social stratum, the palace. We are not told anything about Susanna. All these women contributed their resources to Jesus' ministry. Their hearts were sensitive to God's work, and they expressed this sensitivity through their generosity.

When this discussion of women is set next to that of the sinful woman in 7:36-50, it is clear that Jesus' ministry spanned social backgrounds as well as moral backgrounds. It is striking that here the women's response took the concrete form of support. Just as in the Old Testament the whole nation was to support the priests, so these women, as beneficiaries of God's grace, gave to support Jesus' ministry. Receiving should lead to giving.

The Call to Faith and Christology (8:4—9:17) This fifth section of Luke's portrayal of Jesus' Galilean ministry continues to focus on the issue of Christ's authority, but now the attention turns to the responses to that authority. Luke 8:4-21 shows how the Word of God reveals the way to God. The Word for Luke is the preached word of Jesus. That word can be compared to light, and those who are of Jesus' "family" will obey it. Luke 8:22-56 reveals the extent of Jesus' authority through a series of miracles, starting with Jesus' control of nature and moving to demon exorcism, healing and then a resuscitation. Jesus has authority over everything.

Luke 9:1-17 shows Jesus extending his authority through the commissioned ministry of his disciples. They are to preach the kingdom to surrounding towns and villages. As evidence of their authority they have the ability to heal. They are to "feed" those who have need, as the later miracle of the multiplication of loaves indicates. Meanwhile, there is public reaction. Is Jesus *a* prophet or *the* prophet to come? Is he John the Baptist reborn? The section ends with a demonstration of authority in the feeding of the multitudes through Jesus' provision and the disciples' distribution. The next passage, Luke 9:18-20, contains Peter's confession that Jesus is the Christ. All the events in this section show how Jesus deserves this confession.

The Parable of the Seed and the Importance of the Word (8:4-21) Opinions and ideologies abound in our world. Often we hear the statement that there are many ways to God. But for Jesus the preaching of the kingdom was revelation of a unique message, not one opinion among many in a melting pot of ideas. This portion of Luke highlights the centrality of the word of the kingdom for Jesus. The parable of the seed contains a mystery, one which disciples have the privilege to behold while outsiders are blinded and unable to see its truth. Such revelation is like light, illuminating the way to God. In fact, Jesus indicates that being related to him is a matter of responding to the message he preaches. The parable of the seed indicates the variety of responses to the word Jesus sows in his preaching (see Is 55:10-11 on God's word as a seed). Not everyone embraces his message, but those who do yield a life of fruitfulness that honors God. For Jesus, the kingdom message is special and unique. To heed it is to find blessing.

The picture of the word as seed is important. Often we think of evangelism and preaching as something that happens in an instant. But the picture of a seed makes us think of a farmer who prepares the ground, sows seed, waters and then must wait for the crop. Producing a crop is a process over time. Often the message of the word, too, takes time to bear fruit.

Today Gallup, Harris, Reuters and Barna polls can acquaint us with the range of reactions to any event or idea of interest in our culture. Since everyone is different, the reactions are varied. Responses to spiritual truth

Notes: 8:4-15 The parallels to this parable are in Mark 4:1-20 and Matthew 13:10-23. The parable in these other Synoptic Gospels is part of a larger sequence of kingdom parables. Luke notes only this one in this context. At numerous points Luke's rendering of the parable is distinctive. He appears to be explaining the parable's significance in light of the church's

are also varied. The parable of the seed, or better the parable of the soils, is one of Jesus' most popular. It describes four reactions that Jesus' preaching produces, though the story concentrates on those who make at least an initial response. Of the various options, only one type of soil yields fruit; every other type proves inhospitable to the precious seed.

Jesus lived in an agrarian culture, so his parables often use farming imagery. Such is the case here. As the crowds are drawn to Jesus, he adopts a new teaching style, one he will explain in verses 9-10. Parables are comparisons in which spiritual truth is pictured in vivid terms (Blomberg 1990). In a Palestinian setting a farmer would walk a path through a field and distribute seed from a bag draped over his shoulder. Sowing was done between October and December, since harvest came around June. Between harvest to sowing the field was left alone. In the ancient world the key to a successful harvest was the soil in which the seed fell.

So Jesus tells of four places where seed lands—on a path, on rocks, among thorns and in good soil. The variety of possibilities reflect the kinds of soils the ancient Palestinian would have encountered. Some seed never makes it to the soil; it falls instead on a path, where it is exposed to birds and travelers. Other seed lands on a type of soil that was common in the area—thin topsoil with a hard layer of rock underneath. This allows a plant to grow quickly, drawing moisture from the rock; but with the sunshine that moisture disappears and the plant, unable to send its roots deeper, withers. Still other potentially fruitful fields are infested with parasitic thorns. Palestinian weeds could grow up to six feet tall, gobbling the land's nutrients. The seed on the good soil, however, produces a hundredfold. (Unlike the other Synoptics, which speak of a variety of yields in the good soil, Luke's version notes its fruitfulness with a single example.) Most seed in the ancient world would produce a crop of thirty-five or so times, so the yield here is high (Linnemann 1966:117). When Jesus finishes the parable, he issues his

situation. So he does not compare the seed to "the message about the kingdom" but simply speaks of *the word.* Such changes are not really differences, since Luke 4:42-44 and 9:1-6 make it clear that Jesus and the disciples did speak of the kingdom in their preaching.

standard call to hear (Mt 11:15; 13:9, 43; Mk 4:9, 23; 7:16; Lk 8:8; 9:44; 14:35; compare Ezek 3:27).

After Jesus tells the story, the disciples ask why he is resorting to parables. They know him well enough to recognize that this is not a lesson in agriculture for a 4H class or a polytechnic school. In response, Jesus observes that knowledge of the "mysteries" of the kingdom of God has been given to his disciples. Numerous points are made here. First, Luke places *to you* in the emphatic position in Greek. They have been privileged to understand these things. Second, the passive "is given" indicates that the gift has come from God. Third, what is given involves *secrets* about the kingdom of God. So the message of the seed is related to the promise of the kingdom of God. Fourth, others get parables as judgment.

"Mystery" is an important biblical term. Its roots go back to the image of the *rāz* in Daniel (Dan 2:20-23, 28-30; Bornkamm 1967:814-15, 817-18). There Daniel unlocked the mystery hidden in an already revealed dream. Some New Testament texts on mystery highlight the newness of the revelation (Eph 3:4-6; Col 1:27-29), while other mystery texts note the connection of what is revealed in Jesus to what was revealed in the Old Testament (Rom 16:25-27). Thus the term speaks of new truth emerging alongside old promise. Discontinuity in God's plan emerges within continuity. Jesus is revealing further detail and fresh twists in God's plan, but those details fit together with the program that God has already promised. The twists and turns in the promised and progressing kingdom program are being revealed to the disciples in these parables.

8:10 The concept of mystery (NIV *secrets*) also appears at Qumran (1QpHab. 7:8; 1QS 3:23; 1QM 3:9; 16:11). Only those with direct access to God understand and explain such mysteries.

The Synoptic rendering of Isaiah 6:9 shows an ambiguity in how that text was read in the early church. Matthew says the cause *(hoti)* of parabolic teaching is hardness of heart, while Luke speaks of its purpose *(hina)* as being to keep eyes blind and ears dull. Luke emphasizes the judgment result of the preaching parable, while Matthew stresses that it is used because of the hearers' previous hardness.

8:13-14 There is debate whether seeds two and three produce saved people. For some, the mention of faith in verse 13 is decisive in answering the question positively. But the overall image of the parable makes that conclusion most uncertain. Seed is designed to bear fruit, and fruit is produced only in the fourth example. Whatever belief exists in verse 13, it is not permanent but temporary, as the second part of the verse shows—*they believe for a while.* Faith saves; the absence of faith does not. So to believe for a time is not to believe

But the parables do not only reveal secrets to the disciples; they also conceal truth from outsiders, those Jesus calls *others*. At this point he alludes to Isaiah 6:9. The other Synoptic versions also cite this text, but Luke's version is shorter and more paraphrastic. The goal of such comparative stories is so that *though seeing, they may not see; though hearing, they may not understand*. The danger of exposure to revelation is that if we do not respond in faith, eventually hardness sets in and God acts to judge. Here is a warning about the ultimate perils of rejection: God may sovereignly involve himself in cementing the process. These words are harsh, yet they serve as a warning of the extreme danger of rejecting Jesus' message.

Now Jesus turns to explain the parable. The seed is the word. Contextually it is clear that *the word* here means the preaching of the kingdom (v. 10). Jesus' message is about entry into God's plan and rule. The seed on the path represents those who do not get to respond to the message because the devil comes and takes the seed before it can even penetrate the ground, much less bear fruit. When God seeks to speak to humanity, a cosmic battle breaks out.

The seed on the rock represents a message that falls into a person's heart but penetrates only shallowly. There is initial response, but eventually temptation causes the person to abandon that initial response. Initial receptivity and short-lived belief are followed eventually by a falling away. The engagement the word produced at the start does not last. Both Old and New Testaments issue dire warnings about the consequences of falling away or departing from faith (Jer 3:13-14; Dan 9:9;

in a commendable way, since the end result is not faith. One cannot end up unbelieving and have a faith that saves, for then salvation comes in unbelief. Another way to say this is that genuine faith is permanent (1 Cor 15:3-5; Col 1:21-23; Heb 6:4-6; 10:26-31). Our theological problems may emerge here because we tend to view faith as a response of the moment. The New Testament stresses that faith in Jesus is permanent, being established by a rebirth. Its permanence is suggested by its nature as the product of the regenerating work of God (Eph 2:8-10) and by texts like this one. When the Spirit is present, we recognize that we are his children (Jn 10; Rom 8:14-30). Jesus offers no comfort to those represented by the seed among rocks and thorns. It is clear that this seed is unfruitful.

This picture does not mean that works save; rather, works are merely the fruit of seed that has landed in good soil, soil that has faith. In fact, in this historical setting it is possible that the first seed refers to the leaders, the second and third kinds of seed symbolize the crowds, and the last seed refers to disciples. However, the lack of specific identifications makes this conclusion more inferential than explicit.

1 Tim 4:1; Heb 3:12). Jesus offers no comfort for the person represented here; he merely notes significantly that the seed never bears fruit.

The thorny soil represents those who are choked out of a walk with God by life's distractions. The world's worries, riches and pleasures take any benefit the seed has to offer or any nutrients the soil possesses. They swallow up any opportunity for fruit to come to maturity. Luke often notes how wealth can influence people adversely and become a harmful distraction (6:24; 12:16-21; 14:12; 16:1, 19, 21-22; 18:23, 25; 19:2; 21:1). *Pleasures* translates a Greek word from which our term "hedonism" is derived. Clearly, wrong priorities can kill off the seed of the word.

In the one positively assessed case in the parable, the good soil pictures those who hear the word and hold fast to it. They possess an honest and *good heart* and so bear fruit with patience. The mention of patience *(persevering)* is important, for Luke assumes that believers live under much pressure because of their faith. Associating with Jesus will not help people to win popularity contests. If we care about the world's respect or are too weak to resist temptation, we will not hold on to the word with patience; tragically, we may fall away, or our potential for fruitfulness may be choked out. Three of the examples end with the seed failing to produce that for which it was sown. God sows the word to bear fruit in the heart. Only by clinging patiently to what God offers does the seed reach maturity. In other New Testament texts such reliance is called faith.

This parable is not about a response to the word at any given moment. It sums up the different ways the word is received over a lifetime of exposure. It takes time to fall away from an initial attraction to the word. Only over time do the pleasures of life erode the seed's effectiveness. The parable calls for reflection. We need to cling to the word in patient faith. If we desire to be fruitful, especially given that the obstacles to fruitfulness are so varied, then we must hold fast to God and his message of hope. We focus either on God's promise or on our circumstances. Which we choose makes a difference: one leads to fruitfulness, the other

───────────────────────────

8:16-18 The parallel to this passage is Mark 4:21-25, though Luke has similar imagery in 11:33-36, 12:2 and 19:26. The image's exact force here is disputed. Some equate it to Matthew 5:15 and argue that the disciples are the light. But this makes too great a shift for this Lukan context. It is more natural, given the emphasis on the Word in both the preceding and succeeding passages, to see a reference to the Word here, by which is meant contex-

to barrenness.

After the parable Jesus uses imagery of light to characterize the word. We could call this passage "the parable of the lamp." In the ancient world, such a lamp would have been a candlestick or an oil-burning lamp (Michaelis 1967b:324). Since a stand is mentioned here, an oil-burning lamp is likely to be in view. Jesus' message is put *on a stand, so that those who come in can see the light.* Like light in a dark place, Jesus' message can guide us through life in the darkness of this world (Wisdom of Solomon 6:22; Sirach 39:12). But light does not just shine to illumine the way, it also reveals how things really are. The word shows the way and brings to light the secret things in people's hearts. Whether we realize it or not, the word shines and exposes. It may well be that the picture of Jesus as light influences the portrait of his message as containing light (1:78-79; 2:30-32; Jn 8:12; 9:5).

So Jesus urges his audience to be careful how they listen. The stakes are high. The one who has listened by responding to the word will receive more. But as for those who think they have something but do not have anything (because they do not receive the word), even what they thought they had will be taken away. To refuse to hear God's word is to be left desolate and naked before God.

To drive the point home even more, Jesus contrasts his biological family with his real family. Hearing that his mother and brothers desire to see him, Jesus remarks, *"My mother and brothers are those who hear God's word and put it into practice."* Jesus affirms kinship with those who have heeded his authority and responded to his message. As he has said in Luke 6:47-49 (and as his brother notes in James 1:22-25), we should hear and do what the word calls for. James apparently learned from the Lord's remark here. Kinship with Jesus means responsiveness to his message.

Miracle 1: Jesus' Authority over Nature and Care for Us (8:22-25) Is God there and does he care? No question is more basic to human

tually Jesus' teaching about the kingdom.

8:19-21 The parallels are Mark 4:31-35 and Matthew 12:46-50. Mark's version portrays the family most harshly, but Mark is consistently more severe than the other Synoptics in his depictions of Jesus' family and the disciples. Mark ties this event to the Beelzebub dispute, an event Luke places later. Luke's arrangement may well be topical.

beings' relationship to the creation and to one another. If he is not there, then life is a free-for-all and we must do the best we can for ourselves. Often this worldview means that the one with the most power wins. If God *is* there, then finding him and responding to him is our most basic need. For if he exists, then power resides with him and everyone becomes accountable to him.

Power means different things for different people, and it can be used in a wide variety of ways. It can be put to good use, destructive use or selfish use. As Jesus continues the revelation of his authority in a series of four miracles extending through the end of Luke 8, he uses his power for others—for those to whom he ministers. Authority for Jesus is not a matter of a raw exercise of power; rather, it is a natural resource that is put to positive use as he shows compassion to those with all kinds of needs. Of course these miracles are audiovisuals of deeper realities. The Gospel of John makes this connection very clear (for example, Jn 6), but the Synoptics show this pictorial dimension as well.

The miracles all raise one question. That question cannot be any more clearly stated than it is at the end of this first miracle where Jesus calms the storm: *"Who is this? He commands even the winds and the water, and they obey him."*

This simple miracle account actually contains much teaching. The event itself is rather straightforward. As the disciples and Jesus set about to cross the *lake* (the Sea of Galilee), a severe storm kicks up. We can tell the problem is severe since some in the boat had been professional fishermen and are now in a panic. Such storms are not uncommon on the Sea of Galilee, since the surrounding topography lends itself to sudden weather changes. The sea is some 680 feet below sea level. It is surrounded by hills, the steepest of which lie on its eastern shore. Coming through the hills, cool air reaches a ravine and collides with trapped warm air over the water. As any meteorologist will tell you, this produces volatile conditions.

While Matthew describes the storm as a "shaking" *(seismos)* of the boat, Luke calls it a whirlwind *(lailaps)*, a word that sounds like what

8:22-25 The parallels to this account are Matthew 8:23-27 and Mark 4:35-41. Mark clearly associates the event with the day Jesus taught in kingdom parables, while Matthew places it before his kingdom parable section (chap. 13) and appears to be arranging the material

it describes. Only Jesus is resting, unaware of the danger that surrounds him. The text expresses the danger in a peculiar fashion—*the boat was being swamped, and they were in great danger.* The term for danger means Jesus' and the disciples' lives are at risk, as their later plea to him indicates (Acts 19:27, 40 and 1 Cor 15:30 include other uses of the term). Since verse 22 only mentions one boat, *they* here are the disciples. The storm threatens them. Jesus is physically there but appears to be mentally absent, taking a nap, unable to help them in their hour of need. In their anxiety they awake him, announcing impending doom if nothing is done: *"Master, Master, we're going to drown!"*

The next three parts of the passage are loaded with significance. First Jesus rebukes the wind, so that calm is immediately restored. Called upon to help his disciples, he responds faithfully. The event is the catalyst for two commentaries, one from Jesus, the other from the disciples. Both present aspects of the passage's teaching.

Jesus rebukes his disciples for lack of faith. By asking where their faith was, he is reminding them of his care of them. Often this point in the passage is lost as we marvel over the calming of the sea. Jesus' authority and attributes do not exist in abstraction from his relationships. Even though he seemed to be absent and uncaring, a point Mark 4:38 makes explicitly, he was there and they could rest in the knowledge that he knew what was happening to them. Faith would have told them that God would take them through the terrible storm. So Jesus takes the calming of the storm as an opportunity to remind them that he will care for them. They need to have more faith in God's goodness. They need an applied faith that will hang tough under pressure. This is what he had earlier called holding to the Word with patience (v. 15).

Meanwhile, the disciples are pondering the event. Full of fear and marvel, they ask, *"Who is this?"* The question is a good one, because anyone who knew the Old Testament or Jewish theology would have known that Yahweh has control of the wind and the seas (Ps 18:16; 104:3; 135:6-7; Nahum 1:4; also Wisdom of Solomon 14:3-5). In fact, Psalm 107:23-30 says that God delivers the sailor who is imperiled at sea.

---

topically.

8:24 The use of the double vocative, *"Master, Master,"* is always an indication of high emotion (compare 5:5; 8:45; 9:33, 49; 17:13).

Now this miracle did not automatically prove that Jesus has absolute authority. What it did was more subtle. It raised the question of Jesus' identity for the disciples. Earlier he had forgiven sins; now he calms the seas. Who can do such a variety of things?

Luke leaves the query unanswered here. The reader is to ponder the question. But the topic of Jesus' identity keeps popping up in the Gospel and in Acts (Lk 9:7-9, 18-20; 20:41-44; 23:49; Acts 2:30-36; 10:34-43). In the meantime, faith is called for in the recognition that Jesus is there and is aware of his disciples. Jesus' authority means he has the power to deliver those who depend on him. Calm waves can come only from the One with the power to restore order.

Miracle 2: Jesus' Authority over Disease and the Reversal of Evil (8:26-39) Evil's presence in our world is a fact of life. Every evening news report and every newspaper tells of the damage people do to one another. In fact, evil grabs our attention. The proverb about television news—"If it bleeds, it leads"—indicates how stories about acts of fallenness leap to our attention.

The account of the Gerasene demoniac is such a story. Here is a man in the grip of evil's power. Other human forces and agencies have been unable to contain him. So he lives a destructive and isolated life among the tombs outside the city. Luke is in the midst of presenting a series of miracles that reveal the extent of Jesus' authority. How does he stack up in a showdown with evil?

The account is a fully developed miracle story, giving a clear development of the need, Jesus' response and then the reaction to what took place. The man's condition is serious. First, he is possessed by several

---

8:26-39 The parallels to this event are Mark 5:1-20 and a more abbreviated version in Matthew 8:28-34. There has been some debate about the event's historicity, because of Jesus' permitting the demons to infest the swine. Even beyond the story's miraculous elements, this detail has been hard for some to accept. But once the miracles are seen as events that are also important audiovisuals, the demons' departure into the swine makes sense, since it pictures so graphically the significance of what Jesus did in saving the man from forces that would have driven him to total destruction—forces that did not mind inhabiting "unclean" creatures like the swine. This swine imagery may well suggest the miracle's traditional roots. Though it takes place in a Gentile region, it is told with sensitivity to Jewish imagery.

Matthew has another difference that is much discussed. He mentions two demoniacs (Mt 8:28, 33). The story is simpler if only one character is in view, so Mark and Luke focus on the one character. It seems likely that Matthew has independent access to facts about this

demons (note the Greek plural, *echōn daimonia,* "who had demons," in v. 27). Later it will be said that a single demon speaks (vv. 28-29), but this is simply a single voice for the multitudes that indwell this man. Second, he is naked and has been so *for a long time.* This would make his behavior offensive. Third, the man lives in isolation among *the tombs.* The German scholar Adolph Schlatter has been quoted as saying, "Only deranged people have a desire for death and decay" (Geldenhuys 1951:258 n. 4). This certainly summarizes well the picture Luke has painted here. Everything about this man shows how the presence of evil in his life has left him deserted and alone.

Jesus' presence alone is enough to stir the forces inside the man to react. The demonic power reacts to Jesus' command to leave the man by causing the man to fall before him and say, *"What do you want with me, Jesus, Son of the Most High God? I beg you, don't torture me!"* Several details are important. The evil force recognizes Jesus' authority and ability to exercise judgment (4:34, 41). As in 4:34-41, there is a confession. In Luke 8 the confession is of Jesus' unique sonship. The demons desire to be left alone, to avoid torment. In an aside in verse 29 we are told that this possessed man had often been led into the wilderness by what possessed him—a statement that has both literal and figurative force. Numerous times this diabolical power had enabled the man to break bonds that had trapped him. Such ancient fetters could have been made of hair, cloth, rope or chains, but the Mark 5:4 parallel suggests that these had been chains. This foe is so powerful that other people have been unable to control the man. So they have left him in the solitary confinement of the tombs.

---

event and thus chooses to mention a companion (Carson 1984:217).

Another issue is the event's locale. A textual problem is involved here. The best readings of these texts appear to suggest that Matthew refers to the Gadarene region, while Luke and Mark refer to Gerasene. Some uncertainty exists about the actual locations in the ancient world. It may well be that overlapping regions are referred to here; or one may be a more specific designation than another, just as we could refer to the Dallas region or to the Metroplex and thereby include Ft. Worth, or refer to London and thereby include Gatwick and Heathrow. In every case, one part of the region is quite distant from another portion of it. No matter how the geography works, it is clear that a Gentile region is in view, given the swine's presence.

8:28 *Most High* was the Gentile way to refer to the God of the Jews (Josephus *Antiquities* 16.6.2 §163; Dan 3:26; 4:24; 5:18; 7:18).

Jesus' request for the name of the demon brings the reponse Legion, a reference to a unit made up of thousands of soldiers. No doubt the name indicates the extent of the possession and the difficulty of Jesus' task in dealing with it. Luke makes this explicit: *many demons had gone into him.*

The demons feared Jesus. They did not want to be thrown into the *Abyss,* a reference to the abode of the dead in the Old Testament (Ps 107:26; compare Rom 10:7). Only Luke uses this term in the New Testament, though Hades, Gehenna and Tartarus may be parallel concepts (on Hades see Lk 16:23). In the Old Testament and Judaic writings this term referred to the "depths" and was often associated with the sea (Ps 71:20; *Jubilees* 5:6-7; *1 Enoch* 10:4-6; 18:11-16). The demons feared permanent confinement, so they asked to be allowed to inhabit the swine on a nearby hill. The choice of pigs is interesting, given their association with uncleanliness in the Old Testament (Lev 11:7). It is not clear why the demons made such a request, other than to escape total confinement and judgment.

The demons' request is granted, but their relief is short-lived. The pigs apparently are startled and rush headlong over a cliff and into the sea. In Judaism the sea was a symbol of potential evil (*Testament of Solomon* 5:11; 11:6), so this becomes an illustration of evil's destructiveness, especially since the demons have not only harmed the man but now have led to the pigs' death.

Needless to say, this is not an everyday event in the Gerasene region, so the herdsmen run to tell others in the city and countryside what has happened. When the people travel out to the scene of the miracle, they see a transformed man sitting at Jesus' feet *dressed and in his right mind.* The story of how this change occurred is told, but the people cannot take it; they ask Jesus to go. Luke does not tell us why, although Mark 5:16 suggests that the economic impact of the loss of the swine is a concern. Evidently, however, the encounter with Jesus' power is too threatening for them (v. 37, *because they were overcome with fear*).

The newly healed man wants to go with Jesus, but instead Jesus tells

8:31 The term *Abyss* has a complicated background and may be in view conceptually in

him to remain behind and testify to what *God* had done for him. He obeys and tells the whole city what *Jesus* had done for him. This man, now of sound mind, makes no distinction between Jesus' actions and the workings of God's power.

This miracle account is full of teaching. The miracle itself shows the extent of Jesus' authority over the forces of evil and his ability to transform people's ties to evil. The Gerasene man had been a totally destructive agent under the force of the demons. As a result of Jesus' work, he has been restored to full life. The image of him clothed and seated before Jesus at the end of the account contrasts sharply with the earlier picture of his sojourn among the tombs. The miracle pictures how Jesus can erase the power and effects of evil in a person. This transformation and the ability to overcome evil is why Paul calls the gospel "the power of God" in Romans 1:16-17.

The man's reaction shows that after God's grace works, our attention should be directed to Jesus. He longed to serve Jesus and even assumed that he should join his traveling band of disciples. Such devotion is commendable. Jesus made it clear, however, that this man's testimony should remain in the region. He was to be a "missionary in residence" for God. Of course the man understood that to tell God's story, he must mention Jesus as well.

The demons show how impotent evil ultimately is when confronted with Jesus' authority. The account also reveals how destructive such unseen forces are.

The people's reaction is also instructive. For some people it is very difficult to let God and his power get close to them. These people recognized that Jesus had power. It aroused fear in them, and they chose to have nothing to do with it.

Jesus possesses authority so great that he can reverse the effects of evil. Some are transformed by that power—turned from a path of uncleanliness, destruction and death to life and testimony. But others fear it and want God's presence to be distant from them. They fear what involvement with God's power might entail.

a few New Testament passages: 2 Peter 2:4; Jude 6; Revelation 9:1, 2, 11; 11:7; 17:18; 20:1, 3. For more on this term, see Jeremias 1964a.

Jesus' authority is a given for Luke. It forces choices of association. The world is full of destructive forces, but Jesus is the means for overcoming them. Luke raises a question here. Shall we sit at his feet and let his power free us? Or will we quake at Jesus' authority and ask him to go? Finally, those who have experienced the freedom Jesus gives are called to testify to what God has done.

Miracles 3 and 4: Authority over Disease and Death and the Importance of Faith (8:40-56) Perhaps nothing is so fearful for people to face than disease and death. Nature can overpower us and evil can invade our world, but we feel most threatened when our own body starts to work against us and our mortality becomes painfully evident. In a world full of AIDS and cancer, images of our slow destruction assault our senses on an almost daily basis. We wonder, "Is that all there is—only a few score years and then dust?"

As Luke continues unfolding dimensions of Jesus' authority, he ends his fourfold miracle sequence with a double miracle that attacks both disease and death. Each miracle in the sequence is increasingly inward. Death, the most intimate and comprehensive opponent, is left for last. But these last miracles teach more than the extent of Jesus' authority. They also offer a lesson about response.

These miracles are audiovisuals of important truths related to Jesus' sovereignty. As important as each event is in itself, even more important is the picture involved. The overcoming of disease and death in this passage is but a foretaste of the ultimate, comprehensive overcoming of disease and death. The event points beyond itself to eternal realities, which put the limitations of this life into perspective. Such lessons are Luke's goal in reassuring his readers about Jesus (1:1-4).

The drama of this scene is virtually matchless. Jairus must have been wracked by intense frustration as events unfolded. It certainly appeared as if all circumstances were working against the synagogue leader.

To begin with, the crowds continue to pursue Jesus. Despite the disapproval of many religious leaders, some do sense that Jesus has authority to perform great and powerful acts. Jairus, a synagogue ruler, is among

---

8:40-56 The parallels to this account are Matthew 9:18-26 and Mark 5:21-43. Stein (1992:260) notes a handful of differences among the parallels. Luke does not give as much detail about why the woman seeks to touch Jesus. Only Luke notes that this is Jairus's *only*

these. His only daughter, a twelve-year-old, is dying. Jesus responds by beginning the journey to Jairus's home. But as he walks the crowd squeezes in against him, seeking to draw near to him.

One person in the throng is particularly intent on getting to Jesus. This woman has been hemorrhaging for years, which means she has been in a perpetual state of uncleanliness according to Jewish law (Lev 15:25-31; Ezek 36:17; *m. Zabim* 2:3; 4:1; 5:7). She has been shut out from religious life, a social outcast. Various ancient remedies existed to relieve her condition, like a glass of wine mixed with rubber alum. Additional ingredients might be garden crocuses or onions (van der Loos 1965:511). But these attempts have failed. In despair over her loneliness and condition, she hopes that an underground approach, a surreptitious touching of Jesus, will change her fate. This is why she *came up behind him*. Contact with his garment, either the edge or the tassels hanging from it, may bring her instant healing. Her solution works, but it brings her more than she bargained for. She is not permitted to retain secrecy.

Jesus turns to the crowd and asks, *"Who touched me?"* Amazed at the question, Peter points out that many are crowded around Jesus. It is as if a current celebrity or political leader turned to a herd of reporters upon exiting a building and asked, "Who just took my picture?" Peter's reaction is most understandable, especially since no one in the crowd is claiming responsibility and he knows that getting to Jairus's house is a matter of life or death. But Jesus senses things most of us cannot sense. His timing is different from others'. He is able to deal with many realities at once. At this point he knows that someone who had come near to him had done more than get a glimpse of him. He had ministered to them. He knows that *power has gone out* from him.

For the woman there is no sense in trying to hide from Jesus now. It never is successful to try and hide from Jesus. *Trembling*, she comes forward to give her public testimony of how she has been healed. Despite the embarrassment of her past condition and the timidity of her approach to Jesus, she declares what Jesus has done for her.

In response Jesus issues a simple commendation: *"Daughter, your*

---

daughter. Luke does not mention the criticism of the doctors, but adds more detail on the crowd's laughter and the description of the resuscitation. These changes fits Luke's style of letting the event speak for itself.

faith has healed you. Go in peace. "He makes her faith an example, timid as it was. The one with faith does not need to fear approaching Jesus and his authority. He is accessible and available. Both the woman's faith and her testimony are commended in Jesus' response. Faith trusts in God's ability to meet our needs by his power. God honors such faith.

Or does he? Consider Jairus's mood. Imagine what he must have been going through as this woman impeded Jesus from getting to his daughter and healing her. We can only speculate on what thoughts and emotions swirled through him as this woman became a roadblock to Jesus' work on his behalf. It was rather like the frustration of someone in a hurry to get to a destination who is blocked by a traffic jam. Only Jairus is not just late; he is trying to save his daughter. To make matters worse, now a man from Jairus's home shows up to announce that it is too late. Imagine it: Jesus stops to heal a woman of a nonfatal condition, and as he delays a young life is snuffed out. Where is justice?

But again Jesus responds by reminding Jairus not to jump to conclusions: *"Don't be afraid; just believe, and she will be healed."* Here trust means understanding that Jesus has authority even over death. Everything about this double miracle points to the need to trust God's power, presence and timing over ultimate human well-being.

Jesus travels on to the house. When he arrives, only the family, Peter, James and John are permitted to enter with him. The mourning, which was customarily public in ancient Palestine, is already in full swing (Rengstorf 1965:724-25; Stählin 1965:844-45). Jesus attempts to reverse the mood by telling the crowd that the girl is merely asleep. Their skepticism is expressed in their laughter. Popular sentiment is that Jairus has brought a crank with strange beliefs into his home. The consensus is that death cannot be reversed. However, Jesus is not just any visitor.

Sometimes the majority is wrong. Jesus tells the child to arise. Like the only son of the widow of Nain, the daughter rises to life as *her spirit returned.* Immediately Jesus requests that she be given food. Amazement

8:42, 49 Luke is more detailed here in making it clear when the girl died. Matthew, as he often does, compresses the story and lacks the detailed sequencing of the timing of the girl's death. Such compression in Matthew is also evident in the differences between the accounts of the healing of the centurion's slave in Luke 7:1-10 and Matthew 8:5-13.

9:1-6 The parallels to this text are Mark 6:6-13 and Matthew 10:1-14. In Matthew the passage is part of a much larger unit on Jesus' commission. A comparison of the accounts

grips the parents. Jairus's invitation to Jesus to heal, an act of faith, had revealed that Jesus had power over death. Jesus urges silence, even though what he has done was obvious. His goal is not to become a traveling Palestinian miracle show. His ministry is not about such displays of power, but about what they represent. He knows that miracles would become the major interest, not new life and the basic issue of who it is who can heal a woman and raise a young girl. Jesus has taught a major lesson: faith means understanding that Jesus has the power to deliver life and that his timing and sovereignty can be respected. All Jairus's earlier pain and frustration have been transformed into a new perspective that weds faith with Jesus' authority. In fact, this is the lesson of all four miracles of Luke 8:22-56: God's power is absolute. Death is not the chief end of persons. Trusting and knowing God is.

Sharing the Authority (9:1-6) Often those who have power hoard it as their personal property. But Jesus, in building a community, sought to delegate power and enabled those who ministered with him to share in carrying out his mission. This passage, the mission of the Twelve, picks up a theme introduced in Luke 5:10 (Tannehill 1986:215-16). The disciples will be fishers of people. This is the first of two missions Luke records (see 10:1-24). Only Luke includes two missions. This first mission is limited to the Twelve, while the second will expand the number who take the message of the kingdom abroad. The description of the mission assumes that some may reject them, just as when we go fishing sometimes the line yields a catch, sometimes it doesn't attract a single fish, and sometimes a catfish swallows the line. Jesus has his disciples prepared for any contingency.

The importance of bestowed authority for Jesus cannot be overappreciated (10:16, 19-20; 11:19; Grundmann 1964:310). All ministry, whether in Jesus' time or today, takes place in the context of delegated authority. Those who minister serve Jesus and are responsible to him (1 Cor 4:1-

shows that each Gospel writer has summarized the account in his own terms and with his own emphases. The major difference is that Luke 9:3 and Matthew 10:10 speak of not taking a staff, while Mark 6:8 speaks of taking nothing except a staff. It is clear, either way, that Jesus is stressing traveling light. In all probability the differences represent an attempt to summarize Jesus' instruction not to seek to procure a staff and to take one only if the disciple already had one. For the various options see Liefeld 1984:919.

6). This line of accountability does not mean that we minister without concern for the feelings of those ministered to, but that we're aware that all ministry involves derived authority. The minister is a steward and a servant, ultimately accountable only to God for how the ministry proceeds. Usually being sensitive to that accountability means being sensitive to those we serve. But sometimes the "constituency" may be wrong and may need leading or instruction on the way to go. In this initial effort Jesus gives very specific instructions to the disciples as they seek to serve and be dependent on God.

The disciples' ministry mirrors Jesus' own ministry in Luke 8. Just as he preached the Word of the kingdom and healed, they are given authority over demons and disease as they seek to declare the kingdom of God. It is important to link verses 1-2 to verse 6. The miracles are the audiovisual of God's power at work in the announcement of the kingdom's arrival (11:20). The preached message of the kingdom is called *the gospel* in Luke 9:6. A hint of the message's content is given in 10:9. The healings picture the arrival of God's power. Again, the attention is not on the miracle itself but on what it represents. The fact that the disciples' power is derived is also significant. Jesus is the source of this declared deliverance. The speeches of Acts make the same point (for example, Acts 3:6, 14-26; 4:10-12).

Jesus' instructions for this journey are simple: travel light and keep lodgings basic. The disciples should not burden themselves with excessive provisions. One tunic is enough. No staff, bread, bag or money needs to go with them beyond the basics. The instructions parallel the travel practices of the Jewish Essenes, as well as what Jews instructed temple visitors to do (Fitzmyer 1981:753-54; Josephus *Jewish Wars* 2.8.4 §125; *m. Berakot* 9:5; in contrast are the Greek Cynics and philosophers who sought money constantly—Schürmann 1969:502 n. 24). The disciples are to stay in one place, not move around within a village. In fact, the point may be, Live as the locals do and live with them. If there is rejection they are to move on, shaking the dust from their feet as a repudiation of the village's rejection of them (Strath-

---

9:7-9 The parallels to this text are Mark 6:14-16 and Matthew 14:1-2. Matthew apparently expresses Herod's final conclusion, that Jesus is John the Baptist raised from the dead. Mark

mann 1967:503). It is a way of warning the city (10:9-11). But as Jesus' attitude toward Jerusalem shows, it is done painfully, not with joy (19:41).

The disciples do as Jesus says. Though there is no report on this mission, 10:17-24 communicates what the disciples feel—and what we too should feel as we take God's message to the world. What an honor to carry this message and to experience what the kings and prophets of old had longed to see.

Everything about this mission says that disciples are to depend on God. Their authority comes from him. Their needs will be supplied by him. There is no personal gain to be sought. As a contrast to the cultural peddlers of religion and philosophy of their culture, they carry the gospel so as to signal the character of those who serve the gospel. Modesty is the rule, ministry is the focus. I wonder how often the gospel's credibility has been damaged in more recent times because this modest approach to mission was not followed. As Paul shows in 1 Corinthians 9, ministers should strive to burden others financially as little as possible. On the other hand, God's people should care for those who minister to them—laborers are worth their hire (Lk 10:7; 1 Tim 5:18). According to Old Testament guidelines, the priests were supposed to be able to live comfortably as they ministered through the support the nation provided. The same should be true of the saints. Money and provisions for ministry always raise tricky questions. Those who are ministered to should give; and those who minister should trust God for their provision, traveling light and responsibly as they minister.

Who Is This Jesus Anyway? (9:7-9) Years ago a popular television show often ended with the masked hero riding off into the sunset as someone at the rescue scene inquired, "Who was that masked man?" This passage has very much the same flavor. Reports of Jesus' activity have reached the nation's highest political levels. Herod is hearing about what Jesus is doing, and he is attempting to assess who Jesus is. He is perplexed. Like many who encounter Jesus, he is not sure where Jesus fits.

---

is similar to Matthew in this regard. Luke seems to list the popular options Herod considered.

Is Jesus *John . . . raised from the dead?* (This probably means people speculate that John's spirit now resides in Jesus.) Others have suggested Elijah, which makes Jesus a prophet of the end times (Mal 3:1; 4:5). The third option is that *one of the prophets of long ago had come back to life.* Interestingly, all these options have a prophetic thrust. Clearly God is behind Jesus' activity. But where exactly does he fit? Herod has beheaded John, so why is he hearing such things about someone else? Are prophets proliferating before his eyes? The possibilities pique Herod's curiosity, and he desires to see Jesus.

This passage continues Luke's "who is this?" discussion about Jesus. Here Herod serves an as example of one trying to come to grips with who Jesus is. His curiosity and openness end the passage on a note of reflection. Such curiosity is natural when one looks at Jesus from a distance. But who Jesus really is cannot be discovered through second-hand reports and rumors. Genuine testimony about Jesus comes a little later in Luke (9:20). Those who give testimony there will recognize that the One through whom such powerful works occur is more than a prophet.

Authority to Provide Revealed (9:10-17) With the question of Jesus' identity still at the forefront, Luke narrates a miracle that appears in all four Gospels (Mt 14:13-21; Mk 6:32-44; Jn 6:1-15). The extended commentary on this event occurs in the Bread of Life discourse in John 6, but the miracle's importance is underlined by its appearance in all the Gospels. The event serves two purposes: (1) to help identify Jesus and (2) to teach the disciples something about trust and provision. Both Moses (Ex 16; Num 11—manna) and Elijah (2 Kings 4:42-44) were prophetic vessels in similar miracles of provision. But these connections were only conceptual. This miracle is unusual in that no reaction from the crowd is recorded—a detail showing that the lesson is for the disciples.

The miracle's setting is simply stated. Luke notes that the disciples have withdrawn privately to Bethsaida, a city located on the Sea of Galilee's northeast corner. The effort at solitude failed, for the crowds, having discovered their locale, descend upon them. Jesus *welcomed them,* teaching about *the kingdom of God.* As the subsequent context makes clear, he moves into the desolate countryside outside Bethsaida to accomplish this. Healings also occur, as they often do with Jesus. The pairing of preaching and healing recalls the disciples' mission in verses 1-5.

As the day draws to a close, the Twelve sense a developing problem. How can provision be made for all the crowd? Where will the evening meal come from? In the ancient world, of course, "fast food" was not a possibility. Prompted by a sense of responsibility and the need to wrap up and go home, the disciples approach Jesus. Their request seems very reasonable.

But Jesus' response is surprising. He wants the disciples to provide the meal. This severely limits the options, as well as raising the issue of resources, which were currently limited to *five loaves of bread and two fish*. Buying food would be an expensive proposition and a logistical nightmare. Jesus advises that the five thousand men be divided into groups of fifty. With the groupings in place, Jesus teaches a visual lesson on his ability to provide and the disciples' ability to serve.

All the elements of this miracle focus on Jesus' authority. He is the one who breaks the food and gives it to the disciples after prayer and blessing. Here is a picture of Jesus leading people at supper, suggesting a foretaste of the messianic banquet (Stein 1992:275; Ps 81:16; Is 25:6; 65:13-14). Luke gives no detail as to how the food multiplies, because he is more interested in the result and what it pictures than in detailing the miracle. The messianic association is set up by the context. Herod's question in verses 7-9 and Peter's response in verses 18-20 indicate that this event, sandwiched as it is, provides a point of identification. The picture is of a Messiah who provides and makes full (6:21, 38; of God— 1:53; in the Old Testament, Ps 23:1-2; 37:19; 78:24; 105:40; 107:9; 132:15; 145:15-16, with God's provision of manna in the wilderness as the prototype example).

In addition, the disciples learn that Jesus is the source of provision for their own ministry. They are to model Jesus' style of ministry as they depend on what he can give them (22:24-27). They are to provide the food for the crowd, and through Jesus they do so. He supplies with abundance, and they are the vessels bearing the provision.

Christological Confession and the Road of Discipleship (9:18-50) This section represents a significant turning point in the Gospel.

Peter's confession of Jesus not only answers the question of Jesus' identity but also brings a shift in Jesus' teaching. From this point Jesus begins
to prepare the disciples for his death and for the discipleship of bearing
one's cross daily. In fact, six times Jesus notes his approaching suffering
(9:22, 44; 12:50; 13:31-33; 17:25; 18:31). Three of these notes have
parallels in Mark 8:31-32, 9:30-32 and 10:32-34, but three of them are
unique to Luke.

While the crowds wrestle with the prophetic nature of Jesus' ministry,
the disciples realize that Jesus is the promised one, the anointed ruler
promised by the Old Testament. But despite Jesus' prominent and
authoritative position, God's program is not a matter of the raw exercise of power. The disciples think that kingdom means immediate
victory. Jesus must show them that before the glory comes the cross
and a life of sacrificial service. This is what Jesus portrays as the "new
way" (9:23-27). Other passages in this section show that the disciples
have much to learn, so the voice from heaven at the transfiguration tells
them to listen to Jesus. He offers instruction on the new and true way
to God.

Peter's Confession (9:18-20) This passage begins to answer the
"who is Jesus?" question posed throughout the Gospel, especially in
chapters 7—9. After prayer Jesus checks the disciples for a "Gallup
Poll" reading of the multitudes: *"Who do the crowds say I am?"* The
answers exactly parallel verses 7-9: the crowds believe that Jesus is some
kind of prophet. Many people today also have an elevated view of Jesus;
they see him as a great teacher or someone in touch with God's will.
But for them Jesus is hardly a unique religious figure. This is why Jesus'
question and Peter's answer are so crucial. When Jesus asks, *"Who do
you say I am?"* he is trying to see if the disciples recognize his unique-

---

Notes: 9:18-20 The parallels to this text are Matthew 16:13-20 and Mark 8:27-30. Here
Luke begins again to share parallels with Mark, having not included the content of a large
set of passages in Mark 6:45—8:26. This leap between verses 17 and 18 of Luke 9 is known
as Luke's "great omission." It is not clear why this occurred. Of course, the phrase assumes
that Mark was the first of the Synoptic Gospels. Another issue in the text is the slight
difference in wording in Peter's confession between the Gospels. This difference is a matter
of summarization. Matthew's account is the most complete, while all the versions highlight
Jesus' messianic position. The confession recognizes that Jesus is more than a prophet; he
is a unique agent of God, called to the task of fulfillment.

ness. Prophets have abounded through the centuries, but only one is called the Christ, God's anointed. Peter's answer highlights Jesus' uniqueness.

In considering the uniqueness of Jesus in Peter's answer, it is easy to overstate Peter's meaning in this original context. The disciples eventually came to see that the Messiah is a divine-human figure, but Peter's confession did not have that full force when it was uttered here. The disciples had to learn about Jesus' divinity through his ministry as a whole. The confession of Jesus as Son of God in the Matthean parallel pushes toward this implication, but Peter's attempt to correct Jesus right after this confession in Matthew shows that he was not yet aware that Jesus possessed total divinity. Son could also be a regal title, as Psalm 2 and 2 Samuel 7:11-14 show.

What Peter is confessing is that Jesus is not merely a prophetic revealer of God's way, he is the deliverer who brings God's way, as Jesus has already proclaimed himself to be in 4:16-30. Jesus will stretch this foundational understanding of Peter's into new and higher categories as his own ministry proceeds, but the key step in getting there is to realize that Jesus' uniqueness goes beyond prophetic-teaching categories. Jesus is not the messenger; he is the message. The burden of the rest of Jesus' ministry is to show how that message will be delivered and who the message bearer is.

The First Prediction of Jesus' Suffering and the Way of the Cross (9:21-27) Divine logic sometimes surprises us. We can imagine being among the disciples as Peter confesses Jesus to be the Messiah and thinking, "Great! Now victory, power and authority are right around the corner. Surely God will vindicate the righteous now. We can sit next to the king. We will rule with him!" But immediately after the confession

---

9:21-27 The parallels for this passage are Matthew 16:20-28 and Mark 8:30-9:1. Only Luke notes the prayer that preceded the events (9:18), and Luke and Mark make it clear that these statements to disciples were consciously made before the crowd (Mk 8:34; Lk 9:23).

9:21 This passage along with Peter's confession raises the question of Jesus' "messianic secret," or why Jesus was slow to have himself confessed as the Messiah. The basic reason appears to be Jesus' expectations of what that role would require, especially in terms of suffering, in contrast to popular expectations of the time, which took various emphatically triumphant forms. For more on this issue see Bayer 1986, Tuckett 1983 and Dunn 1970b.

Jesus moves to reorient the disciples' thinking. They continue to wrestle with such questions even as late as Acts 1:6-11, but Jesus is always reminding them that the divine call involves service and witness, not the raw exercise of power. People are to be won over and served, not coerced.

The same truth endures for disciples today. The cross Jesus bore is the cross the church is to bear. Giving oneself on behalf of sinners is just as integral to the gospel today as it was in days of old. Ministry is not a matter of power and privilege, but of humility and service.

Jesus will have to make his point several times before the disciples get it. Divine logic requires a listening ear and an open heart.

This passage has two parts: the prediction of Jesus' suffering (vv. 21-22) and the announcement of the "new way" of suffering, bearing one's cross daily (vv. 23-27).

Jesus' command that the disciples keep his identity secret has provoked considerable discussion. Why would Jesus want to hide his messianic role? This problem is known as the "messianic secret" in New Testament studies. The command for silence has bothered some interpreters so much that they have argued (1) whether Jesus really ever presented himself as Messiah and (2) that a Gospel writer (generally said to be Mark) created this idea to explain why the church later preached Jesus as Messiah though he had not presented himself this way. I mention this view not because I think it is right but because its very existence shows how surprising Jesus' messianic presentation was. Jesus' command shows that he wanted to communicate certain facts about this title to the disciples before it was bandied about in public. There was much potential for misunderstanding about Jesus' task.

So Jesus discusses the approaching suffering of the Son of Man. This is the first "suffering Son of Man" saying in this Gospel. Later Luke will speak of the Christ's suffering (24:26, 46). Both here and in 24:26 this suffering is said to be necessary *(dei)*. The plan is for Messiah to suffer and serve before receiving glory (19:10). Luke emphasizes this point from here on (9:44; 11:29-32; 12:50; 13:31-35; 17:25; 18:31-33; 20:9-18; 22:19-20, 28; 24:7, 46-47).

This passage's teaching is clear enough. Jesus will suffer, be rejected, be killed and on the third day rise again. Subsequent history and the church's continuing proclamation of this point make this message easy to comprehend today. But what strands of Old Testament hope served as the original basis for Jesus' saying that such things must be?

Probably various themes contributed to this portrait. (1) Psalm 118 (117:22 LXX) predicts the suffering of a regal figure. Some even link this imagery with Daniel 2 and 7, but there the presence of regal suffering is not so clear. However, the theme of rejection, as expressed in Luke, is reflected in Psalm 118. (2) The portrait of a suffering representative for the nation in Isaiah 52:13—53:12 easily suggests a representative role for Jesus that includes suffering. (3) The general biblical portrait of the righteous sufferer, as found in many psalms (18, 22, 32, 69), also supports this expectation. God's righteous ones often suffer at the hands of the world. Surely the One who is righteous and represents them would share in their journey. These three strands seem to be the biblical base for Jesus' remarks and his synthesis of Messiah's career. Since an emphasis on suffering was not a standard element of Jewish messianic hope (in fact, no Jewish messianic text found up to this time clearly refers to it), Jesus wanted to instruct his disciples about it and not use the title Messiah publicly to explain who he was until they understood all that was involved. They got the point eventually, as evidenced in Acts 2:24-33 by Peter's linking of the resurrection to Psalm 16, a psalm also about righteous suffering. Jesus will go the way of saints before him, and those who follow him must be ready to travel the same road.

Suffering is by nature hard, and it will take time for the disciples to understand that God's promised deliverer will indeed experience suffering, even death. In fact, the New Testament is clear that it took the events themselves to make the point acceptable to the disciples (24:13-36).

But Jesus' path also meant that these disciples lived in tension. They had access to many blessings through Jesus, but Jesus' departure meant that other blessings the Messiah would bring were yet to come. In addition, the world's harsh reaction to Jesus and those identified with him would continue until he returned.

So Jesus says that to follow him means walking in the path of the cross. Disciples are like their teacher. Whether that path involves "taking up the cross," "losing one's life" or "not being ashamed of the Son of Man," disciples need to understand that life in the world will not involve an easy, stressless trip into glory. The apostle Peter would write later that this road of trial to glory mirrors what Christ himself was predicted to experience—suffering and then glory (1 Pet 1:3-12).

The essence of discipleship is humility before God. That humility expresses itself as self-denial. Taking up the cross daily and following Jesus means approaching ministry in the world as he did. He served and gave of himself daily, even to the cultural ignominy of publicly bearing rejection on the cross (Acts 5:30; Gal 3:13). The Savior bore rejection and death for others, and the disciple must follow in the same path of service. We must be prepared to accept rejection as a given. Everything Jesus teaches his disciples in chapters 9—19 will underscore this point.

The tense sequence in verse 23 is important. Two aorist imperatives are followed by a present imperative. Two summary commands are issued: deny oneself and take up the cross (aorist imperatives). These are basic orientations of the disciple. Then the disciple can continually follow (present imperative) Jesus.

Jesus explains that to seek to preserve one's life will result in its loss, while giving one's life up will lead to its being saved. The remark's context is crucial. During Jesus' ministry, anyone concerned to maintain their reputation in Judaism would never come to Jesus, given the leadership's developing official rejection of him. Someone whose life and reputation in the public sphere were primary would never want to come to Jesus. But if they gave up a life of popular acclaim and acceptance to come to Jesus, they would gain deliverance. Jesus understood that trusting in God means nontrust in self and nonreliance on the security the world offers: *Whoever loses his life for me will save it.*

Jesus' explanation now goes a level deeper by probing the issue of gain and looking at the question spiritually. One can possess the world but lose one's soul and thus have nothing spiritually. By implication, it is far preferable to lose the world and gain one's soul. Such contrast between the world and a person's spiritual welfare is common in the New Testament (Jn 3:17, 19: 1 Cor 1:18-31; Gal 2:20; 2 Pet 1:4; 1 Jn 2:15-

---

9:28-36 The parallels for this passage are Mark 9:2-8 and Matthew 17:1-8. The site of the event is disputed, with Mt. Hermon and Mt. Tabor apparently the most likely candidates (Liefeld [1984:167 n. 27] adds a third suggestion, Mt. Meron; see Fitzmyer 1981:798). More important than the locale is what occurs there. Luke offers a number of unique elements,

16; Sasse 1965:888). Turn to God through Jesus and for his sake. Jesus made a similar commitment himself, when he turned down Satan's offer of all the power in the world (Lk 4:5-8).

So Jesus exhorts his disciples not to be *ashamed* of the Son of Man. The mention of shame reveals Jesus' concern about the persecution that will come to those who identify with him. In ancient Middle Eastern culture, personal shame was to be avoided at all costs. But to suffer shame while serving God can be a badge of honor, if one is in God's will (1 Cor 4:9-13).

Again Jesus calls himself the Son of Man. Only here it is the Son of Man of glory that is in view. One day he will render judgment. If some have not identified with Jesus, he will not identify with them in that day. So the stakes are high: the issue is one's soul. With Jesus, there is no doubt about one's fate.

In the midst of this warning Jesus offers a promise: some will not see death until they see the kingdom of God. Contextually this is a reference to the preview of glory some of the disciples get in the transfiguration, an event recorded in verses 28-36. Seen in light of Luke's development in the book, the arrival of the kingdom also is made visible in Jesus' current ministry (11:20; 17:20-21). In fact, the benefits of promise are distributed in Acts 2 (Lk 24:49 with Acts 2:30-36). So Jesus has in view both the preview of total glory and the initial arrival of promise as a result of his ministry. Those disciples who were present at the transfiguration, as well as those who shared in Pentecost, shared in the sneak preview of the kingdom's arrival before they "saw death."

The disciples are never to forget that they are associated with the Son of Man, the one who bears and comes with the glory of God. In suffering they imitate Christ. After the cross of suffering there is blessing and glory. Allegiance to Jesus in service to God and a needy world is worth the cost.

Divine Confirmation and a Call to Hear (9:28-36) Every time I come to this passage a particular American commercial rings in my ears. It has various versions, but one of them is a scene of people sitting in

---

including discussion of Jesus' approaching "exodus," his *departure* in death from Jerusalem. Another is the indication that the transfiguration was preceded by prayer—a standard Lukan theme. Jesus acts in the context of seeking and following God's will.

the stands at a tennis match, their heads turning to and fro in unison, following the progress of the tennis ball during the point. Then a man in the stands turns to his friend and says, "My broker works for E. F. Hutton, and E. F. Hutton says . . ." Suddenly every head stops and everyone leans in to hear the financial advice. The closing line of the ad is "When E. F. Hutton talks, everybody listens."

That is very much the feel of the transfiguration, except that in this scene the call to listen comes at two levels. There is the divine voice, which stops all discussion between the disciples and Jesus, and there is the central instruction to listen to Jesus. The point in both cases is that instruction is needed, because the path Jesus walks is unexpected. If disciples are to understand that walk and follow in its footsteps, they will need to *listen to him.*

This event is so significant that 2 Peter 2:16-21 comments upon it. The disciples come to preview Jesus' majestic glory, but they also are told to be quiet for a time until they understand what God is doing through Jesus.

Luke locates this event *about eight days* after Peter's confession, which associates the event and its proclamation with Jesus' remarks about discipleship. When the call to listen to Jesus comes, the statements about discipleship are especially in view.

Jesus takes Peter, James and John along as he goes *up onto a mountain to pray.* We are not told why only this inner circle is present. But as Jesus prays, his appearance changes. Luke highlights two details: the changing of his face and of his garments. Luke does not use the Greek verb *metamorphoō,* "to transform," for he wishes to avoid confusion with the Hellenistic picture of the epiphany of a god and its suggestive polytheism. Nonetheless, this is a transformation, not a vision. By describing Jesus' clothes as *bright,* Luke makes associations with the glory of God's presence as in Exodus 34:29-35 (the Greek has no mention of lightning in this context, unlike the NIV). In fact, much in the account suggests imagery of the second Moses, such as the allusion to Deuteronomy 18:15 in the words of the heavenly voice, but the fact that booths for Elijah and Moses would be inadequate tells us that this connection does not exhaust the event's meaning. Jesus is the bearer of a new order and more.

The presence of Elijah and Moses has been much discussed (see Stein

1992:284). (1) Do they represent the different kinds of life endings (burial versus being taken up to God; Thrall 1970:305-17)? (2) Is their presence an indication of endorsement by great prophets and wonder-workers of old (L. T. Johnson 1991:153)? (3) Or is it a contrast between the law (Moses) and the prophets (Elijah; so Stein 1992:284)? (4) Or is it that Moses points to the prophet like Moses, while Elijah suggests the eschaton's arrival (as late Judaism also had the linkage, *Deuteronomy Rabbah* 3 [201c]; Schürmann 1968:557)? This last view is slightly more likely than the third approach. Luke makes the Moses connection explicit in various texts (Acts 3:18-22; 7:35-37), while Elijah is consistently a figure of eschatological hope (Lk 1:16-17, when John is pictured as such a figure). The event suggests two great periods of Israel's history, the exodus and the end-time hope of deliverance.

These great figures discuss the coming fulfillment of the "exodus" (Greek) or *departure* (NIV) in Jerusalem, an allusion to Jesus' death and journey to heaven. He will be gone awhile to return, though the stress is on the journey's launching, his death. The juxtaposition of exodus imagery and his glorious countenance suggests the imagery's broad sweep. Of course the disciples do not grasp this discussion's significance at the time, since they struggle with Jesus' predictions of his death later when they approach Jerusalem (18:31-34).

The disciples are trying to come to grips with what is happening. In their view Jesus is another great figure, like Moses and Elijah. He will found a people like Moses and sustain them through hope like Elijah. So Peter suggests they together celebrate Tabernacles, a feast that looked forward to the eschaton (also called the Feast of Ingathering, Ex 23:16; 34:22; Lev 23:34; Deut 16:13; Zech 14:16-21; Michaelis 1971:369-73; *m. Sukka* 1, 2:9; 3:9; 4:5; Josephus *Antiquities* 8.4.1 §100). They should build three booths in honor of Jesus and his colleagues. The suggestion is eminently reasonable, except that it understates Jesus' relationship to his two witnesses. Peter wants to enjoy the moment and prolong it in celebration. He wants to stay on the mountaintop for as long as possible.

But Luke makes it clear that Peter has spoken because *he did not know what he was saying.* The voice from heaven explains: they need to listen to Jesus so they will understand his uniqueness, call and destiny to suffer. Also, their role is not merely to contemplate Jesus but to serve him.

Celebration awaits in the future, but now is a time for instruction, response and action.

The voice from heaven speaks before Jesus responds. As was the case with the baptism, the voice describes who Jesus is. With the voice came *the cloud* that envelops them and leaves them fearful. The cloud symbolism is significant, though its meaning has engendered some controversy. The cloud could indicate God's presence as the heavens descend to the earth. But more likely is the suggestion of the new age's arrival, an age like that which founded the nation of Israel, when God's glory was present and overshadowed the people (especially Ex 40:35 LXX; also Ex 13:21-22; 16:10; 19:16; 24:16; 40:34-38; Oepke 1967:908-9).

The voice speaks of Jesus as *my Son,* language that recalls Psalm 2:7. *Whom I have chosen* highlights Jesus' unique, elect status. The wording seems to be a conceptual allusion to Isaiah 42:1: here is God's chosen instrument of deliverance. The third remark is crucial, because it adds to the remark made at the baptism. *Listen to him* recalls the language of Deuteronomy 18:15. Jesus is a second Moses who brings a new way for God's people. The disciples must listen to this Jesus. Their tendency is to assume they know who Jesus is and what he is about, but as his instruction shows, there are some surprises coming. He is greater than his extremely illustrious witnesses. The disciples need to sit at his feet and learn.

Instantly everything returns to normal. The disciples are so overwhelmed that they remain silent about this event for years. The testimony of 2 Peter 1:16-21 tells us why. Only in light of the resurrection did they come to understand Jesus' majesty and glory. The transfiguration was confirming testimony to the glory of Christ, and the resurrection was the crowning endorsement. Revealed in light, he is the light. With the "exodus" came understanding—but only after much listening. When we are with Jesus, we experience the cloud of glory, if we have ears to hear.

A Failed Miracle and a Call to Listen (9:37-43) The transfiguration called the disciples to listen to Jesus. The miracle that follows ex-

---

9:37-43 The parallels to this passage are Matthew 17:14-21 and Mark 9:14-29. Luke has the shortest version. In particular, he lacks any discussion of the father's faith and the discussion about why this healing was so difficult. This means that Luke is interested only in the teaching in verse 41, a lesson and rebuke for disciples.

plains why this call was issued. The disciples' failure to heal a possessed boy indicates their failure to trust. The contrast between Jesus' glorious power and the disciples' impotence is significant. Jesus' authority can be trusted, but disciples acting on their own are useless.

This event is the first of several failures the disciples have at the end of this chapter. They will not understand Jesus' passion prediction (vv. 43-45), nor will they understand greatness and cooperation (vv. 46-50). Instincts fail the disciples; they must listen to Jesus.

There is another important lesson in this passage. Even as Jesus turns to face rejection and death, he still overcomes the forces of evil that attempt to bring people down. Listening to Jesus is worth it, because listening to him means triumphing over evil.

The juxtaposition of this event to the transfiguration has always caught the eye of artists. One of Raphael's most famous paintings, *The Transfiguration,* places these two scenes side by side. The mountaintop experience is followed by an everyday failure to trust. Such an up-and-down spiritual record is often the product of failing to trust God.

Jesus descends from the mountain and encounters a huge crowd. Mark 9:14 notes that there was an ongoing dispute between the disciples and the scribes. Luke lacks such detail and keeps the story simple. A man with an only son is in distress over his child's condition. So he asks for Jesus' aid: *"Teacher, I beg you to look at my son, for he is my only child."* Only Luke notes that the boy is an only son. The note adds pathos to the scene, because in ancient culture boys were highly prized and only sons were especially precious. The man's family heritage is at stake here. Matthew 17:14-15 says the boy is "moonstruck" and describes symptoms of epilepsy, a disease that ancient Jews viewed with much apprehension (van der Loos 1965:401-5). The disease brought terror because of its associations with darkness. It was this condition that David feigned as having before Saul (1 Sam 21:13). The detailed description of the possession's effects underline the father's terror as he watches his son controlled by forces that seek to destroy the boy. There is hardly a better metaphor in

9:39 Van der Loos (1965) notes that later Jewish tradition described both Balaam and Saul as suffering from this disease. *Targum to the Psalms* 121:6 notes how one is safe during the day, but at night danger comes. This experience could be compared to the fear a scary horror film evokes during one of its midnight scenes.

the whole Bible for the effects of evil's presence in one's life. So for the child and the father, emotions run high and the need is great.

The father has sought relief once already: *"I begged your disciples to drive it out, but they could not."* We can almost hear the disappointment in his words. Jesus is the last chance for this father. The father's "begging" here recalls the earlier request of verse 38. The entreaty is filled with desperation.

Jesus' response makes it clear that something is awry: *"O unbelieving and perverse generation, . . . how long shall I stay with you and put up with you?"* The rebuke is broad and indicates the futility that imperils the creation because of lack of response to Jesus (Rom 8:18-25). Without him creation runs haywire, going its own way. The hope is that he will reverse its effects one day. Those who refuse to believe live in the same futility. Jesus wants the disciples to learn to trust him and find their way. His rebuke indicts all the disciples, since it is a response to their failure. The description of the generation as perverse has Old Testament roots. The language most closely resembles that of Deuteronomy 32:5, a passage on covenant unfaithfulness (Num 14:27; Deut 32:20; Prov 6:14; Is 59:8). This is a generation that strays due to lack of trust. Such straying calls for much patience on the part of the One who has come to turn humanity onto the path of true life.

Jesus asks that the child be brought to him. Immediately the demon takes hold of the child and tries to seize control, but Jesus issues a rebuke. So the boy returns to his father healed. Jesus' authority and the extent of the reversal of evil's presence emerge before all. *They were all amazed at the greatness of God.* God is gloriously present in Jesus' acts, but the implication, given Jesus' rebuke, is that such a glorious presence demands trust. Only Jesus has the power to reverse the effects of evil. Jesus may have to be patient with some people's unbelief, but when faith like that of this father appears, evil's defeat becomes possible.

A Second Prediction of Betrayal (9:43-45) The previous success should not be misunderstood. Rejection still awaits Jesus. So he again predicts his fate. The juxtaposition of success and rejection is important,

---

9:43-45 The parallels to this passage are Matthew 17:22-23 and Mark 9:30-32. Matthew alone notes the disciples' distress in association with this interaction.

highlighted as it is by the introduction to these remarks: *while everyone was marveling all that Jesus did, he said to his disciples* . . . Even though he is the Son of Man, Jesus will be handed over to others, betrayed and rejected. The betrayal's nearness is underscored by the term *mellei*. It is "about to come." The disciples do not understand the saying. In fact, its significance is concealed from them. And they do not dare to ask about it.

How can the disciples not understand? Matthew 17:23 notes their distress as they hear Jesus' words. That text indicates that the meaning is probably not that they fail to understand the content of what Jesus said. What they fail to grasp is its import. How can the promised one, the recently confessed Messiah, possibly accomplish God's will and be rejected? Is he not to be a glorious, victorious figure? Is he not to bring deliverance? The disciples fail to grasp the answers to questions like these. Their lack of understanding is why they must *listen to him*. The lessons are just beginning, and some expectations need revision.

On Greatness and Cooperation (9:46-50) Our world is consumed with issues of status. Titles, degrees, offices and positions affect one's image and self-esteem. We even speak of wearing power suits and power ties to give an official air of status and authority. The last unit of the Galilean ministry section of Luke addresses the issue of status. The synonym of "status" for most people is "power," and its antonym is "being a nothing." But Jesus calls us away from pursuing status and power. Viewed spiritually, the opposite of status is humility and a lack of concern about where one fits on the corporate ladder. Such an attitude is fundamental for the disciple.

Jesus' remarks emerge because of a debate among the disciples about who is at the "top of the table," as the British say. Who are the top dogs among the disciples? There is an intense irony here: as Jesus discusses the Son of Man's approaching rejection, the disciples are consumed by their own discipleship rankings. In response Jesus points to a child, a person with little status in the ancient world. In that world a child was barely seen and not heard at all. In Judaism, where children were held

9:46-50 This passage is really made up of two units, verses 46-48 and 49-50. The parallels to the first passage are Matthew 18:1-5 and Mark 9:33-37. The one parallel to the second text is Mark 9:38-40.

in more respect than in other ancient cultures, it still was often considered a waste of time to teach one under twelve the Torah. In fact, *m. 'Abot* 3:10 reads, "Morning sleep, mid-day wine, chattering with children and tarrying in places where men of common people assemble, destroy a man." Here children and status issues appear side by side. Jesus does not view children as insignificant. For him every person counts. Mark 9:36 notes that this child is small enough for Jesus to take into his arms.

Bringing the child to his side, Jesus says, *"Whoever welcomes this little child in my name welcomes me; and whoever welcomes me welcomes the one who sent me. For he who is least among you all—he is the greatest."* Jesus' point is that everyone, even the lowest person on the ladder, is important. Receiving a child is like receiving God. Jesus speaks of people in these terms elsewhere (Mt 25:35-45).

In all likelihood the theology behind this statement involves a recognition that every person is made in the image of God and deserves respect for that reason alone. The effect of Jesus' words is to rule out debates over status. Greatness comes from one's status as a human being, as one created by God. Even little children are great. Disciples are to affirm the greatness of all persons; they all have dignity, even those who need to get right with God and deal honestly with sin. Every sinner deserves some respect. No persons are so low on the ladder that they are beyond the reach of divine compassion.

The danger of the pursuit of status is a destructive elitism. Like a cancer, elitism eats into the gospel invitation that is made to all humankind. Cliques and withdrawal into an air of superiority within the church often destroy its ability to draw in those who need Jesus the most. Those in the church who worry about where they rank are thinking too little about how to serve others who need God.

There is another point here. Jesus defines greatness without using explicit comparison to anyone else, as people often measure greatness. Greatness is found in an attitude, humility; it does not require someone else's lack of greatness. All relative scales are removed. Greatness has only one mirror, the reflective eyes of God. He sees greatness in those who

Notes: 9:51—19:44 Of the seventeen parables in this section, fifteen are unique to Luke. I have posited the end of the section at 19:44, though others have found transitions at various other points—18:14, 19:10, 19:27, 19:48. I opt for 19:44 because Jesus is not actually in the

do not need to be great to have stature.

The next event brings to the surface yet another error. Another destructive attempt to project greatness is the attempt to limit the right to share in ministry. When the disciples try to stop a man from performing exorcisms in Jesus' name, Jesus tells them they are wrong. The principle is that *whoever is not against you is for you.* Jesus' point is not that those who are neutral about Jesus are for him; in fact, the man invokes Jesus' name in doing his work. This exorcist is not neutral. Rather, the point is that all disciples are to minister and should be allowed to do so. The disciples who travel with Jesus are not to see themselves as professional ministers who must perform all the tasks of ministry. Rather, all can labor for Jesus and should be encouraged to do so. Ministry is a cooperative venture.

☐ **The Journey to Jerusalem (9:51—19:44)**
Many of the events and teachings described in this section, especially parabolic material, are unique to Luke. In fact, almost a third of the material in this part of Luke is unique. Here teaching is emphasized over miracle, in contrast to the previous section where they were fairly evenly distributed. The section's first few chapters reveal the deepening rift between Jesus and the Jewish leadership. In addition, this section indicates how Jesus instructed the disciples on spiritual matters. His teaching made it clear that their approach to spirituality would differ from that of the Jewish leadership.

The most neutral title for this unit would be "the central section," but many scholars call it "the Jerusalem journey." This name reflects various travel notices that speak of Jesus' heading to Jerusalem or of a journey (9:51, 53, 56; 13:22; 17:11; 18:31; 19:28). This is not a straight-line journey, since Luke has Jesus at Martha and Mary's home in Bethany in 10:38-42 and then has Jesus and the disciples up north between Samaria and Galilee in 17:11. Since John's Gospel tells us Martha's home is in the south (Jn 12:1-2), a straight-line journey is excluded. Luke portrays a journey of destiny in which Jesus must meet his fate (Lk 13:31-35).

city until then. The entire scene of the triumphal entry, including 19:41-44, still places him outside and approaching the city, since 19:28 has him "going up to Jerusalem."

As one considers the unit as a whole, two major themes stand out. The first is the growing rift between Jesus and the Jewish leaders. Much of 9:51—13:35 displays this tension. Jesus' criticism of the Jewish leaders follows the pattern of the deuteronomistic critique of Israel. Like the prophets from the time of Moses on, Jesus notes the ways in which the nation has been repeatedly unfaithful to God (Moessner 1989 develops this theme in detail).

The second major theme is Jesus' preparation of his disciples for his departure. He calls them to be faithful despite rejection by the world. Thus discipleship themes dominate the section. Discipleship is not easy; they must count the cost. They may suffer, but alongside the suffering come explicit promises of God's vindication. Disciples can know that God sees their suffering, and he will vindicate the righteous one day. No passage makes this last point more clearly than Luke 18:1-8. The way of the disciple is a "new way," unlike that of the religious leadership that rejects Jesus.

The Blessing of Decision: Privilege, Mission and Commitment (9:51—10:24) The journey's initial section concentrates on disciples. After some initial failure by the disciples (9:51-62), success follows in the mission of the seventy-two (10:1-24). In light of such success, Jesus instructs the disciples about the special nature of the time in which they live. It is not a time of judgment but of invitation. It is the hour of decision, and decisions about the disciples' message have everlasting consequences.

Knowing God is a blessing and life's highest priority. But that blessing is not automatic for every individual; it must be consciously entered into by embracing the hope the disciples offer. This period is so special that kings and prophets have longed to share in the blessings that the disciples get to experience through Jesus. To minister with power is exciting, but to know God and his grace is even better.

Rejection in Samaria (9:51-56) The section opens with the note in verse 51 that *Jesus resolutely set out for Jerusalem.* The journey begins.

9:52 For more information about the Samaritans from a first-century Jewish point of view, see Josephus *Jewish Wars* 2.12.3 §§232-33; Josephus *Antiquities* 20.6.1 §§118-23; and Sirach

It starts *as the time approached for him to be taken up to heaven.* Imagery of Jesus' fate and destiny appears even in the start to this section. "Setting one's face" to do something is an Old Testament way of speaking about resolve (Gen 31:21; Jer 21:10; 44:12; Lohse 1968:776 n. 45). Jesus is determined to accomplish God's will wherever it leads.

Jesus' path often leads to rejection. The lesson, however, is not rejection's presence but how we respond to it. This short account is unique to Luke. It also is the only passage where Samaritans are portrayed negatively (contrast 10:25-37; 17:11-19). As Jesus heads for Jerusalem, we might think that a change of scenery and an outreach program in a new ethnic area might have more success than earlier efforts. This brief account makes it clear that rejection is not limited to Israel.

In Jewish eyes Samaritans were half-breeds, ethnic traitors, bad guys. When the nation was divided, Samaria was originally a name for the capital of the northern kingdom founded by Omri (1 Kings 16:21-24). Samaritans intermarried with other peoples in the region. They even worshiped at a different site, Mount Gerazim (Jn 4:20-24). Many recognized only the Pentateuch as inspired. Traditionally Jews and Samaritans were hostile to one another. So Jesus' effort to reach out to them is culturally exceptional. It would be like ministering in a crossracial setting today. The reaction might be "What are you doing here?" and "Can you believe he minsters to them?"

Jesus sends messengers ahead to prepare the people for his arrival. Much like an advance public relations team, they were to help plan what would occur when he arrived. But the Samaritans *did not welcome him.* The explanation is that Jesus' face is set toward Jerusalem. In other words, rejection is his fate. Even though that rejection will occur in the capital of Israel, the Samaritan reaction mirrors that coming reality. The world is not responsive to Jesus; rejection is widespread.

The disciples react with the wish to use their connections and power to launch a retributive strike. James and John ask for the ancient equivalent of nuking the enemy: *"Lord, do you want us to call fire down from heaven to destroy them?"* The disciples understand the great power they

---

50:25-26. *Testament of Levi* 7:2 says the Samaritan capital is the "city of the senseless." See also *Jubilees* 30:5-6, 23.

---

have access to, but the question is whether vindictive use of this power is proper. Is their hostile reaction justified? The request for "fire from above" recalls the ministry of Elijah (2 Kings 1). In their view, surely rejection means instant judgment.

Jesus corrects them. The text does not tell us what he said. In a story that is a little unusual in form, it simply notes that Jesus rebukes them and they move on to the next village. Many Gospel accounts end with a climactic saying of Jesus, a pronouncement that is key to the event in question. Here Jesus' action speaks for itself. There is no saying; rather, the disciples' saying becomes a view to be rejected emphatically. The disciples are not to wield their power as a club of judgment. Vindication from God will come later, as he deals with those who reject him. Warnings can be issued, as in 9:5, 10:13-16 or 17:20-36, but God is giving people time to decide to come to him. So the disciples are to preach the opportunity for salvation. If they are not well received, they are to move on. So having left this Samaritan city, Jesus and the disciples continue their mission in another village.

Acts 8 shows that the disciples eventually returned to this region with some success. Second Peter 3:9 may well be a theological commentary on an event like this: God is patient, wanting all to come to repentance; his judgment waits so that more may have time to come to him.

The Demands of Discipleship (9:57-62) In the midst of rejection, it becomes crucial to understand the nature of discipleship. The three sayings of these verses stress what discipleship requires. The presence of the kingdom means not instant power and position but rejection by the world. It requires a focused commitment to be a disciple.

The key to this section is the verb *follow,* which appears in verses 57, 59 and 61. The three examples parallel the threefold call of Elisha by Elijah, except in Luke three different persons are called (2 Kings 2:1-6; L. T. Johnson 1991:162). The three cases are all different. In one case Jesus makes the call (v. 59). In another a disciple offers to follow wherever Jesus goes with no excuses (v. 57). In the third case the disciple has a

---

9:57-62 The parallel to this passage is Matthew 8:18-22. He places this event in the Galilean ministry period. But the difference merely shows how topical Luke's journey section is. Matthew also lacks any equivalent to Luke 9:61-62.

9:58 Though some have argued that *Son of Man* in this verse refers to humanity in general

priority that stands before his desire to follow Jesus (v. 61). The first and third scenes are the only two records of someone offering to follow Jesus. Whatever the approach to discipleship is, the requirement is the same: following Jesus is a priority.

The first volunteer's offer is open-ended; he will go anywhere Jesus goes. Matthew 8:18-19 makes it clear that he is approaching Jesus as a student would approach a rabbi, since Jesus is addressed as "Teacher." Students in Judaism lived with their teachers to learn Torah and see a model of a righteous life. But there is more to discipleship with Jesus than being a student. Jesus' response makes it clear that discipleship is a demanding affair. To follow Jesus is more like following an Old Testament prophet than like studying with a rabbi (Hengel 1981). Jesus, calling himself the Son of Man, says that he has no home. Even foxes and birds have more of a home than Jesus does. Discipleship requires resolve because it means rejection. The premise behind the remark is that disciples will have to follow the same path as the Son of Man. Discipleship requires trusting God in the midst of rejection.

The second scene involves a man who wishes to bury his father before he comes to follow Jesus. Though the request seems reasonable, the potential disciple's premise is that family comes before Jesus. In Judaism, burying family members is a priority (Sirach 38:16; Tobit 4:3-4; 12:12). The request also parallels Elisha's request to Elijah (1 Kings 19:19-21). Jesus, however, represents the arrival of a new, more demanding era. So even carrying out such a burial is insignificant in the face of discipleship. The task must be left for others: *"Let the dead bury their own dead."*

Jesus' response seems so harsh that some have argued the man's wish is to wait until his father has died and can be buried—something that could take years. But nothing in Jesus' request or the reply suggests such a delay. Jesus' command is heavily rhetorical, since the dead cannot bury anyone. It means either that the spiritually dead should be left to perform this task or that such concern is inconsequential in the face of the call

(Colpe 1972:432-33), this would contradict the general teaching of Scripture that God provides for all creation. God cares for humankind more than he does the birds (Lk 12:22-34). Jesus' remarks have proverbial parallels (Plutarch *Lives* 9 [828c]; Sirach 36:26-27).

to discipleship. As important as taking care of a family member's death is, it is a lower priority. Either way, Jesus makes it clear the request should not be honored. Even the "best excuse" possible should not get in the way of discipleship.

Instead, the call is to *go and proclaim the kingdom of God.* This is the responsibility of all disciples. All must be prepared to share the message of God's goodness in Christ. The remark raises questions about the nature of the kingdom. What does such preaching emphasize? The best examples of it, in light of the additional revelation of the cross, are the speeches in Acts. Central to these speeches is the authority of Jesus Christ as Messiah and Lord. He is the mediator of divine blessing and the returning Judge of the living and the dead (Acts 2, 3, 10). Jesus' exercise of authority and rule comes in conjunction with Old Testament promise (Lk 24:43-47).

Though some might wish to distinguish between the kingdom of God and the kingdom of heaven, making the two sets of kingdom texts teach about distinct programs in the plan of God, there is no reason to do so, since parallel texts between the Gospels alternate the terminology in the same saying (for example, Mt 4:17 and Mk 1:15; Mt 13:31-32 and Lk 13:18-19). Apparently "the kingdom of heaven," Matthew's term, and "the kingdom of God" can be exchanged in the same passage and treated as synonyms. The passage in Mark is really significant because there the kingdom of God message is also called "the gospel."

Matthew's and Luke's parable of the mustard seed are important to this discussion because in each case the kingdom is said to come gradually. For those who have argued that the kingdom of God is exclusively future, this is a problem, for when that kingdom comes it will not start out small and then become great as the parable indicates. That future kingdom will be great from the start, set up at Christ's return.

The language about the kingdom's arrival is also crucial, since it shows that what the New Testament means by this term is not the ever-present kingdom of God that is his by right as Creator and that is affirmed as present even in the Old Testament (Ps 145:10-13). Rather, this kingdom is the promised redeeming kingdom of God, where he restores his rule and delivers people from a fallen creation. Such a redeeming kingdom, whose authority and blessing reaches into all nations, is what Old Testament saints anticipated as far back as God's promise to Abraham to bless the world through the patriarch's seed (Gen 12:1-3), even though they believed that in one sense God ruled over all nations already.

If we are to make a distinction in kingdom terminology, we could do so between the concepts of the always-existing kingdom of God and the promised kingdom of God as seen in the Old Testament. But when the New Testament uses kingdom terminology (especially with either nearness, preaching or arrival terminology), it speaks of the kingdom of promise and the program associated with it, a kingdom that did not exist in the Old Testament and was anticipated to come by the saints of old.

Jesus' rulership ultimately involves both material and spiritual elements, as the hymn of Zechariah shows (Lk 1:67-79; Bock 1993). Both elements are always present, whether one is considering Jesus' first coming, his rule from heaven or his rule upon his return. Kingship involves a ruler, a reign and a realm. The presence of God's reign means that regal prerogatives are exercised, so that promised blessings like the Spirit are mediated to those who join themselves to the Messiah (3:15-18; Acts 2:16-41). To reign is to exercise authority over salvation, not just total authority over the total creation as Christ will do at the end. The authority can be present in a variety of ways; some of it can be exercised now and the rest of it at a later time. To save and form a people is one exercise of authority, while to judge is another.

Obviously God exercises his rule through Jesus. The realm of Jesus' current authority is primarily the new community that he is forming (Eph 1:15-23), but ultimately Jesus has claims on all humanity (Col 1:15-20). When he returns he will complete the rest of the promise as described in the Old Testament (Acts 3:18-22). The main prerogatives Jesus exercises now involve the privileges of citizenship in the new community, marked by the distribution of the Spirit (Acts 10:42-43; Eph 4:7-16; Col 1:12-14). In fact, the Spirit's presence itself is the sign of victory and authority, as Acts 2:30-36 and Ephesians 4:7-16 make clear. Future prerogatives include the right to judge humanity (Acts 10:34-43; 17:31).

It is because Jesus is central to God's ruling activity that discipleship in following him is such a priority. To preach the kingdom is to preach the benefits that God has made available because Jesus the Messiah has come.

The third scene involves a request to tell the family goodby. Again, the request parallels Elisha's response to Elijah's call (1 Kings 19:19-20). Jesus' response provides yet another contrast to Old Testament example. The premise again is concern for family. Nevertheless, Jesus interprets the request as a desire to hang on to the old life. This too is emphatically rejected, with a warning that turning back from the task is showing oneself unworthy of discipleship. The disciple's hand is to stay at the plow. The remark makes great sense in a Palestinian setting, since the land there is rocky. The person who looked back while plowing would not furrow a straight row for crops. Jesus' point is that discipleship takes focus.

Only Luke quotes this symbolism of the plow, a detail that stresses the disciple's commitment. Disciples cannot back off from the task. Discipleship is not a second job, a moonlighting task, an ice-cream social or a hobby. It is the product of God's calling and should be pursued with appropriate seriousness.

The Mission of the Seventy-two (10:1-24) The ministry of proclamation is not limited to the Twelve. In 9:1-6 they were sent out on a mission to preach the kingdom, but now a larger group of seventy-two is sent. Jesus does not limit ministry to a select few (see 9:49-50, 60-61). Disciples are called to preach the hope of the kingdom. Luke 22:35 refers back to these instructions when Jesus is addressing the Twelve at the Last Supper. So it appears that the Twelve are part of the seventy-two. They travel *two by two* to prepare different towns for Jesus' arrival. It is clear from what Jesus says that the task ahead of them is large. There will be rejection, but they can also anticipate a large harvest.

Jesus' concept of ministry does not limit it to a professional level. Everyone is called to represent him. The epistles make it clear that gifts

10:1-24 This long section has numerous points of contact with the other Gospels. Matthew 9:37—10:16 serves as a point of contact with Luke 10:1-12. Luke 10:13-15 is like Matthew 11:20-24. Luke 11:17-20 has no parallel, while Luke 10:21-24 is like Matthew 11:25-27 and 13:16-17. But the Matthean parallels involve only the Twelve. What appears to be happening is that the rules that applied to the two missions were the same. What Matthew narrates with reference to the Twelve is what Luke discusses in 9:1-6, but with little detail. Luke supplies the detail when he tells of the parallel mission of the seventy-two. Thus there were two missions of similar style, but of differing numbers.

Another discussed matter is this mission's size: seventy or seventy-two? This is a text-critical issue involving verses 1 and 17, where the evidence is virtually identical in each

vary and various functions allow a diversity of ministry within the body, but everyone is gifted to contribute to the ministry of the community (Rom 12:3-8; 1 Cor 12; Eph 4:1-16). Jesus had an inner circle, but the call of ministry was not theirs alone. This is a major lesson of the mission, but it is only one of many.

Another major concept is that mission occurs in the context of prayer and God's sovereignty. Jesus argues that a ripe harvest is ready for the reaping, but few servants are ready to gather the grain. The association of conversion with agricultural imagery is common (Lk 8:10-15; Jn 4:31-38; Rom 11:16-24; 1 Cor 3:6-7; 1QS 8:5-6; CD 1:7; 1QH 8:4-11; Odes of Solomon 38:17-21; in the Old Testament, Is 27:11-12; Hos 6:11; Joel 3:13). This picture balances out the warnings of rejection that have been prevalent since 9:21. The prayer for more workers links mission and conversion with expansion of the pool of laborers. The assumption is that with conversion come disciples who are ready to share the good news. By asking for more laborers, they are asking for the mission's success.

There is another key point involved in asking God for laborers. Workers need not be coerced into labor; God is to supply them. Jesus calls us to express trust that God will supply additional help for the field. This is why God is called *the Lord of the harvest*. He is the one who will *send out workers* (v. 2).

In an age when marketing and public relations strategies often determine how the gospel is shared, Luke provides a needed reminder of God's lordship over the process of conversion. The gospel is not a consumer-oriented product. The consumer is not always right. Of course knowing one's audience is important, as is being sensitive in framing the gospel's presentation. Acts 17:16-34 shows Paul being sensitive to such

verse. The earliest manuscripts are split on which number to read: seventy (p⁴⁵, ℵ, A, C) or seventy-two (p⁷⁵, B, D). The Vulgate and early Syriac read seventy-two as well. Both numbers could reflect symbolism. Seventy could reflect a parallel to the number of Moses' elders (Num 11:16-17, 24-25) or an allusion to the list of nations in the Hebrew Old Testament (Gen 10—11). Seventy-two is the number of nations listed in the Greek Old Testament version of Genesis 10—11, a number also paralleled in Jewish tradition (*3 Enoch* 17:8; 18:2-3; 30:2). The choice is difficult. Either number could be original. I opt for seventy-two on the basis of slightly stronger external evidence (Metzger 1958-1959 has a full discussion). Textual scribes aware of one type of symbolism or another likely altered the number accordingly.

concerns. But sometimes the gospel is inherently offensive, because it deals with the need to turn to God and understand the debt that sin produces before God. It means admitting to wrongs. Nevertheless, God is at work to change and open up hearts. The disciples' responsibility is to preach and pray, and the results are God's concern.

The difficulty of this ministry means that these disciples should see themselves as *lambs among wolves*. The Samaritan mission of 9:51-56 illustrates the saying. Disciples minister under duress and rejection. They are vulnerable like lambs before a ravenous wolf. Yet despite the risk, they minister. This image is also present in Judaic writings. Psalms of Solomon 8:23 reads, "God was proven right in his condemnation of the nations of the earth, and the devout of God are like innocent lambs among them." In the same book 8:30 reads, "Do not neglect us, our God, lest the Gentiles devour us as if there is no redeemer." Lambs are a figure for God's people. The world is sometimes hostile to them, but that does not mean disciples have the right to withdraw. Proclamation assumes engagement and service. To run and hide from our neighbors or to wall ourselves off into enclaves is to disobey God's call to mission.

The dangerous nature of the disciples' mission means that they must travel light (see discussion of 9:1-6). They should not be weighted down with numerous provisions. Just as God supplies those who will respond, he also will provide for them. There is to be no *purse or bag or sandals*. They are not to *greet anyone on the road*. The mission's urgency and the disciples' lack of attachment to earthly concerns are evident in how they travel. Ministry is the priority. God has supplied others with provision to care for them. This group of traveling ministers is "professional" in the sense that other disciples will receive them and meet their material needs. The labor of such traveling, ministering saints is worthy of material support from those who receive their ministry (v. 7). Believers are to provide adequate support for those who minister full time.

As the disciples travel, they are to stay in one place, not run from house to house in a frenzy. The offer of blessing, *"Peace to this house,"* involves the invocation of God's goodwill (von Rad 1964:402, 406; Foerster

---

10:7 This is one of the few sayings of Jesus to be repeated in the epistles (1 Tim 5:18). In the ancient world, payment was usually made on a daily basis (Preisker 1967a:698).

1964b:413; *m. 'Abot* 4:15). It is like saying, "God be with you." The invocation is not a trivial matter, since the blessing of God's presence can enter or depart. If the disciples are welcomed, it is as if their hosts have welcomed God himself; if not, then blessing retreats from the home (Mt 25:31-46 is similar in tone). Those who serve as hosts will feed them and give them lodging. There is no charge for lodging, because laborers should be paid for their ministry (1 Cor 9:7-14). The Old Testament and Jewish tradition stated the same point negatively by noting how wrong it was to withhold such payment (Lev 19:13; Deut 24:14-15; Sirach 34:22; Tobit 4:14-15). The disciples are to eat and drink whatever is put before them.

Their ministry is proclamation and service. They are to heal the sick in the village and proclaim the nearness of God's kingdom. Since they are commanded to heal, authority is being given to these witnesses like that given in 9:1-6. The ministry of healing includes both the disciples' service and the true healing that comes through their preached message of God's deliverance. Jesus provides commentary on such healing ministry in 11:14-23.

In the New Testament, those who have such gifts are able to heal almost as a matter of course. The only failed healing in the New Testament is the failed exorcism that comes after the transfiguration (9:37-43), though in some locales healings were restricted because of unbelief (Mk 6:5). For healing to be a gift, it needs to happen with high consistency. This ability should be distinguished from God's sovereign acts of healing, which God's people should seek vigorously, trusting his sovereign judgment.

These disciples appear to have been given authority that was unique to this initial period of gospel proclamation, but to say that does not entail a denial that God can heal today. The Christian discussion over healing does not center on questions of God's capability or sovereignty, whether God heals today or whether the Spirit is active today. The question is whether gifts of healing are present today. A genuine gift of healing should evidence a level of consistency like that of the New

Simply accepting hospitality rather than begging for cash contrasts with the practice of Cynic philosophers of the era. Rabbis had similar limitations (*m. 'Abot* 1:13; 4:5; Danker 1988:214).

Testament gifted healers.

Those who claim to possess the gift today or to have seen it exercised do not testify to consistent healing rates. I remember hearing one prominent believer, who claimed access to such gifts, say that he had seen a healing rate of about 2 percent among the very serious conditions he had prayed for. This rate is similar to what I myself have experienced with no claim to a special healing gift. To argue that healing gifts continue, but that the rate of healing today differs significantly from that of the first century, is inconsistent. "Gifts" that are highly inconsistent are probably not full-fledged gifts.

God can and does heal. Healing can and should be prayed for, as James 5:13-18 suggests. A few successes, however, do not indicate that the gift of healing or of exorcism is present. Those few successes do remind us that God is active and sovereign. Without seeking to split hairs, I suggest that the difference is important and worthy of reflection. We can agree that a sovereign God is active and present without confusing his activity with the bestowal of a spiritual gift.

But one more word of caution. Believers today should discuss these issues calmly. In Scotland years ago, a charismatic brother and I shared responsibility for a Bible study in which we agreed not to make our differences on this topic an issue. We worked harmoniously for three years. We had vigorous discussions in private and also covered the topic when others raised it in our study. We were committed to honor each other and to represent our differences fairly as we humbly argued for the truth as we saw it. Though an individual community may have to decide what its practice and doctrinal approach to healing will be, all believers should work hard to respect and understand one another's point of view.

When the disciples gave evidence of God's nearness through healing, they were also to proclaim the kingdom's nearness (a definition of the kingdom is given in the commentary on 9:57-62). Luke 10:11 raises a question: if the kingdom *is near,* does this mean it approaches or it arrives? In the Lukan context the key is not the term *near* but the preposition associated with being near, *upon (epi).* The idiom present here is like Daniel 4:24, 28 (Theodotion), where the *arrival* of a given time is the issue. The preposition is spatial and looks not just to approach but also to arrival. The point is that the healings evidence the presence of

God's rule. The disciples proclaim a special time of divine activity. Luke 10:17-18 confirms this picture with its image of Satan's fall.

To say the kingdom has arrived is not to say that everything associated with it has come. It is clear from texts like Acts 1:6-8 and 3:18-22 that more is expected in the kingdom program. Proclamation and healing form a verbal, pictorial union of word and deed that evidence the truth of the disciples' message. Such a mixture of word and deed is also a powerful testimony today, even when the deed is an act of compassion rather than a miracle. When we proclaim God's love and show God's compassion concretely, the word takes on a dimension it otherwise might lack.

When rejection occurs, the stakes of refusal are also to be made clear. To shake off *the dust . . . that sticks to our feet* is to declare a separation between the city and God (9:5; Acts 13:51; 18:6). The rejection stands in testimony against those who reject. The symbolic act of departing the city, including leaving its dust behind, shows that the city stands alone before God. It must answer for its actions. To reject God and then have to face him is a fearful thing. The cities that reject the message are warned that the kingdom came near, but opportunity was missed. Only accountability remains. The invocation of a more tolerable judgment for Sodom indicates just how serious that rejection is, since Sodom is one of the ancient Scripture's most wicked cities. It was turned to dust by God's judgment against sin.

The disciples' mission reveals basic choices. The kingdom of God is not a trivial subject. Their preaching about it has serious benefits and consequences. The preaching of that message today carries precisely the same significance. The series of woes against Korazin, Bethsaida and Capernaum show how seriously Jesus takes their mission. Tyre and Sidon, two cities whose reputation rivals that of Sodom, will come out better in judgment than these Galilean cities (Is 23; Jer 25:22; 47:4; Ezek 26:3—28:24; Joel 3:4-8; Amos 1:9-10). Those sinful cities would have repented, as evidenced by their willingness to sit in sackcloth and ashes (1 Kings 20:31-32; 2 Kings 19:1; 1 Chron 21:16; Neh 9:1; Esther 4:1-3; Joel 1:13; Amos 8:10). The sackcloth would have been made of animal's hair, usually that of a goat. What Jesus' remarks mean is that these cities stand at the bottom of the list, subject to God's harshest judgment. Lest there be doubt about the reality of the judgment to come, Jesus says to

Capernaum that it *will go down to the depths.* To reject the message of
the kingdom is to face the judgment of rejection by the God who offers
that kingdom. The woes' seriousness is underlined when Jesus says, *"He
who listens to you listens to me; he who rejects you rejects me; but he who
rejects me rejects him who sent me."* The disciples represent him; the
messenger cannot be separated from the One who stands at the center
of the message.

When the disciples return from their mission, they are thrilled at the
power they possess—*"Even the demons submit to us in your name."*
Jesus' response to them shows yet again why the disciples must "listen
to him" (9:35). Their excitement is understandable, but they must be
careful to be excited about the right things.

Jesus does pause to respond to their observation about demons by
giving a verbal picture of their fall. His words suggest the language of
Isaiah 14:12. Jesus' report of the observation suggests that their ministry
represents the defeat of Satan, the archaccuser (Oepke 1965:213). In
Judaism and in later rabbinics, Satan's end was associated with Messiah's
arrival (*1 Enoch* 55:4; *Jubilees* 23:29; *Testament of Simeon* 6:6; *Testament of Judah* 25:3). The New Testament often portrays the cross or the
Second Coming as such a turning point (Jn 12:31-32; Col 2:14-15; Rev
12:10-12; in two final, future rebellions, Rev 20:1-3, 7-10). Luke 11:20-
23 also puts the defeat in terms of events in Jesus' first coming. Of course,
all these points in Jesus' career contribute to Satan's defeat. These are
not either-or options, but both-and. In fact, the following remarks in
verse 19 underscore the connection.

Jesus proclaims the disciples' authority over serpents and scorpions,
creatures that symbolize the presence of Satan (on Satan as enemy,
Foerster 1964d:813-14; Grundmann 1965:400; Foerster 1967:579; 2 Cor
11:3; *Testament of Dan* 6:1-4; 3 Baruch 13:1-3). Here Jesus is not endorsing snake handling but stating that the disciples now possess the

---

10:15 The negative statement on Capernaum is very strong given the *mē* particle attached
to the question in this verse. It indicates that the city will *not* be exalted to heaven. The
subsequent statement about Hades (NIV *down to the depths*) drives the nail home even
more. Hades is the Greek term for the Old Testament Sheol (Ps 89:48; Is 14:13, 15; 66:24)

10:18 There is some discussion as to what event is in view here. Does Jesus really refer
to his current ministry and that of his disciples? Two other candidates are sometimes
suggested: (1) the fall of Satan as described in Isaiah 14 and (2) the future defeat of Satan

power to resist Satan. *Nothing will harm* them. Jesus makes this last statement very emphatically, since the Greek term *ouden* ("nothing") is in the emphatic position and the emphatic Greek particles *ou mē* ("shall not") are used.

Despite all this, Jesus urges the disciples to see that their power is not the major blessing. They should rejoice not so much because evil forces are subject to them, but because their *names are written in heaven*. The real blessing is to possess life and be enrolled among heaven's permanent citizens. Here is the source of constant joy. The present imperative for *rejoice (chairete)* in verse 20 indicates that they should constantly rejoice in the fact that the great census of God contains their names. Jesus alludes to the "book of life" here (Ex 32:32; Ps 69:28; Is 4:3; Dan 7:10; 12:1; Phil 4:3; Rev 3:5; 20:12, 15; 21:27; Schrenk 1964a:619-20; Traub 1967:532 n. 295). Ministry with God is a privilege, and access to God's power is exciting, but the real cause of joy is that we have true and everlasting life before God.

The mission completed, Jesus turns to his heavenly Father and rejoices, underlining the point he has just made. His gratitude and joy are for the Father's sovereign choice to reveal himself to *little children* (1 Cor 1:25-31). As at the beginning of the mission, God's guiding hand is emphasized. The sovereign God did not seek out intellectuals *(the wise and learned)* but the humble. This was his *good pleasure,* his gracious will. He honors those who rely on him, not on their own faculties.

But God is not working alone. He and Jesus are intimately linked. In words reminiscent of those reported in the Gospel of John, Jesus says, *"All things have been committed to me by my Father. No one knows who the Son is except the Father, and no one knows who the Father is except the Son and those to whom the Son chooses to reveal him."* Now the Father's sovereignty is tied to the Son. They share authority. What God has put together, no human being can separate. This is why the kingdom

---

as described in Revelation 20. The second option is highly unlikely, since that would ask Jesus' audience in Luke to understand an allusion to a book not yet written. The allusion to Isaiah requires that Isaiah be read as describing Lucifer only. But that text may well be a typological passage about an earthly king who portrays himself as God and whose arrogance parallels that of Satan, the fallen star. It is much more natural contextually to relate Jesus' comment to the disciples' words, especially given how the imagery of defeat reappears in 11:21-23 in the context of miraculous activity.

message from Jesus should be taken so seriously. To hear Jesus' voice is to hear the authority of the Father. To deal with God, one must deal with Jesus.

The theme of rejoicing continues as Jesus turns back to the disciples and blesses them. They should feel happy and honored because they are seeing things that the prophets and kings longed to see (1 Pet 1:10-12). This passage emphasizes that what Jesus is doing is what the saints of the Old Testament had hoped to see. Many great saints of the old era did not get to experience the blessing, but Jesus' disciples are blessed to be a part of this new era. The statement recalls 7:28: the lowest person in the kingdom is higher than the greatest prophet of the old era.

Sometimes we think how great it would have been to see Moses perform miracles before Pharaoh or watch Elijah defeat the prophets of Baal at Mount Carmel. Jesus says that the situation is in fact the exact reverse—they long to see what we experience, because to know God and life through Jesus is what they had wished to experience all along. In effect, Jesus says, "Count your blessings, for they are many and have been desired for centuries."

Considering the mission as a whole, four points stand out: (1) God is sovereign, and that sovereignty includes the central role of Jesus. (2) Disciples are to serve God in dependence, resting in his provision. (3) The stakes in the gospel message are high, since blessing or divine rejection rides on how one responds. (4) More important than power is the honor of possessing life with God. Such blessing is cause for joy. The great saints of the Old Testament appreciate the unique blessing that belongs to disciples. So we should never take for granted what others longed to have.

Discipleship: Looking to Our Neighbor, to Jesus and to God (10:25—11:13) Now Luke turns from mission and discipleship to basic

Notes: 10:25-37 It is debated whether the parallels to this passage are genuine parallels. The parable is unique to Luke, but the discussion that introduces it in verses 25-28 is very similar to Matthew 22:34-40 and Mark 12:28-34. It is clear that the Matthew-Mark texts are parallel. All three texts involve a scribe and cite Deuteronomy 6:5. But Luke also has several distinct elements. In Luke the scribe answers the question; and the temporal placement in Jesus' ministry differs greatly, since in Matthew and Mark the event occurs in Jerusalem. In fact, the question itself is actually different, since here eternal life is the issue, while in

attitudes the disciple is to possess. In a series of three passages he addresses attitudes toward neighbor, spending time with Jesus and prayer to God. The grouping is important. It suggests connections among the various relationships. How we respond to our neighbor and how we walk with God are connected; in fact, both Jesus and the lawyer connect the two concepts in Luke 10:27-28. Ethics is not an abstract question of options in a particular situation; it is a matter of character developed through a walk with God and a focus on Jesus.

The Parable of the Good Samaritan (10:25-37) One of the most abstract, but important, questions we can wrestle with is the goal of life. Humankind has struggled with this question throughout its history. During my first year at university, I took a course called "The Nature of Man," which devoted an entire semester to this question. We studied and discussed what the great minds in history had said about the purpose of life. I was an agnostic at the time, and it was a fascinating journey. Many people engage in such a quest whether they have religious interests or not. Most of us sense that power and possessions are really meaningless life goals. Surely there is something more.

In this passage a theist asks Jesus how one can inherit eternal life. This Jewish lawyer knows that God exists and that he is accountable to that God, so his question is particularly focused: *"Teacher, what must I do to inherit eternal life?"* If God exists, then the goal of life must be related to his purpose for us. The terminology of the question is unique to New Testament time, but it has a rich background, since the Bible speaks of inheritance in many ways (Mt 19:29; Mk 10:17; Tit 3:7; 1 Pet 3:7; L. T. Johnson 1991:172; Bultmann 1964a:864 n. 274). In the Old Testament one could inherit the land (Gen 28:4; Deut 1:8; 2:12; 4:1). Or one might speak of the Lord as one's inheritance (Ps 15:5 LXX). Mention is made of an "eternal inheritance," but its nature is not specified in the context (Ps 36:18 LXX). Daniel 12:2 speaks of the just who will rise to eternal life.

Matthew and Mark the issue is the greatest commandment. Jesus' command in Luke, *"Do this and you will live,"* is also distinct. The tone also differs. Here the lawyer is clearly challenged by the parable, while in Mark 12:34 he is praised. It is likely that the Lukan event is unique, while Matthew and Mark are genuine parallels (Stein 1992:314-15 n. 39; Stein also suggests that the incident and the parable belong together and were not connected later by Luke).

The lawyer seems focused on this last possibility. He assumes that he must do something to gain life everlasting. In effect he asks how he can be sure to participate in and be blessed at the resurrection of the dead. Jewish scribes would have great interest in such questions, not only for personal reasons but because they were interested in interpreting the law for the community.

The lawyer's question seems to assume that he must earn such a reward, though when Jesus probes him we see that he knows that works are not the issue. Jesus calls for reflection on the law, asking, *"What is written in the Law? How do you read it?"* He is asking for scriptural support.

The lawyer responds well (v. 28) by citing Deuteronomy 6:5, a text that has become known as the "great commandment": *"Love the Lord your God with all your heart and with all your soul and with all your strength and with all your mind"; and, "Love your neighbor as yourself."* This text could well be called "the law of love." The reply shows that the issue is not action per se but the heart. Do I love God fully? That is the starting point. Everything else grows out from that relationship.

This is a relationship of trust and devotion, a truth that lies at the heart of Jesus' reply and explains why Jesus' approval is not an endorsement of works righteousness. When Jesus says, *"Do this and you will live,"* he is saying that relationship to God is what gives life. The chief end of humankind is to love God wholly. We were designed to love; but to love well, we must love the right person. Here is the definition of life that brings life. And the product of our love for God will be a regard for others made in his image, those whom God has placed next to us as neighbors. The New Testament often connects one's relationship to God to one's response to others (Mt 5:43; 19:19; Jn 13:34-35; 15:8-12; Gal 5:14; Col 1:3-5; 1 Thess 1:1; Philem 6; Jas 2:8; 1 Pet 2:17; 1 Jn 4:11). To respond to the law means to love God. To live by the Spirit means to love and do righteousness (Rom 8:1-11).

The lawyer is confused, even though his answer is correct, because he still thinks that eternal life is earned rather than received in the context of a love relationship with God. It is also important to set this discussion in its context. Jesus has just said that to know the Father one must know the Son (vv. 21-24). So to love the Father will also mean to love Jesus.

If Jesus brings the kingdom message, then he must be heeded as well. This is why 1 Corinthians 2:9 describes believers in Christ as those who love God.

But the lawyer latches on to the second part of the reply about one's neighbor. Exactly where does his responsibility fall? Does it have limits? Luke is clear that the lawyer has not understood the thrust of Jesus' reply, for he notes that the lawyer is seeking *to justify himself* by his next question. The question *Who is my neighbor?* is really an attempt to limit who one's neighbor might be. In ancient culture, as today, such limits might have run along ethnic lines. There was a category of "nonneighbor," and the lawyer is seeking Jesus' endorsement of that concept. In contemporary terms, any of various forms of racism may underlie the scribe's question: there are neighbors, "my folk," and then there are the rest, "them." Perhaps the lawyer could appeal to a text like Leviticus 19:16 for support: my concern is for "my people."

Jesus' reply not only challenges the premise but brings a shocking surprise: each of us is to *be* a neighbor and realize that neighbors can come from surprising places. Jesus' words reflect Leviticus 19:33-34: even "sojourners" deserve love. In addition, the ethic of Hosea 6:6 seems reflected here.

The original impact of the parable of the good Samaritan is generally lost today. After centuries of good biblical public relations, our understanding of a Samaritan as a positive figure is almost a cultural given. But in the original setting, to a Jewish scribe a Samaritan would have been the exact opposite, a notorious "bad guy" and traitor (see discussion on 9:51-56 above). That is an important emotive element to remember as we proceed through this parable. The hero is a bad guy. Culturally he is the last person we would expect to be hailed as an exemplary neighbor.

In fact, the parable turns the whole question around. The lawyer asks who his neighbor is in the hope that some people are not. Jesus replies, "Just be a neighbor whenever you are needed, and realize that neighbors can come from surprising places."

The story builds on a common situation, a seventeen-mile journey on the Jericho-to-Jerusalem road. This rocky thoroughfare was lined with caves that made good hideouts for robbers and bandits. The road was notoriously dangerous, the ancient equivalent to the inner city late at night. Josephus notes how some took weapons to protect themselves as they traveled this road and others like it (*Jewish Wars* 2.8.4 §125).

In Jesus' story, a man is overcome by a band of robbers and left on the road to die. As he lies there, his life passes before him. Then a priest comes down the road. The expectation culturally would be relief: "Surely help is on the way now." Luke's statement that the priest appeared "by chance" (Greek) suggests a note of hope that fortune has smiled on the wounded man. The NIV renders this *A priest happened to be going down the same road.* But the priest does not stop. Rather, he crosses to the other side and keeps going. The detail about crossing the road is no accident. It is a brilliant use of literary space: the priest gets as far away as possible from the wounded man as he passes by.

A Levite, another potential source of aid, arrives on the scene. As one who served in the temple, he will surely have compassion, stop and render aid. But when he sees the man, he also crosses to the other side of the road and keeps on moving. So two men of similar Jewish background have failed to render aid. They have failed to be neighbors.

Interpreters speculate as to why they refuse to help. Do they fear being jumped themselves? Do they fear being rendered unclean? The text gives us no reason. As is often the case, the bother and discomfort of helping have kept the man dying on the road. Getting involved is costly, and for many the investment is too high. But to refuse to help is moral failure.

But now another traveler comes on the scene. In Greek the text highlights this man's arrival by placing his ethnic identity, *a Samaritan,* at the front of the description. The scribe hearing Jesus tell the story must be thinking, "There will be no help from this half-breed." But as often happens in Jesus' parables, a twist on cultural expectations yields this story's major point: the despised schismatic will be the model of neighborliness. Maybe "enemies" can love God and be examples.

Jesus focuses his language now. In as many words as he used to

---

10:38-42 This account is unique to Luke, continuing Luke's attention to women. A telling contrast to Martha and Mary's involvement with Jesus is Josephus's *Against Apion* 2.25 §201, which argues that the law says women are inferior to men in all things. Other texts of Josephus show a different side of him, as when he praises Alexandra in *Antiquities* 13.16.6 §§430-31. But she appears to be an exception that proves the rule. In the *Mishna, Soṭa* 3:4

describe the activity of the two Jewish leaders, he details all the Samaritan does to save the man—six actions in all. He comes up to the man, binds his wounds, anoints him with oil to comfort him, loads him on his mule, takes him to an inn and cares for him, even paying for his whole stay. In fact, given the amount the Samaritan leaves with the innkeeper, the injured man probably has about three and a half weeks to recover if he needs it, since the going inn rate was one-twelfth of a denarius and two denarii was two days' wages.

Jesus' question to close the story requires no brilliant reply: *"Which of these three do you think was a neighbor to the man who fell into the hands of robbers?"*

The lawyer knows, but he cannot even bring himself to mention the man's race. The lawyer is choosy about his neighbors. He does not understand the call of God. Nevertheless, he answers, *"The one who had mercy on him."*

This reply is correct, so Jesus simply says, *"Go and do likewise."* Jesus' point is, Simply be a neighbor. Do not rule out certain people as neighbors. And his parable makes the point emphatically by providing a model from a group the lawyer had probably excluded as possible neighbors.

To love God means to show mercy to those in need. An authentic life is found in serving God and caring for others. This is a central tenet of discipleship. Here human beings fulfill their created role—to love God and be a neighbor to others by meeting their needs. Neighbors are not determined by race, creed or gender; neighbors consist of anyone in need made in the image of God.

Looking to Jesus: Mary and Martha (10:38-42) Balancing work and reflection is tricky. Most people in Western cultures are forced to live harried lives. Often their full schedules are full of "good" activity, labor that has merit. One of the demands of a full schedule is that the activity be prioritized. Some things come high on the list; others must wait. Sometimes priorities have to be shuffled at the last minute to meet

---

says that some rabbis were against any instruction of women, while others thought it advisable. Clearly debate about women existed in ancient culture, and opinions varied. For the most part, however, women's role was quite limited (Oepke 1964b:781-82). Luke's attention to women and children shows his desire to reflect Jesus' commitment to touch every level of humanity.

needs. The account of Martha and Mary is about such priorities, especially when the options are good ones.

This short passage is capable of being misread in a couple of ways (Alexander 1992:167-86). First, it is not about women; it is a passage on discipleship. Its point is not that women can get too easily caught up in the busy work of keeping the home. What is said to Martha about Mary would be equally true if Mary were male or even a child. The fact that two women dominate the story would have been shocking in the first-century context, where men often dismissed women as marginal, but the account is designed to make a point about all disciples. Second, the point is not that activity like Martha's is bad. The choice Jesus discusses with Martha is between something that is good and something that is better. Life is full of tough choices, and Jesus is stressing the relative merits of good activities here. For conscientious people, such choices are often the most difficult and anxiety-filled.

Martha receives Jesus at her home as he travels from one village to another. John 11:1, 18 and 12:1 tell us that this home was in Bethany, so Jesus appears to be a few miles outside Jerusalem when this encounter occurs. This is one of several meal scenes Luke will narrate. Besides the host and the teacher, the other protagonist is the host's sister, Mary, who sits *at the Lord's feet listening to what he said.* This is reminiscent of the Jewish saying in *m. 'Abot* 1:4: "Let your house be a meeting house for the Sages and sit amidst the dust of their feet and drink in their words with thirst."

Just as the Samaritan's activity in the previous parable was surprising, so is this portrait of these women with Jesus. Why would a teacher spend time teaching only women? In the first-century culture the question would be inevitable. The fact that Jesus commends Mary and has a meal with Martha shows that Jesus is concerned about all people.

Martha is not comfortable with Mary's approach to Jesus' visit, since

---

10:42 A textual problem here slightly bears on the argument in Jesus' remark. Some manuscripts read, "few things are needed, or one." This makes Jesus' prioritization less emphatic. Either way, he commends Mary's choice, but the question is how strongly Jesus commends her. In favor of the reading cited in this commentary is the external evidence, which includes both major papyri (45 and 75), A, C and most versions. But the choice is a tough one, since the longer alternate reading has papyri support (3), as well as the support of B.

she could use another hand in the kitchen. She requests Jesus' aid: *"Lord, don't you care that my sister has left me to do the work by myself? Tell her to help me."* We know that Martha's viewpoint is questionable not only because of Jesus' reply but also because the text says she makes the comment while being *distracted by all the preparations.* In fact, in Greek she asks the question in such a way that the Lord is expected to give a positive answer (note the particle *ou*). The Lord does care, and Martha fully expects him to tell Mary to get up and help.

But as is often the case when Jesus is asked to settle a dispute, he refuses to side with the one who asks that things be decided in a particular way (compare Lk 12:13; Jn 8:4-7). Yet he responds tenderly and instructs in the process. The double address *"Martha, Martha"* indicates the presence of caring emotion, as such an address does elsewhere (6:46; 8:24; 13:34; 22:31). Jesus questions her not because of her activity but because of her attitude about it: *"You are worried and upset about many things."* By comparing what she is doing to what Mary is doing, she has injected unnecessary anxiety into the visit. *"Only one thing is needed."* With this remark Jesus sets priorities. *"Mary has chosen what is better, and it will not be taken away from her."*

Jesus commends the hearing of the word at his feet. To take time out to relate to Jesus is important. The language of the passage recalls Deuteronomy 8:3 (Wall 1989:19-35). In a sense Mary is preparing to partake in the "right meal" (Deut 6:1-8). What she has done by sitting at Jesus' feet will remain with her. This meal will last. Jesus is not so much condemning Martha's activity as commending Mary's. He is saying that her priorities are in order. To disciples Jesus says, "Sit at my feet and devour my teaching. There is no more important meal."

Looking to God: A Call to Pray (11:1-13) As this section has already shown, discipleship involves concern for one's neighbor and attention to Jesus. As we move "from earth up," the last central focus of

11:1-13 The parallels to this passage are dispersed in the other Gospels. Luke 11:1-4 is similar to Matthew 6:9-13. Luke's version is shorter than Matthew's, lacking reference to God's will being done and the request for deliverance from evil. In addition, Luke's prayer is the result of a private request to be given a community prayer, like the one John the Baptist has, while Matthew's version is voluntarily given by Jesus in public instruction. Because of these differences, I prefer to see the two prayers as separate events, but it is clear that both same basic material would have been used in these two contexts. It may be that both

discipleship is looking to God. Here the stress is on prayer and the attitude we bring to the Father in prayer. God's gift of the Spirit is also highlighted as Luke gives us a version of the Lord's Prayer, as well as a brief parable and exhortation to pray.

As we look at the setting for the Lord's Prayer, a very important point emerges. The prayer is really poorly named, at least in its Lukan setting. Here the prayer is the direct result of a request from the disciples to be given a community prayer such as John the Baptist's community has. Such community prayers were not unusual. The Jews had the Eighteen Benedictions, and the disciples' remarks make it clear that John also had a community prayer. The Qumran community had numerous hymns and prayers (1Q34; 4Q507-9). This makes the Lord's Prayer really "the Disciples' Prayer." It was given to exemplify the attitude of dependence that Jesus' disciples should have.

The disciples' request also reflects the independent identity they were developing as they followed Jesus. The more they followed Jesus the more they realized that he was forming a new community, a distinct expression of Jewish hope. So they wanted to know how to pray to mark their distinctiveness. This is the only time in Jesus' ministry that there is a request for instruction on prayer.

The communal emphasis is seen even at the prayer's start, *Father*. In fact, even in introducing the prayer as a call to the Father, Jesus does it with a pronoun reminiscent of the Southern U.S. idiom "you all": *when you [plural] pray, say* . . . As disciples come before the Father, they are to affirm their unity and share a sense of family. This communal character laid a solid groundwork for the liturgical use of the Lord's Prayer. The communal perspective reflected in the prayer is difficult to appreciate today in a highly individualized society. But community before God, even sharing the same goals in intercession, is a major part of discipleship.

---

versions are very short, and that Luke's is shorter than Matthew's, to highlight Jesus' stress on prayer in private and short public prayer in Matthew 6:5-8. Those who see one tradition present tend to see the Lukan prayer as the older form of the tradition, though the issue of the older form is much discussed (for Lukan form, see Jeremias 1971:193-96; for Matthew's reflecting original wording, see Beasley-Murray 1986:147).

Verses 5-8 have material unique to Luke, while verses 9-13 have a fairly similar parallel in Matthew 7:7-11. The Matthean setting differs from Luke's, as does the wording of the final

A second major theme is to be found in the prayer's content. The prayer does not use an individualized checklist of specific wants and needs as we often hear at prayer meetings. The prayer is focused like a laser beam on expressing a dependent approach to God, on the quality of the community's life with him. It expresses a desire for holiness, for God's ruling presence, for a life of forgiveness, and it recognizes that provision and spiritual protection come from God. It asks God to work on the heart and seeks to be submissive to his will.

The prayer's structure is simple: one address, two statements and three requests. The ABCs of discipleship are reflected in its content.

The address of God as Father is important, since it focuses on the relationship God has with his children. The expression goes back to the Aramaic *abba,* which combines respect for the father's authority with a sense of intimacy. The term has often been misinterpreted as meaning "Daddy," but the ancient evidence for this does not exist (Barr 1988:28-47; for a critical evaluation of Barr's challenge to this standard reading, Witherington 1990:217-18). Jesus' introduction of such intimacy in prayer is perhaps not entirely unprecedented in Judaism, but it certainly is unusual in the context of prayer (Sirach 23:1, 4; 51:10; Dunn 1975:21-26). Disciples should feel close to God, since they are part of his family and have ready access to him.

But intimacy does not do away with respect. So the prayer's first statement is *Hallowed be your name.* The disciple approaches God's person with the recognition that God is holy—that is, "set apart" and unique. There is none like him, and no one has the authority he possesses. This note of submission is the prayer's heartbeat. To sanctify God's name means not only that God is set apart, but also that his uniqueness should be made known (Is 52:5-6; Ezek 36:20-21; Rom 2:24). The Jewish background to this can be seen in a portion of the Kaddish, a prayer that often closed synagogue services: "Exalted and hallowed be his great name in

---

remarks, since Luke refers specifically to *the Holy Spirit* rather than Matthew's more general "good things." Either Luke arranged authentic material topically and highlighted a particular application, and Matthew did the same (if one sees that sermon as an anthology), or they are describing different events. I slightly prefer the latter option. Stein (1992:323) argues that it is hard to see the connection between these verses and what precedes. My arrangement makes that connection clear, so I think the placement makes great literary-theological sense.

the world which he created according to his will. May he let his kingdom rule in your lifetime and in your days and in the lifetime of the whole of Israel, speedily and soon." The disciple desires the visible manifestation of God's presence in the world.

The second declaration is for God's kingdom to come. This hope centers on the full realization of God's promise. More is meant here than eternal life. Rather, the disciple desires that the creation be restored to its fullness and that sin, injustice and chaos be banished. The whole of the disciple's life is lived in reflection of what God will eventually do. The later request regarding forgiveness is built on the premise that one day justice will prevail. Jesus' earlier call to love (6:27-36) also rests on the realization that wrongs done to one who loves with vulnerability will be reversed. The disciples long for the day when God will show his authority in justice. The rest of the New Testament tells us that this hope will be fully realized with Jesus' return. But this awareness was beyond the grasp of the disciples when Jesus originally taught this prayer. They only knew and hoped that one day God would bring full redemption.

With God's character and authority established, Jesus turns to the matter of requests. Basic needs are acknowledged as the Father's provision is requested. Jesus starts with the most basic material need, food. The term *artos* is probably broad in force here, a reference to all kinds of food, not just the most common ancient staple, bread (Lk 7:33; Jn 13:18; 2 Thess 3:8; Behm 1964:477-78). As important as the request is, the attitude it reflects is even more important: the disciples know that God cares daily for his own. In contrast, the Jewish Eighteen Benedictions asks for a annual supply of food (requests 9 and 18). The recognition of God's continual presence and care is fuel for the life of disciples.

Next the disciples ask for God's forgiveness. For the disciple, forgiveness is not a right but comes by God's grace. This is recognized in the clause that follows: in order to ask for forgiveness, one should be ready to give it as well. Judaism shared this understanding (Sirach 28:2; elsewhere in the New Testament, Eph 4:32; Col 3:13). Here sin is described

---

11:3 Perhaps the most notorious lexical problem in the Gospel occurs here with the term often translated *daily, epiousios.* Does it mean necessary provision or daily provision or future provision? The term appears to be coined; thus debate exists as to its exact force. Many argue that the force is "the following day's bread," which still translates out concep-

as a debt to be forgiven. When someone acts against another, he or she incurs a debt. Sensitive disciples recognize that we should not ask God to do something for us that we are not willing to do for others.

The recognition of the need for forgiveness is significant for other reasons. First, it shows that disciples are aware that they live in an imperfect, fallen world and that they contribute to its imperfection. The world is full of victims because it is full of people who sin. Sin should not surprise us, but neither should it be ignored. Without forgiveness and the willingness to forgive, sin and animosity heighten. Second, there is the recognition that sin is not only against individuals; it is an act of opposition to God, an affront to the holiness proclaimed earlier in the prayer. Third, the recognition of the need for forgiveness reflects a humility that is central to healthy discipleship. The world is not divided between "us and them." Rather than pointing the finger at others, mature disciples start with a look at their own attitudes and behavior.

The final request is for spiritual protection. This petition is confusing at first glance. Why would God lead us into temptation? God does not tempt anyone (Jas 1:13-15). But this is a rhetorical statement that we must read carefully to understand its force. Disciples recognize God's power to protect us and keep us from succumbing to temptation, not because God wants to take us there but because he can keep it from "getting us." The first step in such prevention is to recognize this and rely on God to protect our steps. Such constant spiritual inventory serves as preventive care of the soul.

There is some question whether temptation in this context should be read more narrowly as persecution. But the previous remarks about forgiveness suggest a broader sense. In sum, to avoid sin we must go where God leads and embrace the spiritual wisdom, provision and protection God supplies (1 Cor 10:12-13).

The Lord's Prayer is really the community's prayer. What stands out in the prayer is its spirit of submission and dependence. It envisions a community that walks with God and looks to him for everything from

---

tually as daily bread (Foerster 1964c:591-95 has a full discussion but opts for "necessary" or "daily" bread). Fortunately, though the precise force is less than certain, the general conceptual force is clear.

food to forgiveness.

Now Jesus highlights the importance of prayer with a parable. Many features of this parable reflect the culture of the time. In the ancient world, food was not as readily available as it is in modern culture. Most food was prepared daily; preservatives were largely unknown. In addition, ancient culture put a high premium on hospitality (Stählin 1967:20; 1974:161). Guests had the right to a good host who would provide for their needs. So the man who receives a late-night guest faces a dilemma: he has a guest but no food. He must make a choice: either to be rude by not welcoming this guest with food or to seek food from a neighbor, who may be able to help but may be in bed. One final cultural note is key. Most ancient Palestinian homes had only one room. Waking the father would mean risking waking the family.

Jesus turns this scenario into a lesson about boldness in prayer. It is *midnight (mesonyktion)*. A friend has come and needs food. Jesus asks whether his listener would go to a neighbor to try to procure food for his guest. Cultural expectations would push him to try. The neighbor initially refuses to get up, noting that the house "has been closed" for the night and his children are in bed with him. To get the bread would cause great unrest. Anyone who has children and knows what it takes to get them to bed can identify with this reply!

Jesus says, however, *"I tell you, though he will not get up and give him the bread because he is his friend, yet because of the man's* shameless boldness [Greek] *he will get up and give him as much as he needs."* Then Jesus goes on: *"Ask and it will be given to you; seek and you will find; knock and the door will be opened to you."* The juxtaposition of these exhortations shows that Jesus encourages boldness in prayer. The attitude here is like that of Hebrews 10:19-22. The key term is *anaideia* (NIV *boldness*), because it contains two ideas at once: both boldness and

---

11:8 When the parable is read as setting up a contrast between the neighbor's response and God's, the argument has a Jewish "how much more" quality: if this is how a neighbor will respond, how much more will a good God respond! Such a force is explicitly present later in verses 11-13. I reject the interpretation that God responds to avoid shame, just as the neighbor would do. Such an understanding undercuts God's character as revealed in the rest of the passage. The parable's stress is on the petitioner, which is why verses 9-10 stress the disciples' need to ask. This is also why the parable is not about the householder's shame. The major figures in the parable are the petitioner and God.

shamelessness. This kind of prayer has gall. Nothing will stop such a request from being set before God. The response is still God's choice, but the door is open for the request.

In verse 10 Jesus indicates God's openness to receive such bold petitions. In the context of the Lord's Prayer, Jesus is asking the disciples to pursue both the spiritual goals and the request for basic needs indicated in the earlier prayer with great boldness. Unlike the neighbor who is disturbed in the night and perhaps responds only grudgingly, God is ready and waiting to respond to us. All we need to do is ask, seek and knock. These are not blank-check promises that God will give us anything we want, but promises that requests for our spiritual welfare will be heard. The reference to the Holy Spirit in verse 13 shows this spiritual emphasis. God is especially willing to give spiritual aid to those who seek it.

So Jesus compares the disciple to a son who asks for something essential to eat, like a fish. A father will not feed him a poisonous snake, will he? If he asks for an egg, his father will not give him a poisonous spider, will he? Jesus knows the answer is "Of course not!" *"If you then, though you are evil, know how to give good gifts to your children, how much more will your Father in heaven give the Holy Spirit to those who ask him!"* As disciples bring their spiritual requests to the Father, they know that he is ready to help them. He longs to work in them and supply the Spirit for their needs. Like a father who feeds his child, so the Father will supply his disciples with the Spirit they need to be guided in their spiritual life. At the foundation of all discipleship is trust in the Father's goodness. He loves to provide for all our spiritual needs.

Controversies, Corrections and Calls to Trust (11:14-54) This third portion of the Jerusalem journey section deals with themes of opposition to Jesus. Religious leaders question the source of Jesus' heal-

11:14-23 The possible parallels to this text are Matthew 12:22-30 and Mark 3:22-27. The event's distinct placement, so early in Mark and before the great Caesarea Philippi confession in Matthew, has raised some questions. Interestingly, the Lukan version has verbal contact with both Matthew and Mark. None of the accounts opens with a tight temporal indicator. Mark's account occurs in a section of controversies that itself may be topically arranged. Given that this section of Luke also has topical features, Mark's early placement is not a problem, and neither is Luke's placement here. In all likelihood all are describing the same event, which each writer has placed differently within his Gospel.

ing power. They think Satan is responsible. Next Jesus warns about response to him. The portion closes with Jesus' strong condemnation of the Pharisees and scribes. The lines are being drawn, and positions about Jesus are hardening. In the midst of this growing opposition there is the call to know what miracles mean and to understand the times. To think Jesus' power comes from Satan is to miss the arrival of God's kingdom and thus to make a grievous mistake.

Why Miracles? (11:14-23) Contemporary Western culture is highly visual. As I teach, I can hardly think of lecturing without considering what audiovisuals I might use to reinforce an idea. And we can hardly watch television or use a computer without being amazed at the visual variety and creativity in our electronic world.

Visuals are powerful. They say things that words cannot say. As the saying goes, a picture is worth a thousand words. Pictures reach places that words may fail to reach, penetrating the closed vault of our hearts and allowing us to see things that words only obscure.

This passage is probably the most strategic text for explaining why Jesus performed miracles. In other miracle stories considerable attention is given to the occasion, setting and nature of the miracle. In some texts, such detail spans thirteen verses (Mk 5:1-13). But in Luke 11:14-23 all these elements appear in a single verse. The rest of the account gives the reaction to the miracle. It is a miracle story turned upside-down. Here it's the commentary on the miracle that counts. The fact that this passage's form departs from the standard shows its importance. What Jesus tells us here is that miracles are an audiovisual, a graphic display of how God's plan and power advance.

The event that leads to the discussion is an exorcism of a demon that had caused its victim to be struck dumb. The exorcism makes the man able to speak again, so *the crowd was amazed.* Speculation begins regarding the kind of power Jesus possesses. His healings must be explained. That they are taking place cannot be denied.

Two options are suggested by those who have doubts. First, some attribute his capabilities to *Beelzebub, the prince of demons.* They clearly have Satan in mind and imply strongly that Jesus is demonically controlled. The name *Beelzebub* in its English form comes from the Latin; it appears to refer to the Philistine god Ekron (2 Kings 1:2-3, 6, 16). In all probability the name means "Lord of the flies" (on this discussion and other options, see Fitzmyer 1985:920-21). The name was a derisive characterization of Satan.

The second alternative is a wait-and-see approach. Some want more proof through some *sign from heaven.* It is unclear what this might have involved—a heavenly portent or just more miracles? In any case, not all are persuaded that demonic control is the answer.

These two possibilities well summarize reactions to Jesus today. Some reject him; others want to see more from him. But clearly, those who were exposed to Jesus realized that they could not ignore his actions or claims. His ministry demanded that people consider his identity.

Significantly, the opponents did not doubt Jesus' miraculous power. The opinion of skeptics today, that miracles do not happen or that whatever Jesus did was not miraculous, was not a line Jesus' opponents took in his day. This is very significant. Surely if this nonmiraculous option existed, it would have been taken. But the opponents and those they hoped to persuade were too close to Jesus to deny that something supernatural was happening. Unfortunately, historical distance can so blur reality that explanations not considered possible at the time of the event can seem possible later. We can reject Jesus, but to doubt his miracles is to question not only him but also, curiously enough, his opponents.

Jesus, knowing *their thoughts,* responds. He raises the issue of the divided house. How can Satan stand against himself if he wants to survive? A divided kingdom does not stand. Jesus argues that it is a strategy of foolishness if Satan has sent one of his henchmen to undo his own work of destruction.

Then Jesus makes a second argument. By whose power do their own *followers* cast out demons, if Jesus casts out demons by Satan's hand? Now this argument is making one of two points. Jesus may be saying, I do the same exorcisms as Jewish exorcists do, so to attribute my exorcisms to Satan is to attribute theirs to Satan as well. Do you wish to demean the activity of your own exorcists in this way? Another possibility, and the one I prefer, is that Jesus is arguing that their "sons"—that is, his disciples—also do this work. So if the people are going to question his work, they must also question the work of those who follow him. I prefer this argument because I am not sure Jesus would endorse the activity of Jewish exorcists and, more important, predict their positive role in the future judgment, since they are currently outside God's will in their rejection of him. More likely Jesus is arguing that he is not alone in this ministry. Either way, the argument that Jesus is enabled by Satan falls like a house of cards.

So Jesus offers another alternative, in a statement loaded with theological significance: *"If I drive out demons by the finger of God, then the kingdom of God has come to you."* Jesus says the miracles are evidences of the arrival of God's promised, redemptive rule. They are audiovisual testimony to God's power and rule.

The key term in the verse is *ephthasen* (from *phthanō*), "has come." Theologians debate this arrival language. Some question whether arrival is in view and argue that Jesus is simply saying the kingdom has drawn near, as in Mark 1:15. They note that this term can carry that force (Mt 26:45; Lk 15:1; Jn 21:1). However, against this view is the presence of *epi* with the verb. Daniel 4:24, 28 (Theodotion) show the force of this combination of terms. The combination means "arrive." In addition the contextual emphasis in verses 18 and 21-23 indicates that it is current events that are pictured and current power that is described (Kümmel 1961:107 n. 8). The miracles trumpet the arrival of God's ruling power in such a way that Satan's display of power on earth is challenged and is in the process of being defeated.

To say the kingdom has arrived is not to argue that consummation has come, only that its presence has begun. The process of establishing kingdom authority is a long one, as Jesus will reveal, and it will take his return to bring the full promise of the kingdom to completion (for more on the kingdom see above discussion of 9:57-62). God is breaking peacefully into the creation through Jesus to reclaim humanity from Satan's grip.

Jesus overcomes the presence and power of evil in the world. His power is greater than that of demons. He is stronger than Satan. His power and authority reverse the effect of sin. This exercise of power through Jesus is why Paul can call the gospel "the power of God" in Romans 1:16-17. The story of the gospel is the story of how Satan, sin and the flesh are overcome through Jesus' provision of the Spirit. So Paul calls the kingdom of God a matter of power (1 Cor 4:20) as well as justice, peace and joy inspired by the Spirit (Rom 14:17). And Ephesians 1:15—2:10 and 6:10-18 refer to the battle we have against the forces of evil and note how Jesus has a position of authority over them. These theological realities are pictured in Jesus' words.

The parable that follows in verses 21-23 shows that this cosmic struggle is the point and that the miracles provide evidence for Satan's defeat. The *strong man* in the palace at the parable's start is Satan. But *someone stronger* than he comes and overpowers him, takes his armor and divides the spoil.

Here is the ultimate cosmic war. Jesus and Satan stand toe to toe in battle. The miracles are an audiovisual that Satan's cause is ultimately lost. He can do great damage, as any enemy can; but the die is cast. He will lose. The picture of the "stronger one" alludes back to 3:15-16. The stronger one is the promised Messiah who brings fire and the Spirit. The dividing of the spoil recalls the imagery of Isaiah 53:12 (see also Is 49:25-26). Jesus' work means that Satan is no longer in control of the palace.

Other New Testament texts highlight this theme of cosmic victory and refer to the cross and resurrection (Eph 4:7-16; Col 2:14-15). The entirety of Jesus' first coming sets up the kingdom's coming and Satan's defeat. The *spoils* in these texts are the benefits of salvation distributed to those who have been redeemed. Thus Paul presents Jesus' lordship as an expression of grace as Jesus richly bestows his blessings on all who call upon him (Rom 10:9-13). Our sins can be cleansed, and Jesus can pour out the Spirit because of our Savior's victory.

There are no Switzerlands in this cosmic war. *He who is not with me is against me, and he who does not gather with me, scatters.* Jesus says that neutrality to him is opposition to him. To decide for God, one must decide for Jesus. In a cosmic war there are no spectators; everyone lines up on one side or the other. The implication is to be careful which side you choose. The miracles not only make a statement about Jesus' authority; they ask a question about our response.

But even where there is opposition, the opponents are not abandoned to their fate. Evangelism is infiltration into enemy lines. Rejection is not a cause for abandonment, since we never know when a Saul might become a Paul.

Warnings About Response (11:24-36) The previous passage has shown that Jesus' presence forces a choice. This unit reinforces that idea. In a series of short sayings Jesus warns of the dangers of rejection and states the benefits of responding to him. Images of threat are juxtaposed to images of light. As often in this Gospel, the question has to do with how we respond to Jesus.

It is popular in our day to be neutral. In a culture where tolerance is highly valued, nonpartisanship is attractive. In religious discussions we try to avoid stepping on toes, for in Western cultures religious views are generally considered private. We want to avoid offending others in a culture that is diverse. But neutrality is not always a good thing, and neither is polite disengagement. Some issues are important enough to require our considered choices. That is Jesus' premise in this passage.

If God exists, should we think of him as having a laissez-faire attitude, not interested in how we relate to him? Jesus argues that is not the case. Religion by its very nature is a public affair, since it deals with how people relate to reality and to others. Though religious coercion such as marred European history in the Crusades and the Thirty Years' War is wrong, so is our culture's tendency to relegate religious concerns to the fringe world of private reflection. The issues are too important to be kept peripheral. Ultimately we must ask each other, What centers our lives, what do we accept as truth, what defines our character? And so in this short passage Jesus calls us to consider what directs our lives.

In the first of five short units, Jesus tells a parable that urges us to make a spiritual response. Blessing provides an opportunity for response to God, but ignoring the opportunity brings tragic results. Having just discussed exorcisms, Jesus maintains the theme by speaking of an unclean spirit that looks for a place to reside after an exorcism. The man who has had the exorcism is compared to a *house* that is *swept clean*. Nothing

---

11:24-36 While verses 27-28 give material unique to Luke, the rest of this passage has contact with the other Synoptics. Verses 24-26 are like Matthew 12:43-45. Verses 29-32 are like Matthew 12:38-42 and Mark 8:11-12, though Luke's version is closer to Matthew's. Verse 33 parallels Matthew 5:15 and Mark 4:21, while verses 34-36 are like Matthew 6:22-23. The parallels in Matthew come from the Sermon on the Mount, but the sayings are short enough and proverbial enough to have been repeated. The coherence of the sequence in Luke 11

has replaced the demon that once took up space in the house. Empty, it is fit to be reinhabited. So the spirit brings *seven other spirits more wicked than itself,* and they take up residence there. The man's situation is now worse than it was before.

Jesus' point is simple. When you are blessed by a cleansing of evil that allows you to receive fresh spiritual input, do not leave your inner "house" empty. The risk is that the void will be refilled with something even worse than what had been banished. Neutrality is emptiness, a void that eventually is filled by something—often something like what was there before. When we do not respond to God, opportunity becomes tragedy, and the chance for permanent reversal is lost.

Jesus has used exorcism as a graphic example of the principle he wants to convey. He says that we should make sure our inner house is not empty and that we take in light, since emptiness will likely lead to darkness.

Perhaps because all this talk of demonic confrontation has been making the crowd nervous, one woman now offers a blessing for the mother who nurtured Jesus to life. Jesus deflects her praise and replaces it with a blessing that calls for reflection. His beatitude is for *those who hear the word of God and obey it.* Reminiscent of 8:21, this blessing encapsulates a major theme of Jesus' teaching. In short, Jesus is saying, Respond to the preached offer of the kingdom. Believe the gospel.

The call to respond also provides an opportunity for rebuke. The rebuke extends to the fence-sitters of verse 16, those who want more signs. Neutrality always seeks more evidence. Now careful consideration of truth is a good thing, but to delay decision in the face of repeated demonstrations of power is really avoidance. Jesus calls this generation an evil one for seeking a sign. He implies that the time for signs is passing away. For having refused to believe God's Word, the people will not believe a sign either (16:30-31). Only *the sign of Jonah* remains to be given.

---

may suggest that though Matthew's and Luke's sayings are similar, they come from distinct events.

11:24 The concept of a spirit looking for a place to reside was common in Judaism (Tobit 8:3; Lk 8:29-31 also reflects this idea). In contrast to this image is that of God's Spirit indwelling believers (1 Cor 3:16; 6:19; 2 Cor 6:16; Eph 2:22).

A surface reading might lead us to think that by *the sign of Jonah* Jesus means resurrection, since a striking feature of Jonah's career was his three-day reflective sojourn in the belly of the fish. But when we look carefully at Jesus' remarks in Luke, we find that the sign he means is Jonah's preaching of repentance. Jesus mentions both Jonah and the Queen of the South in making his point (1 Kings 10:1-13; 2 Chron 9:1-12; Josephus *Antiquities* 8.6.5-6 §§165-75). In both cases he mentions teaching or preaching as the point of contact.

So Jesus argues that someone greater than Solomon or Jonah is present. Response is demanded, and looking for more signs is not the way to proceed. Rather, the preached word is the issue. It is time to decide, not sit on the fence. At risk is condemnation from those of a former era who did respond to the preached word. The Son of Man is a sign to this generation in the sense that he brings the Word of God to light, so people can come to know God. Thus Jesus issues both a rebuke and an exhortation here: Do not be evil and seek more miraculous signs; believe the Word as the Ninevites did and as the Queen of the South did. Jesus is the bearer of God's wisdom (7:31-35; 10:21-22; 1 Cor 1:24, 30).

Finally Jesus turns to the image of light. Again he makes his point through comparison. Lamps are not lit to be hid, but to be set on a stand where the light can do some good. Then the light allows those who enter a room to know where they are going. The image is very much like that of 8:16. In the ancient world such light usually was kindled in an oil lamp; what the KJV calls "bushel" (*bowl* in NIV) was a vessel for grain. Light did not go in bushels but on stands. Here Jesus' teaching is compared to light. Jesus has not failed to discuss what God is doing. Guidance is available through Jesus' teaching. But it guides only when it is seen and received.

Receptivity is Jesus' final point. The metaphor shifts slightly as the eye is now compared to a lamp for the body, but it can either be lit or be

11:37-54 The parallel to this text is Matthew 23:1-36. In Matthew, Jesus issues the woes publicly in Jerusalem. The different settings have prompted much discussion. Most see Luke as formulating this teaching around the meal scene but view it as the same tradition as Matthew contains (Stein 1992:339), though a few argue Matthew has shifted its setting (Marshall 1978:491). I prefer to see Luke dealing with special Lukan material that conceptually is similar to Matthew 23. Certain omissions, like Jesus' rebuke of the Pharisees for their

dark. Be careful what you take into your soul. The opportunity exists for the body, the person, to be *full of light,* if he or she takes in what God makes available. Jesus emphasizes the positive here; thus in the span of the entire passage he has both warned and exhorted. A healthy eye is a clear or pure *(haplous)* eye that takes in the light and benefits from this illumination. For Jesus there is no automatic inner light; light must be received. And the possibility of taking in *darkness* means that some things received are not the light. In sum, we must take in the teaching Jesus offers, for it is our source of spiritual light and spiritual health.

Jesus Rebukes the Pharisees and Scribes (11:37-54) Luke loves meal scenes and often reports discourses of great significance at the table (5:29; 7:36; 10:38; 14:1; 22:14). This meal is no exception. If diplomats had been present at this meal, the press release afterward would have said, "The two parties held frank and direct discussions, but no agreement was reached." In typical diplomatic terms that description would be an understatement. Jesus takes the occasion of this meal to condemn his host's religiosity. The harshness of his critique strikes our modern, sophisticated taste as almost rude, but in ancient culture, as in many non-Western cultures today, discussions about religion were very open and direct. So Jesus delivers his honest opinion about the leadership's spiritual life. Here is a checklist of potential pitfalls in the pursuit of piety. The differences between Jesus and the leadership are not small; a great gulf yawns between them.

The evening starts simply, with Jesus responding to a Pharisee's invitation to dine with him. As Jesus begins he does not *wash before the meal,* a fact that astonishes the host. Jewish tradition made a point of washing (Gen 18:4; Judg 19:21; Josephus *Jewish Wars* 2.8.5 §129; especially *m. Yadayim* 1). The Old Testament describes such washings, but they are not commanded. Later writings from Judaism speak of washings both before and after a meal. The Pharisees are concerned with ritual purity before God, but Jesus will view this concern as adding burdens

---

failure to keep God's commands and the allusion to Isaiah 29:13, are hard to explain if these are parallels. Virtually none of the wording matches, though there are conceptual parallels. The order of the woes is very different. If Luke's order is compared to Matthew's, the sequence is 6, no parallel, no parallel, 1, remark, 3 and 5. This seems very odd if the same tradition is being quoted.

to God's revelation.

Jesus' host is thinking about these things—there is no indication he says anything to Jesus. Nevertheless, Jesus responds. What follow are a general condemnation and then six woes. The first three are directed at the Pharisees and the last three at the scribes. The general condemnation is for hypocrisy, and in the woes Jesus specifies the subtle variety of forms such hypocrisy takes.

He begins with the picture of a cup that is clean on the outside but filthy with extortion and wickedness on the inside. When I read this text, I often recall walking over to my children's sandbox after a rainstorm. The cups the children played with would be covered with sand and dirt on the outside but, because they were turned upside-down in the sand, absolutely clean on the inside. They were so filthy that I almost hated to pick them up. Though Jesus' image is the reverse of this, what he is evoking is similarly distasteful. Jesus creates a powerfully emotive visual.

Jesus' reply moves beyond hand-washing to address issues of character. In speaking of cups that are clean on the outside, Jesus alludes to the precise care that went into washing utensils so as to avoid ritual uncleanliness. Often this was called "fly impurity," for if an unclean or dead bug fell onto a cup or plate, that would render the dish unclean (Goppelt 1968b:149). The practice was grounded in Leviticus 11:32-33 and 15:12 (in later Judaism, *t. Berakot* 5:26; see Booth 1987:119-50, 194-203). Jesus is not condemning physical cleanliness. However, he is reacting to the contrast between compulsiveness in external cleanliness and an absence of concern for the heart. The two vices Jesus names are *greed* and *wickedness*. Both are broad terms for immorality of various types, usually attitudes that lead us to treat people and possessions as objects to be used and manipulated. Luke 20:45-47 is similar in tone. The rebuke has Old Testament roots (Is 1:10-17; 58:4-8; Amos 5:21-24; Mic 6:6-8). From the very start of his rebuke Jesus shows that a person's heart concerns God most.

As he completes the general rebuke, Jesus turns his attention to God's role as Creator, the One who made both the outside things and the inside. God cares about both. To think otherwise and act otherwise is foolish. In calling the Pharisees *foolish people* Jesus harks back to the book of Proverbs' many rebukes of the fool. The fool exhibits the exact opposite of the wisdom the Pharisees think they possess. To be a fool in the Old Testament is to be blind to the things of God (Bertram 1974:230-31). The question whether God created both the outside and inside is structured for a positive answer (note the use of the Greek particle *ouk*). God made both, and both cups and hearts are subject to him!

Jesus' next remark is difficult. To what does the reference to giving alms refer? In the ancient world giving alms meant contributing to those who had material needs. The practice reflected a sensitive religious concern for the unfortunate (Bultmann 1964b:485-87; Sirach 7:10; Tobit 12:8-9). To give alms is to show mercy (Is 1:10-31; Hos 6:6). Giving alms requires conscious action. But what do alms have to do with hypocrisy? The saying "Give alms for those things that are within" (Greek) means one of two things. (1) Most read it to mean that one should be generous from the heart (NIV). Such generosity makes for spiritual cleanliness. The opposite of extortion and evil is generosity. (2) But another meaning is possible: to apply the consideration we give to almsgiving to the issues of the heart. If we give special attention to the heart, then cleanliness is the result. Given the heavily figurative language of the context, this second sense seems more natural and sets the theme of Jesus' remarks: true piety begins when we pay careful attention to the issues of the heart.

Now Jesus begins the woes. A woe is a cry for God's just judgment in light of an action that deserves a divine response (see 6:24-26). The first woe says to the Pharisees, *"You give God a tenth of your mint, rue and all other kinds of garden herbs, but you neglect justice and the love of God."* Another religious practice of Jesus' day was giving one-tenth of all one had back to God for the temple and its ministers. This practice also had Old Testament roots (Lev 27:30-33; Num 18:21-32; Deut 14:22-27). In fact, there were various types of tithes, including tithes of produce and tithes involving livestock. By tithing minute herbs the leaders showed themselves scrupulously faithful. Elaborate rules existed for such tithes (*m. Ma'aser Šeni; m. Demai* 2:1). But two large relational imperatives were ignored—justice and love for God. It is no accident that these two ideas are linked, as they were also linked in 10:25-28. The basic call of God is to love him and respond properly to others (Mic 6:8;

Zech 7:8-10; Col 3:12-13). Jesus corrects the Pharisees by saying that they should tithe without neglecting the pursuit of love with justice.

The second woe addresses pride. Why do the Pharisees seek *the most important seats in the synagogues and greetings in the marketplaces?* Judaism had elaborate greetings for rabbis, and the prominent seats drew attention to the leaders' status. Jesus offers no correction here, only the rebuke.

The third woe is the most direct. The Pharisees are *like unmarked graves, which men walk over without knowing it.* Here is the height of uncleanliness. Jesus suggests not only death but also uncleanliness. Jesus' view of the Pharisees is exactly opposite of their self-image. In fact, what they thought about Jesus' not washing his hands is true of them. The "cleanliness tables" have turned! Jews were careful about their contact with dead bodies or things associated with death (Num 19; Lev 21:1-3; *m. Demai* 2:3). Yet Jesus says the Pharisees, far from being paragons of purity, are bearers of burial, death and uncleanliness. Only they carry their uncleanliness in a stealthy, underground fashion. Unfortunately, few knew just how deadly they were.

At this point a scribe tries to come to the Pharisees' rescue: if Jesus is going to attack the Pharisees, he'd better realize he is also attacking the scribes. The logic seems to be that surely Jesus would not want to throw his net of rebuke quite so wide. In fact, the scribe actually accuses Jesus of insulting *(hybrizeis)* them all. Does he really want to take them all on, and does he really want to tell them all to repent? Surely the religious leadership is above reproach.

Briefly, Jesus' answer is yes, they all need to repent. So he continues to issue woes and turns his attention to the scribes. There is plenty of guilt to go around. The first woe for them is because "you load people down with burdens they can hardly carry, and you yourselves do not touch the burdens with one of your fingers" (Greek). This woe can also be read in one of two ways: either (1) they are hypocrites, asking others to do what they do not ask of themselves, or (2) they are heartless, asking others to labor hard at spirituality while doing nothing to help those

---

11:49 The concept of "the Wisdom of God" (NIV *God in his wisdom*) has rich roots. In the Old Testament it referred to God, especially the expression of his will (Job 28; Prov

people accomplish the task (NIV *will not lift one finger to help them*). The term for *burdens* in the verse *(phortion)* is normally used to describe a ship's cargo. So the burdens are indeed heavy ones. Given the Pharisees' reputation for being very careful to keep the letter of the law, it is unlikely their kind of hypocrisy is the point. Since the other passages refer to failures at a relational level, we might expect a similar failure to be cited here. The rebuke is for a failure to show mercy and encourage others in their pursuit of God (view two above). Quick to point the finger but slow to lend a helping hand—that is Jesus' complaint.

True devoutness is never cold and withdrawn. The scribes' hypocrisy lies in claiming to know God's will yet being cold to others. The leadership was loading others down with a U-Haul or lorry full of demands and then standing by and watching them get crushed under the load. The scribes were so right in their own eyes that they unconsciously but constantly did wrong. What a rebuke to those whose life was focused on getting the law exactly right.

The second woe for the scribes is for their support of the slaying of the prophets. Now this woe contains irony: *"you build the tombs for the prophets, and it was your forefathers who killed them."* They built these tombs, no doubt, to show how they honored the prophets. But Jesus argues that in fact it shows their support for killing these divine agents! By building the tombs, he says, *you testify that you approve of what your forefathers did.* Here is one of Jesus' fundamental critiques of the leadership: they have been disobedient as their ancestors were. This evaluation also has Old Testament roots. It has been called the "deuteronomistic" critique of the nation, for throughout the books of Samuel and Kings the nation is condemned for consistent unfaithfulness before God in light of standards God proclaimed for the nation in Deuteronomy (Moessner 1989).

Jesus, speaking for "the Wisdom of God" (Greek), goes on to predict that another line of sent prophets and apostles also will be slain (NIV has simplified the construction by removing the personification of the

1, 8). God speaks here out of his knowledge of the history of the nation's response.

Greek). This will be proof that Jesus' point is correct. This generation will have to answer for the slaying of all the prophets, since all the prophets preach the same call to obey God.

The final woe to the scribes is a stinging rebuke for their assumption that they know the way to God and hold *the key to knowledge* (Weiss 1974:48). Jesus argues that in fact they *have taken away the key.* In fact, not only have they not entered into knowledge themselves, but they have put up barriers for those who were entering! They are doing the exact opposite of what they assume. No one enters the house of the knowledge and blessing of God through them. They are a wall instead of a door.

The woes are a devastating critique of pride and self-assurance in religious practice. Amid concern for external righteousness, the heart was neglected. Rules existed for everything except for how to relate honestly to God and to others. Self-importance replaced humility, and destruction replaced pursuit of God's will. These remarks are strong because they show how deceived people can become if they do not rely humbly on God. Sometimes the obsessive pursuit of what is right results in some very serious wrong.

The reaction to Jesus is strong. The leaders press around him and try to think of questions that may provoke him. Lying in wait, they hope *to catch him in something he might say. Enedreuō* ("to lie in wait") and *thēreuō* ("to catch") are hunting terms. The opposition to Jesus has become a hunt with Jesus as the prey. But this time the hunters will be shooting themselves.

Luke is showing not only how the opposition grew but also how they failed to heed Jesus' earlier call to repent (11:29-32). Luke also reveals what piety does not look like. The way to God is not that of the Jewish leadership. The way to God is not in a piety of pride and rules without care and compassion. The God-lover should not point the finger but lend a helping hand.

Notes: 12:1-12 Discussing parallels for this passage is difficult because of the complex nature of the connections. Verses 1-2 have similarities with Matthew 16:5-6 and Mark 8:14-15. Verses 3-9 have a potential parallel in Matthew 10:26-33, while verse 10 has an equivalent in Matthew 12:31-32 and Mark 3:28-30. Verses 11-12 look like Matthew 10:19-20, Mark 13:11 and Luke 21:14-15. The way these passages are scattered across the other Gospels is what

Discipleship: Trusting God (12:1-48) Since the way of Jesus is different from that of the leadership, understanding the nature of discipleship is crucial. This section treats such concerns. Disciples must fear God and stand up for him in the midst of persecution. They must avoid dependence on material things. They must trust God and realize that they are accountable to him. The essence of discipleship is fearing God and putting him first. To share God's priorities is the disciples' call. To learn from God means to follow him.

Fear God and Confess Jesus (12:1-12) The pressure of the Pharisees' example, along with the rise of persecution, prompts Jesus to warn his disciples about whose opinion they value. Peer pressure is a given in any culture. The power of those who seek conformity is very strong. Persecution methods can be strong, controlling and painful. The book of Acts tells of beatings, floggings and stonings. Economic pressure was also sometimes applied, along with social ostracism. The pressures to conform are still great. But Jesus issues a call in this passage to be strong and resist such pressure.

In the midst of growing crowds and official opposition Jesus issues a warning. The setting of his words is not insignificant. Even though people are practically crawling over one another to get to Jesus, the disciples should not be fooled by current popularity and should recall the level of opposition Jesus has faced. Popularity can breed a desire to remain popular and thus to soften the hard truth of our sinfulness before God. So Jesus warns, *"Be on your guard against the yeast of the Pharisees."* Leaven (NIV *yeast*) was a symbol of corruption (Ex 12:14-20; 1 Cor 5:6). The Pharisees' hypocrisy has just been discussed in 11:39-41. Jesus is saying that the desire to impress can lead to a double life. The way of the Pharisees is not the way for Jesus' disciples.

Hypocrisy will not work, because everything is revealed before God. The secrets of people's hearts will be revealed (Rom 2:15; 1 Cor 4:5). God's omniscience means that *there is nothing concealed that will not*

---

makes the discussion complex, as does the appearance of a similar passage later in Luke itself. It shows how similar sayings can be repeated in separate traditions. It is possible that here Luke has pulled together a thematic unit of Jesus' teaching. Another option is that some of these sayings were repeated on distinct occasions. There is no way to prove which option is correct.

be disclosed, or hidden that will not be made known. This includes words said in the dark or whispered in private rooms. A private room *(tameion)* was the innermost apartment in a house. So even things said deep within one's home and mind are known to God. Even these things will be proclaimed from the housetops one day. What is done in the basement will be revealed on mountaintops. We may divide our activities into public and private, visible and unseen, but there is no such division with God's vision. The walls we build up to protect our psyche and rationalize our behavior cannot keep out the eyes of God.

Now we might debate whether the passage stresses the revealing of sin or the exposure of righteousness. The previous statements about hypocrisy make a negative force likely here, but the following call to fear God may also suggest that God's positive response is in view. The choice between the options may be a false one. God responds to all that we do, and his justice in the future will balance any injustice that exists today.

So given the pressure to do one thing in public and another in private, Jesus reminds the disciples that they should fear God. They should fear not *those who kill the body* but the One who has *power to throw . . . into hell.* Human beings' power over life is limited. The life that counts is the life to come. We should not fear rejection or even martyrdom. The Jews understood this as well: "Let us not fear him who thinks he kills; for a great struggle and peril of the soul awaits in eternal torment those who transgress the ordinance of God" (4 Maccabees 13:14-15). There is no prosperity theology here, nor is there any glossing over of the rejection disciples may face. Standing up for God will mean opposition; they had better be prepared.

But they can also be assured that God is aware of their situation no matter how bad it gets. Even *five sparrows* that sell for a few pennies do not escape God's attention. These sparrows were the cheapest thing sold in the ancient market, and an *assarion* (Greek form of a Latin loanword) was the lowest valued Roman coin, being worth one-sixteenth of a denarius or a half-hour's minimum wage. God cares for those insignificant birds, and he cares for the disciple. He knows the number of hairs on one's head, and he knows that people are more valuable than sparrows. So we need not fear even the direst of persecutions, because

God knows what is taking place.

What it all comes down to is a choice of allegiance, an identification with Jesus. Those who acknowledge Jesus before human beings will receive due reward. *The Son of Man,* that is, Jesus, will acknowledge them before the angelic witnesses of heaven; they will stand accepted for eternity. A picture of this truth is Stephen's martyrdom in Acts 7:54-59. On the other hand, those who deny Jesus will face a similar denial before the angels.

Jesus raises the issue of blasphemy against the Spirit, a sin that cannot be forgiven in contrast to a word spoken against the Son of Man. This statement has led to considerable debate. Is the blasphemy attributing Jesus' work to the power of Satan (11:14-20)? Is it a reference to apostasy? Is it rejecting the apostles' preaching about Jesus, since that was Spirit-empowered preaching? Or is it not so much a single act as a persistent rejection of the Spirit's testimony about Jesus? This last option, the obstinate rejection of Jesus, is the most likely meaning. Not only does this remark fit all the Synoptic contexts in which this saying appears, but it fits with the importance Jesus places on the preached gospel message (Lk 24:44-47) and corresponds to the warnings the apostles issue at the end of their preaching (Acts 3:22-26; 13:38-41). To fear God means to choose Jesus. To reject him is to reject the Spirit who testifies constantly to him. Exposure to Jesus and church attendance are not the same thing as receiving the testimony of the Spirit and embracing the hope of the gospel. The Son of Man accepts only those who respond to the testimony of the Spirit (1 Cor 2:14-15).

Jesus' remarks prepare anyone thinking about responding to him for a world that will pressure those who embrace Jesus. The world may persecute disciples, but Jesus will honor those who seek him.

The pressure to deny Jesus may be great, but so is God's provision as disciples stand up for him: *"When you are brought before synagogues, rulers and authorities, do not worry about how you will defend yourselves or what you will say."* Jesus promises that the Spirit will come to their aid. Again, examples of fulfillment of this promise occur in Acts (4:13-22).

The disciple may face a hostile world, but loving God means standing up for him. Behind that backbone and resolve to face the opposition is an understanding that we must fear God and know that he sees both the disciple and the accuser. What is done in secret will be revealed in public before God one day. Then the disciple will stand though others fall.

The Parable of the Rich Fool (12:13-21) Now Jesus turns from issues of trust and conviction to discuss a major distraction to the spiritual life. The parable of the rich fool is unique to Luke. Rather than taking sides in a family dispute, Jesus warns about greed. Often disputes over inheritance are really about greed, symptoms of the disease of "possessionitis." Jesus attacks this disease directly in this parable, making a point Luke repeats often in his Gospel (4:4; 8:4-15; 9:24-25; 12:22-34; 16:19-31; 18:18-30). It appears that greed and the pursuit of possessions constitute one of the greatest obstacles to spiritual growth. This is especially true in modern culture, where possessions are readily available and their technological glitz is always being enhanced, as splashy advertisements for the latest gadget make clear.

Jesus will tell the parable in response to the arrival of a man who wishes to settle a dispute over an estate with his brother. Often rabbis served as mediators in such disputes, and so this man approaches Jesus as he would a leader of the Jewish community (on Jewish inheritance, Num 27:1-11; 36:5-9; Deut 21:15-17; *m. Baba Batra* 8:1—9:10). The details of the conflict are not clear. Often in the ancient world families kept their property together and shared its resources for business purposes, even though ownership was technically distinct. Did the brother want out of a family business so he could take his share and go out on his own? It should be noted that the brother really does not want an arbiter but an advocate on his behalf: *"Teacher, tell my brother to divide the inheritance with me."* This may have been Jesus' clue that there was a danger of greed in the situation.

Jesus refuses to judge between the two. He has not been appointed their judge, but he cannot avoid the opportunity to turn the request into an opportunity for instruction: *"Watch out! Be on your guard against all kinds of greed; a man's life does not consist in the abundance of his possessions."* When Jesus makes this warning, he has more in mind than monetary accumulation. If Jesus were alive today he would see the attitude behind the expression "The one with the most toys wins" as a prescription for failure in life. The ancients knew, as moderns also know, that life consists of more than the accumulation of wealth. Scripture repeatedly warns against greed and includes it in lists of moral vices (Mk 7:22; Rom 1:29; Eph 4:19; 5:3; Col 3:5; 1 Tim 6:10; 2 Pet 2:3, 14; in the Old Testament, Job 31:24-25; Ps 49). The ancient historian Plutarch said, "Greed never rests from the acquiring of more" (*On Love of Wealth* 1 [Mor. 523 E]; L. T. Johnson 1991:198).

When possessions are the goal, people become pawns. In fact, a reversal of the created order occurs, as those made in the living image of God come to serve dead nonimages. It is this inversion of the created order that makes greed such a notorious sin; it is even called idolatry in some texts (Eph 5:3; Col 3:5). When I think of this story and its lesson, I picture a Buddha with a dollar attached to its stomach. For some, the material world is god. Many of us end up serving our dollars or pounds and bowing before their demands rather than relating sensitively to people. In the process relationships can be damaged and marriages destroyed. False worship involves bowing before something that is not worthy of honor and that cannot deliver life's true meaning. The pursuit of wealth is the pursuit of false religion.

So Jesus tells an example parable, in which the example is negative. It involves the fortune of one man and how he handles that fortune. The man remains nameless, as is the normal pattern in such parables, because he represents a type of person. This farmer has a banner crop year. So great is the yield that he lacks storage space for it all. Rather than letting his resources waste away, he devises a plan to create more storage space. Now it is crucial to realize that the decisions the man makes to address his dilemma are perfectly normal and prudent, but the rationale, philosophy and desires that result from the decision are the problem.

This man believes that what he has is his in no uncertain terms. Several times in the next few verses he speaks in first-person terms about what he has: *my crops . . . my barns . . . my grain . . . my goods . . . myself.* There is no hint of an awareness of stewardship or responsibility to others as a result of his fortune. There is only self-interest. In his view he, like the famous American investment company, has made money the old-fashioned way—he has earned it! So after he stores his grain, he can relax into a totally self-indulgent life of ease: *"Take life easy; eat, drink and be merry."* The language recalls the biblical and Jewish texts of hedonism, as well as Greek culture (Eccl 8:15; Is 22:13; Tobit 7:10; *1 Enoch* 97:8-10; Euripides *Alcestis* 788-89). Almost every culture recognizes that using the creation for strictly selfish ends is a distortion.

As the man contemplates his future as one of the rich and famous, God has another account to render: the man is about to join the dead and departed. When God addresses the man as *fool,* he indicates the man's blindness in judging life's priorities. The man's soul is being weighed in the balance. On that scale the possessions the man has and the social résumé he has built register no weight whatsoever. He cannot take these things with him to the bar of divine justice. Only his naked character will be on that balance. The man whose life is possessions makes himself a paperweight at the final judgment. The one who defines life in terms of possessions comes up empty when the time comes to assess whether eternal life will be gained. The parable ends on a note of tragedy: *"Who will get what you have prepared for yourself?"* One thing is for sure, his treasures will not be his anymore.

Jesus underscores this tragedy as he closes the parable with a final commentary: *"This is how it will be with anyone who stores up things for himself but is not rich toward God."* Jesus' point is that the seeker of wealth ends up with an empty soul and an empty life. Possessions are like "lite" beer; they may taste great, but they are really less filling.

All this teaching suggests the importance of proper priorities regarding possessions. They are a stewardship, not to be hoarded selfishly but to be used to benefit those around us. Jesus is not saying possessions are bad, but that the selfish pursuit of them is pointless. When the creation is inverted, the value of possessions is distorted. Those who climb over people or ignore them in the pursuit of possessions will come up empty on the day God sorts out our lives. What a tragic misuse of the gift of resources this man had gained! What could have been an opportunity for generosity and blessing became a stumbling block to the soul.

Do Not Be Anxious (12:22-34) If we are not going to pursue material things, then how should we deal with our physical needs? Jesus' answer to this question is really fairly simple: "Trust God." Using crea-

---

12:22-34 This material is very similar to Matthew 6:25-34, while the final two verses are like Matthew 6:19-21. Both Matthean sections are part of the Sermon on the Mount. There is enough agreement *and* disagreement in wording (vv. 24, 26, 29, 32-33) to suggest to some

tion as the example, Jesus points to the tender care of the heavenly Father and asks people to consider how gentle God is. If God can care for his other creatures, he can care for you.

This passage's basic exhortation is *Do not worry.* Given God's care, we can be generous with the things God provides. The contrast between Jesus' attitude here and that of the rich fool could not be greater. Jesus' concern is with food and clothing (v. 22), the basics of life, a perspective Paul also shares (1 Tim 6:7-10). Jesus' exhortation begins with a call not to *worry (mē merimnate).* He uses a present imperative in Greek to indicate that a constant attitude is in view. Paul has a similar exhortation in Philippians 4:6-7.

Jesus explains his call away from worry by noting that life is more than food or clothing. The deepest dimension of life is relationship with God and with others. In 10:25-28 Jesus made it clear that real life has to do with relationship. Living is more than having; it is being in relationship with God and relating well to others. Placing concern for our daily needs in God's hands is part of what it means to have relationship with God (11:3-4).

Jesus now turns to support his exhortation with three illustrations from natural life: the birds (v. 24), the lilies (v. 27) and the grass (v. 28). *Ravens* refers to a wide variety of crows that inhabited Palestine. Interestingly, they were unclean creatures in Old Testament thinking (Lev 11:15; Deut 14:14; Job 39:13-14; Ps 147:9). They were among the least appreciated of birds, so the example is important because of the cultural perception of these creatures. Jesus has gone to the "bottom of the creature barrel" for this example. God cares for them by giving them food, and just think *how much more valuable you are than birds!* In other words, if he cares for them, he certainly will care for you.

Beyond the illustration from creation, there is a practical reason not to worry: it does no good. Does worrying "add a cubit" (Greek) to one's span of life? Now a cubit is about eighteen inches. There is debate whether Jesus is using the term to speak of ability to increase one's stature or the length of one's life. Neither option alters Jesus' point,

that two versions of a tradition are present (Marshall 1978:525). Such variation in the tradition may also suggest distinct events.

though the more natural possibility is the idea of adding to the length of one's life (so NIV). Either way, worrying does not help! In fact, anxiety should have a surgeon general's or health minister's warning attached to it: "Warning: anxiety may be harmful to your health." Jesus does not issue such a medical warning, however, only a practical one.

If worrying is futile in adding even a small increment to your life span, *why do you worry about the rest?* Worry is wasted energy, an emotional investment that yields nothing. Worry actually reflects the tension we have when we feel that life is out of our control; it is the product of feeling isolated in the creation. Disciples, however, should know that God cares for them. Biblically, the opposite of worry is trust. That is why after offering some more illustrations Jesus addresses his audience as *you of little faith* in verse 28. He wants them to come to trust God again.

So Jesus turns to his second and third natural illustrations. Both the lilies and the grass manage to be clothed with beauty. Lilies are arrayed more beautifully than courtly garments in the golden age of Solomon. Grass is cared for, even though it is soon tossed into the oven for fuel. Grass is often a figure for what is transitory in creation (Job 8:12; Is 40:6-8). If God cares for these basic, short-lived plants, *how much more will he clothe you.* Just as the ravens illustrated God's care to feed, so the lilies and the grass picture God's ability to adorn. Food and clothing are basics God knows we need. With them we are adequately adorned.

So we should not be anxious. *"Do not set your heart on what you will eat or drink; do not worry about it."* Such an attitude may be hard in our culture, where unemployment and the future are often not very secure. But Jesus is calling on disciples to realize that *the pagan world runs after all such things, and your Father knows that you need them.* It is no accident that Jesus refers to God as the Father in this context, for our intimate relationship with God should encourage us that we will receive his care. Once again, security comes from our relationship to God.

Seek his kingdom: disciples' priorities differ from those of the world. Unlike those in the world who consume themselves with the pursuit of food and clothing, disciples are to focus on seeking God's kingdom. This means we pursue relationship with God, his will and the evidence of his rule and guidance in our lives as we seek to serve him. Matthew 6:33 has a longer form of this saying: to pursue God's kingdom is to pursue his righteousness.

Jesus offers a promise with the exhortation: God will provide these other things as well. We can major on what God desires for us because he is committed to our care.

As Jesus concludes his exhortation, he turns more directly to the application. *Little flock,* his address for the disciples, suggests imagery of tender, easily frightened sheep who need the care of a shepherd. Jesus is deliberate in comparing believers to these fragile creatures rather than to lions or bears. The Father is the shepherd (Ps 23), and he promises to give everything associated with the kingdom to his sheep. We may be fragile, but God promises to care for us and make us strong.

Jesus' statements here fit well in a context of persecution and rejection. Whatever risk comes from trusting Jesus, whatever ostracism and isolation, know that God will care for you. Kingdom blessing will be provided. This is not a promise of abundant material blessing but of sufficient provision to do what God really desires.

In fact, so certain can we be of this care that we can be generous with what God provides. Jesus encourages the disciples: *"Sell your possessions and give to the poor"* (Greek "give alms"). The stress here is on how unattached disciples should be to the world, since they serve the kingdom of God. The virtue is not in giving up one's possessions but in being generous with resources, as the mention of alms indicates (on alms see 11:41).

There are two kinds of treasure: that which grows old and rots and that which lasts. Trust in God frees us to treasure the relationships that are at the center of life. To serve for the sake of God is to live. Do we value others, so that we serve them in giving and through service? Or do we value self and things, so resources are hoarded? Jesus says, Look at your treasure and what you do with it. That will show where your heart is. Since the Father gives, so should the disciple. (Zacchaeus becomes an example of a commended giver in 19:1-10.)

Jesus is talking about our basic approach to life. Are we anxious and lacking trust in God, constantly trying to gain control of things that often are beyond our control? Or do we trust God to provide and concentrate on honoring relationships by pursuing righteousness and serving others with our resources? Two things tell us the answers to these questions:

our heart and our pocketbook. Our heart can tell us if we are anxious, and our pocketbook can tell us if we are generous. Both tell us if we are trusting God.

Be Faithful Stewards (12:35-48) Perspective is crucial. Sometimes when we are going through particularly difficult situations, everything seems hopeless and pointless. Only after some time do we gain perspective so that events come into focus and the lessons become obvious. Perspective in life can work in two directions. Usually it is reflective, as we look back and consider what has happened in relation to subsequent events. But perspective can also be prospective. We can act now in light of what we hope will happen in the future. A couple who saves prudently now for their children's future education or for their own retirement lives prospectively. That kind of perspective is harder, because it requires faith and counts on events that have not yet occurred. It is very different from living strictly according to present needs and gratification.

Christians are supposed to live prospectively. Believers know that Jesus is returning and that all will give an account for their stewardship. So in this passage Jesus gives a series of three images to underline the importance of living prospectively. The parable of being prepared (vv. 35-36), the parable of waiting for the Son of Man (vv. 39-40) and the parable of the kinds of stewards (vv. 41-48) call us to reflect on our view of the future. The nature of the future helps to determine present priorities. Jesus wants to make sure disciples are prepared for what is to come. Faith means trusting God, not only for the present but also for the future, by walking faithfully with him until he returns. What God will do affects what we do.

Jesus launches right into the exhortation and parable: Let your loins be girded (Greek) *and keep your lamps burning.* These two images both suggest being prepared. So the NIV rightly renders the first as *be dressed ready for service.* Tying up one's garment around the waist is a picture of constant readiness to move quickly (Ex 12:10-11; 1 Kings 18:46; 2 Kings 4:29; 9:1; Is 59:17; Eph 6:14; 1 Pet 1:13). The perfect participle, acting as an imperative, makes the point: keep yourself ready. The image

12:35-48 This passage is similar to Matthew 24:42-51. What Luke has as part of the journey to Jerusalem, Matthew has in the Olivet Discourse during Jesus' last week in Jerusalem. Also some material in the Lukan version has no parallel (vv. 35-38). Though many regard the

of lamps burning adds to the sense of watchfulness. Even in the dark hours of the night you must be ready. Watch at all times. A variation of the image is Matthew 25:1-13.

Now Jesus makes a comparison. Like servants who wait for their master to return from a wedding celebration, disciples should be ready for their Lord to appear anytime at the door. Wedding feasts could last for as long as a week, so the time of someone's return was not always predictable. Servants had to be ready to serve whenever the master broke loose from the party to return home. Disciples should live in the same expectation.

Jesus offers a beatitude for those who heed his advice (v. 37); NIV introduces it with *it will be good*. The NRSV more closely follows the Greek: "Blessed are those slaves whom the master finds alert when he comes." The beatitude has an interesting twist: when the master returns, he will serve the servants who are faithful. Jesus has always placed a high premium on service, and here he shows that he will honor faithfulness with service. It is not at all common for masters to serve slaves, but God's grace shows the extent of God's love. The chief steward leads the stewards in service. He will share the meal at the table of fellowship and serve the food. The imagery suggests the blessing of being totally accepted by Jesus.

But Jesus does not tell his disciples when the master will return. The allusion to *the second or third watch* gives a general time frame, though the exact time is uncertain because it is not clear if Luke intends a Jewish three-watch or a Roman four-watch schedule. Either way the time frame is "deep night," somewhere between midnight (Roman time) and 2:00 a.m. (Jewish time). Luke uses the Roman schedule elsewhere (Acts 12:4), but a Jewish setting might suggest the other possibility. Either way the point is clear: the disciples must be ready because the return may be at any moment, even deep in the night when one normally would not be prepared. Constant vigilance is expected.

Jesus extends the call to readiness by comparing his return to a thief's robbing a house at night. Just as a man would never leave his house exposed if he knew a robber was going to try to enter it, so the disciple

material as coming from the same source, I prefer to see distinct versions and events because of differences in content and setting.

should be ready for the Son of Man's return. For just as we do not know when a thief may come, so we must be ready at all times. The Son of Man will come at an unexpected hour. There is spiritual exposure in lack of preparedness. The thief image suggests that the risks of unpreparedness are great.

Peter catches the importance of Jesus' remarks and asks who the parable's audience is. He may be distinguishing between the crowds and the disciples, or he may be asking about distinctions between the disciples and the leadership. The answer is not as easy as it might at first appear. That leaders are included is obvious from the passage's stewardship imagery. The problem is that when Jesus returns to render judgment, all are subjected to it. But only some disciples are asked to care directly for the Lord's children. If the judgment is for all, then the ministers to the community are any who associate with the community. So it would appear that Jesus has in mind all disciples, not just the leaders and not all humanity.

If there is an evaluation of stewardship, then what is good and bad stewardship? What will the evaluation be like? Jesus begins by noting what a good steward is like. A steward in ancient culture was a slave who was left in charge of domestic affairs when the master was away (16:1; 1 Cor 4:4-5; Michel 1967:149-51). The steward's major responsibility was to care for the other servants' welfare, especially to allot food to them. Food might be handed out daily, weekly or monthly. A steward's job was to serve, not to exercise power. This may well be why Jesus uses the image (Manson 1957:118).

Jesus praises faithfulness with another beatitude much like that of verses 37-38. The good servant, the one who waits and is ready, is the one who serves faithfully during the master's absence. Often we think of waiting as an attitude, but Jesus sees it as translating into action. Life lived prospectively is marked by constant service to God. The Lord blesses those living faithfully as they await his return. The reward will be further, expanded responsibility. Then the steward will have responsibility not only over the house and its servants but over the whole estate. What this "promotion" represents is hard to specify. Certain texts suggest that Jesus will continue to administer the creation upon his return (19:17; 1 Cor 6:2-3; Rev 20:1-6). Administrative assistants will be needed to exercise this responsibility. The reward seems to involve the future period of Jesus' rule, at which time faithfulness will be honored with more service.

But other outcomes are possible. What if the steward's service is blatantly unfaithful? Jesus raises this other side of the coin next: *But suppose the servant says to himself, "My master is taking a long time in coming," and he then begins to beat the menservants and maidservants and to eat and drink and get drunk.* In light of the subsequent verses, Jesus is discussing a stewardship that goes exactly opposite of what Jesus requested. Instead of the servants' being cared for, they are abused. Resources are wasted on the steward and not shared with others. How will the Lord evaluate those who don't care that the Master is returning and who live like it, abusing others along the way?

The master of that servant will come on a day when he does not expect him and at an hour he is not aware of. He will cut him to pieces and assign him a place with the unbelievers. For such a steward there is no reward, only severe judgment. The key to the passage is the dismemberment *(dichotomeō)* imagery and the idea of having a portion with the unfaithful. The Greek speaks of the "unfaithful," but contextually, given the judgment imagery, the NIV is correct to render this term *unbelievers.* The steward is not given a mere beating, but a mortal blow and a total separation. It represents a total rejection—a painful death as opposed to a punishment. This type of punishment is the most severe possible. The imagery of dismemberment is rendered too softly in many English translations (for example, "punish him" in RSV; see Betz 1964). This servant is rejected—as Matthew 24:51 says, placed among the hypocrites where there is weeping and gnashing of teeth.

Such servants may also include those who destroy God's temple in 1 Corinthians 3:16-17, who in turn are destroyed by God. These are the false teachers Acts 20:26-35 warns about and leaders like those condemned in 1 Timothy 3:3. In sum, they do not end up in heaven but are exposed for their unbelief and end up in hell with the rest of the totally unfaithful.

Jesus elaborates on other degrees of stewardly unfaithfulness—unfaithfulness that falls short of eliciting the total judgment Jesus has just described. In verse 47 it appears the servant exercises poor stewardship by not acting to *do what his master wants*. This is something less than a blatantly disobedient stewardship. This servant suffers a beating *with many blows*, as opposed to the dismemberment described in verse 46 for blatant disobedience. This is the discipline of a unfaithful steward, but one with some knowledge.

Second is the unfaithfulness of *one who does not know*. Here the servant is still culpable for his failure, but his punishment is a few blows, a discipline less severe than the previous two. Both the possibilities in verses 47-48 have conceptual parallels in Paul's remarks in 1 Corinthians 3:15—these are saved, but as through fire. The more one knows, the greater one's responsibility.

To be associated with Jesus is to have responsibility before him. Those who are sensitive to his return and their accountability to him will serve him faithfully. God will richly reward the faithful. Those who take this accountability less seriously will be sorted out according to their deeds. Those who never really responded to the Master and ignored his return by doing the opposite of what he asked for will seal their place among the unfaithful. Those who are knowingly negligent will be disciplined, while those who act in ignorance will be less severely disciplined.

The end of the passage helps to explain its start. We should live prospectively, sensitive to the accountability of discipleship. We should wear our work clothes and keep the lamps burning, looking for the Lord's return by serving him faithfully.

12:46 To argue that this verse is about a steward (NIV *servant*) who has no reward and is judged with the unbelievers is not to argue that one can lose one's salvation or that salvation is not of grace. The servant's attitude indicated that he did not know the master or even care about what he desired (Mt 7:21-23). This steward had no faith in the master, only selfishness. The fact that his stewardship went so totally in the opposite direction of the master's request evidenced this. There had been no heart-change indicative of a genuine faith. Instead the unfaithful steward seems to represent someone who had associated with the new community without any genuine, heartfelt commitment. To feel no accountability to Jesus in light of his return is evidence of absence of relationship with him. The fruit only indicated what the heart had always lacked.

These texts are difficult. The parable is told from the perspective of how one sees oneself in relationship to Jesus, as an insider, as most of the New Testament warning passages are told. Thus some who appear to be inside the community, but really are not, are addressed as if they were inside, because that is how they would see themselves. Addressing them as outsiders might lead them to ignore the warning, since they would not put themselves in

**Know the Time: Israel Turns Away but Blessing Still Comes
(12:49—14:24)** In this section the tension with Israel continues to
grow, so that by its end the Jewish nation's rejection of Jesus is virtually
inevitable. Warnings, rejected sabbath miracles and prophetic laments
set the tone. Perhaps typical of the unit is 13:31-35, where Jesus issues
a prophetic declaration that Israel's house is now desolate. Its isolation
will remain until it recognizes the Messiah. After this section Jesus' attention will turn to instructing his disciples in light of his approaching
departure. They must be made ready to live in his absence.

Know the Time (12:49-59) In three short passages Jesus characterizes the times. Things are not going to go smoothly. Jesus' ministry will
bring division (vv. 49-53). But anyone who is observant can read the
times and know that God is at work (vv. 54-56). Most important, the
disciples had better settle their spiritual debts with God. A failure to pay
up will mean one will pay every last penny (vv. 57-59). This final remark
sets up the discussion on repentance in 13:1-5. The theme of all these
statements is the need to understand the time that encompasses Jesus'
ministry. He is not one of many options for knowing God; he is the way.

Jesus came to do God's will. In his first statement he shows how ready
he is to get the job done: *"I have come to bring fire on the earth, and
how I wish it were already kindled!"* This is one of several mission
statements Jesus makes ("I have come to . . ."): 5:32; 7:34; Jn 3:2; 5:43;
7:28; 12:27, 47; 16:28; 18:37). The reference to fire appears to suggest
judgment (Lk 3:9, 17; 9:54; 17:29). In the Old Testament fire often refers

that category. Also, an outsider address might cause some who were inside to think they
were out. Usually if someone is concerned about whether he or she is in or out, such
spiritual sensitivity indicates the Spirit's work in the heart and thus a genuine belonging to
the community.

12:47 Some argue that *that servant* in this verse refers back to the servant of verse 46,
so that this verse elaborates on the judgment described there, and this steward is among
the children of God. But it is better to see the parable as going through the possibilities
that exist for any one steward. *That* steward can be faithful, totally unfaithful, disobedient
with knowledge or disobedient with ignorance. The evaluation differs in each of the four
possible cases.

12:49-59 The parallels for this section are less than certain. Matthew 10:34-36 and Mark
10:38 are like Luke 12:49-53. Matthew 16:2-3 is like Luke 12:54-56. Similar to Luke 12:57-
59 is Matthew 5:25-26. But none of the parallels have much verbal overlap; the connections
are more broadly conceptual. This allows the possibility that Jesus' teaching has been
reproduced in various forms from different settings.

to the stinging word that came through the prophets (Jer 5:14; 23:29). Division is clearly the result, as the following verses show. Sometimes the truth is painful and divides.

Jesus speaks of the *baptism* he must face before he can finish his work. This must be a reference to his approaching death (Mk 10:38-39). So Jesus fully anticipates that the opposition forming about him will lead to his death. More specifically, baptism probably alludes to the "inundation of the waters of divine judgment" (Oepke 1964a:538-39; Job 9:28-30; the "floods of persecution," Ps 18:4, 16; Is 8:7-8). So Jesus understands that he will bear the force of judgment, a judgment that will be propelled by persecution and rejection. Luke later will portray Jesus as "accursed" in his death by hanging on a tree (Acts 5:30-31; 10:39-43). God's plan and the Spirit's judging work cannot come until Jesus dies.

The judgment work of separation will split families; it will not bring peace. *"There will be five in one family divided against each other, three against two and two against three."* Fathers and sons, mothers and daughters, mothers-in-laws and daughters-in-law will stand on opposite sides of the divide. Jesus forces choices about what God is doing, and family members will choose differently. The imagery is from Micah 7:6. Jesus' point is simple: "Expect division. Opposition to me is a given."

As Jesus speaks of his ministry, he asks the multitudes to think of a weather forecast. Unlike meteorologists today, who work with satellite images and Doppler radar, the ancients had one weather tool, their eyes. They could predict the weather in Palestine by making a few simple observations. A westerly wind meant that moisture from the Mediterranean was riding in and clouds and rain would follow. Southwesterly breezes meant that heat from the desert was on the way and a rise in temperature could be anticipated. The signs of the times were indicated by the breezes.

Such meteorological expertise is common among the people Jesus addresses. But they cannot tell what breezes are blowing through their lives from Jesus' ministry. Or as Jesus says, *"Hypocrites! You know how to interpret the appearance of earth and sky. How is it you don't know how to interpret this present time?"* The signs of the time are everywhere, and so was spiritual blindness. Not reading this weather correctly is dangerous—more dangerous than missing a hurricane.

Having issued warnings of approaching division and the nature of the times, Jesus calls on the multitudes to make one other judgment. He actually calls for their reflection: *"Why don't you judge for yourselves what is right?"* The picture is a simple one. The judgment in view is a legal, civil dispute, since Jesus mentions settling accounts before a *praktōr* (NIV *officer*), a tax collector and general financial official. In this context the official figure is a sort of bailiff in charge of the debtors' prison (Maurer 1968:642; Rengstorf 1972:539). Jesus' advice is simple: better settle up accounts and avoid prison. In fact, his imagery is graphic, for those who fail to settle accounts and are found guilty will be "dragged away" to prison. The warning of shame is obvious. Jesus closes by assuring them that negligent debtors will certainly have to pay the debt, down to the very last copper coin. The use of the Greek double negative *ou mē* makes his statement emphatic—you will *never* get out without payment. A *lepton* (NIV *penny*) was the smallest coin in circulation, worth only a fraction of a penny. In the ancient world, family members had to pay the full debt before a jailed debtor could be released.

Such a prospect is painful and embarrassing, though of course the comparison is not exact. The point is our accountability before God— at least this interpretation makes the most sense contextually. Jesus is not talking about relationships with other people here but about our relationship with God. Having warned about division and failing to read the sign of the time correctly, he warns of the need to repent. We all have debts before God that need paying. To settle accounts with God, we must come to grips with Jesus. His presence forces choices and brings the potential for division. We need to look at the ledger. Bankruptcy and debtors' prison will be the results of rejecting God. Only Jesus can pay our debt.

Lessons for Israel (13:1-9) The presence of evil in our world is always disturbing. Tragedy surrounds us on every side. Whose fault is it? In the ancient world, unlike the modern, people were slow to attribute evil to the deity's carelessness or noninvolvement. Certainly they believed in evil spiritual forces, but they assumed that tragedy generally reflects God's judgment for sin committed. If tragedy comes, responsibility lies with the person who experiences the tragedy.

This supposition leads Jesus to respond to public comments about a pair of recent Palestinian tragedies, in a passage that is unique to Luke. Jesus takes popular assumptions and turns them into an opportunity for public reflection. Rather than engage in abstract discussion about others, he asks questions about us.

Extrabiblical sources tell us nothing about either of the incidents the crowd raises. The first event involved Pilate: the state had slain some Jews and allowed their blood to be mixed with that of the sacrifices at the temple. We do not know if this was a reaction to an act of rebellion or if it was a pure governmental abuse of power. Only the result is noted. Five candidates for this event have been suggested out of the writings of Josephus, but none of them is an exact fit in timing or detail (*Jewish Wars* 2.1.3 §§8-13; 2.9.2-3 §§169-74; 2.9.4 §§175-77; 13.16.4 §372; *Antiquities* 18.4.1 §§85-87). What these extrabiblical texts do show is that such incidents did occur periodically.

It is hard for us to appreciate how significant this event would have been in Jewish circles. Such an attack in a sacred setting was sure to raise religious passions to a high level. Imagine if someone marched into church and started slaying people as they prayed, as happened recently in South Africa. Or recall the 1994 slaying of Muslims at a mosque in a region Israel controlled. The reaction was emotional and widespread.

In Jesus' time this atrocity may have raised nationalistic questions as well. Did Jesus think Rome was right? Was this a judgment for sin? So Jesus asks, *"Do you think that these Galileans were worse sinners than all the other Galileans because they suffered this way?"* Such a question would be natural to a Jewish mind (Strack and Billerbeck 2:193-97). Often in the Old Testament a tragic event is seen as the product of sin— this was the interpretation of Job's friends.

But before the philosopher-theologians in the crowd can get lost in the various possibilities raised by the question, Jesus personalizes it. *"I tell you, no! But unless you repent, you too will all perish."* There is a more fundamental issue than "them" and "their sin." Mortality is evidence of the presence of sin in our world (Gen 3). More important than the timing or cause of death is this: only repentance can change death from a tragic end into a bridge to a new kind of life (Lk 3:8; 6:24-26; 10:13; 12:58-59; 15:7). The event shows life's fragility. Disaster looms for the unresponsive.

Now some see Jesus' remarks as national in character, in light of verses
6-9; in other words, Jesus is calling for national repentance. But this
seems unlikely, for it requires a very indirect allusion to corporate needs.
It is better to see the individual call in verses 1-5 and the national one
in verses 6-9. The individual reading has continuity with the debtor
imagery of 12:58-59, the general call to repentance through the gospel
and the Jewish view that repentance is a part of the eschaton (*1 Enoch*
98:3, 16; 99:9; 103).

Jesus cites a second event to make the same point. Rather than a
political tragedy, this is a natural catastrophe, something akin to a hurricane or tornado: a tower at Siloam collapsed and eighteen died. Siloam
was the location of a water reservoir for Jerusalem on the south and east
walls of the city (Josephus *Antiquities* 18.3.2 §60; *Jewish Wars* 2.9.4
§175). Here was an event apparently beyond anyone's control. Perhaps
the persons who died were worse sinners, or, as the Greek text puts it,
"worse debtors" (NIV *more guilty*). Maybe natural disasters are different.

Jesus' interpretation is exactly as before. Without repentance all die
similarly. What is imperative is that each person repent.

The passage is significant because Jesus constantly avoids letting the
question get off-track; he keeps people considering their own sinful
state. I am reminded of the standard question that comes up in evangelistic contexts, often to shift the subject: "What about the heathen in
Africa [or some other remote area]?" This abstract question is often
posed to deflect a personal confrontation with our sin and our need for
God. In former days when confronted with such a question, I would wax
eloquent on the evangelistic possibilities or lack of possibilities for those
distant folk in need. Recently, thinking of this Lukan exchange, I have
tended to quickly refocus the question by assuring the listener that God
is perfectly capable of handling the needs of those distant folk, but the
real question for us to discuss is what *we* will do with God and his call
to turn to him.

Also, Jesus is again stressing that the real fact of life we must face is
mortality, not the timing of death. More important than determining
death's cause or timing is dealing with the fact of death and subsequent
judgment. This quickly levels the playing field and calls on each person
to consider where God stands in the equation—or better, where one

stands before him.

Now a parable expands Jesus' point by raising a national dimension. The fig tree is a common scriptural image. Israel is often compared to some botanical plant, especially a vine; vines were plentiful, and their destruction was a sign of judgment (Hunzinger 1971:755-56; 1 Kings 4:25; Ps 80:9-18; Is 5:1-7; Jer 5:17; Hos 2:12; Mic 7:1). The problem is what to do with a tree that uses up scarce nutrients but yields no fruit. Jesus' words are a clear rebuke to Israel. If the nation is at risk of judgment, then so are its individuals. The owner desires to chop the tree down because it has had the necessary time to bear fruit and has failed to do so. The vineyard keeper asks for one more year to fertilize—just a little more time. Perhaps extra care, a little loosening of the soil and fresh nutrients will do the trick. If after a year the tree still hasn't produced fruit, then . . . The conclusion is obvious: judgment draws near unless there is a change. Unless repentance comes to the nation, the national tree will be judged. But God's willingness to hold off shows his patience (2 Pet 3:9).

Jesus tells both individuals and the nation that the clock is ticking. God is watching over his vineyard. If his plant does not bear fruit, he can find other ways to get fruit. The commentary on this passage is Romans 11, where Paul speaks of grafting in new branches. In this passage it is clear that God did not cut away the vine; instead he did radical botanical surgery on it. Romans 11 also makes it clear that God is not yet done with that surgery. One day Israelite branches will be grafted in again (Rom 11:26).

A Sabbath Healing Rejected (13:10-17) The healing of the bent-over woman is not just another miracle. Luke has been silent about miracles since 11:14 and the Beelzebub controversy. He has not included a detailed miracle report since 9:37-43. In the meantime he has called for repentance. This miracle repeats work Jesus did earlier in his ministry (4:31-41; 6:6-11). It is a "mirror" miracle, for it repeats earlier work in the hope that perhaps Jesus' warnings have been heeded. In

---

13:6-9 A vine usually had three years to grow before it was considered ready to bear fruit, so this parable suggests that six fruitless years were already invested in the vine.

13:9 The verse is presented in Greek as a third-class condition, so the parable gives no hint of the outcome within the clause. The only difference in how the options are laid out

addition, the discussion of conflict with Satan is continued in verse 16, as is the theme of God's compassion. In many ways this scene and another like it in 14:1-6 summarize the reaction to Jesus' ministry. Since the account is unique to Luke, we can assume it is particularly important.

Once again Jesus is in a synagogue teaching. This is the last time in Luke that Jesus appears in a synagogue. As he is teaching, a woman possessed by *a spirit for eighteen years* is in the audience. *She was bent over and could not straighten up at all.* The mention of the spirit is important, because the woman's opponent is not merely mortality or the natural process of aging but a spiritual agent. The age of her condition indicates how serious it is. This is not a cramp; it is an ongoing condition. Considered medically, the condition has been interpreted as a type of bone fusion or muscular paralysis (Wilkinson 1977:195-205). Unable to stand, the woman pathetically pictures the crippling effect that evil can have on us.

Jesus takes the initiative—a significant act in a culture that tended to shun women (see discussion of 8:1-3). He shows his authority when he declares, *"Woman, you are set free from your infirmity."* With the laying on of hands, her back is made straight and she praises God. For the first time in almost two decades she can stand up straight. She has been released and is no longer in bondage. Her praise confesses that reality.

Indignant because Jesus had healed on the Sabbath, the synagogue ruler speaks to the crowd. Rather than address Jesus directly, he complains to the people, *"There are six days for work. So come and be healed on those days, not on the Sabbath."* He ignores the liberation of this woman from her pain. He ignores the release of power through Jesus that has allowed this to take place. He gives no indication of compassion or of joy that God has worked.

This is too much, so Jesus responds: *"You hypocrites! Doesn't each of you on the Sabbath untie his ox or donkey from the stall and lead it out*

---

is that the possibility of no fruit is presented in more vivid terms, suggesting by the difference in style the likely outcome.

13:13 Luke mentions the laying on of hands (NIV *put his hands on her*) only here and in 4:40. This action serves to indicate Jesus' compassionate identification with the woman.

to give it water? Then should not this woman, a daughter of Abraham, whom Satan has kept bound for eighteen long years, be set free on the Sabbath day from what bound her?" It is a stinging rebuke, as well as an indication that the leadership has failed to heed any of Jesus' calls to repentance. They have learned no lessons.

Sabbath activity such as Jesus describes was often allowed. The Mishna lists rules allowing cattle to drink, along with the "forty less one" practices that were prohibited on the Sabbath (*m. Šabbat* 7:2; 5:1-4; 15:1-2; *m. 'Erubin* 2:1-4). In contrast, at Qumran such aid was often denied to animals (Cairo Damascus Document 11:13-14). Jesus' point is simple: if animals can receive basic care on the sabbath, how much more human beings, especially a woman of promise, a child of Abraham! In effect, Jesus says, what more appropriate day to release her than the sabbath? What better day to reveal Satan's impotence? The synagogue leader's and Jesus' views could not be more opposed. The great division Jesus predicted is evidenced here.

Luke summarizes by noting that Jesus' opponents were put to shame by his words, at least in the eyes of the people, who *were delighted with all the wonderful things he was doing.* Thus the passage ends by noting the choice people must make about Jesus. Will we side with the leaders or react with the people? Jesus' exercise of power and compassion requires that we choose sides. Do not ignore the sign of the times. Will you choose Jesus or take the view that Jesus acts at the wrong time and in the wrong place?

Two Kingdom Parables (13:18-21) Jesus preaches about the kingdom and illustrates it with parables. Two such parables appear here. What is the kingdom's character? What does it look like? The mustard seed and the leaven help us to grasp how the kingdom operates.

The general Jewish expectation was that the messianic kingdom would be established suddenly and decisively. So the surprise in these parables is the almost subtle initial form that the kingdom takes. Both mustard seed and yeast are very small in the beginning but pro-

---

13:18-21 The parallels for this material are Matthew 13:31-33 and Mark 4:30-32. In the other Gospels this material appears in the midst of the kingdom parable discourse. In this case it seems one tradition is behind all the uses, though Jesus' teaching on such a major

duce something much larger. The kingdom as described in the parables is a presence that begins almost invisibly yet eventually comes to dominate.

It is perhaps fitting the parables are set here after the account of how a woman under the grip of Satan was healed. Once again Luke associates Jesus' healing activity with a picture of the powerful presence of the kingdom. One illustrates the other.

Most of Jesus' parables have a surprise, a twist, that helps to explain their point. The parable of the mustard seed is no exception. The mustard seed's growing to become a tree is surprising, almost unnatural. Here is supernatural, creative growth. Some readers miss the surprise (or complain that the image's unusual nature shows it does not come from Jesus); but the entertaining and instructive "twist" in many of Jesus' parables is a characteristic device that helps to unlock his teaching. The type of tree Jesus is envisioning here is debated. Is it the twenty-five foot *Salvadora persica* or the ten-foot *Sinipis negra?* If the latter, then he is talking about a member of the mustard family. It is not clear which is meant, though the birds in the limbs suggest Old Testament imagery (Ezek 17:22-24) of a large cedarlike tree. The point, either way, is what starts out small will end up big—big enough to make a home for many birds.

The bird imagery is significant. Three Old Testament texts have this image (Ps 104:12 and Dan 4:10-12, along with Ezekiel mentioned above). Daniel's image is interesting: the great tree of the worldly kingdom of Nebuchadnezzar is reduced to a stump by God. But the closest parallel is Ezekiel. Picturing the restoration of Davidic rule, his cedar tree sprouts from a sprig (is the sprig in turn an allusion to Is 11:1-2?). This goes in the exact reverse direction of the Nebuchadnezzar image. In this tree the birds, representing the people of the nations, will dwell in peace. In sum, the kingdom grows in surprising ways but is a place of shelter and calm for those who rest in its branches. God is restoring the work of the house of David, and all the world benefits.

theme would naturally be repeated on many occasions. This explains the variety of Gospel locales for this material.

The parable of the leaven is similar. Yeast slowly permeates bread dough and eventually penetrates it through and through. The woman in this parable is making a huge loaf. Three measures (Greek; NIV *a large amount*) of flour would probably be three seahs, or about fifty pounds. The point of this parable is not so much growth as contrast. What starts out as a pinch of yeast in a huge batch of dough ends up present throughout it. Permeation is inevitable once yeast is introduced. Implied is a growth that is slow, almost invisible, but this is not the point. Be sure of one thing, Jesus says: we may seem like a small movement, but eventually we will permeate the world.

These parables issue a call to trust the way God is developing his program. They also serve as a kind of commentary on the previous healing. Luke's reader can have hope that despite the humble beginnings of this community, the kingdom will come to have a dominating presence and will provide shelter and calm. God's plan is advancing. Opposition, whether human or spiritual, cannot stop its realization in the world. Trees built with earthly hands, like that of Nebuchadnezzar, will become stumps, but the branches of God's kingdom provide shade forever.

The Narrow and Soon Shut Door (13:22-30) The time is short, and the kingdom comes, but how important is it that a decision be made? Jesus' parable of the narrow and soon shut door makes it clear that making a decision, and the right one, is crucial. In Western culture many people believe that there are many ways to God, that the road to heaven is like the interstate highway (or motorway) system—there are many available routes. In contrast, Jesus compares spiritual blessing to entering a banquet room where, once the door is closed, entry is no longer allowed.

After noting that Jesus continues his journey to Jerusalem, Luke turns to a parable that responds to the question *"Lord, are only a few people going to be saved?"* Apparently Jesus' teaching has created the impression that salvation will be restrictive. Again Jesus takes a general theological question and personalizes it.

13:22-30 Despite conceptual parallels with Matthew 7:13-14, 25:10-12, 7:22-23, 8:11-12 and 19:30, this parable is really unique to Luke's Gospel, though it does represent a fusion

Jesus is clear from the start: *"Make every effort to enter through the narrow door."* The verb here, *make every effort,* or better "strive" (NRSV; Greek *agōnizomai*), suggests great labor and struggle in the effort to get through the door. The verb is used in other contexts of an athlete in training (1 Cor 9:25). Our world places many obstacles before us, as does our own pride. Access to God is not a wide-open, take-any-route-you-want affair. He sets the route's ways and means. So *many . . . will try to enter and will not be able to.* Such restrictiveness would not surprise this Jewish audience, since it was already taught that Israel was God's elect nation (*m. Sanhedrin* 10:1; 2 Esdras 7:47; 8:4—9:22). Second Esdras 8:3 reads, "Many are created, but few are saved." The surprise in Jesus' reply is not that access may be limited, but who gains entry.

There will come a time when the householder arises and shuts the door, announcing that the time for filling the room has come to an end. Those on the outside of the closed door will knock, seeking entrance, but it will be denied. The basis of the refusal is the Master's declaration that he does not know those who knock. Earlier, when there had been opportunity to get to know the Lord, those outside had not been interested. So the Lord now says, *"I don't know you or where you come from."* The Lord's denial perplexes those who appeal for entry, since they once had meals in Jesus' presence and listened to his teaching in the streets. But Jesus' reply makes it clear that exposure is not knowledge. Something more than presence is required in coming to know Jesus. So he tells them, *"I don't know you or where you come from. Away from me, all you evildoers!"* Outward contact with Jesus means nothing; inward reception is everything (6:46-49; Jn 1:12). There is no bargaining with the Lord here. The issue is simply, Did you know him?

Rejection means weeping and gnashing of teeth, the pain that comes from knowing one has been excluded from blessing (Mt 8:12; 13:42, 50; 22:13; 24:51; 25:30). Contrary to some popular perceptions of the deity, he can and will say no. Jesus' audience will see *Abraham, Isaac and*

---

of many ideas Jesus taught on other occasions as well, as the Matthean texts indicate.

Jacob and all the prophets in the kingdom of God, but you yourselves thrown out. The parable warns people not to assume they are in the kingdom on the basis of exposure to Jesus or on the basis of elect ethnic origin. The patriarchs of Judaism will be there, but that does not mean every physical descendant of Abraham will. One had better decide for Jesus while the door remains open and there still is time. A responsive heart to Jesus is what God seeks.

In fact, there is another surprise: *people will come from east and west and north and south, and will take their places at the feast in the kingdom of God.* This means that the nations will be blessed at God's table. The blessed of God will come from everywhere. The disciples did not immediately grasp this truth and its implications. The special vision of Acts 10 was needed to reveal how it would work. Even today, though Israel has a special place in God's plan, others are not excluded from blessing. We all have equal access to God's blessing through Jesus (Eph 2:11-22). Even the promise to Abraham stressed how the world would eventually be blessed through the patriarch's seed (Gen 12:1-3). Galatians 3 explains how that promise is realized now in Jesus.

So Jesus closes his parable of warning with a note of eschatological reversal. Expectations are overturned as *there are those who are last who will be first, and first who will be last.* Many will get to the table, including some surprises. All are on the same footing. In today's context the warning of this passage might be that those who are first (who have exposure to Christ through attendance at the church) may turn out to be last (excluded from blessing) if they do not come personally through the door by personally receiving what Jesus offers. Simply put, knowing Jesus is the issue. As John 10:7 puts it, Jesus is the door for the sheep.

But really Jesus has turned the question around. His questioner had asked, "Will the saved be few?" Jesus replies with the question, "Will

---

13:31-35 Verses 31-32 are without parallel, but verses 33-35 are conceptually like Matthew 23:37-39. Those who see only one tradition here debate who has relocated the teaching, with most suggesting Luke is responsible (Marshall 1978:569-70, 573-74; Fitzmyer 1985:1028, 1034). This explanation, though quite possible, is not the only possibility. What Jesus has said about the Jewish nation could be repeated in various relevant settings.

the saved be you?"

Lament for the Nation (13:31-35) Jesus has warned Israel repeatedly of the consequences of rejection. Now with language reminiscent of the Old Testament prophets, he begins to spell out the result of the nation's failure to embrace him. As sand trickles through the hourglass, a warning about Jesus' well-being prompts his expression of concern for the nation's welfare. As occurs frequently in this journey, words addressed to Jesus lead to a challenge of popular perception.

The warning is that Herod wishes to kill Jesus. It is debated whether the warning was sincere or a ruse to get Jesus out of the area. Nothing hints at a ruse. Regardless, Jesus does not fear Herod. He tells the Pharisees who warn him, *"Tell that fox, 'I will drive out demons and heal people today and tomorrow, and on the third day I will reach my goal.'"* By calling Herod a fox Jesus may be saying either how clever Herod is, as in the English idiom, or how destructive he is, more consonant with ancient expression (Neh 4:3; Lam 5:17-18; Ezek 13:4; Darr 1992:240-46 prefers the latter). Contextually an allusion to destructiveness is slightly more likely. Jesus' fate *on the third day* has to do with completing his course with his death. He has nothing to run from.

Jesus knows his fate. Prophets perish in Jerusalem. His ministry will continue until that time has come. If this Gospel were a movie with music in the background, the beat and mood would suggest time's quick and fateful passing. Jesus knows the clock hands are moving toward to midnight and the bell will toll for him. But he will face this as his destiny (note in v. 33 the use of *dei*, "it must be").

But even though Jesus is headed for death, the tragedy is not his. It is Israel's. In a strong prophetic lament, Jesus cries out for the nation and its capital city: *"O Jerusalem, Jerusalem."* Its life story has been to kill and stone the prophets. It has made a pastime of rejecting God's will. Speaking for God and using the first person, Jesus declares how God has

---

Concepts as basic as the nation's fate and the consequences of rejection would likely be repeated. I prefer to assume that the same point is made at different times.

13:32 Note the figurative use of *day* for a period of time in this verse. Jesus lives knowing that his time is short but that he will accomplish God's will in the process.

---

longed *"to gather your children together, as a hen gathers her chicks under her wings."* Here is a tender portrait of God's mothering love. It has been God's desire to love and protect his people. But *you were not willing.* Israel has consistently rejected such gentle care.

So the judgment comes: *your house is left to you desolate.* The language recalls the words of the prophet of exile, Jeremiah (Jer 12:7; 22:5), warning of approaching exile for a disobedient nation. Jesus makes clear later that what awaits the Jewish nation now is a similar judgment at the hands of Rome (Lk 19:41-44). Rather than being under God's shadow and protective wing, they are exposed, empty and at risk. That is what sin and rejection of God's way often bring.

The suffering has a duration. The desolation will last until they say, *"Blessed is he who comes in the name of the Lord."* When they recognize that Jesus has been sent from God, blessing will return. The language of this statement is from Psalm 118:26. The original psalm described the priests' blessing of the worshiping entourage as it approached the temple, probably led by the king. The Jewish people must acknowledge "the one who comes" (Lk 3:15-16; 7:18-19, 22).

Jesus' words appear to hold out hope for the nation's future. In fact, Luke 21:24 and Acts 3:12-26 suggest that the Old Testament hope for Israel has not died. The "time of the Gentiles" does not permanently shut out Israel. As Paul says in Romans 11, branches that were broken off can be grafted back in. But for now Israel is in an exposed condition. And though the warning here is national in scope and points to Israel, the implied application is clear enough: for any of us to live outside of relationship with Christ is to live exposed, desolate in a world of spiritual promise.

Another Sabbath Healing Controversy (14:1-6) In another sabbath setting, Jesus continues to evidence God's presence yet faces the leadership's rejection. Even after all the warnings, Jesus' healings fail to bring a change of heart. Eyes controlled by sin are stubborn in refusing to see and respond to God's hand. The meal setting of this text extends through 14:24. But this is not an ordinary dinner party, nor is the con-

---

14:1-6 This is one of several sabbath incidents in Luke (4:16-30, 31-38; 6:1-5, 6-11; 13:10-17) and the last sabbath healing. The passage itself is unique to Luke.

14:5 There is a small textual problem here. Some manuscripts speak of a donkey rather

versation normal table talk. On the menu is theological and ideological reflection about what God is doing.

As Jesus dines with the Pharisees, the religious leaders are watching him. Luke's noting of this is no idle remark. The phrase used for *carefully watched* means to watch surreptitiously and ominously (*ēsan paratēroumenoi;* Riesenfeld 1972:147), rather as an undercover agent would today. The suspicion is deep, the mood somber. At the meal is a man with dropsy, which means his limbs are swollen with excess body fluids—a condition much discussed in later Judaism and associated with uncleanness and immorality (*Midraš Rabbah Leviticus* 15:2; Strack and Billerbeck 1926:2:203; van der Loos 1965:504-6). Jesus does not shy away from the situation. He asks whether it is *lawful to heal on the Sabbath.*

Having had experience with this predicament, the leaders remain silent. And Jesus heals the man. After sending the man away, Jesus notes, as he did in the healing in 13:10-17, that they would quickly offer aid to a son or even an ox that had fallen in the ditch on the sabbath.

A softer, more lenient version of the sabbath law appears much later in the Talmud (c. A.D. 500), alongside a contrary, harsher opinion (*t. Šabbat* 128b). That source allows exceptions for pulling an animal out of a pit, while the harsh ruling argues that all one can do is place food in the pit for the animal until the sabbath has passed.

The leaders' silence continues. Nothing has been learned; nothing has been confessed. Despite a constant barrage of divine activity, their position has not changed. The passage confirms how strong sin's stubbornness can be. It also shows how even after warnings about judgment and its consequences, God graciously still gives evidence of his presence. His grace still reveals itself, but closed eyes can never see the evidence of God's power. The division between Jesus and religiosity remains, and so does the question of which way we will choose if we want to know God.

On Humility and Generosity (14:7-14) The rising note of opposition does not prevent Jesus from instructing regarding discipleship. Yet

than a son falling in the ditch. The basic point is little altered by the difference, but the weight of external evidence favors the reading *son.*

here too the Pharisees provide a negative, contrasting example. Pride and status are social issues in any culture, and the ancient Jewish culture was no exception. Status brings power, and power often begets pride. Jesus regards this equation as destructive to spiritual health. Jesus' disciples are marked by humility. Both how we operate socially and whom we invite to dinner indicate the type of person we are. Humility means ignoring rank or class. Friends can be made anywhere. The lesson is a hard one, as some of the New Testament epistles show (1 Cor 11:17-22; Phil 2:1-11; Jas 2:1-5; 4:6; 5:1-6). But Jesus' picture parable (v. 7) shows that he regards this attitude as fundamental to discipleship.

Jesus' teaching, though it addresses a discipleship issue, is really a rebuke to many at the dinner table. Luke notes that Jesus speaks because he has noted *how the guests picked the places of honor.* At a big ancient meal, these seats would probably have been those closest to the host. Couches for a meal were usually set in a U, with two to four guests reclining on each couch. The host would sit at the base of the U, with the most honored guests on his left and right. Power and prestige resided closest to "the chair." Seating would have followed the washing of hands for cleansing (Mk 7:3; *m. Berakot* 6—8, especially 8:2).

Jesus notes that there is danger in pursuing seats of honor. He tells the story of a wedding where someone quickly grabs the high seat of honor. But then *a person more distinguished* walks in, and the host asks the one holding the seat of honor to move. So *humiliated,* the presumptuous one must head to the last seat. The description of the move down the social ladder is drawn out in Greek to underline the person's shame (you begin . . . to head for the last seat; NIV *you will have to take the least important place*). It is as if every step hurts.

How much different it is if the guest takes the last seat at the beginning. Then the host will tell that humble one to move up to a higher seat, honoring him before everyone. Jesus uses the term "glory" *(doxa)* to characterize the honor that results. In fact, a principle is in view here: *For everyone who exalts himself will be humbled, and he who humbles himself will be exalted.* This theme of eschatological reversal has Old

14:7-14 The passage is unique to Luke, though its themes are not (Mt 18:4; 23:12; Lk 18:14; Jn 5:29; Jas 4:6; 1 Pet 5:6). The Old Testament roots for this teaching are in Proverbs 25:6-7.

Testament and Jewish roots (Ezek 17:24; Sirach 3:19-23). It is also a significant Lukan theme (1:52-53; 6:21, 25; 10:15; 18:14).

Jesus' point is not that we should connive to receive greater honor. Rather, he is saying that honor is not to be seized; it is awarded. Jesus is not against giving honor to one who deserves it, but he is against the use of power and prestige for self-aggrandizement. God honors the humble, and the highway of humility leads to the gate of heaven. Those who are truly humble persons recognize their desperate need for God, not any right to blessing.

Jesus expands the picture of humility by exhorting his audience to invite to their dinner table the needy and those who cannot repay such kindness. Hospitality should be open to all. So whether at the early meal *(ariston)* or the main evening meal *(deipnon)*, hospitality should be shown not to the rich and famous nor to family members, but to those who cannot repay the favor. In ancient culture, the one who hosted a festive meal would be placed on the invitation list for future meals at the guests' homes. Jesus argues that such "payback" hospitality has no merit. The best hospitality is given, not merely exchanged in a kind of unspoken social contract. If God reaches out to all, then those who seek to honor him should reach out also. So *the poor, crippled, the lame, the blind* should be invited. (This list looks much like the list of Luke 7:22, with a few differences; it is repeated in Luke 14:21.) The poor and the powerless should be welcome. For such hospitality and humility, God promises blessing at the resurrection of the dead. Jesus allows no class mentality.

The Parable of the Great Supper (14:15-24) The third part of the discussion around this very eventful meal involved the telling of a parable. Jesus' rebuking was making some of the guests nervous, so someone at the table pronounced a blessing on those who *will eat at the feast in the kingdom of God.* Surely it will be a great day when eternal fellowship with God comes. No doubt the person who speaks up thinks that all at the table will agree with this blessing. But Jesus takes even this occasion to issue yet another warning through a parable. In

14:15-24 Many see this parable as parallel to Matthew 22:1-14, as well as to *Gospel of Thomas* 64—65. But the numerous differences between the parables (there are at least eight) make this conclusion unlikely (Blomberg 1990:237-39).

effect, he says, "Do not count your chickens before they hatch. And do not count your blessings too early. There will be surprises at God's banquet table."

The parable revolves around a man's invitations to a grand occasion, a *great banquet*. In the ancient world such a meal would have been preceded by invitations, which would have been accepted by those planning to attend, much like our RSVP. The next step was to hear from the host's servant that the meal was ready, which is exactly what happens in verse 17.

But a surprising thing happens on the way to the dinner. Last-second refusals pour in, despite the RSVPs. As the text says, *they all alike began to make excuses.* Jesus notes three in particular.

The first excuse involves the need to check out a recently bought field. Some ancient purchases did require a postpurchase inspection. So the excuse is a culturally natural one, but it also reveals priorities: something else is more important than this celebration.

The second excuse involves the purchase of five oxen. Since most ancient landowners had only one or two oxen, this man is clearly wealthy by ancient standards (Jeremias 1972:176-77). Of course the reaction again reflects priorities.

The third excuse involves a recent marriage and the desire to spend time with the new bride. The Old Testament allowed one to be freed from certain obligations in case of marriage (Deut 20:7; 24:5). But it is hard to see why this would be sufficient reason to keep the man from attending this party, especially since he had already accepted the invitation. Again, he is choosing other priorities.

The servant tells the master of the refusals. The master decides, however, that his party will go on anyway. Nothing is to be delayed. The promised celebration will be held as announced.

The celebration pictures the arrival of salvation in the kingdom's initial phase. There is no delay to the kingdom's arrival associated with Jesus. There are only others who will be invited to come. The cultural imagery and timing control the meaning of the imagery in this text.

So the host, angered but not defeated, sends the servant out into the streets and lanes so the poor, maimed, blind and lame may come. This list recalls Jesus' earlier remarks about who is receptive to his message and shows the spiritual connection in the story. God now will invite all kinds of people to the table, and some who had appeared to be in line for an invitation will miss the meal, by choice: when the time to celebrate arrives, they refuse what is on offer.

The servant reports back, noting that many have come but the room is not yet full. So a second invitation goes out to those on the highways and in the hedges (on "hedges" see Michaelis 1967c:68); thus the invitation is now extended to travelers from outside the city who may not know the host.

It seems that the allusion here is to Gentiles. There is no great temporal break between the invitations, so Jesus is likely foretelling the apostolic mission beginning in Acts 10. Jesus views the current time of his ministry as a celebration, a time when the groom is present (Lk 5:33-39).

He concludes the parable by noting that those who were originally invited will not share in the banquet. At this point the parable becomes a rebuke. The warning is that many in the nation of Israel who were in line for divine blessing and who had responded to an initial invitation to be engaged with God's promise have failed to step forward now that the wedding day has come. The parable obviously pictures Jesus' invitation to experience the blessing of God's kingdom by responding to him.

It is crucial to understand here is that the party goes on despite the reneging of the original invitees. The party is not postponed; others are invited to take their place. Opportunity has been lost by some, grace has been extended to others, but the meal is still served. The question is on which side of the divide Jesus' listeners and Luke's readers fall. God's grace continues, but we can miss blessing if we do not respond to Jesus. Even those who seem to be first in line will miss the party if they refuse to come to the celebration. To use Jesus' words elsewhere, "the first have become last, and the last have become first."

Pure Discipleship (14:25-35) With this very short subunit in the journey section, Jesus' attention turns almost totally to his disciples. The leadership has been warned and rebuked. But what does following Jesus really require? The previous parable had hinted that other issues became higher priorities for the original invitees to God's kingdom. This single unit will make it clear that disciples should count the cost of following Jesus, because success will not come easily.

This passage is unique to Luke, though verses 26-27 are like Matthew 10:37-38 and verses 34-35 are similar to Matthew 5:13 and Mark 9:49-50. It is extremely significant that this passage is addressed to *large crowds.* Jesus offered himself to all, but he also was honest from the very beginning of his preaching about what the journey would involve. What Jesus asks for is first place in one's heart. That is what successful discipleship requires.

So Jesus calls for a follower who will *hate his mother and father, his wife and children, his brothers and sisters—yes, even his own life.* The point of the list is that no other relationship is first for a disciple. "Hate" is used figuratively and suggests a priority of relationship. Jesus is first. To follow Jesus means to follow Jesus, not anyone or anything else. A disciple is a learner, and the primary teacher in life is Jesus. This total loyalty is crucial, given the rejection and persecution that lie ahead. If his followers care more about family than about Jesus, when families are divided under pressure of persecution, they will choose against Jesus. This is what lies behind Jesus' remarks. Discipleship is not possible if Jesus is not the teacher.

This is why bearing the cross and coming after Jesus is *the* issue of discipleship. Learning from Jesus means following him, experiencing the rejection he experienced and so bearing the cross he bore. We cannot "learn Jesus" without being prepared to walk this path. Discipleship is basically allegiance. To follow Jesus is to rely on him. Paul makes the same point in different imagery in Romans 6.

Two pictures illustrate the teaching, though each has a slightly different point. The first picture involves the building of what is probably a watchtower for a vineyard. To be a success, this building program must be planned out carefully; otherwise the builder may well start the project but not finish it. Failure to finish would make the builder a laughingstock to neighbors, as his half-finished shell of a tower casts its incomplete shadow over the land. So Jesus asks what person does not *first sit down and estimate the cost to see if he has enough money to complete it.* How sad it is to start something and not finish it. The failure is evident to all.

Verse 30 expresses the public response in very mocking terms, as all around belittle *"this fellow."* The shell of the building echoes the shell that remains of this man's reputation. The implication is that embarking on discipleship is just the same: we do well to reflect on what it will take to finish what we have started.

The second picture is of a king who finds his forces outnumbered as he considers going to battle. After calculating the cost in terms of destruction, he decides that appealing for peace is a better idea. The king reflects, then acts.

Many readers take this to be a second example of taking stock, just like the first illustration. But there may be something more here. In the case of building the tower, all the options lay with the builder. In the case of potential war, the situation is forced on the king. Only a foolish king would try to take on a stronger foe when he is outnumbered two to one. So it is prudent to seek peace with the stronger foe. There is a "more powerful one" than Satan to deal with in life: God. It is wise to count the cost of facing him. There are benefits in allying ourselves with God rather than having him as the decidedly stronger enemy.

The application Jesus states without apology: *"In the same way, any of you who does not give up everything he has cannot be my disciple."* Jesus must be first. Those who are disposed to oppose God's will should count the cost. Much better sue for peace with God on his terms. His terms for peace are gracious, but disciples must acknowledge that he is the source of life and spiritual well-being.

A final warning closes the exhortation. Salt is good as long as it is salty. If not, it is thrown away. Now salt in the ancient world was used in several ways: as a catalyst for a fire, as seasoning, as a preservative and as fertilizer. In each case the presence of salt facilitated some function. But once salt ceases to perform its role, it is good for nothing. Similarly, the disciple who loses "saltiness" can become useless to God. There are a couple of possible ways to interpret *thrown out* here. It could refer to being rejected for never having been genuine to begin with, like the "odd man out" in many of Jesus' parables (12:46; 19:21-26; Mt 25:20), or it could warn of the physical judgment that comes on those who displease God (1 Cor 11:30). Jesus' remark is ambiguous and may be purposely so to allow for both possibilities. Clearly, however, the warning should be heeded, since Jesus closes his remarks with *"He who has ears to hear, let him hear."*

Discipleship is serious business to Jesus. To be a disciple and complete the task, we must count the cost. It is a good idea to sue for peace and come to terms with God. But that means we must humbly come to him on his terms. Successful discipleship requires that God be first.

Why Pursue Sinners? (15:1-32) This chapter contains three linked parables that explain why Jesus associates with sinners. The linkage is evident in the terms *lost* and *found* (vv. 6, 9, 24, 32) and *rejoice* and *celebrate* (vv. 6, 9, 24, 32; Stein 1992:400). All three parables end with similar statements (vv. 7, 10, 32). The theme of Jesus' association with sinners is key (5:29-32; 7:36-50; 19:1-10). The unit involves a "twin parable" typical of Luke (5:36-39; 14:28-32) followed by an elaborate parable of the type often called an example story (another example story is the parable of the good Samaritan in 10:25-37).

Parables of the Lost Sheep and Coin (15:1-10) These parables introduce the importance of sinners for Jesus, and thus for disciples. The parable's drama is built on the tension of an attempt to find something that has been lost. Anyone who has lost anything or loses anything on a regular basis can identify with this tension. In our house it is keys and the remote control for the television that most often go AWOL. At such times an all-points bulletin sends my children on a hunt for what their absent-minded father has misplaced. When it is found, all are relieved. So in these parables with the sheep and the coin.

Jesus tells these parables to tax collectors and sinners. Thus the stories offer comfort, especially in the face of the Pharisees and scribes' grumbling that Jesus *welcomes sinners and eats with them* (compare 5:30, 37; 7:34, 39). The fact that tax collectors and sinners listen to Jesus while the leadership does not is a cultural reversal of expectation. Sometimes hearers are found in surprising places. The issue of listening to Jesus is a major one in Luke (5:1, 15; 6:17, 27, 47, 49; 7:29; 8:8-18, 21; 9:35; 10:16,

Notes: 15:1-32 There is a story similar to the parable of the lost sheep in Matthew 18:12-13, but the lost coin and the prodigal son are unique to Luke. This leads to discussion of the connection. Some argue that the linked parables give evidence of being pre-Lukan. Nolland (1993:769) posits all kinds of specific Lukan editorial work in these parables. But

24, 39; 11:28, 31; L. T. Johnson 1991:235). To experience God's blessing, we need to listen to him.

Jesus begins with a pastoral scene that would have been familiar in Palestine. A shepherd had a hundred sheep—a count that would indicate he is modestly wealthy, since the average flock ranged from twenty to two hundred head (Jeremias 1972:133). Such flocks were an economic resource, since they provided wool and mutton. During the count as he gathers the sheep at day's end, the shepherd notices that one is missing. Jesus' original hearers probably assumed that the shepherd asks a neighbor to keep an eye on the ninety-nine so he can search for the missing sheep, though the story does not offer this detail. The sheep needs to be found; otherwise it may be permanently lost or attacked by hungry predators. It is risky to be a lost sheep.

The search proves fruitful: the shepherd finds the sheep and lifts it onto his shoulder to bring it home. (Compare Is 40:11; 49:22. Shepherd imagery in the Old Testament is rich—see Ps 23; Jer 31:10-14; especially Ezek 34:11-16; Mic 5:1-4; in the New Testament see Jn 10:11-12.) Given the possibility that the sheep could have been devoured, the shepherd rejoices at finding it.

The parable pictures God's desire to find sinners and bring them back into the fold. Thus the owner throws a party, asking his neighbors to celebrate with him since the lost sheep is found. In the same way, Jesus says, *there will be more rejoicing in heaven over one sinner who repents than over ninety-nine righteous persons who do not need to repent.* When a sinner turns to God, heaven throws a party. The prospect of such joy keeps Jesus associating with sinners.

The second parable parallels the first. Here a silver coin has been lost. It sounds as if the coin is a drachma, which equals a denarius—a day's wage for the average worker (Josephus *Antiquities* 3.8.2 §195). As with many things that are dropped and lost, the search begins with the certainty that "it must be in here somewhere." The search is likely to be taking place in the evening, since the woman must light a lamp to look

others argue that there is no way to sort out these details (L. T. Johnson 1991:239). I agree with this latter approach and wonder whether in fact Luke had an independent version of this one parable. For this reason I question whether one should even debate whether Luke or Matthew has the parable's original setting.

for the coin. She sweeps the house clean, looking carefully, until it turns up. We can almost hear her "there it is!" relief as the search ends successfully. Like the shepherd, this woman calls her friends together to celebrate the discovery of the lost coin. So *there is rejoicing in the presence of the angels of God over one sinner who repents.* The reference to angels is a circumlocution for God's joy. The courts of heaven are full of praise when a sinner turns to God.

Is there any significant difference between the two parables? At their most basic level they make the same point. The second parable, however, stresses the search a little more than the first. Recovering a lost sinner can take diligent effort. But the effort is worth it when the lost is found. Sinners should know that God is diligently looking for them. Disciples should diligently engage in the search for sinners on behalf of the Master they serve. Jesus provides a clear example for us to follow. Finding lost "sheep" and missing "coins" is a disciple's priority. Jesus involved himself with sinners; so should disciples.

Parable of the Forgiving Father (15:11-32) The third parable of Luke 15 is a more elaborate treatment of the seeking-of-sinners theme. The parable's popular title "prodigal son" probably puts the focus in the wrong place. Actually the story gives more attention to the father and his reaction than to the son's return. The father's response to the elder son's resentment also shows how central a character he is in the parable. So a better title might be "the parable of the forgiving father" or "the parable of a father's response to his two sons."

The parable is unique to Luke and is almost allegorical. The father pictures God. The prodigal symbolizes the lost, especially the tax collectors and sinners of verse 1. The elder brother represents the self-righteous leadership, the Pharisees and scribes of verse 1 or anyone else who claims to serve God and yet is harsh toward the possibility of forgiveness for sinners. The situation described is not all that unusual, as shown by a short letter from a man named Antonios Longus to his mother, Neilus (Preisigke 1922:72-73): "I am writing to tell you I am naked. I plead with you, forgive me. I know well enough what I have done to myself. I have learned my lesson." These sentiments parallel those of the prodigal on his return. Because of the basic nature of parent-child relationships, as well as sibling rivalry, the story has a human poignancy that makes it one of the most touching of all of Jesus' parables. The major issue is repentance before God and God's willingness to forgive. The parable is Jesus' final defense of the offer of good news in the face of official criticism of his association with sinners.

The parable opens with the younger son's request to have his *share of the estate*. Since the boy is still single, he is probably in his late teens. The Greek term for the inheritance is suggestive, "the life" *(ton bion)*. He wants his portion of what his father's life will leave him. In a Jewish context the younger brother would receive half of what his elder brother received (Deut 21:17). In Jewish thinking a father should not divide the estate too early. Sirach 33:19-23 begins, "To son or wife, to brother or friend, give no power over yourself while you live; and give not your goods to another so as to ask for them again." Nevertheless, in this parable the father grants the son's request. It pictures God letting a sinner go his own way.

Having divided the living or the *property* (NIV) between the two sons, the father watches the younger son depart. On his own, the son loses everything *in wild living*. No other details are given. In fact, the text says he scatters *(diaskorpizō)* his resources: he *squandered* his inheritance and throws his money away. Following his financial failure comes natural disaster. Famine strikes the land, and he is in need. Finding a job, he ends up feeding swine, a job of great dishonor for a Jew (Lev 11:7; Deut 14:8; Is 65:4; 66:17; 1 Maccabees 1:47; Jeremias 1972:129). Now as a Jew working for a Gentile and caring for swine, he can sink no lower. It is clear that he has taken whatever job he can get.

Though employed, he still suffers. *He longed to fill his stomach with the pods that the pigs were eating.* These pods were either sweet beans from a carob or locust tree or else bitter berries. No one has anything to offer him. Even unclean animals are better off than he is. Here is the lostness of the sinner.

The son reflects on his condition and realizes that his father's servants have it far better. Thus the sinner discovers his desperate situation because of sin. To be outside of God's family is to be utterly alone.

The son devises a plan of action. He will confess his sin before his father: *"Father, I have sinned against heaven and against you. I am no longer worthy to be called your son; make me like one of your hired men."* This expresses the humility of one who turns to the Father.

Sinners have nothing to rely on except the Father's mercy. They recognize that they have failed and can claim no blessing.

So the son comes home. The father's reaction is telling: *But while he was still a long way off, his father saw him and was filled with compassion for him; he ran to his son, threw his arms around him and kissed him.* The action breaks all Middle Eastern protocol; no father would greet a rebellious son this way (Jeremias 1972:130). But as is often the case in Jesus' parables, the twist in the story makes the point. Literally, the father drapes himself on his son's neck (v. 20, *epepesen epi ton trachēlon*). He is pleased and thrilled to see his prodigal return.

The son proceeds with his confession, but the father interrupts. The son is satisfied to be a slave, but the father will restore him to full sonship. So the father orders the servants to bring the *best robe, a ring* for the son's hand and *sandals* for his feet. A *fattened calf* is prepared, and a party will be held. Fatted calves were saved for special occasions like the Day of Atonement. This is not just any party; it is a rare and complete celebration. There will be rejoicing for the lost son, now found (vv. 7, 10).

The note of joy about the son's return is crucial in the passage, as is the father's restoration of sonship privileges. The son has come from destitution to complete restoration. That is what God's grace does for a penitent sinner.

The elder son has been laboring in the field, so he has missed all the action. Returning home, he hears the commotion of *music and dancing.* In fact, the word used for "music" is the Greek term from which we get our word "symphony"; but in ancient Greek *symphōnia* was a broad term for music or singing. There is a real celebration going on. One of the servants explains to the older brother what is taking place. The servant gives an accurate summation: celebration and a fatted calf for a returned brother who is safe and sound.

Enraged, the elder brother does not go in to join the festivities. Here is one of the parable's great ironies, made graphic by Jesus' use of literary space. The brother who had been on the outside is now on the inside, while the brother who had been on the inside is now on the outside. Again Jesus' words echo, "The last has become first, and the first has become last." The repetition of this theme shows how important it is not to be in the wrong place in the line!

The father's compassion does not cease. He comes out to the angry brother and tries to calm him down. The elder brother pleads his faithfulness despite the lack of celebration for him at any time in the past. Not even a "kid" has been butchered for him. (The contrast he draws is as if steak were now served for the returning son while a fast-food meal has never been served for him.) The elder makes a serious complaint— "I am worthy," he pleads; "you are ungrateful. This is unfair!" What parent has not heard such a complaint from one child about another? The elder's problem is his self-righteous, self-directed focus. There is no joy that his brother has come home. The elder is too self-consumed with issues of justice and equity to be caught up in the joy. (The scene recalls the synagogue leader's complaint that someone had been healed on the sabbath.)

Other things are more important to this elder brother than showing forgiveness and compassion. His anger is so great that he refers to his own brother as *"this son of yours."* He speculates that the brother has wasted his money on harlots. As far as the elder brother is concerned, there is nothing to praise here.

The father has a ready reply aimed toward reconciliation between the brothers. He accepts his elder son and acknowledges that all the father has belongs to him. There is no reason for jealousy. In a sense the elder son has always had access to celebration: the animals are his! But there is one other fact. The father says, *"We had to celebrate and be glad, because this brother of yours was dead and is alive again; he was lost and is found."* Note the reminder that the returning son is a brother. Justice means that the son should be received back with joy and celebration. The focus should be outward, on the transformation that has occurred. The sinner should be welcomed back into God's family with joy.

The parable has two major points. First, repentance means an absolute reversal of status. The lost son has become a family member again. The father's acceptance of the penitent son is total. This is God's grace. This is why God pursues sinners. Second, others should have joy when the penitent returns. Reconciliation involves not only God and the individual but also the individual and the community.

The story is left hanging. The elder brother is left to contemplate the father's words. We do not know if he comes in to celebrate or not. In literary terms, this is an open ending. What will he do? Jesus' listeners are to contemplate their own response as well. The parable is truly a story of reversal. It is hope of such a reversal that causes Jesus to seek the sinner. The potential of God's grace drives him to love others and actively pursue them.

Generosity: Handling Money and Possessions (16:1-31) The use of wealth is the major topic of Luke 16. Wealth can be a blessing or a curse, depending on whether it is used as a means to exercise power, a tool of self-indulgence or a resource to serve others. Wealth's danger is that it can turn our focus toward our own enjoyment, as the rich fool showed in 12:13-21 and as the rich man of 16:19-31 will show. Money is a tool. It is an excellent resource when put to the right use. It can help to build many things of use to others. But to possess money is also to hold a sacred stewardship. Our resources are not to be privately held and consumed but are to be used as a means of generosity, as a way of showing care for our neighbor, as the good Samaritan showed in 10:25-37 and as a restored Zacchaeus will show in 19:1-10.

Two parables unique to Luke make this twofold point about wealth. Between the two parables comes a short description of the two periods in God's plan, with Jesus' declaration that the new era demands faithfulness in our commitment to others, just like the commitment a spouse makes in marriage.

The Parable of the Shrewd Steward (16:1-13) This story is probably the most difficult parable in Luke. Its point is clear enough—be generous and responsible with your resources—but how it makes the point is much discussed. The parable centers on a steward who is *accused of wasting* the master's goods. The description of the steward's activity is like that of the prodigal son in the previous parable (15:13). He has been scattering *(diaskorpizō)* his master's resources. Such mis-

---

Notes: 16:1-13 This parable is unique to Luke, but verse 13 is like Matthew 6:24 and verses 10-12 are conceptually similar to Matthew 25:20-30 and Luke 19:17-26.

16:3 The type of labor the steward wishes to avoid was viewed as shameful in Judaism (Sirach 29:22; 40:28). Even more shameful would be to beg on the streets, probably from those he had previously served as bill collector!

16:5-6 The bills here are large and suggest major operations by the master. The oil bill reflects a yield of 875 gallons, since a bath is 8¾ gallons or about 40 liters. It is the yield

management requires a response.

The characterization of the steward's activity is crucial, because some distinguish between what is said here about the steward's ineptitude from what is said about his dishonesty in verse 8 (Stein 1992:412). If such a distinction is made, then the steward's actions in verses 5-7 are seen as dishonest. On the other hand, others argue that the "wasting" itself in verse 1 involved outright dishonesty. As Nolland (1993:797) suggests, "It is tempting to think of the steward as siphoning off funds for his own consumption from transactions made in the name of the master." The need to choose between these two options is what makes the parable so difficult, since either can be easily defended as fitting the story's framework. Though for reasons I make clear below I prefer the latter option—that the steward's dishonesty led to his dismissal—it must be acknowledged that either understanding may be right.

In any case, the steward's reputation leads to his dismissal. The master calls for an accounting, but it is not to see if the charges are true. For with the accounting comes the steward's pink slip—he is fired. His accounting will be his last task for this master. Facing unemployment and having no marketable skills beyond being a steward, he is in a dilemma, since he does not wish to beg or resort to demeaning physical labor. He decides on a course of action that will bring him into his neighbors' good graces.

The steward introduces a high deflationary trend in his master's bills. The cultural background to the 50 percent reduction in the oil bill and the 20 percent reduction in the wheat bill has been much discussed. What exactly does the steward do? Three options are often suggested: (1) The steward wields his authority as steward and simply lowers the price. This act would undercut his boss by showing what a shark he is. (2) The steward removes the interest charge from the debt, following Mosaic law (Ex 22:25; Lev 25:35-37; Deut 15:7-8; 23:20-21). The differing

of 146 olive trees. The oil would cost 1,000 denarii, or about five years' salary for an average laborer. The wheat debt was 1,100 bushels or 3,930 liters. This debt was 2,500-3,000 denarii, or twelve to fifteen years' salary for an average laborer. Of course those saddled with such bills would probably not be average wage-earners, but still the amounts are large. The reductions would be significant. By the way, these rates fit ancient standards, at least as regards the grain (Derrett 1970:66-68).

rates of reduction seem to be against this view, however, unless different materials carried different interest rates. (3) The steward removes his own commission, so what he sacrifices is his own money, not that of his master (Derrett 1970:48-77). Differing rates are less of a problem here. The commission might well have varied depending on the item sold.

The first position, that the steward simply unilaterally lowers prices, is the traditional view. The argument is that the master later praises the steward for his shrewdness as well as recognizing his dishonesty. By exposing the master, he creates goodwill for himself. This view argues that the first sentence of verse 8 is about the actions of verses 5-7, not verse 1. The view tends to be argued with a challenge to the third view, the commission option.

There are several main arguments against the commission view (Stein 1992:412; Ireland 1992:79-83). I will note these objections and then reply, since I believe the commission view is slightly more likely than the other options.

1. Some complain that the commission view reads a subdivision of charges into the text. But Derrett's work on first-century commissions shows cultural background that may be assumed without being stated explicitly. Such a reading of cultural background is common (Keener 1993: introduction). Today I could tell a story of the purchase of a house without mentioning the relationships among my bank, the mortgage company and various insurance companies involved in the loan. Often such cultural details are assumed in Scripture as they are today and are not stated for an audience.

2. Some question how the manager is really helped by acknowledging the size of the steward's commission. It is argued that it would have been better to keep the favor of the debtors and master by not revealing the master's share of the profits. But the steward does not need to reveal that the reduction represents his commission. The debtors may not know that it is. He appears to portray his reductions as acts of kindness. For the debtors, the reductions must create a favorable impression of both him and the master, just as today businesses earn our loyalty by offering us "good deals." What is harder to believe is that the master would commend the steward if the steward has really cheated him.

3. Some argue that verse 5 indicates only that the master is receiving

the money. This objection is really a variation on the other two and ignores the fact that the steward may not have publicized the source of the cut. In fact, this action would preserve the master's integrity (though it would pressure him to keep prices down in the future) as well as give the debtors good feelings about him. The shrewdness is in the "sweet" twist in the deal.

4. Some argue that verse 8 describes the steward as dishonest only after the actions of verses 5-7. This is more assumed than proved. It is not a harsh reading to take the description of dishonesty back to verse 1, as was noted above.

I favor the commission view because I find it hardly credible for the master to commend a steward who has just cheated him. If the reductions are dishonest price cuts, they constitute further injustice against the master beyond the steward's earlier squandering. If so, the master now has two charges against the steward: ineptitude followed by dishonesty. The traditional view hardly allows the steward to gain credibility and respect. Another problem is that Jesus himself praises the steward's actions in his subsequent remarks. Would he really commend such immoral behavior?

It is better to see that the previously dishonest steward learns something by his failure and comes up with a generous solution, one that can be commended. In my view, the master commends his formerly dishonest steward for a shrewd solution. The steward has sacrificed what he could have taken now and has given it to others so that he can receive gain later. The implicit moral about perspective in the use of resources is exactly the application Jesus makes in verse 9.

Jesus' applications extend in various directions. First he notes that people of the world are more shrewd than *the people of the light* (the disciples) are. People of this world think about how they use their resources. Even if they misuse them, they still give it thought. They think about the long-term benefits of what they acquire. Disciples should apply themselves to honor and serve God by their use of resources. They should think through their actions, both short and long term.

To this Jesus adds three further applications in verses 9-13. We should use resources generously *"so that when it is gone, you will be welcomed into eternal dwellings."* What "welcoming committee" is Jesus referring to? Some argue that "they" may be the poor who receive the benefits of disciples' stewardship, while others argue that they are either angels representing God or God himself (as a plural of majesty). Since the context has to do with present actions that are taken in light of the future, it is best to see a reference either to angels or to God here. *Eternal dwellings* has to do with entering into heaven (Michaelis 1971:378-79).

Money cannot come with us to heaven. Its value is limited when it comes to everlasting life. So recognize its limits and use it for others, not selfishly. To *gain friends* by means of mammon is to use money in such a way that others appreciate you for your exercise of stewardship, your kindness and generosity.

Jesus calls mammon "unrighteous." The NIV is too soft here, calling it simply *worldly wealth* (NRSV has "dishonest wealth," which is not quite right either). Mammon is called unrighteous not because it is inherently evil but because of the unrighteous attitudes the pursuit of money can produce. If money were inherently unrighteous, then all uses of it would be evil. But that is not Jesus' view (see 19:1-10). The attitude reflected here may be similar to that of 1 Timothy 6:10, where Paul says that the love of money is the root of all evil. Money is evil because of how it brings out distorted values in people. Pursuing money can make people selfish, leading them to take advantage of others, to treat other people as objects and to be unfaithful to God. It tends to reflect an excessive attachment to the world. So it is better not to be attached to the pursuit of wealth.

Possessions are a responsibility. Their use is a test of character, values and stewardship. The one who is faithful in little is also faithful in much. So also the other way around—to be dishonest in little things is to be dishonest in much. Faithfulness with the "little thing" of money indicates how faithful we are with the big things, the *true riches* of our relationships to God and to others. So if we *have not been trustworthy* in handling possessions that produce unrighteousness, who will trust us with

---

16:9 "Mammon" *(worldly wealth)* is the Aramaic term for wealth or possessions (Hauck 1967:389-90).

16:14-18 This composite of sayings has different points of contact within the Synoptics. Verses 14-15 are unique to Luke. Verses 16-17 are like Matthew 11:12-13, though Matthew lays out the elements in reverse order, and the statement about heaven and earth passing

true riches? The true riches in this passage seem to involve future kingdom service—that is, service for God and to others. True wealth is faithfulness in serving him.

The theme of responsibility continues as Jesus raises the question
about being faithful with something that belongs to another so that later
one can receive reward for oneself. If someone is unfaithful as a steward,
why should that person be entrusted with ownership? Handling wealth
is a preparatory lesson for other responsibilities before God.

So Jesus warns that we cannot have two masters. In the end, when
push comes to shove, we will choose to serve God or mammon, to love
one and hate the other. The implication is that we had best make the
choice early. Choose God over mammon.

Responses to the Pharisees' Scoffing (16:14-18) This brief inter-
lude is among the more perplexing passages in the book of Luke. It
comes between two passages that are clearly about wealth and possessions. Luke introduces it by noting that the Pharisees scoffed at Jesus'
teaching because they *loved money*. Yet though Jesus proceeds to rebuke
the Pharisees, he does not mention money directly at all. On the surface
the unit is so disjunctive that many interpreters despair of trying to
ascertain where it fits in the chapter's literary argument.

But one approach is likely to explain the connection. The issue Jesus
raises in this middle section has to do with values and Jesus' authority.
Coming under the authority of God's kingdom influences disciples'
values (Tiede 1988:285-88). Kingdom causes call us to renounce divided
loyalties (vv. 10-13), to have idolatries revealed, since God hates them
(vv. 14-15) and to raise standards of obedience to reflect total integrity
(v. 18). Verses 16-17 make up the hinge, suggesting that the kingdom's
arrival means that Jesus' preaching comes with authority. His way will
fulfill what the law and the promise anticipated. The passage ends up
being yet another rebuke of the Pharisees. Their way is not the way to
God. It is kingdom preaching that transforms people, not the way of

---

away appears in Matthew 5:18. Verse 18 has parallels in Matthew 5:32 and 19:9 and Mark
10:11, though the Matthean texts mention exceptions for divorce that Mark and Luke lack.
These variations at several points, along with the independent character of the rest of Luke
16, suggest that this section came to Luke independently of the similar sayings in the other
Gospels.

these leaders.

So the Pharisees are *sneering* at Jesus' call to be generous and responsible stewards of the resources God gives. The Greek word for sneer, *ekmyktērizō,* is particularly graphic. It means "to turn one's nose up" at someone (Preisker 1967b:796-99; Lk 23:35). They thoroughly reject Jesus' teaching. The Pharisee's consistent attitude toward Jesus' teaching reveals hard hearts dead set against him. There is no attempt to hear him; there is only contempt.

The official approach does not impress Jesus. They seek *to justify* themselves *in the eyes of men.* But God knows their hearts. It is what God thinks that counts. Accountability before the divine is more important than the world's opinion. What human beings value is an abomination before God. The term "abomination" *(bdelygma)* is strong (Foerster 1964a:600). An abomination is the opposite of an acceptable offering before God. In other words, their values stink and are rejected as repugnant by God. The NIV rendering *is detestable in God's sight* is on the mark. God hates their loving attitude toward money. Similar complaints from Jesus are recorded in 11:39-41 and 18:9-14.

Jesus turns his attention to getting the right perspective on these events. The new era means that the Pharisees do not have an exclusive claim on God's will: *The Law and the Prophets were proclaimed until John. Since that time, the good news of the kingdom of God is being preached.* Here are the two basic eras as far as Luke is concerned. There is the era of promise and the era of preaching of the good news of fulfillment. The dividing line is John. He prepared a people (1:15-17), and now the new era is being preached. Jesus' arrival means the new era's arrival. The way of God is found in his kingdom preaching. Thus it is not the Pharisees' scoffing that carries authority, but Jesus' exhortations about how to walk with God.

But Jesus says more. He notes that "all are urged insistently to enter in." This translation is somewhat unusual and needs defending (for this approach, Fitzmyer 1985:1117-18). Most versions read *everyone is forcing his way into it* (NIV; NRSV has the variation "everyone tries to enter it by force"), but such a statement is manifestly not true. Everyone is not in a rush to enter in; many choose to reject the kingdom utterly. The key here is the Greek term *biazō,* which means "to apply force." But the voice of the verb is ambiguous in Greek. Is it middle, so the force is applied *by* everyone? Or is it passive, so force is applied *to* everyone— and if so, in what sense? I would argue that the term is passive and thus that Jesus is speaking of the persuasion applied to all through preaching (for details, Cortés and Gatti 1987:247-59). The preaching of the good news offers the opportunity to enter into kingdom benefits. Through this message all are urged to enter in. The time of fulfillment has come, and all are asked to share in its blessing. But to do so one must hear Jesus, not scoff at his authority.

Then Jesus sets the remark in a larger context. Nothing about the law will pass away. What does this mean? In the context of law and promise, it must mean that it is the kingdom program that realizes the law. Authority is associated with that program (Banks 1975:214-15). The goal of the law is Jesus. Through him its promise is realized. The verse must be read contextually.

The term *law* in Luke-Acts has various functions depending on the context of its use. In fact, to consider Luke's view of the law is to take up a question that surfaces again and again in the New Testament (for views on New Testament handling of the law, see Bahnsen et al. 1993). In Luke three themes dominate. First, in terms of relating to God and to others, the law instructs and gives moral guidance (16:27-31). Second, when law is considered in terms of promise, as in this passage, it stands fulfilled in Jesus. Third, law has passed away when it is considered as individual laws or what the Jews would call "halakoth," practices that identify a person as Jewish as opposed to Gentile. Rites like circumcision and concern about clean foods are no longer necessary (Acts 10—11, 15). These three senses summarize how Luke sees the law; each time the term appears, the reader should examine the context to see which force is being applied (Blomberg 1984).

Jesus' point in 16:16-17 is that the kingdom's arrival represents the culmination of the law's function. Values and morals are determined by the kingdom's presence. Jesus' preaching and teaching are part of the kingdom program and thus reflect God's will. The Pharisees' responses, including their scoffing, do not lead one to God.

But this administrative move from law to kingdom does not mean that commitments are to be ignored. An example of Jesus' authoritative teaching is the handling of the divorce issue. Jesus lays out the standard that marriage is to remain intact. It is a commitment made before God. To break it is to set up adultery, since remarriage is likely to follow. This saying in Luke is not designed to be a detailed presentation of Jesus' view of divorce; it merely sets out the most basic standard as an illustration of the moral tone Jesus desires. More complete biblical statements on divorce come in Deuteronomy 24:1-4, Malachi 2:16, Matthew 5:30-32, 19:1-12, Mark 10:1-12 and 1 Corinthians 7:8-16. Jesus' point here is that he sees the marriage commitment as intended to be permanent. The theological basis is the recognition that marriage involves a vow before God as God forms the couple into one flesh, a point made clear in Matthew 19 and Mark 10. Jesus' pronouncement illustrates his authority. The way of righteousness sees divorce as wrong, because to divorce is to break a promise made before God and is to deny what God does in making a couple one flesh. Kingdom values honor commitments made to others before God. In the kingdom integrity and faithful devotion to God are the essence of character.

Parable of the Rich Man and Lazarus (16:19-31) After a brief note about kingdom values, Jesus turns back to the use of resources. Raising a negative example, he discusses kingdom ethics and values in caring for others. God's concern for people also becomes evident. The disciple is to be giving and outward in orientation, as the rich man painfully discovers through his failure. As Jesus shows, wealth is not always what it is assumed to be.

Donald Trump, Aristotle Onassis, J. P. Morgan and John D. Rockefeller

---

16:18 A full discussion of divorce and remarriage is beyond the scope of this commentary, since it involves a discussion of the verses noted above. Matthew's exception clauses prompt all the debate. House 1990 surveys a variety of views, from no divorce or remarriage to remarriage in the context of God's forgiveness. For a defense of divorce in the case of adultery or unbeliever desertion without the right to remarry, see Heth and Wenham 1984. For the view that remarriage is permitted in various situations, see Keener 1991. For my own view argued in more detail, see Bock 1995 on 16:18. In my view, divorce is permitted on biblical grounds in the case of immorality or unbeliever desertion. Though with less certainty, I believe that remarriage is permitted for the nonoffending party in those two exceptional cases.

16:19-31 This account is unique to Luke. Some even debate whether it is a parable, seeing it as a real event (Gooding 1987:227). The arguments for an event include (1) no parable or comparison language like that which normally introduces a parable, (2) the naming of a character, which is unprecedented for parables, and (3) the fact that a specific, one-time

are among the extremely rich figures of history. Every generation has its very wealthy, those who live high. American culture calls this "the good life," "success," "making it," "reaching the top" or "living in the pent-house." In short, the very rich person "has arrived." For many, wealth is the essence of life. It means self-sufficiency, independence and plenty of opportunity to enjoy material pleasures. Though few people attain such wealth, many strive for it.

The parable of the rich man and Lazarus is not really about money. It is about much more than the dollar, yen, mark or pound. There may not be many Donald Trumps in the world, but appeals to greed and the desire for self-indulgence abound, especially in advertising. Jesus wants disciples to see the great spiritual danger in that path.

The account is an example story, not a parable. It pictures reality through a two-character story that mirrors life. "The rich man" is never named. He is nameless because he represents the danger of wealth. He could be anyone. The name of the second character, Lazarus, is derived from Eleazar, which means "God helps." He is the only named character in any of Jesus' example stories or parables.

Two people and two contrasting sets of life circumstances drive this story. On the surface the rich man has all the cards and all life's blessings, while Lazarus has nothing. The rich man is "in" with style, while Lazarus is definitely "out." But often the way we read circumstances and the way God does are not the same.

The contrast is set up from the opening of the account. The rich man is finely clothed and eats well. Fresh linen and clothes of *purple* dye

---

event is in view, rather than a repeatable event as is often the case in parables. But replies to these arguments exist (Blomberg 1990:205). Parables often open with reference to "a certain man" (NIV *a rich man;* compare Lk 10:30). The story has a three-point structure like other parables (compare 14:16). Parables can lack introductions (Mk 12:1; Lk 15:11). Lin-nemann (1966:4-5) calls the account "an example story," which is probably the best name for it. It is like the parables of the rich fool and good Samaritan in recounting a single event that reveals a lesson.

The parable's second feature is its discussion of the afterlife. Since it is an example story, some of these features are no doubt literary. To see literary elements does not mean, however, that we should deny the existence of the afterlife or a place like Hades. However, the conversation related should be seen as a literary device to make the story's point. If a *great chasm* indeed exists between the blessed and condemned (v. 26), then could the rich man actually engage Abraham in conversation? Also, the man's torment by *fire* may be simply symbolic of horribly painful torment.

indicate his wealth, as do his daily feasts inside his mansion with its own gate. Clothes of purple dye (derived from a snail) were very expensive (Strack and Billerbeck 1926:2:20). *Linen* may allude to expensive undergarments; the two terms together suggest a "power dresser" (Fitzmyer 1985:1130-31). This man lives like a king (Prov 31:22; 1 Maccabees 8:14; 1QapGen 20:31).

While some people eat heartily and can afford expensive underwear, others have nothing. So we meet Lazarus. He is very poor and probably crippled, since he lies down at the gate. If he is not crippled, he is very sick. He is looking for food. Even crumbs will do. His hope of sustenance is alms, the offerings of those who have something. His skin is a snack to lick for the wild *dogs* that roam the streets. These dogs were considered unclean, because it was likely that they had previously licked animal corpses. The image is purposefully gruesome: they lick *his sores* and render him unclean (see 1 Kings 14:11; 16:4; 21:19, 23-24; 22:38; *1 Enoch* 89:42-43, 47, 49, on dogs as a negative figure of those that devour; Michel 1965b:1103; Danker 1988:283). Lazarus wears his poverty's pain on his ulcerated skin—a graphic contrast to the rich man's soft clothes. If the panhandlers of our cities' streets look bad, Lazarus would serve as a worthy ancestor. Later rabbis would have seen Lazarus's life as no life at all, since they had a saying that three situations resulted in no life: depending on food from another, being ruled by one's wife and having a body covered with sores (*t. Beṣa [=Yom Ṭob]* 32b). According to this saying, Lazarus is doubly deprived.

The story's initial impression is clear: the rich man has a great life, while the poor man does not. The rich man throws away food; the poor man must scrounge for it. Some people have nothing, while others have expensive underwear. Observing this scene, we might well conclude that God has blessed the rich man, while the poor man must be the object of God's judgment. Lazarus must be lazy or sinful, paying for his depravity with his destitution. But the parable will show that appearances can be deceiving. Jesus' parables often come with a twist.

In this parable Lazarus never speaks. His situation is so pathetic that no one would likely hear him if he did. Here is dire need that the rich man could easily meet, even with leftovers sticking to a discarded finger towel. The ancient finger towel was used to wipe up the last bites of bread and gravy. After use it was often thrown out or given to dogs. Lazarus would have regarded such a tossed-out napkin as a feast, a generous, life-comforting gift.

It is amazing what we take for granted when we have much. Right after the Berlin Wall fell in late 1989, I had the chance to visit Romania within six weeks of the change of government there. We went in with supplies of food and clothes for believers. To go to Eastern Europe then was to enter a time machine and travel back in history and culture. In some cases the journey crossed several decades. The most precious food people had to offer us was eggs from their own chickens. For four days all we had was eggs. The people could not count on bread at the stores. The shock of seeing how people lived daily has never left me. But it did not take long to realize that we were receiving the best they had to offer and to appreciate the meals as a result. Often as we ate the hosts serenaded us with hymns in their own tongue to thank us for bringing them needed supplies. We slept in the beds of these generous hosts while they took the floor outside. For them life was simple, and they were rejoicing in their newfound freedom to worship God openly. So it did not matter what they lacked materially.

Others from the West who traveled into that region during the same period were similarly stunned by what they saw. Several marveled to me about what we take for granted and how frivolously we use resources. One Christian woman who lives in a very wealthy area of Dallas said her life—especially her shopping practices and her attitudes toward the needs of others—was changed permanently by her trip to Eastern Europe. Both she and I learned a lesson the rich man never did: we should never forget to look out our window and consider those less fortunate than ourselves. I pray that I never will.

If this parable were a television docudrama, it would take a commercial break here. Imagine how advertisers might flood images of their wares into the pause, entreating us to participate in the high life. Life often gets defined in terms of things or activities, as we ignore people and souls in need. Our advertising differs little from the rich man's attitude. Only the occasional public-service announcement is the exception.

Imagine you were a guest from another planet and television was your "eye" into this world. How selective is the eye of television? How much does it reflect real life and our world's pain? The news often does, but people do not enjoy watching that, nor do they often try to do much about the harsh realities that are portrayed. We feel helpless to do much to help, even if we want to. So documentaries that shed light on the hurting world are zapped away with the touch of a remote-control switch (no ratings, no TV time). Often people have to fall into totally desperate straits before others' concern translates into action—and for many the action never comes. So we hide behind our gates and hope the world's neediness will go away. Are we more like the rich man than we think?

This parable is not about money. It is about roots, the roots of our heart. Where do they reach? What nourishes them? Are our roots tied to earthly treasure? Are we looking to line the walls of our life with things and leisure? Are we too busy to notice the screams of human desperation? Or are the roots of our life drawing from the spiritual well of God's concern and compassion, which ministers comfort to a world in pain?

A film that stormed the evangelical world on the sensitive issue of abortion was called *The Silent Scream*. Yet some cultural critics have charged that Western Christians have great compassion about life while it is in the womb but could not care less about the lives of persons once they are born. Could that charge, though certainly overstated, be partially true? Is there another silent scream which we ignore, a scream that would assault our senses as a protest and an eyesore in every corner of our world, including the corners of our own inner cities? Is it possible that this parable addresses the pain of living in areas where human life itself is constantly at risk and where dogs live better than people? Could this parable be about us?

The parable exposes our values as it now considers Lazarus from an eternal perspective. Some time has passed—how much is not said. The rich man and Lazarus have both died. Each has a ticket for a permanent destination, one that money cannot buy. Who is "in" and who is "out" now, and why?

A remarkable reversal has taken place. Now Lazarus is in and the rich man is out. This is known as an eschatological reversal. It is a true rags-to-riches story, only eternal destinies are the prize. Lazarus is by *Abraham's side*, while the rich man is in dire need of relief, living *in torment.*

The term for torment here, *basanos,* was often used for the kind of punishment meted out to a slave to elicit a confession of wrongdoing (Wisdom of Solomon 3:1-10; 4 Maccabees 13:15; Schneider 1964a:563). The passage's mood is set by the distance and difference between the two figures. Everything is reversed, and the changes are all very permanent.

Lazarus is next to Abraham, the figure of promise, sharing in blessing (Schweizer 1974:647 n. 182). This is another way to say that he has been "gathered to the fathers" (Gen 15:15; 47:30; Deut 31:16). *The angels carried him to Abraham's side,* to heaven, in one of the greatest funeral processions of all time. Here as elsewhere, Luke emphasizes that sometimes the poor are headed for glory. One's social status on earth need not dictate one's spiritual status before God.

On the other hand, the rich man's new address reads "Hades" (Greek; NIV has *hell*). Mr. Deep Pockets has found the road to nowhere, the deep pocket of the universe. A selfish life is a rootless life, for everything it yields withers and fades. The rich man has joined a new kind of country club where the dues are permanent.

Interestingly, however, the rich man still sees Lazarus as his pawn, his social inferior. Having learned nothing in his new situation, he begins trying to negotiate his way to relief. There is now no drop of water for him, just as there had been no food for Lazarus before. The measure by which the rich man had lived was now being measured to him. Irony abounds. The wealthy man had not even acknowledged Lazarus in his earthly circumstances, but here he knows his name. Maybe he had seen the poor man all along and had ignored him. Lazarus had been good for nothing to him, only the object of a casual uncaring glance. God sees the potential of the poor very differently (Jas 2:5).

Divine riches do not take notice of earthly wealth or social status. The rich man's chance to use his wealth in a way that pleases God had passed. Now he is outside the gate of the mansion of eternal blessing (see 6:20-26; Jas 5:1-6).

I am reminded of a wealthy man whom God "blessed" with bankruptcy during the recession of the 1980s. Interpreting the experience positively, he said it made him reconsider his values. He called himself a "recovering materialist." Sometimes to lack is to realize what blessings one does possess.

Now Jesus is not against wealth. He is concerned with how it is used. The story of Zacchaeus shows Jesus commending a wealthy and formerly corrupt man who became generous with his resources (19:1-10). But Jesus wants to warn about the danger of abusing resources. This story of an unrepentant rich man reveals the tragedy of learning this lesson too late. His deep pockets had been sewn tight when it came to others, and thus he had sewn up his fate.

His personal appeal fails. Abraham tells him a grand "canyon" (*chasma;* NIV *chasm*) lies between them. No crossing is allowed. The distance he kept from others' needs in his earthly life has become a distance he cannot cross. The Greek term used for crossing here, *diabainō,* is often used of crossing a river that serves as a boundary between regions. There are no bridges between heaven and hell. When Abraham tells the rich man, *"Remember that in your lifetime you received your good things, while Lazarus received bad things,"* he is saying it is too late. Lazarus will be comforted, and the rich man is destined for anguish. Many today reason that a loving God will change his mind in heaven and grant eternal life to many who do not honor him now; they say there is no permanent judgment or condemnation from God. Abraham disagrees. The parable is a negative illustration of 16:9.

So the rich man gives up on himself and begins thinking of others. He has learned the lesson, but too late to help himself. Still, maybe he can help others avoid his error. There is irony here also, for what the rich man is denied the story's imagery supplies. No one will be sent to warn the rich man's brothers, not even Lazarus. Nevertheless, the rich man's plea provides the parable's lesson, a voice of one who has seen God's judgment: Be warned—wealth does not mean spiritual health. How exactly the rich man thinks the dead can contact his brothers is not clear—a resurrection, a vision? What is clear is that his brothers share the same philosophy of life that has condemned him. He knows they need to be warned. Many follow the same philosophy as he: to enjoy pleasures while ignoring the needs of others. Research shows that residents of the United States, for example, use a substantial amount of the earth's resources but give only a few percentage points of what they earn to charities of any type. What conclusion must we draw about our values?

Even when the government extends aid to other nations in need, we often complain about the burden we bear to help.

The rich man now wants to warn others who are like him and let them know what God desires. But what would this warning be? In the parable's context it seems clear that the warning would center on values and lifestyle. The rich man's perspective on such questions had been his downfall. The call would be to repent before God and be more generous to others. Those who love God and wish to honor him will have compassion on those like Lazarus. They will not confuse material blessing with divine blessing.

The man's request that a messenger be sent to his brothers is denied for a crucial reason. Abraham simply declares that *Moses and the Prophets* are good enough. The Old Testament makes clear what God desires of those who know him. "Deep pockets" that are holy have holes. God wants us to love him and to love our fellow human beings. He wants generosity. A text like Deuteronomy 24:10-22 seems to be in view, with its call to be generous and remember what it was like to be a slave in Egypt. So God's people were to care for the stranger, the fatherless and the widow, even leaving some of their own precious harvest for them. In fact, numerous Old Testament texts make the same point, with many prophets calling for compassion (Deut 15:1-3, 7-12; 22:1-2; 23:19; 24:7, 14-15, 19-21; 25:13-14; Is 3:14-15; 5:7-8; 10:1-3; 32:6-7; 58:3, 6-7, 10; Jer 5:26-28; 7:5-6; Ezek 18:12-18; 33:15; Amos 2:6-8; 5:11-12; 8:4-6; Mic 2:1-2; 3:1-3; 6:10-11; Zech 7:9-10; Mal 3:5). Just reading Moses and the Prophets should make it clear that those who hear God serve others, because they recognize that in ministering to others in need they show God's compassion. Love for God changes one's values, so that persons made in God's image become more valuable than things. Money is a resource, not a reward. It is to be used, not hoarded. It is to serve, not become master. Jesus said as much in his own ministry (Mt 6:24; Lk 10:25-28). To love God is to love and show compassion to the humanity he loves (Lk 6:26-36; Jn 3:16; Gal 6:10; 1 Jn 3:18).

The rich man does not give up. He suggests trying a sign. He seems to argue that the Word of God is not enough, but a message from the dead would be convincing. The reply is equally clear: revelation is better than a sign; besides, signs are ignored. Abraham insists, *"If they do not listen to Moses and the Prophets, they will not be convinced even if someone rises from the dead."* Jesus has already warned that signs other than the call to repentance will not be given (11:29-32). If God's prophetic Word cannot convince and put a crack in a hard heart, neither will miracles. Jesus' own resurrection is testimony to the point: only an open heart sees the evidence for God's presence and hears his voice.

This parable is ultimately about the heart. Where our treasure is, there our heart is. Where is our treasure being stored? Jesus says, "Healthy seed reflecting God's desire is not planted in riches. Rather, it should penetrate the heart and be planted into people, especially people in need." Jesus warns that treasure invested for the self yields emptiness, while treasure invested for God yields compassion.

False Teaching, Forgiveness, Faith and Service (17:1-10) This short section highlights four aspects of discipleship. It is hard to be certain if these four characteristics are simply listed or whether there is some relationship between them. If a relationship exists, a warning about sin and false teaching serves as a contrast to more positive exhortations about showing forgiveness, having faith and serving without demanding a reward. Faith understands forgiveness and leads to duty. In all these exhortations there is awareness of community. Christianity is not a privatized experience of faith.

Christianity is not a private affair, but a family one. Luke 17:1-10 is about our familial responsibilities. In America controversies are often framed in terms of the individual and his or her rights; but that is not the scriptural picture of how we relate to one another. Our text makes it clear that no Christian is an island unto himself or herself. We have responsibilities to each other. Unlike Archie Bunker of *All in the Family*, we should not see things only in terms of how they impact us. Service is not selfishness.

The first aspect of discipleship here is expressed in a warning not to be a cause of sin (vv. 1-3). It is inevitable that sin will come through false

_____

16:31 In Greek the *if* clause in this verse is a first-class condition; this means that the *if* is presented as if failing to hear is the case. The grammatical choice creates a presumption in the parable that many are failing to hear Moses and the prophets.

17:1-10 Teaching similar to this section's four units exists in the Synoptics. Only the

teaching. But *woe to that person* who brings it. The offense *(skandalon)* Jesus discusses here is probably serious sin that causes stumbling and a fall from faith. In the LXX this Greek term is used for the Hebrew concept of luring someone into a trap or of causing stumbling (Lev 19:14; Judg 8:27; 1 Sam 25:31; Ps 119:165; Stählin 1971:344-47). The rhetorical picture of verse 2 indicates that serious sin is in view. Those who fail to come to Christ trip over the "scandal" of the cross (Is 8:14; Lk 20:18; Rom 9:33; 1 Pet 2:6-8). So the warning addresses teaching that leads to a loss of faith and a life of sin.

God's concern for his children is seen in Jesus' characterization of them as *little ones.* Caring for God's children is baby-sitting: the responsibility is great because the children are precious in their parents' sight. Children need attentive care. And teaching carries special responsibility (Jas 3:1).

In fact, those who lead others into error are at risk before God. So Jesus issues a warning: a Mafia-style death is better for the one who leads others into apostasy. Jesus pictures an execution with a concrete block tied around the necks of the condemned as they are cast into the sea. A *millstone* was a large, heavy stone used at the top of a grinding mill. It was a millstone that crushed Abimelech's head in Judges 9:53. The picture is of severe judgment. You are accountable, Jesus says, *so watch yourselves.* Be careful to avoid sin (Ps 141:8-10).

Family relationships require us to be responsible to be careful about sin and error. Jesus' stress here is that individuals must guard themselves in such matters. But the possibility of error needs to be balanced with forgiveness. So Jesus calls for rebuke for sin but also a quickness to forgive (vv. 3-4). The assumption behind such mutual accountability is the community's commitment to pursue righteousness (Gal 6:1). Jesus assumes that we encourage one another and honestly support one another's relationship with God. But the rebukes are personally directed, as they are personally experienced. Jesus is not suggesting that a kind of underground righteousness squad be appointed to watch for sin.

parable of verses 7-10 has no conceptual parallel. Matthew 18:6 is like verses 1-2, as is Mark 9:42. Matthew 18:15 is like verses 3-4. Matthew 17:19-21 is similar to verses 5-6, as is Mark 9:28-29. All the parallels are more conceptual than strictly verbal. It seems best to see similar teaching here that circulated in a variety of traditional forms.

Rather, when people wrong one another in the flow of relationships, they are to sort things out. That is why Jesus speaks of when someone *sins against you* (Mt 18:15-20; Gal 6:1; 1 Thess 5:14-15; 2 Thess 3:14-15; Tit 3:10-11). Sin should be rebuked, but repentance should be greeted with forgiveness. We should be quick to move on once the wrong is acknowledged. Just as there is a commitment to righteousness, so there is a commitment to restore relationships promptly. In Matthew 18:21, as here, the repetition of sinfulness does not preclude forgiveness. Whether seven times a day or seventy times seven, forgiveness is called for, since the goal is to restore relationships within the community. Such values existed in Judaism as well as in the church (*Testament of Gad* 6:3-5, 7; Rom 12:16-21).

Deep and honest relationships presuppose a grounding in relationship with God. So verses 5-10 deal with this other level of relationship. Sensitive to this linkage, the disciples ask for an increase in their faith. Jesus is concerned not about faith's volume but about its presence. God can work with even a little faith. So Jesus says, *"If you have faith as small as a mustard seed, you can say to this mulberry tree, 'Be uprooted and planted in the sea,' and it will obey you."* The mustard seed was among the smallest seeds in Palestine (Michel 1965a:810-11; Mt 13:31-33), while the sycamine tree (Greek), probably a black mulberry tree, lived up to six hundred years. It required a vast root network to draw up the ground's nutrients. Jesus is arguing that a little faith can do surprising things, especially if merely through a spoken word it can pull up a tree with a huge root system and hurl it into the sea. Of course, the remark is a rhetorical picture of faith's power. It is like Jesus' remark about a camel's ability to go through the eye of a needle. It makes the point hyperbolically: do not fret about how great your faith is; only apply what you have and watch it work. The disciple's main responsibility is to trust God.

Out of such faith should come service. Jesus' final parable describes *a servant* (NIV), or more precisely a slave. "Slave" *(doulos)* was Paul's favorite self-characterization (Rom 1:1; also Lk 1:38; Jas 1:1). The service of God's servant is not a matter for negotiation but is a duty. The ancient household servant was responsible for many activities, from working the fields to preparing the meals. A ancient servant's work never seemed to be done. Such is also the case here. Jesus pictures a servant coming in from a long day of farming or shepherding, only to be asked to prepare the owner's dinner. The servant will not get a meal until the master is served. Not only that, the servant will not be thanked as if he had done something special. Rather, he will do it because it is his duty: *"We are unworthy servants; we have only done our duty."* This attitude is in sharp contrast with that of the Pharisee in 18:12. There is no selective obedience here, no bargaining to do something for the master if he does a favor in return. Our closest contemporary analogy to this obedience is the discipline of military life. Servants display humility *(unworthy servants)* and know their position. The servants of God know that God is not obligated to them, as if they were his equal, but they are obligated to him, because he is their Creator and Redeemer.

In the Jewish Mishna, *'Abot* 2:7, a rabbi says, "If you have studied the Torah, do not claim merit for yourself, since you were created for this." The same is true of service for God. Committed service is a disciple's privilege.

So the disciple's life is lived in community with others and God. Be careful not to lead others into sin, Jesus says. When sin occurs, rebuke it, but be quick to forgive when there is repentance. Don't worry about having great faith; just let the faith you have do its surprising work. Finally, serve God as a matter of duty. If you trust God, you can serve him.

Faithful in Looking for the King, the Kingdom and Its Consummation (17:11—18:8) Here Luke's attention turns to the program of God's rule, the kingdom. A miracle highlights Jesus' central role and reminds us that we should honor God. Then in a long discourse Jesus declares the kingdom's availability and speaks of the events associated with its future decisive manifestation. The unit closes with a parable that calls the saints to pray for divine justice and not lose heart, for God will vindicate them. Everything Jesus teaches here serves to reassure saints like Theophilus.

Ten Lepers and a Samaritan's Faith (17:11-19) This passage appears to be a simple healing account. But this miracle is not like most other miracles, since the healing itself is not emphasized as much as the reaction to it. As with all five miracles in the journey section, the miracle is less important than its results. Jesus heals as he continues his journey to meet his fate in Jerusalem. Luke often notes the journey's progress, but the notes become more frequent as Jerusalem nears (9:50-52; 13:22, 33; 14:25; 17:11; 18:35; 19:1, 11, 28, 41, 44). Jesus is passing between Samaria and Galilee. Moving east to west, his journey of destiny continues. That he would meet a Samaritan in this setting is not surprising.

The lepers of ancient society were rejected. They were treated as outcasts, like many who have AIDS today (see discussion of 5:12-16). They were required to live outside the city in leper camps (Num 5:2-3) and were to cry out to warn others to keep away from then as they walked the streets (Lev 13:45-46).

The ten of this story cry out, only this time it is for mercy. Such calls to Jesus are common in the Gospels (Mt 9:27; 15:22; Mk 10:47-48; Lk 16:24; 18:38-39). The lepers are perceptive: they understand that merciful acts constitute a major aspect of Jesus' ministry. The address of Jesus as "Master" is Luke's way of saying that Jesus has authority, since Luke uses it in texts where the other Synoptics have "Teacher" or "Rabbi" (Lk 5:5; 8:24, 45; 9:33). There is no significance to the number ten, though later the fact that one is different from the other nine will be significant. The only question at this point is whether Jesus' work of compassion will continue, given the strong rejection that has arisen against him.

The answer comes quickly. When Jesus tells the men to go to the priest to prove that they have been cleansed, it is clear that Jesus has acted to heal them (Lev 13:1-8; 14:1-11; Mk 1:44; Lk 5:14). Jesus mentions going to *the priests,* using the plural, because there are so many of them. The priests will be busy receiving testimonies about Jesus' work! The request calls for faith, since the men must turn and go to the priests without having experienced the healing first. In that sense the miracle

Notes: 17:11-19 This miracle is unique to Luke, but some have tried to regard it as a duplicate of Mark 1:40-45. The connection is very doubtful, given the account's differences, not the least of which are the number of lepers involved and the focus on Samaritans in Luke, not to mention the presence of a clear parallel to Mark 1 in Luke 5:12-16. Also of interest is the miracle's similarity to the healing of Naaman in 2 Kings 5:9-19. Though it is wrong, given the vast differences, to assume that Luke created the story based on this earlier account, there is a mirroring in the rendering of certain details that indicates this healing is like Elisha's telling Naaman to go wash himself in the Jordan (2 Kings 5:10-15). As they depart, they are cleansed. Jesus does not touch them as he had the leper of 5:12-14. The messianic times are present as Jesus heals from a distance (7:1-10, 22). The prospect of normal life has returned to the ten through the Master's work.

The lessons of the healing follow. There are several points: (1) God's mercy should yield thanksgiving. (2) God works through Jesus (v. 15). (3) Getting close to God is a matter of trusting him. One who seems far away can really be near. (4) The outsider, the foreigner *(allogenēs)*, is the most sensitive to Jesus. Those who respond to God may not be the ones we expect to respond. (5) God's blessing can be appreciated or underappreciated.

It is this last point that Jesus highlights when he asks, *"Were not all ten cleansed? Where are the other nine?"* Only the foreigner has returned to give thanks. Now what Jesus praises here is the Samaritan's initiative. Jesus had instructed the men to go to the priest. All of them had turned to do so, apparently. But only one has taken the trouble to return and thank Jesus. God's graciousness is often ignored and unappreciated. In addition, often those who have blessed forget to take time to thank those God uses. Jesus appreciates the Samaritan's sensitivity and commends it.

So Jesus asks, *"Was no one found to return and give praise to God except this foreigner?"* Yes, he was the only one who gave thanks. Those who do not take blessings for granted make up an exclusive club of surprising people. In our small group at church we recently studied joy. In the materials we used there was a discussion of how some Americans had gained fortunes in the early 1980s: "The average salary for Fortune 1000 CEO's is over $500,000/year. The actor Marlon Brando is said to have collected a fee of $3.7 million plus $15 million in profit percentages for a mere 12 days work in the 1978 film *Superman*—a rate of $1.5 million a day." Many people in Western nations are showered with mate-

---

is like the great works of old (Nolland 1993:845).

17:16-18 There are some nice Greek touches in these verses. The reflexive pronoun *autos* in verse 16 emphatically highlights the Samaritan's nationality. Jesus' first question in verse 17 uses the particle *ouchi*, so it expects a positive answer. In the second question, the interrogative *pou* trails, adding a note of emphasis to the query. The question's mood is, "The nine . . . where are they?" The question in verse 18 uses the particle *ouk* and also expects a positive answer.

rial blessing. Yet an article in *U.S. News & World Report* on the wealthy of the same period reported, "Half of those considered successful by their peers are unhappy." Why is this so?

Maybe it is because success and meaning are being defined in the wrong places by the wrong things. Life's real blessings are not valued and appreciated, while things that cannot really bless are assigned value and worth they do not really possess. Often our families and friends and, more important, the God of life are underappreciated, taken advantage of or ignored—not necessarily to their detriment, but always to ours.

There is one other lesson in the exchange between Jesus and the Samaritan man. God's grace, even though it is extended to all, does not mean that all gain salvation. God blesses humanity in a general way, but only the responsive who appreciate what he has done in Christ receive his full blessing and acceptance. Among the ten former lepers, only the Samaritan hears the comforting words *"Your faith has made you well."* His gratitude has revealed his faith. Jesus commends him for his response and assures him that the appreciation he expressed is also appreciated.

When one surveys the Scripture to see what we are called to be grateful for, an interesting point emerges. Often biblical texts simply call on us to thank God. No specific reason is cited. It is a "fill in the blank" exercise, an exercise in reflection on how God has been good recently. The perspective seems to be: Look for the sun; do not dwell on the clouds. Don't focus on events or things, but on people and on God. Perhaps if we responded to God and other people in this way, life would be brighter. A typical passage is 1 Chronicles 29:10-13, in which God is to be thanked for his presence and availability. But if we live apart from God, who is there to thank? The pursuit of things, status or power ultimately is a lonely existence.

A perusal of the Word provides a full list of large reasons to be grateful.

17:20-37 The unique positioning of this material has led to much discussion about parallels. Verses 20-21 have no parallels, but much of verses 22-37 possesses conceptual points of contact with Mark 13 and Matthew 24 (vv. 23, 24, 27, 31, 35, 37b). On the other hand, some of this material too is unique to Luke (vv. 22, 28-29, 32, 34, 37a). So Luke, at the least, splits up conceptually what Matthew and Mark keep in one place. There are numerous explanations for this situation (for details, see Wenham 1984). Most conclude that Luke chose to split the material for thematic reasons. But I prefer to argue that Luke had

God is thanked for his deliverance (Ps 35:18), for loving us and being faithful (Ps 52:9; 107:8), for hearing our cry (Ps 118:21), for safe arrival after a long, arduous journey (Acts 28:15), for other believers and for the testimony of their faith (Rom 1:8), for the gift of salvation that enables one not to sin (Rom 6:17), for delivering us from our tendency to sin (Rom 7:25), for the spiritual gift of being able to address God (1 Cor 14:18), for resurrection hope (1 Cor 15:57), for testimony, deliverance and victory in the midst of persecution (2 Cor 2:14), for the support of a colleague in ministry (2 Cor 8:16), for other believers (Phil 1:3; Col 1:3; 2 Tim 1:3; Philem 4), for those who respond to God's Word (1 Thess 2:13), for being able to serve others for God (1 Tim 1:12) and for his attributes (Rev 4:9). Those are just some of the options for thanksgiving.

Notice that this list includes not one item having to do with things, with possessions. The occasions for gratitude all have to do with relationships or circumstances in relationship to others. Colossians 3:15 says to "be thankful." That is what the foreigner was. That is what disciples are to be. Remember thank-yous, especially to our good, gracious and great God—and let the sun shine in.

How Does the Consummation Come? (17:20-37) If you ask a student of the Gospels where Jesus gives his eschatological discourse, he or she will answer, "The Olivet discourse." During the last week of Jesus' ministry, both Matthew 24—25 and Mark 13 indicate that Jesus spoke of events that would signal the return of "the Son of Man" with power. Of course, this phrase refers to Jesus' return. Interestingly, what Matthew and Mark set in one location, Luke sets in two. Luke 17:20-37 is the first discourse on the end; 21:5-38 is the second discourse, the one that matches most of the Matthew and Mark texts.

Jesus has two goals in relating this material. First, he wants it to be unmistakably clear that the kingdom program is inextricably tied to him (vv. 20-21). Second, he wants to encourage his disciples (v. 22) that

---

three sources for this material: one he shared with Matthew (Q?), Mark (or a version like the discourse in Mark) and his own independent version. This latter version included a discourse outside of Jerusalem, which Luke then records. Such independence is also suggested by Luke's handling of another eschatological passage, 12:35-48. In addition, chapter 17 highlights what the end is like on its own terms, while chapter 21 shows how the destruction of Jerusalem is the precursor and picture of the end.

although times will be tough and they will long for the day of the Son of Man, it will eventually come suddenly and bring harsh judgment for those who resist him. The implication is that disciples should be prepared, dig in and hang in there.

The first portion of the discourse is a response to the Pharisees. They want to know when the kingdom of God is coming (on the kingdom, see discussion of 9:57-62). Jesus explains that the kingdom does not come "with signs to be observed, nor will people say, 'Here it is,' or 'There it is,' because the kingdom of God is in your midst." My rendering here sticks close to the Greek, for reasons I will make clear.

The reply has caused no lack of discussion, because it suggests the immediacy of the kingdom's presence. The question is very practical: When will God manifest his rule and consummate his plan? Though Judaism did not have a unified picture of the expected Messiah's coming, in most conceptions it was a powerful and glorious arrival (Frerichs, Green and Neusner 1987; Charlesworth 1992). A famous example of Jewish expectation is Psalms of Solomon 17—18, where a powerful Messiah rules in Israel and rescues it from the nations. According to Jewish teaching, the arrival of Messiah would be clear and obvious to all. The question's implication may well be that whatever Jesus' ministry is, it does not reflect the anticipated glory. So his ministry cannot reflect the kingdom's presence.

But Jesus challenges the premise. The kingdom does not come "with observation." This phrase's meaning is disputed (Marshall 1978:654; Fitzmyer 1985:1160; Nolland 1993:852). Does it mean through legal observation, so Jesus denies that faithfulness to the law is required before he returns? Does it mean the kingdom comes mysteriously? Or—most likely—is it an allusion to the apocalyptic signs that are supposed

---

17:21 The various options noted here are attempts to define Jesus' kingdom concept precisely, especially as it relates to Old Testament hope and God's plan. The imagery is important, because in it are wrapped up views about God's plan, Jesus' authority, the church's mission, its relationship to God's promises to Israel and its sense of community. Jesus' rulership over a kingdom (or his headship over the church) is one of the most fundamental relational images of Jesus in the New Testament. This is why Jesus is confessed as the Christ. However, the kingdom involves more than the church and thus is distinguishable from it though related to it, since a future distinct phase exists for the kingdom program, a phase inaugurated by the events tied to Jesus' return. The church is the kingdom in the

to accompany the kingdom's coming? Jesus argues that the kingdom's coming does not require apocalyptic observation, since that was the normal expectation. The initial phase of the kingdom does not come that way.

Why? Because "the kingdom of God is in your midst." This phrase is one of the most discussed in Luke's Gospel. It is one of the few statements of Jesus that puts the kingdom in the present. In fact, so unprecedented is this statement that some argue the idea is really futuristic. The idea is, The kingdom is as good as present, since I am here. You need not miss it when it comes (Nolland 1993:853-54; Mattill 1979:198-201).

But a futuristic meaning is unlikely here. The verb that normally takes a futuristic present is *erchomai,* not *eimi,* which is the verb in verse 21. Thus Luke's shift of verbs in this context is significant, as is his shift of tenses. Moreover, the verb is placed in an emphatic position in the Greek text. More important, the remark about signs in verses 20-21 is specifically denied if a future sense exists, for Jesus appears to go on and enumerate the signs! It is better to interpret this phrase as referring to the initial coming now with a consummation to come later. Then Jesus' reply is, "You do not need to look for the kingdom in signs, because its King (and so its presence) is right before you. But its display in comprehensive power will come visibly to all one day. You will not need to hunt to find it then."

When Jesus says it is "in your midst," he does not mean in one's heart (but so NIV: *the kingdom of God is within you*). Jesus is speaking to Pharisees who have rejected him. They do not have the kingdom in their heart. And nowhere else in the New Testament is the kingdom described as an internal entity. He must mean something else here.

Two senses are possible. Jesus could mean "in your grasp or power."

---

sense it is an initial phase of the promised kingdom program of the promised Christ (Lk 24:44-49; Acts 2:16-41; 13:16-41; Heb 1:1-2). The church is part of God's promised kingdom program, since it has a ruler (Jesus), evidence of reign (salvation authority exercised as the Christ: salvation itself, the distribution of the Spirit, baptism in his name and Jesus functioning as the Judge of the living and the dead) and a realm (believers in Jesus). For two different views on the kingdom, see Beasley-Murray 1986 and Blaising and Bock 1993:128-283. For the hermeneutics behind this approach to kingdom questions, see Bock 1993, Bock 1994c, and Blaising and Bock 1993:57-105. For interaction among evangelicals on the question of the structure of God's plan, see Blaising and Bock 1992:331-94.

The kingdom's presence is related to one's ability to repent (Beasley-Murray 1986:102-3). The view depends on substantiating the presence of an idiom claimed also to be found in various Greek papyri, but that reading of the papyri is challenged (Riesenfeld 1949:11-12; Wikgren 1950:27-28). Also against this view is that it appears to be a nonanswer. To say the kingdom is within your grasp is not to say where it is or how you can get it—at least not very explicitly. In contrast to such vagueness, the second possible sense is that the kingdom is "in your midst"—that is, "in your presence." It is present in Jesus, so he and it stand before you. You do not have to look for it, because it is right before your face! This answer is very much like 7:22-23 and 11:20. It also fits the time perspective of 7:28 and 16:16, as well as the explicit declarations of current fulfillment in 4:16-23.

Now some in challenging this reading argue that Jesus is saying he is present but the kingdom is not. But that approach makes no sense here. Why would Jesus mention his personal presence in distinction from the kingdom's and then use an expression that mentions the kingdom? The whole point is to discuss the kingdom, not just him. The Pharisees know Jesus is present, and they know he claims to bring the time of fulfillment, so they are asking where the kingdom is. Jesus' reply is that the kingdom program comes with him, even in the present.

The program of God's reclamation of creation starts and stops with Jesus. Signs are not necessary because Jesus is the sign. As the entire discourse shows, the kingdom has an "already-not yet" character (Bock 1994d:193-97, 116-17). Luke 1:67-79, Acts 2:25-36, Romans 1:2-4 with 16:25-27, 1 Corinthians 15:25, Ephesians 1:18-23, Colossians 1:12-14, Hebrews 1:5-13, 1 Peter 2:4-10 and Revelation 1:6-8 share this two-phased kingdom perspective. Efforts to tie the presence-of-the-kingdom language of the New Testament to the ongoing presence of God's universal kingdom fail, since the context of these kingdom texts is an announcement of the arrival of something that previously was missing. In addition, efforts to argue that Jesus rules over a spiritual kingdom now that is distinct from the promised rule of the Old Testament also fail to note the declarations of explicit fulfillment in the contexts in which the statements are made (for example, Lk 4:16-23; 7:22-23; 24:43-49; Acts 13:16-41; Rom 1:1-7; Heb 1:1-2). Finally, attempts to argue that the kingdom is present but rule is not ignore the fact that when Jesus saves he exercises regal, executive authority as the promised Christ (Acts 2:16-41). Since Christ is a regal title, and since authority is a function of person and office, an expression of rule is present, though the full coercive rule of Jesus the King over all the creation will come in the future.

If the Pharisees had read the sign of the present time correctly, the question would not even be asked (12:54-56). Jesus has declared that the process of kingdom growth has started, so they should not assume it is absent, though it has made such a humble start (13:18-20). They need to respond to the King.

At this point Jesus turns to his disciples and elaborates on the ultimate answer to the Pharisees' question, the kingdom's future nature. That our attention turns to the future is clear by the words "days are coming," a phrase that can indicate the approach of decisive judgment (Is 39:6; Jer 7:32; 16:14; Ezek 7:10-12; Amos 4:2; Zech 14:1). The NIV renders this in the idiomatic *the time is coming*. Ultimately the kingdom's manifestation will include its powerful and coercive establishment on the earth, with total authority over all of humanity. That period could be described as *one of the days of the Son of Man*. When the Son of Man returns with authority to vindicate the saints and exercise power on their behalf, it will be a grand day of judgment (Dan 7). For a time, disciples will long to see it, but it will not come. That day does not come immediately. People will claim that it has come, but Jesus warns that the disciples should not go to check for his arrival. Those claims are not the real thing. When it comes, it will be sudden and visible like the lightning across the sky.

But first *he must suffer many things and be rejected by this generation*. Luke uses his frequent *dei* here ("it is necessary" that these things occur). Before that day of great rule can come, the Son of Man must suffer at the hands of humankind. Jesus' rejection is an intervening reality. That rejection is why he heads for Jerusalem (13:31-35). The description of its necessity is put in decretal terms, since *dei* speaks of the direction of God's plan. Before glory there is rejection and suffering. The kingdom's decisive arrival will be obvious, but for now rejection dominates. One day the kingdom will wield a gavel, but for now it bears a cross.

Scholars often argue that the church suffered from the "delay of the parousia": Jesus predicted a soon arrival, and when it did not come the church struggled to explain why it did not come. In Lukan studies the major name tied to this view is Hans Conzelmann (1961). He taught that much of Luke is dedicated to concern over the fact that Jesus did not come as quickly as the church had expected (or, in some views, as quickly as he had led them to believe). But in this speech and in the Olivet discourse Jesus is outlining a series of events that precede the return. He makes clear in texts like Mark 13:10, 32 that the exact timing is not known and that other things must happen first, like his suffering and the church's preaching of the gospel. These discourses function to reassure disciples that God has a plan, even if we cannot know the exact timing of all these events. If there is a problem with "delay," it is because the church failed to reflect on the whole of Jesus' teaching.

Jesus compares the day of that arrival to the times of Noah and Lot. The two examples are parallel. Life went on with eating, drinking, marriage, buying and selling—and then judgment came. For one it was the flood, for the other fire and sulfur. But to be outside the family that day was to face instant judgment. The time of the Son of Man will be no different: *it will be just like this on the day the Son of Man is revealed.*

Last of all, Jesus tackles the conditions of the return. When the judgment comes, he says, it will be swift. There will be no time to gather possessions from your home, whether you are on the roof or in the field. Unlike Lot's wife, do not look back, longing for what you are leaving behind. To seek to protect your life is to lose it. But to lose your life will be to gain it. In other words, if you identify with God, suffering and persecution may result, but God will redeem you. If you fear the rejection of persecution, you will not come to Christ, but neither will you be redeemed by God. Jesus' words here recall 12:1-12. Again the point is, Expect suffering but persevere with patient faith. Redemption comes,

---

17:34-37 It should first be noted that verse 36 is absent from some translations because it is lacking in many of the best Greek manuscripts of Luke. Its absence is not significant, since it simply provides a third illustration of the separation. Another question is whether the "rapture" is alluded to here, since it is the departing who are saved. Against the suggestion is that the day of the Son of Man is portrayed consistently here as a grim day of judgment (vv. 26-30), whereas the rapture is an event of hope (1 Thess 4:16-17). An explicit reference to the rapture is unlikely, given the context of judgment. In addition, since there is the option to pick up one's goods and look back, it does not appear that God is taking

and so does God's vindication.

Picturing what the day will be like, Jesus portrays a division within humanity. Two pictures make the same point. Whether two are asleep or two women are grinding at a mill, on that day one will be taken and another left. It is debated whether the one is taken into judgment and the one is left for salvation or the other way around. Given the Noah and Lot metaphors, as well as the picture of the birds gathering over the dead bodies in verse 37, it seems that it is those who are left behind who experience the judgment. Those who flee, like Noah and Lot, are spared.

When the disciples ask, *"Where, Lord?"* they appear to be asking where this will occur or what will happen to the bodies. Jesus replies that where the bodies are, the eagles (or better *vultures*) are gathered. Though the term for the birds *(aetos)* can mean eagles, in this context of judgment it should be rendered *vultures,* as it is in other such contexts (Lev 11:13; Deut 14:12; Job 39:30; Mt 24:28). Eagles do not seek carrion; vultures do. The image is grim. The Son of Man's return means massive judgment; it will be final and will carry the stench of death. The return will be deadly serious. You should not be on the wrong side when it comes. Be assured that the vindication of the saints will come (18:1-8). The Son of Man's return means humanity's separation into two camps: those who were for him enter into everlasting life, while those who were against him face an everlasting judgment.

Parable of the Nagging Widow (18:1-8) To the theologically so-phisticated prayer can sometimes seem to be an odd spiritual practice. If God is all-knowing, sovereign and all-caring, then why bother him with our requests? Interestingly, Luke's portrait of Jesus highlights prayer. He prays before receiving the Spirit (3:21-22), all-night prayer precedes the selecting the Twelve (6:12), and two parables focus on prayer (11:5-13; 18:1-8). The answer to the dilemma of prayer is that it is not intended

---

anyone anywhere. Rather, the language of these verses simply describes rhetorically and graphically the dividing up of humanity into two groups. Those who remain behind are left for the vultures. The others, who are present when the Son of Man returns to earth, have fled, knowing that judgment is coming on those who have rejected him. They have been taken to safety.

18:1-8 This parable is unique to Luke. Conceptually it is similar to 11:5-8. Another conceptual parallel is Sirach 35:13-18, especially verses 13-14.

to do something for God, but for us. It is one of the mechanisms of relationship that God gives to his children to be in touch with him. God may not need prayer, but we do.

This parable highlights that point, as verse 1 makes clear: *Then Jesus told his disciples a parable to show them that they should always pray and not give up.* Since Jesus was speaking to his disciples in 17:22-37, the same audience is assumed by the NIV to be present here, since the Greek says only that he told them a parable. Jesus shows that God responds to prayer and listens to his children. He does not wind up the universe like a watch, as the deists of old argued. He does not merely send the universe ticking on its merry way and sit back to observe as an uninterested spectator; God relates to his creation. This is especially the case when our prayers cry out for justice and the righteous treatment of his children. In such cases, when God acts, his response will be swift and certain (v. 8).

One of the strengths of Jesus' parables is that they are filled with interesting characters. This is especially true of this parable. Two characters are central to the story: a nagging *widow* and an independent *judge* who does not show preference to anyone. I am sure all of us know someone we would call a nag. Such persons are always complaining about something, and if there is an important issue or principle involved, they will not let it go until it is fixed. Such a woman is the example in this parable. We are to pray just as she nags, especially when we desire God's vindication of our commitment to him. We are to pray and keep praying for this.

Now, of course, we need not whine in our prayers to God, but simply express our sincere desire to see him and those who are his vindicated. Often when we pray we do not share our true feelings with God (as if he does not know them already!). It gives me pause to realize that the most common type of psalm in the Psalter is the lament. The mature Old Testament saints were honest about their feelings before God. Yet often as we voice our concerns to God, he renews our faith and trust in him. So when we pray, we should express our deepest feelings, even our

---

18:5 I reject Nolland's argument for translating *hypōpiazō* as "shame," even though he argues the meaning "wear out" is unattested. "Wear out" is a good translation because it indicates how the figurative term should be rendered as an emotional description. The

complaints, as we urge God to bring justice. Perhaps the prayer found in Acts 4:24-32 is an example. There God's people pray, in essence, "Lord, give us boldness and show your presence."

Yet it is significant that the encouragement not to grow weary in such prayer (Lk 18:1) indicates that God's response may not always come when we want it. We may have to wait for it. Jesus did teach that God's vindication of the saints might take some time. Prayer can help us stay in touch with God and stay patient in the interim.

It would be a mistake to assume that the woman in this story is old. In the ancient culture, women married in the early to mid teens, and the life expectancy for men who reached adulthood often did not exceed "thirtysomething" (Jeremias 1972:153). Yet being a widow, she was among the most vulnerable people in her society. She was to be cared for by others (Deut 10:18; 14:29; 16:11, 14; 24:17, 19-21; 26:12-13; 27:19; Ps 94:6; Is 1:17, 23; 10:2; Jer 5:28 LXX; 7:6; 22:3; Ezek 22:7; Mal 3:5; as God does, Ps 68:5; 146:9; in Judaism, *m. Ketubot* 4:12; 11:1-6; *m. Giṭṭin* 4:3; L. T. Johnson 1991:269). Her precarious position parallels the risk believers experience in an often-hostile world.

One other bit of cultural background helps us understand the account. In a civil dispute the judge would be responsible for dealing with the woman's claims. Since she is alone, if she is to find justice, the judge must supply it. Although the judge is not known for his compassion— he *neither feared God nor cared about men*—he still is responsible to hear her case.

The woman takes her problem to the judge again and again and again and again! Like a great defensive lineman rushing the passer or a famous goal-scorer sweeping down on the goal, she just keeps coming. Her message is, *"Grant me justice against my adversary."* Simply put, she wants justice. *For some time* the judge resists. Exactly how long he holds out we are not told. Apparently he thinks his nonaction will get rid of her. He does not wish to act on her behalf. But every time he holds court, she is there. She had the right to keep coming back, because in that culture her case had to be heard (Stählin 1974b:450 n. 86). Finally he

---

woman's continual requests had "beaten him black and blue" emotionally. That means the same thing as "wearing out."

responds: *"Because this widow keeps bothering me, I will see that she gets justice, so that she won't eventually wear me out by her coming!"*

The description of the judge being "bothered" is rather picturesque. What she does is "cause him trouble" *(to parechein moi kopon).* She gets on his nerves. In fact, the judge characterizes himself as "beaten down," using figuratively a term that refers to having a black eye *(hypōpiazō).* Though some argue that the judge is worried about being shamed (Nolland 1993:870), this cannot be the meaning, since he does not care about his public reputation. The woman has just worn him out. Her constant intercession has brought success.

Jesus applies the picture to prayer for God's action to bring justice for his children. Like 11:5-13, this is not a carte blanche to ask for whatever we want. Rather, it is designed to encourage us to pray for God's righteous ways to be revealed. The argument follows the popular Jewish "how much more" style: if an unrighteous judge responds this way, how much more will a righteous God!

In two rhetorical questions Jesus makes it emphatically clear *(ou mē)* that God will vindicate his elect and that he will not delay over them (or he will have patience concerning them—see discussion of views below). Vindication is clearly the issue, since it repeats the terms of verses 3 and 5. Judgment against those who persecute the righteous will come (Ps 149:7). *Chosen ones* is a term Luke uses only here to describe believers. Their constant calling to God *day and night* will be heard.

The idea of God's nondelay has caused much discussion, given that the final judgment has still not come. Though many explanations have been offered, two are more likely (Bock 1995: on Lk 18:8).

The first possibility is that rather than meaning God will not delay long over them, it means God will show patience to them (L. T. Johnson 1991:270). In other words, he will be patient about their request and honor it by vindicating them. This view fits Sirach 35:19 LXX, which appears to be a conceptual parallel. Texts like 2 Peter 3:8-9 show that God's patience reflects his merciful desire that more come to know him.

Another possible meaning is that God will prevent excessive persecution of the community until the vindication comes (Catchpole 1977:81-104). "Patience" can refer to the delaying or putting off of a consequence of an action (Ex 34:6; Num 14:18; Joel 2:13; Sirach 5:4). Thus God will lighten his people's suffering until vindication comes.

It is hard to be certain which of these ideas is meant, though the first option seems less subtle. Regardless, it is clear God will vindicate his saints.

Jesus closes by making two more points: (1) God will act quickly. (2) When Jesus returns, will he find faith on earth—that is, will people persevere in looking for his return? Jesus' second remark assumes that his people will need faith and trust as they consider how history is proceeding. This notion helps to explain the first point. Jesus is not promising that God will come soon—that is, in a short period of time; otherwise God's people would not have become discouraged, which seems to be the assumption behind Jesus' second point. Rather, his coming is soon in that it is next on the eschatological calendar. Prophetic texts often foreshorten the timing of events to show their sequence (for example, Is 61:1-2 and the two comings of Jesus). God has not forgotten the elect. Next on the calendar is his bringing their vindication in justice. Until the vindication comes, it seems a long way away, especially in the midst of persecution, but after it comes and is established for eternity, it will not seem so delayed.

So Jesus urges prayer and perseverance. God will vindicate his saints. Trust him to do so and keep praying for his return, which is the vindication of the saints. We should pray because, unlike the judge in the parable, God is not grudging about granting our desires for justice. And we should keep asking for the vindication of the people of God; our patience and willingness to make this request should never run out. By continuing to make the request, we stay sensitive to the need for justice to come. So like the nagging widow, just keep asking.

Humility and Trusting All to the Father (18:9-30) Three passages make up this discipleship section. In each case, figures provide examples. The Pharisee and tax collector contrast pride and humility. The blessing of the little children shows God's openness to all. The rich man shows how difficult it is for the rich to turn to God, while the disciples are the positive example of giving everything over to service for God. In each case, what is commended is putting everything into the Father's care. Such simple, humble faith is what God desires.

The Parable of the Pharisee and Tax Collector (18:9-14) This parable, like the previous one, deals with prayer, but here the issue is the content of the heart as one prays. The parable is one of contrast and is unique to Luke. It contains common Lukan heroes and villains. The hero is the tax collector; the villain is the Pharisee. Humility is the exalted virtue. The parable serves as a rebuke, since it is told *to some who were confident of their own righteousness and looked down on everybody else.* The Pharisees are the specific targets in Jesus' audience (Jeremias 1972:142-43; Josephus *Jewish Wars* 1.5.2 §110).

What is most dangerous about pride is noted right at the start. First, we come to trust in our own abilities rather than trusting God. Second, we come to regard other people with contempt and disrespect rather than seeing them as created equal in the image of God.

This is a danger inherent in professional ministry: ministers and other Christian leaders can come to look down on laypeople. Here we are reminded, however, that God honors those who realize that their ministry does not commend them before God or make them superior; rather, we are all the objects of his grace and mercy.

The parable takes place at Israel's most holy site, the temple. The two visitors are on opposite ends of the social spectrum. The Pharisee is a respected religious member in a most honored social group, while the tax collector belongs to one of the most hated professions possible for a Jew.

The two prayers also make a contrast. The Pharisee is sure that he is a blessing to God: *"I thank you that I am not like other men—robbers, evildoers, adulterers—or even like this tax collector. I fast twice a week and give a tenth of all I get."* Clearly, God's program could hardly advance without this man's contribution. In fact, his prayer's form is revealing. It starts out like a thanksgiving psalm in which God is praised for something he has done. But the form is perverted, since the occasion of thanksgiving is what the man has done for God. Here is trust in oneself. His real prayer is "God, I thank you that I am so marvelous." In his own "humble" eyes he is not unrighteous. He fasts above and

---

Notes: 18:15-17 This passage has parallels in Mark 10:17-22 and Matthew 19:16-22. The location of these parallels in Mark and Matthew match the passage's location in Luke. This

beyond the call of duty, twice a week, in contrast to the one fast a year on the Day of Atonement required of Jews. He gives tithes from everything (Lev 27:30-32; Num 18:21-24; Deut 14:22-27). He probably tithes down to the smallest herbs (Lk 11:42). God needs to do nothing for him. He makes no request of God, he offers no honor to God. This religious man has done it all. After reading his prayer, we wonder whether God should apply to be his assistant!

In contrast, the tax collector senses that he approaches a holy God, a great and unique being. This man comes with timidity, from a distance, not lifting his eyes to heaven. While the Pharisee had stood right at the front and addressed God, the tax collector beats his breast in an obscure corner to reflect his contrition. A similar sign of emotional dependence in the New Testament is the lifting of hands to God to show one's need of what he provides (1 Tim 2:8). Both practices indicate an awareness of one's humble position before God.

The tax collector knows he is a sinner; the Pharisee is confident of his own righteousness. The contrast could not be greater. Here is another brilliant use of literary space and contrast by Jesus.

The tax collector asks for mercy. He desires to improve his spiritual health, not rest on any personal laurels. He is aware that the only way he has access to God is through divine mercy (Dan 9:18-19). Such access is not earned; it is the product of God's grace.

When Jesus evaluates the two prayers, only one petitioner *went home justified*. The tax collector's prayer honored God and was heard, not that of the Pharisee. To drive the point home, Jesus concludes, *"For everyone who exalts himself will be humbled, and he who humbles himself will be exalted."* Such reversals in God's judgments are common (1:51-53; 6:20-26; 14:11; 15:11-32; 16:19-31). The parable's point is summarized in this saying. The tax collector has a humble heart. He is honored by God. Since this parable is an example story, the call is to be like the tax collector.

Receiving Children and Childlike Faith (18:15-17) In this short passage we see that God is no respecter of persons—not in the sense

is the first passage with clear extensive parallels to Mark since Luke 9:49.

This section teaches nothing about infant baptism. The availability of God to children

that he could not care less about them, but rather he cares for all of them. In ancient culture, children could be seen but not heard. They were left on society's fringe until they were old enough to be useful. This fringe role magnified the impact of what Jesus says here. If he has time for children, he has time for anyone.

The child's age is indicated through a combination of terms. Though *brephē* usually refers to "little ones" who are *babies* (so NIV here), the other term used, *paidion,* seems to indicate that at least some of children are beyond the toddler stage. Second Timothy 3:15 uses the term "little one" to refer to Timothy's age when Scripture was read to him, so we need not think these were all infants. Mark 10:16 has some of the children small enough to be picked up by Jesus.

Yet whatever their age, they were too young to be considered important by some in the crowd. The disciples saw the attempt to bring children to Jesus as inappropriate. Surely there was a better use of his time and energy. Such trivialities should be prevented.

But the disciples had it wrong. They should not hinder the children's approach. Jesus turns the event into a two-level lesson, one about children, the other about disciples.

The lesson about children is that they are welcome in God's kingdom. He is available to them. God's care for them shows that he cares for all. The kingdom is not only for adults.

The lesson for disciples is that children are good models for a disciple. Children trust their parents and rely on them. So disciples should rely on their Father. To be a part of the kingdom, we must receive it in the way a child walks through life. Entry is blocked to those who do not trust the Father. God accepts those who run into their Father's arms, knowing that he will care for them.

The Rich Ruler and the Disciples (18:18-30) This passage builds yet another contrast between the disciples and the response of others

does not carry an implication about the rites they can participate in, especially as infants. That issue is decided in light of other concerns and texts. What the text does indicate is that every person, even the youngest, is valuable to God.

18:18-30 This passage has parallels in Matthew 19:16-30 and Mark 10:17-31. In each of these accounts the discussion about children precedes. All the versions are similar, but Luke is closer to Mark, while Matthew has a few unique details. Luke agrees with Mark in having the man address Jesus as *good.* Luke uniquely tells us the speaker is a *ruler,* while Matthew

in the Jewish nation. The rich ruler represents the wealthy lay leadership in the nation and allows Luke to deal again with a theme that he has consistently kept before his readers: wealth and generosity (3:11; 5:11, 28; 6:23-26, 34-35, 38; 7:5; 8:3, 14; 10:34-35; 11:41; 12:13-21, 33; 14:12-14, 33; 16:9-13, 19-31; 18:22; 19:8; see Stein 1992:459). In fact, this passage reflects a theme that is central to Luke 18—19: the disciple's trust should lead to humble service (18:17).

The rich man lacks the trust of the blind man of verses 35-43, as well as the penitent heart of Zacchaeus (19:1-10). The rich man's attitude is more like that of the Pharisee of 18:9-14. The self-confidence he reflects, along with his sense of sinlessness, is condemned by Jesus. In contrast, by trusting and following Jesus, the disciples have given what he has asked for. They will have a rich reward, both now and in the life to come (vv. 29-30).

Most of the account's difficult aspects come at the start. When the rich ruler calls Jesus *good,* the teacher rebukes him. Apparently Jesus wants to warn the man not to be impressed by human credentials—a problem Jesus will face later in his own life, when the Pharisees challenge his authority (20:1-8). Being excessively tied to credentialed teachers might distract the man from pursuing God. God alone is good; he is the One who deserves attention and allegiance, a key Old Testament theme (1 Chron 16:34; 2 Chron 5:13; Ps 34:8; 106:1; 118:1, 29; 136:1). Jesus is not replying to deprecates himself, but qualifying how the man views the teaching office in general. The teaching role, even for one who does it well, is not to be overly exalted. Jesus' refusal to accept the man's flattery also warns the man that Jesus will shoot straight with him.

More important is the man's question. It matches what a lawyer asked in 10:25: *"What must I do to inherit eternal life?"* He wants to know how he can be sure he will share in the life to come. Jesus' reply focuses on the standard of righteousness as represented in portions of the Ten

and Mark speak only of "one" who asks. In addition, Matthew has the question uniquely phrased as "What good must I do . . . ?" This means that Jesus' statement about only "One" being good (Matthew) or only God being good (Mark, Luke) is not misconstrued as a reflection on his own status. The Markan and Lukan form of the question *("What must I do . . . ?")* clearly implies what Matthew says, namely, "What good must I do . . . ?" Both are adequate summaries of this discussion.

Commandments. Avoiding adultery, murder, stealing and lying, as well as the positive call to honor one's parents, are specifically noted. The spirit of Jesus' reply fits with what was said in 10:25-28, where the commandment to love God and others was cited more generally. In this context the reply is significant, because the issue of money, which will surface shortly, can make us view others as means to an end, rather than as people. So Jesus concentrates here on commandments dealing with how we relate to others. In fact, in Judaism honoring parents might imply financial responsibility for them in their old age (Tobit 4:3; Sirach 3:3-16; L. T. Johnson 1991:277).

Jesus' reply has troubled some as being "too Old Testament" in tone. Where is the appeal to follow Jesus? One could argue it is implied in Jesus' words. By steering the man toward faithfulness to God, Jesus steers the man toward following him. Jesus could steer people to him through his teaching (6:46-49; 11:29-32) or remind them of the ethical standard God desires, as he does here. There is no contradiction in this for him. As Stein (1992:455) says, "For Luke true faith involved loving God with all one's heart and one's neighbor as oneself. . . . Likewise loving God with all one's heart . . . and one's neighbor as oneself involves faith in Jesus."

To trust God means to rest in him and his way. To pursue such a path is not works, but relationship with God. The entry into grace and relationship saves; the path and pursuit of righteousness follow.

Now the man's problem begins to surface. He is confident that he can stand before God on his own merit: he has *kept* all the commandments since boyhood. His confidence recalls the Pharisee of verses 9-14: he has kept the law.

Jesus wishes to check this confidence with a further demand that will reveal two things: (1) how generous the man is and (2) whether he will listen to Jesus. He still lacks something. Here Jesus is not asking the man to do something he asks everyone to do, since he will commend Zacchaeus's generosity in 19:1-10 without asking him to sell all. What Jesus does is test the man's heart and attachments. Is God placed ahead of worldly possessions in this man's life? Does the man really love God and others? So Jesus tells him that he lacks one thing: he must sell all his possessions.

But to stop here is to miss the point. Jesus goes on to promise the man treasure in heaven if he will follow Jesus. The need to come to Jesus, to trust him, is not absent from the passage. It is merely defined by reference to the obstacle that stands between the man and God: his security in his wealth.

The man's response says it all. He is *very sad.* The choice is a painful one, and he refuses to consider it. Grieved at the options, he chooses his wealth.

There is another premise in Jesus' response that may prompt the disciples' reaction. Wealth was generally seen as evidence of divine blessing and pleasure. If Jesus is implying that wealth is not such a guarantee, then how can one know God's blessing? Jesus had answered this question in 10:20 with regard to power, but here he raises it again with the issue of wealth and status, since to sell all and follow Jesus would mean that the rich man's social status would be changed forever. Jesus responds to the rich man's somber mood by driving the point home: *"How hard it is for the rich to enter the kingdom of God!"* He looks at the man as he says it. Wealth and the false sense of security that comes with it can prevent one from meeting God.

Jesus is not done. He explains that a camel can get through the eye of a needle more easily than a rich person can enter the kingdom. Now some have argued that Jesus is talking about a small gate at the entrance to Jerusalem named the "Needle's Eye Gate." But this view clearly blunts the force of his statement. How hard is it for a camel to go through a small gate? Not very hard, yet Jesus and the disciples agree that he is expressing an impossibility, at least for human beings (vv. 26-27). So Jesus is using his common style of rhetorical hyperbole (compare 6:41; 17:2). The hyperbole here makes it clear that a rich man on his own will never make a choice for the kingdom. It is impossible. The priorities it requires demand a new heart.

The disciples catch the tension and are shocked. If the rich cannot be saved and experience ultimate divine blessing, *who then can be saved?* If those at the top of the ladder who enjoy God's rich material provision do not get in, where is hope for anyone else?

Jesus notes that God can do the impossible. He can change hearts and priorities. God's power and grace yield the change. People do not save themselves or earn God's blessing; God provides it. This is why Paul calls the gospel the power of God in Romans 1:16-17. God deals with sin and changes the heart.

Now the rapid-fire dialogue reaches a high point. Peter remarks, probably seeking reassurance, that the disciples have done what Jesus has asked of the rich man. They have left home to follow him.

In the reply is the passage's major point. Jesus reassures Peter and the disciples that God is blessing and will bless their decision. Even given Peter's upcoming denial of Jesus, he has made the choice to follow Jesus. Not only is what Jesus has asked for possible with God, but indeed the Father has wrought it in the hearts of Jesus' followers, who live in relationship to *the kingdom of God* through him. So they have left many things, but they have received *many times as much* in this life *and, in the age to come, eternal life.* In Judaism, "the age to come" is another way to speak of future eternal life (4 Ezra [2 Esdras] 7:47; 8:1; *Pirqe 'Abot* 2:8; L. T. Johnson 1991:279). What the rich man hoped for, but refused to embrace by following Jesus, these disciples are receiving. The lesson is in the contrast. The disciples, for once, provide the positive example. God has made the seemingly impossible possible for them (see 10:20-22).

Messiah Turns Toward Jerusalem (18:31—19:44) Jesus is on the final leg of his fateful journey. He has prepared his disciples for his departure by instructing them about the walk of faith. Now he reminds them of what he will face in the capital. Then follows a miracle performed by Jesus as the Son of David. Next Jesus commends a tax collector for his newfound generosity. A parable will stress accountability to a master who will return. As he enters the city amid shouts acclaiming him as king, he laments that the city will reject him. Jesus is Messiah, but he is a rejected one.

A Final Passion Prediction (18:31-34) Now comes the sixth prediction of Jesus' death in Luke, three more than Mark notes (Lk 9:22, 44; 12:50; 13:32-33; 17:25; the Markan parallels are in Lk 9 and here). Luke

Notes: 18:31-34 The parallels are Matthew 20:17-19 and Mark 10:32-34. Luke's account is more detailed. It highlights the fulfillment of Scripture and the Gentile involvement in the rejection of Jesus. The Son of Man and death are connected in 9:22, 44 and 17:25. The

stresses these predictions to keep the specter of Jesus' approaching death before the reader and to make the reader aware that Jesus was fully preparing the disciples for life after his physical departure from the earth.

Here Jesus addresses *the Twelve.* Throughout the entire journey he has stressed that he will suffer, and throughout the entire journey the disciples have struggled to understand how this can be. The Old Testament indicated that suffering would occur in Jerusalem. Which Scriptures are in view is debated. Daniel 7 is not really a good possibility, since the Son of Man's suffering is not referred to in that passage. Daniel 7 serves only as the eventual background to the Son of Man title, a connection Jesus explicitly reveals in Luke 21:27. The suffering imagery must come from another set of texts. Jesus seems to be combining various motifs. The suffering servant is a major theme of this teaching (Is 50:6; 52:13— 53:12). Another key may well be the "deuteronomistic" critique which describes continual national unfaithfulness and suggests that a prophet will not suffer outside of Jerusalem (Lk 13:31-35). In addition, opposition to Messiah may play a role (Ps 2; Lk 24:44-49; Acts 4:24-28).

In moving to specifics, Jesus does not discuss the chief priests and scribes. Rather, he highlights the handing over of Jesus *to the Gentiles.* The text does not specify whether the handing over is part of a divine permission (reading a theological passive) or is a subtle way to depict national unfaithfulness. But the appeal to scriptural realization means this is not an either-or question. God will permit the nation to hand over the Messiah. The act reflects its hardness of heart (Acts 2:22-24). Jesus will be mocked. The fulfillment comes in Luke 22:63-71 and 23:11, 36, where Jesus is subjected to the ridicule of proud scoffers (Bertram 1972:306).

Jesus will be flogged, die and be raised. This was either the dreaded *verberatio* or the less severe *fustigata.* Usually before crucifixion, *verberatio* was used; for discipline *fustigata* was applied. The criminal was flogged until blood was drawn (Suetonius *Claudius* 34 and *Domitian* 11; Hengel 1977; Sherwin-White 1963:27-28).

Old Testament roots to this prediction were discussed in the commentary on Luke 9:22 and 44.

All this detail does not enlighten the disciples. The point about their lack of comprehension does not mean that they do not understand his words, but that they cannot grasp how this will fulfill Scripture or how Messiah could suffer. They just cannot see how fulfillment can come this way. The unveiling occurs in 24:13-49.

Jesus knows where his journey leads. He will suffer the rejection of his own and of the world. He suffers knowingly and willingly. He has the courage to stand up for God and to suffer according to his will.

Healing by the Son of David (18:35-43) The journey's fourth and final miracle (the previous ones come in 13:10-17; 14:1-6; 17:11-19) involves *a blind man* who sees spiritual reality very clearly. The blind man is one of two examples of faith who shine at the end of the journey; Zacchaeus is the other. The blind man's humble appeal echoes the humility of the tax collector and the child of faith earlier in chapter 18. He contrasts strongly with the rich ruler, who had everything and saw nothing. The blind man has nothing but sees well. So this passage brings together many themes of the section. Thus the miracle is climactic.

If there were any question about Jesus' continued availability to heal, this miracle ends it. Jesus was always ready to serve. A poor, blind beggar cries out to Jesus as *Son of David* to have mercy on him. The crowd rebukes him, seeing the request as annoying and perhaps seeing him as unworthy. But a second time he cries out, *"Son of David, have mercy on me!"* The request is a recognition that Jesus, as the promised regal Son of David, has saving power. This title's juxtaposition to the title "Jesus of Nazareth" forms an answering echo to 4:16-30 and 7:22-23. There Jesus proclaimed himself the fulfillment of promise, but because of his heritage the synagogue crowd in chapter 4 did not want to accept him. The blind man has no such reservations. He knows opportunity is present. Possibly the underlying Jewish tradition is that the Son of David, as exemplified by Solomon, was seen as full of wisdom and thus had

---

18:35-43 The parallels are Matthew 20:29-34 and Mark 10:46-52. There are a few differences of significance in the parallels. One of the most significant is this healing's locale. Mark and Matthew place the healing as Jesus departs Jericho, but Luke apparently upon his entering Jericho. The other difference is the number of men healed. Matthew refers to two, while Mark and Luke mention one. Though many have appealed to two Jerichos as a solution to the locale question, only one locale was inhabited in the first century. This approach could still be correct, but it is not the most likely. More likely is a literary option.

power to overcome Satan (Strack and Billerbeck 1926:4:533-34; Wisdom of Solomon 7:17-21; *Pseudo-Philo* 60:1; Josephus *Antiquities* 8.2.4-5 §§41-49; Duling 1975:235-52). The expectation was that the end time would be a period of healing and restoration (Lk 7:22-23). So as the blind man calls for Jesus he reveals the extent and clarity of his spiritual vision. With boldness he continues to call for Jesus despite others' attempts to hush him.

Jesus stops and asks that the man be brought to him. When he asks what the man wants, he requests his sight. Jesus gives him what he asks for and explains the secret of the man's success: *"Receive your sight; your faith has healed you."* The Greek uses the verb "to save" *(sōzō)* to refer to the healing. The double entendre is intended. Faith is key, as in other texts (7:50; 8:48; 17:19). By commending the man's faith, which had demonstrated itself in his persistence, Jesus points to a lesson for all in the man's attitude. In addition, the healing shows the appropriateness of the title the blind man used to get Jesus' attention. It is the Son of David who heals. Messiah draws near to Jerusalem, and his authority is at work.

Healing comes immediately, and the man follows Jesus, *praising God* (on immediate healing, 4:39; 5:25; 8:44, 47, 55; 13:13; glory to God, 2:20; 4:15; 5:25-26; 7:16; 13:13; 17:15). The picture is poignant. God is thanked for his work through Jesus. Having gained physical sight, the man finds that new light dawns as he focuses on following Jesus. Even the crowd is changed. Scoffers at the start, the people turn to praise God in the end. Seeing Jesus means being transformed.

Saving the Lost: Zacchaeus (19:1-10) Luke has consistently shown how Jesus cared for those in need and for those rejected by society. In the Zacchaeus account these themes are summed up in beautiful detail. The account is unique to Luke's Gospel, just as the parables of the lost sheep, the lost coin and the compassionate father are. Luke always portrays tax collectors favorably (3:12; 7:29; 15:1; 18:10). In return to Jesus'

Luke may have reversed the order between the blind man and Zacchaeus, so the blind man's healing could be first and frame the Zacchaeus story. In this case, the idea that Jesus heals upon entering Jericho is more an issue of appearance. Another approach argues that the verb *engizō* can mean "to be in the vicinity of" rather than "to draw near to" (NIV *approached*). If this is correct, then the issue of entry dissolves entirely (Porter 1992:91-104). As to the number of healed blind people, Matthew often mentions such pairs (Mt 8:29-30; 9:27; 20:30). Luke and Mark seem to keep their story simple at a literary level.

openness to him, Zacchaeus makes the proper response. Having accepted Jesus' initiative, Zacchaeus becomes generous with his resources, even seeking to make restitution for past wrongs. He is a rich man who gets through the eye of the needle.

Jesus proceeds into Jericho. His visit has attracted a large crowd. Zacchaeus, a rich *chief tax collector,* also is interested in Jesus. In Luke's literary context, the introduction of Zacchaeus sends both positive and negative signals. Tax collectors have been portrayed with favor, but rich men with disfavor. We often confront such ambiguities of connection. Stereotypes are often just that. However, in his culture Zacchaeus would be regarded totally negatively because his wealth was "extorted" from fellow Jews on behalf of occupying Rome. This explains the public reaction to Jesus' invitation later in the story. Luke will seek to reverse that perception.

The tax collector is too short to see over the crowd, but his desire is so great that he exercises creativity in attaining his goal. A *sycamore-fig tree* is like a short oak tree, with a squatty trunk and wide branches. So Zacchaeus has a high camera angle on the event.

Jesus takes the initiative, calling for Zacchaeus. The text does not discuss how Jesus knows his name, but Jesus announces that it "is necessary" *(dei)* for him to stay with this eager spectator. In the ancient culture, the request revealed Jesus' acceptance of Zacchaeus; thus it stuns the crowd (v. 7). Luke underlines the request by using the frequent Lukan term *today,* even placing it in an emphatic position (*sēmeron:* 2:49; 4:43; 9:22; 13:16, 33; 15:32; 17:25; 22:37; 24:7, 26, 44). The request meets with public skepticism, which allows Jesus to make a point about the nature of his mission. Zacchaeus's attempt to glimpse Jesus has become much more.

Zacchaeus responds by coming down the tree and receiving Jesus with joy (NIV: *welcomed him gladly*). The theme of joy, coming as it does after a story about the Son of David, may suggest messianic joy. What is clear is that joy is an appropriate response to God's initiative on our behalf (1:14; 2:10; 10:20; 13:17; 15:5, 32; 19:37; 24:41, 52: Danker 1988:305).

19:2 The reference to *a chief tax collector* is unprecedented in ancient literature (Michel 1972:98, 104-5). Since collecting taxes involved a series of contracting relationships, it is clear that Zacchaeus is at the top of the ladder; he would be the one to hire the actual tax

Here joy is the response of a man who has fulfilled God's will despite the protests of many who surround him. The crowd's grumbling recalls earlier grumbling about Jesus' associations (5:30).

Zacchaeus's response to the crowd's charges raises the passage's major interpretive issues. The remark's exact timing is not clear. Does it come immediately after Jesus' request, as the grumbling becomes audible? Or does it come afterward? What is clear is that the statements are made in a public setting. Zacchaeus makes a defense. But does he state that he recently has been faithful in being generous, with the verbs of this verse as progressive present tenses (Fitzmyer 1985:1220, 1225)? Or is he vowing to make generous restitution in the future, the verbs being futuristic presents (Stein 1992:466-67)?

The latter reading is much more likely. Numerous reasons suggest its superiority, but a few are decisive (Stein lists seven reasons for this view). A present tense would portray Zacchaeus as a boaster, which is unlikely in this context. Second, it would be harder to understand the crowd's hostility, if Zacchaeus has already mended his ways. Statements about salvation coming to Zacchaeus's house this very day and about the lost being saved have less power if the salvation is not connected to this current event. The context is full of events where salvation has just been offered (18:9-14, 15-17, 18-30, 35-43). Though faith is not explicitly mentioned in this context as it is in the previous account of the blind man, Zacchaeus's actions represent a concrete expression of faith's presence— a theme that goes back to John the Baptist's call (3:8-14).

So Zacchaeus responds: *"Here and now I give half of my possessions to the poor, and if I have cheated anybody out of anything, I will pay back four times the amount."* Two actions substantiate Zacchaeus's new approach. A new generosity means that half of his assets are going to those in need (contrast 12:13-21; 16:19-31; see 1 Tim 6:6-10, 16-18). In addition, anyone who was robbed will be paid back with the highest penalty the law allows, a fourfold rate (Ex 22:1; 2 Sam 12:6). Normal restitution added only 20 percent (Lev 5:16; Num 5:7). The Mishna tended rarely to apply a more severe 40 percent penalty (*m. Ketubot* 3:9;

collectors who gathered the funds (see Lk 3:10-14). Since Zacchaeus would get a cut of the various commissions that came with the tax, he would be seen as "extorting" money at the top of a bureaucratic pyramid.

m. Baba Qamma 7:1-5). This rich man, touched by Jesus and responding with faith, exemplifies the restoration of a "lost one" and opens up his resources to be shared with others. He does not have to sell everything to receive Jesus' commendation. His heart is in the right place when it comes to possessions. So Zacchaeus becomes an exemplary rich disciple.

Jesus announces, *"Today salvation has come to this house, because this man, too, is a son of Abraham."* He speaks of the tax collector's spiritual heritage here. Now this one has been joined to the great patriarch of faith (Rom 4:11-18; Gal 3:9, 29). Zacchaeus's access to God's blessing has been gained through faith. Not only that, but Jesus' mission has been fulfilled (note the explanatory use of the Greek term *gar* ["for"] that begins v. 10). *"The Son of Man came to seek and to save what was lost."* Jesus does what the nation had failed to do in the past, become a shepherd to lost sheep (Ezek 34:2, 4, 16, 22-23—the hope of the Davidic king restored to the nation may be alluded to here and in Jn 10). Jesus' initiative is a requirement of his mission. In order to find the lost, he must seek the lost. In such cases even the rich and rejected can be a part of the flock. Faith brings Jesus home to stay in Zacchaeus's heart and the lost sheep back to the Shepherd.

Parable of Stewardship and the Minas (19:11-27) The final parable of the Jerusalem journey highlights the disciple's stewardship in the interim between Jesus' death and return. It continues the theme of his preparation of the disciples for life after his departure. His servants must recognize that the consummation of the kingdom is yet future and they are accountable for their service in the meantime. Those who reject Jesus' kingship face judgment, whether they reject that kingship directly or view the King as harsh rather than gracious.

The motive for this parable is explicit. Jesus wishes to correct the view that because he was near Jerusalem *the kingdom of God was going to*

19:11-27 This parable has been the subject of much discussion. Potential parallels in Matthew 25:14-30 and a similar saying in Mark 13:34-35 have sufficient differences to raise genuine questions whether this is the same story or a variation on a similar theme. As many as ten differences suggest a separate parable from Matthew's version (Blomberg 1990:217-20; Bock 1995: see introduction to the passage). The historical background to this parable is Herod the Great's and Archelaus's journeys to receive political authority from Rome. Herod received kingship in 40 B.C., while Archelaus was so disliked that he received an

appear at once. Of course what is meant here is the decisive demonstration of regal authority that Jews expected of Messiah and that the disciples were still asking about in Acts 1:6. Luke wishes to steer attention away from that event to the responsibility that disciples have in the meantime.

The story is simple enough. A man goes to a faraway land to receive a kingdom. This portion of the parable portrays Jesus' departure in resurrection to receive the kingdom at the side of the Father, a major Lukan theme (Lk 24:26; Acts 2:36; 5:30-31; 7:55-56; 13:33-34; 17:31; Stein 1992:473). In the meantime certain servants associated with Jesus are called together and given a mina each—about one hundred drachmas, or three months' average wage. They are to trade with the money and are responsible to make it grow in value. Some of his subjects, however, want nothing to do with the leader and send a delegation to ask that this one not be chosen to rule. Those who refuse the rule are the Jewish leaders, while the servants represent all those who tie themselves to Jesus.

The servants need to be carefully described, since a key to the interpretation of the passage lies in their identity. Some assume that these are all genuine believers because Jesus calls the servants to himself. If so, the rejection of the third servant would mean either loss of rewards upon entrance to heaven or loss of salvation—a choice that generally depends on one's theological tradition. But the third servant's attitude is crucial to an understanding the parable. This third servant views the owner as harsh, even a lawbreaker, by reaping that which he does not sow (Josephus *Against Apion* 2.31 §216). He would exact large sums of money from those who serve him. He would run over people. Now this servant's portrait of the owner suggests an attitude contrary to trust and faith. Though this man serves the master, he is not really allied to him. The failure of his stewardship is no surprise in light of this attitude. This

ethnarchy only in 4 B.C. The story's scenario was very well known.

A challenge to reading this text as discussing the interim period until Jesus returns comes from L. T. Johnson (1991:293-94). He argues that the parable foresees no delay of the kingdom's consummation and is about current events of Luke's Gospel story only. But such a reading ignores the parable's parallelism with 12:35-48, which is clearly a parable about the return.

servant represents a person who has only an association with the Master. Perhaps the individual illustrated here is Judas.

The parable's story is simple. The master returns to evaluate the stewardship of his servants. The first servant has gained ten minas for his one, a 1,000 percent increase. This man has been totally faithful. The reward is more service—responsibility for ten cities. The second servant is also faithful. A 500 percent increase is his contribution. He gets five cities. In contrast, the third servant has done nothing to invest his money, for reasons noted above. He does not think the king is worth laboring for, because the king would rob him. Commendation and more service follow faithfulness, but what follows such a harsh rejection of stewardship?

The master accuses the man of hypocrisy. If he *knew* the king was *a hard man,* then he should have at least put the money in the bank so it could earn a little interest. At least there would have been something to collect! So Jesus calls this slave *wicked (pornēros).* His mina goes to the first servant, who has been faithful. The third servant ends up with nothing. As Jesus says in conclusion, *"But as for the one who has nothing, even what he has will be taken away."* These words echo 8:18. It matters little whether this conclusion is the word of the master or Jesus' commentary, a detail that is disputed; the point is the same either way. Those who have nothing receive nothing. In fact, they lose whatever they thought they had. The stubborn slave is the "odd man out" who appears in so many of Jesus' parables (Mt 13:29-30, 41, 49-50; 18:32-34; 22:11-13; 25:41). Some are associated with Jesus only superficially, and their lack of faith will be revealed at the evaluation of their life's stewardship.

19:28-44 The parallels are Matthew 21:1-11, Mark 11:1-11 and John 12:12-19. There is no parallel for verses 41-44. Verses 37 and 39-40 are also unique to Luke. These verses all highlight the leadership's reaction and Jesus' concern for the nation—major themes in Luke's Gospel.

The event's historicity is much discussed. Most challenged is its messianic flavor. Could a crowd so overwhelmingly favorable to Jesus as the Messiah reverse itself in the space of one week? Was Jesus' entry on a donkey inherently messianic? John's Gospel even suggests that some of the event's significance was not obvious to the disciples until after the resurrection. Luke's version carefully notes that it is the disciples who begin the chants of welcoming Jesus as the King. Since Psalm 118 is used, the hope of God's coming is invoked. The crowd joined in, not necessarily because they were hailing Jesus as the Messiah, but because he was widely believed to be a prophet and thus his presence suggested that God was at work. The crowd may have sensed a declaration of the eschaton's arrival in God's respected representative, while the disciples knew more (Stein 1992:478; Witherington

In contrast, the faithful are rewarded: *"To everyone who has, more will be given."* Jesus acknowledges faithfulness with commendation and more service. To use the Lord's gifts is to prepare to serve him further.

One group remains to be dealt with, the rejecters. They will be slain. Their rejection is total. The parable follows the reality of ancient politics. Refusing the rule of the one in power often meant paying with one's life. Here is the judgment of God. For the leadership in the short term, this would mean Jerusalem's destruction in A.D. 70 (19:41-44). But in the long term there was a more permanent rejection to face. It is a terrifying thing to fall into the hands of a judging and rejected God.

Jesus Enters Jerusalem and Weeps for the City (19:28-44) The event traditionally known as Palm Sunday is fraught with meaning. It is hard to think of any close contemporary equivalents that would parallel the mood of this entry and presentation. It could be compared to a political convention where the party leader is selected and proclaimed to the nation. The figure is usually known to the public before the selection, but at the convention the campaigning gets serious: the leader is now an official candidate. Another analogy would be the "coming out" of a debutante at a ball. As the young woman is officially presented to larger society, there is a public recognition that a new and significant stage in her life has arrived. We could also think of a regal coronation ceremony, but that does not work in this case, because Jesus is being presented as a regal figure but not crowned as one.

Of course, the event is crucial and transitional for Luke. He has built up the journey to Jerusalem as full of significance. Jerusalem is the city

---

1990:104-7).

It is not certain that the entry took place on a Sunday or in A.D. 30, as tradition and consensus have it. Hoehner has argued persuasively that the year was A.D. 33 and, taking John 12 as the key, that the entry took place on a Monday (Hoehner 1977:95-114).

With regard to the lament in verses 41-44, it is often argued that this is *vaticinium ex eventu,* or "prophecy after the fact." But Jerusalem's fate as described by Jesus will echo the standard divine reaction to covenant unfaithfulness, the overrunning of the capital. Anyone in the first century who knew the nationalist strains in some forms of Judaism might have foretold the Romans' attacking and overrunning the city to protect their interests. Given that political possibility and the nation's covenant unfaithfulness, Jesus' prediction is not very surprising. Of course, in addition, there is the worldview issue of the possibility of prophetic gift. To those who consider it possible for God to speak this way, such a prediction need not be a surprise at all, especially given the other factors (for more discussion of this issue, see Bock 1995: exegesis of these verses).

of Jesus' fate and destiny. From Luke's perspective Jesus is still approaching the city and has not officially entered it, since his condemnation of Jerusalem's rejection in verse 41 takes places as he *approached.* Events move quickly from this point, so that after the procession and the lament over Jerusalem, Jesus moves inexorably toward his death. Announced as the king, he is rejected as king.

Luke continues the journey motif as he introduces the entry: *After Jesus had said this, he went on ahead, going up to Jerusalem. As he approached Bethphage and Bethany* . . . Still outside the city, moving through villages just a few miles to the east, he prepares to enter the capital. He takes control of events as well, instructing two disciples to procure an animal for him. Jesus' riding of the young colt fulfills Zechariah 9:9, though Luke does not mention this text specifically. The fact that the colt is young may suggest purity (Num 19:2; Deut 21:3; 1 Sam 6:7). The animal is commandeered because *"the Lord needs it."* Here culture and divine design meet. In the culture a major religious or political figure could request the use of livestock, a custom known as *angaria* (Derrett 1971:243-49). Someone who knew Jesus or his disciples might well have been ready to lend an animal to them. The detail with which the Lord prepares the disciples to find the colt adds another note: for him the coming events will include no surprises. He has announced the sequence of events. When the disciples' experience exactly fits what he has predicted (vv. 32-34), this theme is strengthened.

Outer garments are laid over the animal to make a saddle, and Jesus is placed on it. The language used to describe Jesus' riding the animal recalls 1 Kings 1:33 and David's selecting of Solomon, while the mention of the colt alludes to Zechariah 9:9. The imagery is regal and even messianic, though it is a humble Messiah who makes the ride.

As the people spread their garments (NIV: *their cloaks*) on the road, a "red carpet" of sorts is produced. This part of the entry recalls Jehu's entry for royal accession in 2 Kings 9:13. Luke makes no mention of branches, possibly because they may have had revolutionary, nationalistic overtones he wishes to avoid connecting to Jesus (2 Maccabees 10:7-9; L. T. Johnson 1991:297). The entry is regal without being revolutionary or threatening.

As often in Jesus' ministry, word and deed are hand in hand. The event suggests a regal entry, while the praise points to God's presence. God is being praised for the mighty works he has done through Jesus. The concept of works of power (NIV: *miracles*) is frequent in Luke (4:32-33, 41; 5:17; 6:19; 8:46; 9:1; 19:37; Acts 4:33; 6:8; 8:13; 10:38). For the crowd the miracles mean Jesus is a great prophet (7:16; 9:7-9). But for the disciples Jesus is the promised King (9:18-20). Only Luke inserts the reference to a king into the quote from Psalm 118:26: *"Blessed is the king who comes in the name of the Lord!"* These events signaled a unique time and a unique figure (Lk 11:29-32; 13:10-17; 14:1-6; 17:11-19; 18:35-43; Acts 10:38).

The use of the psalm is significant, because in Jewish worship it was seen ultimately as celebrating God's plan. One day the one greeted as coming in the Lord's name would be the Messiah (Bock 1987:118, 125). The psalm was used in the Feast of Tabernacles for just this reason (*m. Sukka* 3:9; 4:5). So joy and cries of peace surround the verse's use here. Just as heaven rejoices when a lost sinner is found, heaven rejoices as the King enters the city.

But the moment is not so triumphal in the minds of some. The religious leaders regard the crowd's claims as excessive. They approach Jesus to get him to calm the disciples' enthusiasm. Maybe these followers have gone overboard, as zealous supporters often do: *"Teacher, rebuke your disciples!"* Using an urgent Greek aorist imperative *(epitimēson),* the leaders ask that the eschatological demonstration be stopped by Jesus' rebuke. They have again failed to see the sign of the times (12:54-56; 13:31-35).

Irony drips from Jesus' response. He cannot silence his disciples, for if he did, then creation itself would take up the song: *"If they keep quiet, the stones will cry out."* Even inanimate creation understands events better than the leaders do—so deep runs their blindness. All the way back to Abel's blood crying out to God, when rhetoric portrays the creation as speaking, there has been serious misunderstanding of God's ways (Gen 4:10; Hab 2:11; Jas 5:4). The blindness is tragic, as a weeping Jesus will reveal in verses 41-44. Only Luke notes this exchange between the Pharisees and Jesus.

So the candidate has entered the city. His supporters have acknowledged his role. But opposition stands in the way. A divided Israel receives the king into its capital, just as humanity is divided over Jesus today. If one listens to Jesus and to the creation, Luke says, it is obvious who is on the side of truth and right.

The entry encompasses the different kinds of responses to Jesus. Some know who he is and serve him, following his instructions. Others are open, but not with much understanding. Still others are hostile toward him. Even the creation has a response to what is occurring. A famous saying goes, "All the world is a stage and we are merely players in it." Yet as the heavens watch, the question remains: which response do we support (Eph 3:8-10)?

The rejection causes Jesus so much pain that he is weeping as he draws near to the city. *"If you, even you, had only known on this day what would bring you peace."* The nation is missing its moment. Peace with God is not possible for those who reject Jesus. Though this rejection produces Jesus' tragic death, the national consequences of the people's blindness are even more tragic and staggering. Peace is now *"hidden from your eyes"* (Ps 122:6; Jer 15:5). What follows is a "searing oracle of doom" (Tiede 1980:80): national sin will pay its price in judgment on covenant unfaithfulness. The oracle is introduced with the foreboding phrase *days will come* (1 Sam 2:31; 2 Kings 20:17; Is 39:6; Jer 7:32-34; 33:14; 49:2; Zech 14:1). When this phrase appears, judgment follows.

What Jesus proceeds to describe is a Hellenistic military siege that will slowly choke the city to death. This anticipated disaster recalls the judgment that befell the pagan nations when God acted against them and the judgment Israel experienced in going into exile (Ps 137:9; Is 3:26; 29:1-4; Jer 6:6-21; 8:18-22; Ezek 4:1-2; Nahum 3:10; Hab 2:8). The enemy "will cast up a bank around you and surround you, and hem you in on every side, and dash you to the ground, you and your children within you, and they will not leave one stone upon another." The defeat will be total. The city and the temple will be destroyed. Josephus's description of the defeat of A.D. 70 shows just how true Jesus' prediction was (*Jewish Wars* 5.11.4 §§466-72; 5.12.2 §§502-10; 7.1.1 §§1-4; 7.8.7 §§375-77).

The reason for the destruction is simple—"you did not know the time of your visitation." Messiah has come and Israel has said no. Opportunity for peace has come, but the nation has opted for destruction—a destruction that will not be permanent, as later texts like Acts 3:18-22 and

Romans 11:27-29 make clear. Still, this soon-to-come destruction will be devastating. What Jesus has hinted at in Luke 13:31-35 is now described in graphic and painful detail. Israel's house will be desolate. A first-century Auschwitz awaits it. Unlike the twentieth-century version, where repulsive ethnic hatred brought death, the Jewish nation of the first century brought catastrophe on itself. The ancient Jewish historian Josephus blamed the nationalists, the Zealots, for the nation's demise, but Jesus has a different answer. By rejecting him, Israel has chosen the way of judgment. It has missed the day and the moment.

What was true of the Jewish nation can also be true of individuals. To miss Jesus is to miss the time of visitation and face accountability before God.

□ Jerusalem: The Innocent Slain and Raised (19:45—24:53)

The final section of Luke's Gospel proceeds through various controversies in the city about Jesus' authority and his eschatological discourse. After the discourse come the final meal and Jesus' arrest. Luke notes four trials: one before the Jewish leadership, one before Pilate, one before Herod and one before the crowd. The masses persuade Pilate to slay Jesus at the Jewish leadership's instigation. On the cross Jesus is portrayed as slain in innocence. The soldier's confession in 23:47 sums up Luke's view. In the resurrection, which catches the disciples off guard, Jesus is vindicated and reveals himself to them, reviving their hope. His life has fulfilled the Scripture, and so will the preaching of repentance by the commissioned and empowered disciples (24:44-49).

Three themes dominate this section: Jesus is in control of events, the disciples need to be faithful and ready, and God is directing his plan. The "must" of Messiah's career comes to realization here. The issue is not so much how Jesus' death achieves God's will. That is a theological concern Paul explores in his picture of substitutionary atonement. Rather, Luke emphasizes *who* God vindicates and exalts through resurrection. Jesus is the slain innocent. He is risen and exalted to be Lord and Christ (Acts 2:22-39). With Jesus' departure, his disciples prepare to take up his work. The Gospel has an open-ended conclusion that leads to the story of the church, not only the church in Acts but beyond that early era to the church of today. For the story of the influence of the raised Jesus in the world continues to this day.

Controversy in Jerusalem (19:45—21:4) This section is one of end-less controversy, from Jesus' cleansing of the temple to his commenda-tion of the widow who gave all. Even this woman, whom her culture sees as a helpless nobody, stands for Jesus in a favorable contrast to the Pharisees and the wealthy. The various debates in this section are at-tempts to trap Jesus, especially in light of the leadership's reaction to the temple cleansing. Jesus offers two rebuttals, one in a parable showing that the leadership is on the way out and another in a short question designed to focus on Messiah's lordship authority.

Make no mistake about this final section. It shows a battle for the claim to lead God's people. The leadership thinks it has earned that right. Jesus suggests it has been his, as David's heir, all along. Given Jesus' view of himself and the leaders' inability to trip him up, they will move to stop him. Their action will appear to work at first, only to undergo a mirac-ulous reversal. The entire unit raises the question, Where does God's authority reside?

The Cleansing of the Temple (19:45-48) This event is like a stick of dynamite in the relationship between Jesus and the leadership. As if throwing a flame onto oil, Jesus raises the issue of his authority most directly by his act of cleansing the temple. In fact, the leadership clearly sees this as the issue, as 20:1-8 makes clear. Their plotting in verses 47-48 follows the cleansing and shows the action's importance in pushing them to act. In the other Synoptic Gospels, when the trials of Jesus start it is his attitude toward the temple that is the prosecution's launching point.

The custom Jesus attacks is the selling of various items necessary for

---

Notes: 19:45-48 This event has parallels in Matthew 21:12-13 and Mark 11:15-19. Another potential parallel is John 2:13-17. At the least, the event Luke records is similar to these others. Whether John's account is of the same event or not is a very complex question. Either approach could be correct, since one or the other author could have placed the event differently for literary reasons. Nonetheless, John's use of Psalm 69 and the way his placement works in the account suggest a distinct event, especially as it is linked to John 2:23-25.

Even more debated is the significance of this event historically. Though some scholars have doubted its historicity, most acknowledge that Jesus probably did act decisively in the temple. Sanders suggests that an actual total cleansing did not take place but only a pro-phetic prediction and a small-scale action—Jesus simply overturned some tables. This is the work of the prophet Jesus (Sanders 1985:61-76). Others argue that a cleansing is in view.

sacrifice: animals, wine, oil, salt and doves (Jn 2:14; *m. Šeqalim* 1:3; 2:1, 4; Eppstein [1964] notes that some of these practices may have been just recently moved into the temple courts). Money changers also collected Roman and Greek coins and exchanged them for the half-shekel temple tax required by the Torah (Ex 30:11-14). The exchange had a built-in surcharge, a portion of which may have gone to the high priest's family.

Is the cleansing of the temple prophetic or messianic? It must be admitted that little in the event itself has a messianic character. But its literary and temporal juxtaposition to the entry is crucial to an understanding of its character. Jesus has just left a dispute over whether the disciples should call him king—a confession he accepted. Now he is acting on the temple. Though his temple actions are prophetic in character, his acceptance of the earlier acclaim cannot be ignored. The confession is still ringing in his opponents' ears.

Many historical-critical scholars are used to treating events in Jesus' life in isolation from each other, as independent units of tradition. However, in the case of these Jerusalem events of Jesus' last week of ministry, such a separation is historically artificial. The connection between Jesus' entry and his first public act in the temple should not be ignored. The linkage makes Jesus' act one of messianic and prophetic authority. It may well be that Jesus acts here as a leader-prophet, much like Moses.

Now prophets, even those like John the Baptist, could be tolerated. But a prophet who also saw himself as a king had to be stopped, especially if he was going to impose himself on the nation's worship. If the nation had to repent for its actions at the temple, the priests would have to acknowledge their own culpability before God. They could not accept such a challenge to their authority.

Jesus' rebuke is a prophetic act that also raises issues of his authority, since the temple is such a sacred site in Judaism (C. A. Evans 1989:237-70; Witherington 1990:107-16).

For Jesus, the first-century temple has become excessively commercial, sinfully so *(a den of robbers),* rather than being a site for worship and prayer. The money changers helped those who had come to Jerusalem from a distance exchange their money so they could pay the temple tax in the proper currency, shekels (Philo *Embassy to Gaius* 216, 313). To pay the tax was an act of piety. Pilgrims also could purchase animals or birds for the necessary sacrifices (compare Lk 2:24). Jewish tradition had no problem with the money changers' presence (*m. Šeqalim* 3:1; 6:4-5), but the Qumran community did not like it (Cairo Damascus Document 6:15-16; 1QpHab 9:1-7; L. T. Johnson 1991:299-300). There were as many as thirteen tables in the temple area and thirteen chests for funds.

Luke's version of this event is very concise. He does not supply many details the other Gospels include, especially the descriptions of how physical Jesus' actions were. Rather, Luke goes right to the heart of the event, focusing on Jesus' rebuke with its Old Testament allusions: *"It is written,"* he says, *" 'My house will be a house of prayer,' but you have made it 'a den of robbers.' "* The quote combines Isaiah 56:7 and Jeremiah 7:11. Isaiah expresses the hope that the temple will be a house for all the nations, while Jeremiah condemns the Israelites' hypocrisy and injustice as they worship at the temple. (Interestingly, here Luke does not develop the point about Gentiles, even though he loves the theme.) The Jeremiah speech is one of that prophet's most scathing. It calls the Jewish people "robbers," bandits just like the thieves of Luke 10:30.

It may well be, given Jesus' lament and the leadership's protest which precede this event, that Jesus' rebuke for hypocrisy is not limited to commercial practices in the temple but extends to the nation's refusal to worship God and recognize the day of visitation. Either way, Jesus is the issue, and the subject is properly honoring God. Israel thinks God is honored at the temple. Jesus claims the exact opposite. The nation is divided; choices are required. They cannot both represent God's will. The warning also illustrates the danger of combining religiosity and commercialism at the expense of true worship—a danger to which we also must be sensitive today.

The leaders begin *trying to kill* Jesus before he becomes even more dangerous (the Greek means "to destroy"). The plot to get Jesus, originally raised in 6:11 and 11:53-54, is hardening. Something must be done. Jesus is appearing at the temple daily. But because of his popularity the leaders cannot yet act. *All the people hung on his words.* Believing they have power, the leaders are in fact powerless to act until they get a break. That break will come from within the ranks of Jesus' inner circle.

Nothing has changed between Jesus' declaration that the nation's house is desolate (13:34-35) and his weeping for the nation upon entering the city (19:41). The nation's rejection, like the plot against Jesus, has hardened into resolve—and as sin calcifies it becomes even more dangerous. The "Jesus problem" goes in search of a "final solution." But like the Iron Curtain, this attempt to control the situation through isolation and containment will fail; even death cannot hold God's agent back from doing God's will.

By Whose Authority? (20:1-8) Today religious claims are a dime a dozen. If you survey the media it is not hard to find all types of claims about what God is doing. Ultimately the issue is not the claim but what stands behind it.

The Pharisees' question about Jesus' religious authority is in many ways a natural one. He has had no official training. He comes from Galilee, an area not known for its religious instruction or anything else of stature (Jn 7:52). He has never sat under a rabbi. Where does his authority come from? How can he justify the things he has been doing? This is really a fundamental question for the entire Gospel (4:32, 36; 5:24; 9:1; 10:19). It also opens a series of five controversies in 20:1-44. In these disputes the answer to the Pharisees' question becomes obvious, even though no direct reply is offered here. Though an answer is not forthcoming from Jesus, anyone who has followed Luke's story up to this point knows the reply, which is why Jesus' analogy with John the Baptist is so powerful. *By whose authority* does Jesus do these things? He responds, By the same authority John the Baptist possessed.

This controversy arises as Jesus is teaching in the temple, something he is doing daily (19:47). The fact that Jesus is teaching the gospel shows that his message has never changed. But the leadership wants to know the basis for Jesus' actions. Whether it is his teaching or his cleansing of the temple, where did he get the right to do such things? In Greek the question puts *by what authority (en poia exousia)* in the emphatic position, at the front of the question. In the questioners' view the leadership represents God's will and has the right to teach it. Where does Jesus get the right to challenge their teaching?

In good Jewish and Hellenistic fashion, Jesus answers the query with one of his own. This style of disputation was popular in the ancient world. It was designed to show who could ask the wiser question and expose weaknesses in the opponent. Such an approach also produced reflection about the proper approach to a problem. Jesus' question is a

---

20:1-8 The parallels to this passage are Matthew 21:23-27 and Mark 11:27-33.

simple one: *"John's baptism—was it from heaven, or from men?"* The
question is both obvious and subtle. By dealing with a public action, he
has excluded a war of words merely over public claims, titles or credentials. There will be no appeal to derived authority by means of lineage
or mere assertion. Did John give evidence that God stood behind his
deeds? Only two options exist: either he did or he did not. The subtlety
in the question lies not only in its appeal to concrete events but also in
the popular consensus that has developed. The multitudes know the
answer to this question: John came from God. God's presence manifested itself clearly in his ministry. Rejection of that conclusion can only
reflect blindness.

So the leadership is in a dilemma, since they had not responded to
John. They caucus to determine an answer. Either way of replying would
leave them exposed. If they acknowledged divine authority, they would
be hurting on two counts. First, they would raise the question why they
had not embraced John. Second, they would concede a major point to
Jesus: that one need not come from the Jerusalem school of rabbinic
studies in order to teach the way of God.

Now the text only mentions the first reason, but surely the leadership
senses the trap and knows that more than a historical religious dispute
about John is wrapped up in the question. Jesus is building a solid
analogy, and the leaders want to stay out of that building.

However, if they took the other option and said *"From men,"* they
would run the risk of being stoned, because the people know *John was
a prophet.* Though the concern about stoning may be figurative for the
rejection their answer would face, technically to reject a true prophet of
God did merit stoning (Deut 13:1-11).

Faced with a catch-22 and sensing they have been successfully cor-
nered, the leaders do what politicians often do when faced with a no-
win situation: they dance around the query and refuse to take a position.
Fence-sitting is always a tempting option when one is faced with a losing
proposition. The leaders' private dialogue reveals the blatant hypocrisy
of their answer. Clearly they regard John's authority as simply human, but

---

20:9-19 The parallels to this passage are Mark 12:1-11 and Matthew 21:33-44. The Lukan
version has many differences in the details, but the setting and extent of agreement show
that this is the same parable. It is clear that each Gospel writer has summarized the parable

they don't have the nerve to tell the crowd so. Rather than acknowledge their view and its unpopularity, they try to finesse the question. By doing so, they give up any moral ground for challenging Jesus. If they cannot decide about John, how can they decide about Jesus?

Jesus refuses to answer their original question, though the force of his analogy in his reply is obvious. The power behind Jesus is like that behind John. God has stood behind the actions of both, as Luke's narration had already made clear. In this case Jesus' silence lets the story of his ministry speak for itself. Claims of authority are not necessary since authoritative actions mark his entire ministry like giant footprints. Religious claims may be a dime a dozen, but some claims prove themselves to be true.

In this face-to-face battle, like a shootout in the Old West, the leadership had tried to destroy Jesus. But after the two sides had marked off their ten paces and turned to fire their questions, it was the leaders who blinked.

Parable of the Wicked Husbandmen (20:9-19) As a child and now as a parent, I have always enjoyed story time. I enjoyed hearing stories as a child, and I have received the special fun that comes from telling and acting out stories with a rich variety of voices for my children. There is something special about sitting on a parent's knee or watching a child's eyes light up as a story is read. Even more, if the story is a good one, it does more than just entertain: a lesson comes with it.

When Jesus turns to review Israel's history of response to God, he presents that history through a story, a parable. This final parable in Luke is really an allegory. Where a parable may have one to three points of contact with reality, an allegory has a whole set of correspondences to reality (Blomberg 1990). Since there are many points of correspondence between this story and the history of God's activity in salvation, it really is an allegory. Like many of Jesus' parables, it is a rebuke to Israel, especially its leadership (v. 19). But the people also reject the story (v. 16). So it is unlike a parent-child story time in that the message is not a pleasant one for the audience. Nonetheless, there is a point to the story, a lesson to be learned. Though the Son will be removed through death,

in his own way, though the basic parable goes back to Jesus. *Gospel of Thomas* 65 also contains a version of this parable, though efforts to argue that it is the original version are not sustainable (Snodgrass 1974-75:142-44; Hengel 1968:1-39; Schoedel 1972:548-60).

the promise will not remain in the leadership's hands; it will go to others. They can destroy neither the Son nor the promise.

Jesus opens the story by referring to a *vineyard*. This image is rich with Old Testament and Jewish background, alluding to the presence of promise in Israel (Ps 80:8-13; Is 5:1-7; 27:2; Jer 2:21; Ezek 19:10-14; Hos 10:1; *1 Enoch* 10:16; 84:6; 93:5). When Jesus places tenants in the story, he enriches the Old Testament imagery by setting up the role of the nation and leadership as caretakers for the promise. This addition is significant because the parable concludes with the vineyard given *to others,* a reference to Gentile inclusion in the promise.

The servants represent the series of prophets whom the nation rejected. This theme has been constant in Luke (11:47-51; 13:31-35; Acts 7). The concept builds on texts such as Jeremiah 7:21-28 and is Jesus' response to the plot of Luke 19:47. The nation is a poor tenant, lacking fruit and abusing those sent to check on its work (13:6-9). The calls for fruit and repentance for its absence have gone unheeded—in fact, they have been rejected and ignored. Three times the owner's representatives are cast out. There is no significance in the number three other than to point out that God sent prophets to the nation repeatedly.

The vineyard owner, God, decides to send *"my son, whom I love"* (3:22; 9:35), hoping that the stubborn tenants will at least *respect him.* The owner anticipates that his son's visit will be fruitful. But with logic that illustrates sin's blindness, the tenants decide that if they slay the son, they will inherit the land. When land belonged to someone without an heir, inheritance followed a certain custom: when the owner died, the land usually passed on to those who worked the land. Their scheme, of course, assumes that the murderers will not be discovered. There is a major blind spot in their thinking. Given their past track record with the owner's servants, wouldn't these tenants be among the first murder suspects? Hardness of heart does strange things. *So they threw him out of the vineyard and killed him,* an allusion to Jesus' death outside Jerusalem. Jesus knows the leaders have rejected him so that death is his fate. In Luke's telling of the parable, the violence steadily increases as each messenger comes. The rejection is firmer all the time. The nation has gone the opposite direction from repentance.

So what will the owner do? *He will come and kill those tenants and give the vineyard to others.* The vineyard goes to those outside the leadership, even the nation, as the promise will encompass many people of the nations. Acts fills in this part of the story, though it is also clear that Israel still has a place in God's plan (Acts 1:6-11; 3:18-22; Rom 11:25-27). The point of God's judgment on the nation is clear as the crowd responds, *"May this never be!"* The point is clear and shocking to all—this should never happen, they respond. Yet this very act of murder is days away from taking place!

A Scripture sums up the lesson. Jesus cites Psalm 118:22 and asks why it is recorded there: *The stone the builders rejected has become the cornerstone* (NIV margin). This psalm, already cited in 13:35 and 19:38, indicates that God will vindicate his rejected leader. This building-stone imagery made a great impact on the church (Acts 4:11; Rom 9:32-33; 1 Pet 2:7). The psalm uses the symbolism of the foundation stone that is crucial to a building. Jesus is the foundation stone of God's plan. Though some may reject him, God will make him the centerpiece of his plan. Rejection by the Jewish nation is not the end of the plan. There is no replacing this precious and chosen stone.

In fact, judgment resides with "the rock." To fall on that stone is to be broken to pieces. When the stone falls on someone, it crushes. The point is clear: anyone opposing God's stone will be crushed by it. A Jewish proverb has a similar thrust: "If the stone falls on the pot, alas for the pot; if the pot falls on the stone, alas for the pot!" (Midrash Esther 3:6). Imagery for the passage does not allude to a specific text, though the concept is reminiscent of Isaiah 8:14 and Daniel 2:34-44. Rejecting the "beloved Son" has grave consequences—not for the Son, since he will be raised up by God, but for those who reject him. The parable is Jesus' statement regarding the source of his authority. He is the beloved Son, and God will vindicate him and exalt him. His death will be followed by resurrection and exaltation into a place of authority (Acts 2:22-39).

The leadership wanted to seize Jesus on the spot. They knew he had told the parable against them. They could not allow their authority to be challenged anymore. Still, the problem was Jesus' popularity. So opinion polls caused a degree of restraint but did not bring a change in resolve. They would find a way to get Jesus, despite his clear indication that the ultimate outcome would be their dashing themselves against God's precious cornerstone. You cannot kill a solid rock.

The Temple Tax (20:20-26) The next controversy is political and
is a clever attempt to get Jesus into trouble either with Rome or with the
Jews. The background is the "poll tax," which symbolized the Jewish
subjugation to Rome, a sensitive social issue. Nationalist Jews questioned
whether the poll tax should be paid, since it went directly to Rome. On
one reading of the leaders' test of Jesus, they were really asking Jesus
whether he was loyal to Rome or to God's nation, Israel.

The question's setting is clearly hostile. *Keeping a close watch on him,*
they sent spies, who pretended to be honest. They hoped to catch Jesus in
something he said so that they might hand him over to the power and
authority of the governor. The entire effort is hypocritical. Appearing to
ask a sincere question, they are really trying to set a trap. To add to the
hypocrisy, they flatter Jesus, saying that he does not show partiality and
teaches God's way truly. If they really feel this way, why have they not
become followers of Jesus? Such shallow flattery is similar to the arguments of those who say Jesus is a great teacher but ignore his claims to
unique authority.

Nonetheless, the question is whether the tax should be paid. Jesus
pursues the answer, even though he is aware of their *duplicity* (the
Greek term *panourgia* really refers to trickery [Bauernfeind 1967:726]).
His answer will frustrate and expose their hypocrisy at the same time.

Jesus asks them to produce a coin. The fact that they carry the coin
reading "Tiberius Caesar, Augustus, son of divine Augustus," shows that
they already function under Roman sovereignty. The denarius was about
the size of a dime and was the average pay for a day's labor. The men
carry these coins as a matter of course. When Jesus asks whose inscription is on it, they reply, *"Caesar's."*

Jesus' reply is brief: *"Then give to Caesar what is Caesar's, and to God*
what is God's." Government has the right to exist and function, but its
presence does not cancel out one's allegiance to God (Rom 13:1-7; 1 Pet
2:13-17). To what had been posed as an either-or question Jesus gives
a both-and answer, avoiding the trap.

20:20-26 The parallels to this text are Matthew 22:15-22 and Mark 12:13-17. All the
accounts are very similar, though Luke stands closer to Mark.
20:27-40 The parallels are Matthew 22:22-33 and Mark 12:18-27. Again, Luke is verbally

There are many points the passage does not discuss. What happens when there is a blatant moral conflict between the affairs of state and one's union to God? The reply does not endorse a doctrine of separation of church and state, as if these were two totally distinct spheres. What it does suggest is that government, even a pagan government, has the right to exist and be supported by all its citizens. Its existence is not an inherent violation of Christians' commitment to God. The passage does reject the Jewish Zealot approach. Jesus was not a political revolutionary, nor was he an ardent nationalist. He could not have rightly been charged with being politically subversive, though his opponents will misrepresent his words to make this charge in 23:2-3.

Once again, an attempt to trap Jesus has failed. His work transcends politics. His opponents are *unable to trap him* in his reply. In fact, they are silenced by his response. Frantic attempts to corner Jesus have failed. Another way to get him has to be found. A final point emerges from the drama: Jesus looks to be wiser than the leadership. He knows God's way; they do not.

A Theological Dispute over Resurrection (20:27-40) It's easy to assume that questions about resurrection and life after death are modern concerns. Surely only the Enlightenment's empiricist tendencies led to such doubts. Weren't the ancients all very open and malleable when it came to the supernatural? The theological controversy presented to Jesus next shows how wrong such thinking about the ancient world is.

The Sadducees, who ask Jesus about the wife of seven men through levirate marriage, did not believe in resurrection or in the existence of angels (Josephus *Jewish Wars* 2.8.14 §§163-65; *Antiquities* 13.10.6 §§297-98; 18.1.4 §§16-17; Meyer 1971). For these priestly and lay aristocrats, who controlled much of the religious and political situation in first-century Israel and whose rich heritage stemmed back to Zadok, the natural world and the Torah were the only religious authorities (Ezek 40:46; 43:19; Josephus *Antiquities* 18.1.1 §4; Fitzmyer 1985:1302-3). The Sadducees were ideological rivals to the Pharisees. Their movement collapsed in A.D. 70, and the Pharisees took control from them. So all our

closer to Mark's version, though Jesus' reply in Luke is more extensive. All the versions are very similar.

descriptions of them come from those of the prevailing party, the Pharisees. They reacted strongly against the oral Torah of the Pharisees and
were theologically conservative in their commitment to the Torah alone,
yet they were very pragmatic in their relations with Rome, possibly because of their high social status. In the sense that modernist religion
abandons any supernatural belief and keeps only moralism, then the
Sadducees were modernists. Thus the controversy is important not only
among the ancient Jewish camps but also for modern times. This is the
Sadducees' only appearance in Luke's Gospel, but their effort here means
that most of the major Jewish groups have taken their swing at Jesus.

The law of levirate marriage was designed to perpetuate the line of
descent for a man who had died childless (Deut 25:5; Ruth 4:1-12; *m.
Yebamot*). If a man died without progeny, his brother would take his
widow as his own wife and raise their children in the name of the
deceased brother. Preserving the line of descent also kept land in the
family, so numerous social consequences resulted from the practice.

Hoping to embarrass Jesus theologically, the Sadducees use the practice of levirate marriage to pose a question with a satirical edge. They
are trying to show how foolish resurrection teaching is. Their question
seeks to discredit resurrection much like another text, *t. Niddah* 70b,
which asks whether the dead need to be ritually cleansed after resurrection since their contact with the dead and the grave renders them unclean. The question shows how carefully such issues were considered.
This was no trivial matter for them.

So a man's brother dies married and childless, and the brother takes
up his familial duty, marrying the widow. The only problem is that this
man also dies childless. In fact, a total of seven brothers come and go
as the woman's husbands, yet no children are produced. The supersti-
tious person might wonder whether marriage to this woman was haz-
ardous to one's health! Finally the woman dies. On the premise that
resurrection follows, *"whose wife will she be, since the seven were married to her?"* The dilemma is clear. This woman has too many men to
be responsible to and for in heaven! The Sadducees have fired their best
theological shot, and it looks pretty damaging.

Numerous premises stand behind the question: (1) Relationships in
the afterlife will be like those in this life. (2) The absurdity of the woman's

dilemma reveals the absurdity of resurrection. (3) With the possible exception of levirate responsibility, monogamy was recommended—a key point since this woman has been committed in marriage seven times!

Jesus' reply undercuts the basic premise before stating emphatic support for resurrection: *"Those who are considered worthy of taking part in that age and in the resurrection from the dead will neither marry nor be given in marriage, and they can no longer die, for they are like the angels. They are God's children, since they are children of the resurrection."* After the resurrection relationships change. "Putting on immortality" means there is no more need to create new mortals (1 Cor 15:50-54). With God as Father, families are no longer necessary. There is no more death, nor is there any need to worry about continuing one's family line. This makes the afterlife a new paradigm of existence to which the problem the Sadducees have posed is irrelevant. People do not marry in the afterlife, and the issue of whose spouse the woman is becomes vacuous.

By mentioning *the angels,* Jesus has made a second dig at the ancient modernists. The Sadducees also denied the existence of the spirit world (Acts 23:8). Jesus' point is that resurrection life takes on the qualities of eternity and sheds the limitations of mortality. The Sadducees' lack of appreciation for the new dimensions of resurrection existence, not to mention their hesitation to embrace alternate forms of existence at all, has caused them to frame a question that exposes their ignorance. Their denial of the spirit world is significant, since God himself is spirit. This is why Jesus says being like an angel means being a child of God in resurrection. The transformation of resurrection is what makes eternal life possible.

In fact, Jesus goes on, to deny resurrection is to deny the teaching of Scripture, such as that revealed at the burning bush. When Moses, years after the patriarchs died, called the Lord *the God of Abraham, and the God of Isaac, and the God of Jacob,* he was asserting the continued existence of the patriarchs. Here Jesus exploits an absent verb in the Old Testament passage. God *is* the God of the patriarchs. That conclusion follows on another premise: *"He is not the God of the dead, but of the living."* For Moses to speak about God's relationship to the patriarchs means that they must be alive—and raised. The beauty of this allusion to Exodus 3:2-6 is that Jesus argues for resurrection from within the

Torah, the only portion of Scripture that counted for a Sadducee. God's promises live on for the patriarchs because they still live. In fact, life is in his sovereign hands, and all live for him.

Luke notes that some of the Jews—Pharisees in all likelihood—commend his reply. And having failed to trap Jesus politically and theologically, his opponents stop asking Jesus questions. Jesus has passed his oral exams too well. They will have to find another way to trap him.

This passage is important because it shows again that Jesus' understanding of God's way and will is superior to his opponents' perception. In addition it shows Jesus' affirmation of a resurrection and an afterlife that is different from life now in certain particulars. There is no reincarnation, nor is this life all there is. In the face of modern doubts about resurrection and rising belief in reincarnation and other theories of cosmic recirculation, this text makes it clear that this life is our one mortal moment and that after it we are accountable to God for how we have spent it. Death is not the end, only a beginning. The question is, the beginning of what? Only one's response to Jesus determines the answer to that question. Childless levirate wives need not worry which man is their husband. All should worry whether they are a child of God.

Jesus' Question About Messiah (20:41-44) Who is Jesus? Who is the Messiah? For Christians this is one of the basic questions of faith. This passage deals with that question by noting a short controversy between Jesus and the leadership. Previous attempts to stump him had failed, but now Jesus will silence his opponents with a question about the most important figure in Jewish promise, the Son of David, Messiah. It is Jesus' turn to ask a question and seek answers. How will the leadership fare in the hot seat?

Jesus raises a rabbinic antinomy. The question is asked both before and after a quotation of Psalm 110:1. *"How is it that they say the Christ is the Son of David? David himself declares in the Book of Psalms, 'The Lord said to my Lord: "Sit at my right hand until I make your enemies a footstool for your feet." ' David calls him 'Lord.' How then can he be his son?"* Jesus' goal is not to deny either premise but to show a rela-

---

20:41-44 The parallels are Matthew 22:41-46 and Mark 12:35-37. Unlike Matthew and Mark, Luke lacks the controversy about eternal life and the great commandment before this

tionship between two concepts that otherwise might appear to be in tension. In effect, Jesus is saying, more important than Jesus being David's son is that he is David's Lord. Or to answer Jesus' final question: that he is David's son is less significant (as significant as this is) than that he is David's Lord. Davidic sonship is not being denied; in fact, Davidic sonship is an important concept to Luke (1:31-35; Acts 13:23-39; also Paul, Rom 1:2-4). Rather, the point is Messiah's authority, and thus by implication Jesus' exalted position.

In fact, Jesus does not answer the question, nor does his audience. Instead the audience and Luke's reader are left to ponder it. In literary terms the answer comes in Luke 22:69 and Acts 2:22-39. The Son of David exercises divine prerogatives from the side of the Father in heaven. His authority is shared heavenly authority. To understand who the Son of David is, one must understand that he shares authority with the Father. As Acts 2 shows, authority over salvation comes from the Father through the Messiah, who sits at the Father's side functioning in "coregent" fashion. Thus the Lord Jesus reigns at the Father's side. Jesus does not make this explicit point here. But Luke 22:69 and Acts 2 show that ultimately this is the answer to the question.

Psalm 110:1 is the explanation for the answer; this is among the Old Testament passages most often quoted or alluded to in the New Testament (Acts 2:30-36; 7:55-56; 13:33-39; 1 Cor 15:22-28; Eph 1:19-23; Heb 1:3-14; 5—7). This royal psalm described the authority of the promised son of David. The picture of him at God's right hand is a picture of rule with God. A modern analogy would be to think of a corporate boardroom where the chairman of the board and the CEO sit together to manage the corporation. Only here the boardroom is God's heavenly court and the corporation is Creation and Redemption Inc. The Son of David shares authority and rule with the Father. So David, even though he is the ancestor of the Son in terms of family line, is under him in terms of authority.

All these points are only implied here. It took the resurrection to fully reveal who Jesus is, but the psalm shows the promise that through

---

passage. But the omission is easy to explain, since Luke 10:25-28 was so similar.

David's son eventually all the king's enemies would be defeated (Lk 1:67-79; Rom 1:2-4). Messiah's authority has the highest possible connections and reflects the highest possible position. When hymns declare, "He is Lord," passages like this explain what they mean.

The Scribes Stand Condemned (20:45-47) The lines between the Jewish leadership and Jesus were drawn since the journey to Jerusalem began. In 11:37-54 the Galilean teacher pronounced a series of woes condemning both the Pharisees and the scribes. Nothing has happened in the interim to change that assessment. So Jesus issues a warning to his disciples that also comes within earshot of the people. Because of the scribes' pride and hypocrisy, the disciples are to *beware.* The warning is like 12:1.

Pride reveals itself in the scribes' public behavior as they wear their long robes and receive greetings of honor in public places. In fact, rabbis received special salutations (Windisch 1964:498; Lk 11:43). The robes were nicely decorated and ostentatious (Josephus *Antiquities* 3.7.1 §151; 11.4.2 §80). Pride was also evident in the scribes' taking the first seats in the synagogue or at feasts. Jesus had condemned such pursuits of honor in 11:43 and 14:7-14. So Jesus is reviewing his displeasure at attitudes he considers unworthy of disciples.

Hypocrisy surfaces in the scribes' treatment of others. The estates of vulnerable widows are devoured, while long prayers create a façade of caring about God and others (11:39; 18:9-14). The scribes' actions contradict their surface practice. *"Such men will be punished most severely"* (10:14; 11:31-32, 51). Luke often mentions widows or the poor to indicate those God cares for (2:37; 4:25-26; 7:12; 21:1-4; Acts 6:1; 9:39).

How the leadership abused widows is debated. Was the widows' property now dedicated to the temple handled in a way that defrauded them? Did the leaders take undue advantage of their hospitality? Did they accept debt pledges that they knew could not be repaid? Did

---

20:45-47 The parallel to this text is Mark 12:38-40. Matthew 23:1-36 has a long discourse of condemnation against the entire Jewish leadership that is like Luke 11:37-54 in tone. The repetition of a short condemnation here may indicate Luke's awareness of Jesus' longer indictment of the leadership in Jerusalem.

21:1-4 The parallel to this text is Mark 12:41-44. If this refers to the temple receptacles,

they charge for legal advice against the dictates of the law? Scholars are not sure. But abuse occurred.

Disciples should avoid such superficial, destructive piety. True devotion comes from the heart, is marked by humility and cares for others; it does not use people.

The Widow Who Gave All (21:1-4) In contrast to the leadership's pride and hypocrisy come the simple actions of a poor widow. She also stands tall in contrast to the rich who are passing by and contributing to the temple treasury. While noting the rich who give in passing, Jesus draws attention to a *poor widow* who puts *two very small copper coins* into the treasury. These two coins, lepta, were the smallest coins possible. They were worth about 1/100 of a denarius, or five minutes' labor at minimum wage! Hers is a minimal gift, at least on the surface.

Nonetheless, Jesus calls it the greatest gift. She *"has put in more than all the others. All these people gave their gifts out of their wealth; but she out of her poverty put in all she had to live on."* This last phrase can be translated "out of her poverty put in all her living" *(ek tou hysterēmatos autēs panta ton bion)*. The contribution really came from "all that remained of her life." Jesus' point is not so much to rebuke others' contributions as to exalt a contribution that otherwise would have been underappreciated.

Sometimes little gifts cost a great deal more than big gifts do, and their merit is in the sacrifice they represent. In fact, real giving happens when one gives sacrificially. Interestingly, research has shown that when people's income increases their proportion of charitable contributions tends to drop. We tend to give less the more we are blessed. How would Jesus assess this trend?

In contrast to the scribes' pride and hypocrisy stands this woman who has sacrificed out of her life to honor God. So Jesus says, "Beware of the scribes, but follow this widow." When God measures the life of service, he does not just count, he weighs.

---

there were thirteen of them in the temple forecourt by the court of women. They were in the form of trumpets (*m. Šeqalim* 6:5; Neh 12:44; Josephus *Jewish Wars* 5.5.2 §200; 6.5.2 §282; *Antiquities* 19.6.1 §294; 1 Maccabees 14:49; 2 Maccabees 3:6, 24, 28, 40). The passage may simply allude to the room where these receptacles were located. Such offerings would be free-will gifts to the holy place.

Jerusalem's Destruction and the End (21:5-38) Luke's third prediction of Jerusalem's fall is by far the most detailed (the others come in 13:34-35; 19:41-44). Because of the speech's importance and complexity, I take a slightly more didactic approach in my overview of it.

The speech's character emerges when one examines the parallels within the Synoptics. Parallels of this Olivet discourse occur in Matthew 24:1-35 and Mark 13:1-37. A comparison of these parallels shows how Luke has drawn out some additional teaching and made some distinct points. Some of these points emerge from the additional material Luke includes (vv. 18, 21-22, 24, 28 are certainly additional material; vv. 19-20, 23b-26, 34-36 are probably additional). Other emphases surface because of the way Luke has presented the traditional material. Where Matthew speaks specifically of the "abomination that causes desolation" (Mt 24:15), for example, Luke simply refers to the "desolation" (Lk 21:20).

The significance of these differences becomes clear as one carefully compares the accounts. Luke emphasizes the destruction of Jerusalem in A.D. 70 in a way the other Gospels do not. All the Synoptics anticipate the fall of Jerusalem in the way they introduce the discourse, but Luke focuses on the short-term event in a way Matthew and Mark do not. His temporal indicators (vv. 9, 12) draw the reader back toward the present before really focusing on the end in verses 25-28. A transition begins to appear in verses 20-24, but until verse 19 the focus is still on events before the judgment of the capital in A.D. 70, which is not yet the end.

How can Luke make such a shift? What Luke does is easier to understand when we grasp how divine history was read by the Jews, as well as by the prophets. The belief was that God's judgment followed certain patterns. How he judged in one era resembled how he would judge in another. Because God's character was unchanging and because he controlled history, such patterns could be noted. Thus deliverance in any era was compared to the exodus. One event mirrored another. Exilic judg-

Notes: 21:5-38 This speech has a rich transmission history that has been much discussed in New Testament studies. Since the work of Timothy Colani in 1864, the speech has been called the "Little Apocalypse." Colani attempted historically to separate the speech from Jesus, arguing that it is too apocalyptic for him. Others have tried to show that the discourse is authentic (Wenham 1984; Beasley-Murray 1954). It is widely held, by all parties to the debate, that this speech circulated in the church as an independent piece of tradition because of its importance. Some have argued that the speech's roots go back to Jesus but

ments, whether Assyrian or Babylonian, were described in similar terms. This "mirror" or "pattern" interpretation of history has been called a typological-prophetic reading of the text, with the "type" reflecting a basic pattern in God's activity. This way of reading history sees events as linked and mirroring one another. Sometimes the events are described in such a way that we modern readers would not readily notice that distinct events are being discussed. Sometimes a text offers clarifying reflection after more events detailing God's program have been revealed.

Jesus' eschatological discourse links together two such events, the destruction of Jerusalem in A.D. 70 and the events of the end signaling his return to earth. Because the events are patterned after one another and mirror one another, some of Jesus' language applies to both. Mark and Matthew highlight the mirror's long-term image, while Luke emphasizes the short-term event. Either focus is a correct portrayal of Jesus' teaching. Failure to appreciate the typological background to this speech, however, has led to an overemphasis of one image against the other within the Synoptics. Some readers insist that the portrait of one writer must exactly match that of another. Instead, complementary emphases are possible. Appreciation of typology allows each author to speak for himself and allows the accounts of all the Synoptic writers to be viewed not in contradictory or one-sided terms but as complementary.

The speech makes several points. First, Luke clearly shows how the destruction of A.D. 70 is distinct from but related to the end. The two events should not be confused, but Jerusalem's destruction, when it comes, will guarantee as well as picture the end, since one event mirrors the other. Both are a part of God's plan as events move toward the end.

Second, Jesus' prophetic character is highlighted by this section. God is speaking through Jesus about unfolding events in the plan. Such prophetic gifts were highly respected in the ancient world (Philo *Life of Moses* 2.9.50-51).

---

that the speech was modified twice—once in the time of Caligula, A.D. 40, and again after Jerusalem's destruction in A.D. 70 (Kümmel 1957:95-104; Theissen 1991:121-65). This last view assumes a post-A.D. 70 date for the Gospels, which I think is unlikely, while the actual evidence for an A.D. 40 revision is speculative. As I explain below, it is better to see the speech as a typological presentation of Jesus, referring to the fall of Jerusalem in A.D. 70 as well as to the end. From this dual perspective the writers of the Synoptics draw appropriate, distinct, but complementary emphases.

Third, the Jewish nation's fate was clearly tied to its reaction to Jesus. The reader is not to question that the events Jesus describes will result from the nation's failure to respond to him (19:41-44). In fact, if one were to ask why Jerusalem was being judged, Luke has given many reasons. It is filled with hypocrisy (11:37-54), has oppressed the poor (18:7; 20:47), has rejected Messiah (13:33-34; 20:13-18), has missed the day of visitation (19:44), has rejected the gospel (Acts 13:46-48; 18:5-6; 28:25-28) and has slain God's Son (Lk 9:22; 18:31-33; 19:47; 20:14-19; 22:1-2, 52; 23:1-25; Stein 1992:521).

Fourth, the passage offers reassurance to disciples that God will enable them to face persecution and deliver them from it, whether by giving them words to say in their own defense or by saving them after martyrdom.

Fifth, the call is to remain steadfast because God is in control.

So the speech offers information and exhortations. It provides a general outline but not a detailed, dated calendar of future events. Such a general portrait without detailed dates is a common form for biblical apocalyptic material. We must be careful not to get more specific than Scripture does about the events of the future. Even though the portrait Jesus gives is general, he is saying, in effect, "Rest assured, God's plan is being fulfilled."

For simplicity's sake I have split the speech into two parts, though it is really one discourse: the events associated primarily with Jerusalem's fall (vv. 5-24) and the return and its significance (vv. 25-38).

Toward the Fall of Jerusalem or Before the End (21:5-24) The structures of earthly empires often are very impressive. They give the sense that they and what they represent will last forever. Visiting the great ruins of civilizations from Babylon to the Aztecs, one imagines the people must have assumed that their glory would endure forever. Humanity tends to suffer from delusions of immortality.

The rebuilt temple of Herod created such an impression. When the disciples praised its grandeur to Jesus (v. 5), the temple was in the midst of an eighty-three-year building program. Started about 20 B.C., it continued until A.D. 63-64, just a few years before Jerusalem's fall in A.D. 70. Assuming an A.D. 33 date for the crucifixion, the program was over fifty years old at the time the disciples marveled at it. The temple clearly made a deep impression on all who visited it. Josephus gives detailed descriptions of its beauty (*Jewish Wars* 1.21.1 §401; 5.5.1-6 §§184-227; *Antiquities* 15.11.1-7 §§380-425). The Roman historian Tacitus also describes the temple as containing great riches (*History* 5.8.1). Some of its stones were 12 to 60 feet in length, 7.5 feet in height and 9 feet in width (Josephus *Jewish Wars* 5.5.1-2 §§189-90 gives these measurements in cubits; a cubit is eighteen inches). The temple loomed over the city like a "snow clad mountain" (Josephus *Jewish Wars* 5.5.6 §223). Not only was the building impressive, but it was decorated with gifts from other countries and had elegantly adorned doors and gates of fine craftsmanship (Josephus *Jewish Wars* 5.5.3-5 §§206-18).

No wonder the disciples felt national pride as they surveyed the awesome temple, exclaiming at its *beautiful stones and . . . gifts dedicated to God.* Surely something so magnificent and God-honoring, something that had taken so long to build, would last a very long time. God's presence finally had a secure home.

Jesus' response must have come like a knife in the heart: *"As for what you see here, the time will come when not one stone will be left on another; every one of them will be thrown down."* It is hard for us to appreciate the effect on Jewish ears of what Jesus predicts here. When Jesus speaks of "days coming" or a time coming, he is predicting in prophetic terms the arrival of judgment, just like the one Israel had experienced (Jer 7:1-14; 22:5; 27:6; 52:12-13; on the phrase see Lk 5:35; 17:22; 19:43; 23:29). The magnificent temple, the center of the nation's worship and the sacred locale of God's presence, will be destroyed and turned into a heap of rubble. Centuries of worship and years of reconstruction will be brought to an end. The only way this can occur is if Jerusalem is overrun.

Be assured, Jesus tells the disciples, these things are not permanent. The phrase *these things (tauta)* becomes central to the discourse, since the disciples ask in verse 7 when *these things* will be: *"What will be the sign that they are about to take place?"* When will the temple's destruction come, along with the city's devastation?

The broad scope of the question is significant, since a judgment of Jerusalem that wipes out the temple suggests a time of great catastrophe and a turning point in the nation's history (Danker 1988:330). Such an event can only signal that God's plan for the nation is moving along. Though Luke's form of this question is more focused on the temple than the questions in Matthew 24:3 and Mark 13:4, its implications clearly cover the same span.

Two features of this discourse should not be overlooked. First, in verses 8-12 Jesus works from the end backwards and then in verse 25 leaps forward again in time, beyond Jerusalem's destruction to the end. Such a rewinding backwards in time is clear in light of the statement in verse 9 that *the end will not come right away* and the note in verse 12 that *before all this*—that is, the events of verses 8-11—other things will occur. With verse 12 and following, Jesus moves forward again, toward the description of Jerusalem's fall and the persecution that will accompany it. The issues of the end and the return of the Son of Man are deferred mostly until verse 25, with the reference to *the times of the Gentiles* in verse 24 serving as a transition into Jesus' statements about the end times. After Jerusalem falls, the period of Gentile rule will continue until the Son of Man returns.

Second, the events of the end and those of Jerusalem's fall are presented side by side in the entire discourse, as is typical in prophetic presentation, even though we can now look back and know that the events are separated by a large period of time. Such prophetic foreshortening is designed to indicate that one event mirrors and is linked to the other. When the initial event occurs, Jesus' followers can be assured that the rest is coming. But—and this is the key point—for the initial listeners it would be next to impossible to distinguish the times of these mirrored events. More important than these events' time relationship to each other is their linkage in meaning. Both the end and Jerusalem's fall are part of the divine movement toward fulfillment of promise. Anyone originally hearing Jesus' discourse might have assumed the end would come with Jerusalem's fall, but the real indication of the end is not Jerusalem's fall but the return of the Son of Man.

So Jesus warns first about events that are not yet the end. Messianic

---

21:9 Some argue that *the end* here must refer contextually only to Jerusalem's fall. Two facts are against this reading. First, Jesus brings up issues regarding the Son of Man's return; this shows that Jesus addresses events all the way to the consummation. Second, regardless of which Synoptic Gospel order one prefers, here Luke is using traditional material that

pretenders will abound, so the disciples must not be deceived. *"Do not follow them."* Josephus describes such claims in *Jewish Wars* 6.5.2-3 §§285-88, 300-309. In addition, social chaos, civil turmoil, wars and other tumultuous events will precede the end. The disciples should not be surprised when the world is in chaos. There is no need for alarm. These things must take place (the *must* here is the *dei* of divine decree). Paul expresses a parallel concept when he speaks of creation groaning until redemption is complete (Rom 8:18-25). Sin will be with us until Christ returns. Pain and persecution in the world should never surprise us.

Despite the chaos, God's plan is moving on. *The end will not come right away.* Jesus prepares the disciples for the era to come by reassuring them that worldwide chaos does not mean the cosmos is spinning out of divine control. Such chaos should not cause shock or emotional distress.

Still more chaos will come before the end. *Nation will rise against nation,* and *earthquakes, famines and pestilences* will come. All the typology of Jesus' descriptions has roots in judgment scenes of the Old Testament (2 Chron 15:6; Is 14:30; 19:2; 29:6; 51:19; Ezek 36:29-30; 38:19; Amos 8:11; Zech 14:5). *Fearful events and great signs from heaven* are signs of God's activity. (Mark 13:8 mentions the beginning of birth pangs here, but Luke lacks such explicit apocalyptic language.) In sum, chaos of all sorts will precede the end.

But before all these things will come persecution. Disciples will need to stand prepared for its coming. They will be delivered to *"synagogues and prisons . . . brought before kings and governors, and all on account of my name."* The mention of synagogues shows that the period of the early church is in view. In fact, the initial fulfillment of this prediction comes in Acts, starting after the proclamation of Jesus in chapter 3 leads to arrest and persecution in Acts 4. Virtually every chapter after that describes the persecution of the earliest church.

Luke uses a key term to characterize disciples: *witnesses* for Jesus (v. 13; compare Acts 1:6-8). Between now and the end, they are called to

clearly emphasized the long-term events described in this speech. Though Luke highlights short-term events, he is hardly likely to cancel out the long-term view altogether. The fact that the Son of Man's return is discussed shows that Luke's vision, like that of the other Synoptics, is long-range.

witness to him. Part of that witness is how they face persecution. From Stephen's martyrdom to the suffering of many in the formerly communist Eastern Europe, testimony to Jesus in the face of persecution has had a compelling impact throughout history.

Again Jesus tells his people not to worry. They need not be overly concerned with how they might defend themselves. They don't need a defense attorney, for Jesus himself will be their defense: *"I will give you words and wisdom that none of your adversaries will be able to resist or contradict"* (compare Acts 4:8-12; 7:54; 26:24-32). Though Jesus does not explain here how this works, Luke 12:11-12 and John 14—16 make clear that the gift alluded to here is the Holy Spirit.

The persecution will be painful, because it will involve *parents, brothers, relatives and friends.* This is why discipleship requires putting God ahead of family (14:26). Some of God's people will even meet death. Put bluntly, *"all men will hate you because of me."* Part of the chaos before the capital's fall and before the end is the persecution of those allied to Jesus.

But the disciples will receive comfort. *"Not a hair of your head will perish."* In light of verse 16, this cannot mean that none of them will die. Rather, it must mean that even if they die, they will live (12:4-7). There is no way real harm will come, since Luke uses the emphatic Greek negative here *(ou mē).* In short, *by standing firm* with Jesus, one gains life—or to use Luke's language, you *will gain life.* Thus Luke again emphasizes perseverance. Those who cling to the Word with patience bear fruit (8:15). Luke has made it clear that standing firm requires resolve and counting the cost (14:25-33), properly assessing the cares of life (8:14; 14:15-24) and not overvaluing material possessions or the pleasures of life (8:14; 12:19).

In verse 20 Jesus describes Jerusalem's destruction in detail. The sign of its destruction will come when armies surround it. Jesus had already predicted this in 19:41-44. Because of his focus on the near event of

21:24 This reference to *the times of the Gentiles* suggests that God's plan includes a period that is especially focused on Gentile involvement. It implies that Israel's central role will reemerge later in the plan, as does Peter's appeal to Old Testament teaching in Acts 3:18-21. Assuming a premillennial approach, it is likely as well that the break between Daniel's sixty-ninth and seventieth week fits with this scenario (Dan 9:24-27). When the Messiah is cut off, the judgment of Israel begins. Its house is desolate (Lk 13:33-35). The advance of

Jerusalem's fall, Luke's version of this discourse does not include certain details from the other Synoptics. He does not include Jesus' words about this being a time of unprecedented tribulation. He does not mention the Lord's decision to cut short these days so humanity will survive. He lacks any comment about events not coming in winter. Most important, he does not discuss "the abomination that causes desolation"; he mentions only *its desolation*. The focus throughout is the city's destruction, a destruction that encompasses, but is not limited to, the temple. This will be a time of tension, but it is not yet the end. A phrase unique to Luke shows the distinction. *Jerusalem will be trampled on* until *the times of the Gentiles are fulfilled*. The judgment on Jerusalem remains until that time is completed.

When the time of destruction comes, it will be time to flee and hide. *Those who are in Judea* should head for the mountains, where they can hide in safety, while *those in the city* should get out. *Those in the country* should avoid the city. The destruction will be total; the nation will suffer. These events will fulfill *all that has been written*. The allusion is to prophetic warnings of the price of the nation's covenant unfaithfulness (Deut 28:32; Jer 7:14-26, 30-34; 16:1-9; 17:27; 19:10-15; Mic 3:12; Zeph 1:4-13). The reference to God's pattern of judgment suggests a typological connection here: this judgment is like others before it and like ones that will follow it.

The destruction will be a dreadful time for the most vulnerable people, especially pregnant mothers. Distress and wrath will overwhelm the people and the land (19:44; 23:29). Death and imprisonment will be the fate of many citizens. *Jerusalem will be trampled . . . until the times of the Gentiles are fulfilled*. Be assured, Jesus warns, the nation will be judged and the temple abandoned. Israel's fall is not the end of God's plan, however, for one more decisive stage remains.

The End—the Coming of the Son of Man (21:25-38) The final stage in God's plan will begin with the Son of Man's return, a theme Luke

God's plan for Israel is on hold, even though God's promised kingdom and plan arrive and move along. This dichotomy between advance and suspension is the great mystery revealed in Jesus' ministry. Both occur side by side. Jerusalem's destruction, which is the result of its rejection of Messiah, is the final sign of the arrival of the times of the Gentiles (Lk 19:41-44). Nonetheless, the fact that the duration of such a time is limited suggests that Israel too will have its day in the future (Rom 11:25-27).

has emphasized (9:26; 11:30; 12:8, 40; 17:22, 24, 26, 30; 18:8). The question of Jesus' return has always been captivating for believers. People have always speculated whether their own time might be the end. Four factors fuel such speculation. First, Jesus taught that his return was imminent; it could come at any moment. Since the time was not specified, such a "next event" hope naturally has led many to wonder if and how it might come soon. Second, Jesus' return is longed for, since his coming represents the saints' redemption. What Christian would not look expectantly for the day when justice and righteousness are established and God's people are vindicated? Clearly Jesus called disciples to have an expectant attitude toward events of the end—not just to assume that "it will all pan out in the end." Third, it is natural to try to fill the gaps in revelation and put pieces of the eschatological puzzle together. People enjoy trying to solve mysteries. Unfortunately, sometimes such speculation strays into date-setting or leads to dogmatism about exact timing and sequence. Our speculations must be tempered by humility about the gaps in our scriptural knowledge, and we need to carefully distinguish what is clear in Scripture from what is only implied. Fourth, Jesus told his disciples to keep awake and be on the watch (v. 36). So we do need to consider the end if we are to be sensitive to Jesus' instruction. Jesus called on disciples to be "end-time minded" without withdrawing from ministry under the assumption that the time is here.

Jesus does not give a calendar of end-time events as much as a portrait of the moment. Old Testament imagery abounds in his words, since the event will mark the culmination of God's promise to his people. Disciples are to keep watch, in part because the exact time *is* uncertain (Mk 13:32). The Son of Man is at the door, but no one knows exactly when he will come in. So we should keep watch, while humbly realizing that Jesus did not ask us to determine the exact moment. As this section indicates, we can know the general character of events surrounding the return even if we cannot know the exact timing.

So what will the return look like? Luke 21:25-28 tell us. Its apocalyptic imagery indicates that God is about to work in a major way. Heavenly *signs* will abound as the cosmos releases its power. Sun, moon and stars will signal the time. In particular, the sea is mentioned, since human beings have often feared its power (Ps 46:2-4; 65:7; 89:9; 107:23-32;

Wisdom of Solomon 5:22). Such cosmic signs will indicate a shaking up of the natural order (Is 3:24—4:1; 13:7-13; 24:18-20; 33:9; 34:1-15; Jer 4:23-26; Ezek 32:7-8; Dan 8:10; Joel 2:10, 30-31; 3:15; Amos 8:9; Nahum 1:4-5; Hag 2:6, 21; *1 Enoch* 80). Such imagery also foreshadows portions of the book of Revelation. To imagine the fear an unleashed, out-of-control creation might generate, think of being caught in a major hurricane, flood or tornado. *Men will faint from terror, apprehensive of what is coming on the world, for the heavenly bodies will be shaken.* There will be a sense of being trapped and tormented. *Faint from terror* pictures someone hyperventilating and collapsing because of anxiety. Some argue that Jesus' words about heavenly chaos are figurative for severe destruction. However, a chaotic, destructive situation was already described in verses 8-11, while the chaos of verses 25-27 is of a completely different order. Even creation itself will be in convulsions. Then disciples will know that God is about to act.

Jesus describes the return of the Son of Man in terms that recall Daniel 7:13-14. There the phrase is not used as a title but as a description: "one like a son of man." This one rides the clouds like a god but is a human figure (Ps 104:3; Is 19:1; in the cloud, Ex 34:5; 14:20; Num 10:34). He has human traits superior to the animal traits of the other nations mentioned in Daniel 7. Most important, he shares authority with "the Ancient of Days," a clear reference to God. That authority especially entails the right to judge and make vindication for the saints. Jesus says the Son of Man will return *in a cloud with power and great glory.* When Jesus does return, it will be to take rulership over all the earth and exercise judgment on behalf of his people (Rev 19:8—20:15). So the saints can *lift up [their] heads, because [their] redemption is drawing near.* At that moment hope will become confidence (Judg 8:28; Job 10:15; Ps 24:7, 9; 83:2). God's promises to his own are being consummated. As the world shrinks back in fear, the saints will look up in expectation. *These things,* the immediate signs of his return, will show that God is in control of events—that trust in him has led to vindication.

The discourse changes its focus at this point. Now Jesus applies his teaching. He gives a picture of assurance about what he has predicted (vv. 29-33) followed by an exhortation (vv. 34-36).

Jesus draws a comparison with a fig tree beginning to bud. When that beloved tree with its sweet fruit begins to show shoots and leaves, it is the sign of summer. Winter's barrenness is left behind. Signs of life are visible. A new season has come.

So it will be at the end. When these cosmic signs are displayed, Jesus' followers can rest assured the end is near. In fact, when the whole discourse is taken into account, Jerusalem's fall—predicted as it is and mirroring the end as it does—also serves as a sign guaranteeing that what Jesus says about the end and redemption will come to pass. So Jesus says to look for two things: the fall of Jerusalem and cosmic signs. With these heavenly portents (vv. 25-26), *the kingdom of God is near.* In this text Luke speaks of the kingdom as not yet arrived, in contrast to earlier texts where it had already approached or come (10:9, 18; 11:20; 17:20). As has been noted, Luke sees the kingdom in two phases: an initial, already-present phase and a consummating, yet-to-come phase. The consummation will wrap up the promise in total fulfillment. Anticipation will become realization. The kingdom will be present in its fullness.

There is much "sign-watching" today, but this text along with others in the New Testament warns against getting too specific about predictions. The history of the church is littered with those who, though well intentioned and sincere in their belief that they had found the key to the timing of end-time events, were proved wrong. Assembling the puzzle of apocalyptic pieces is a difficult interpretive exercise, since it involves making judgments about many difficult and variously interpreted texts (for a discussion of the hermeneutics involved, see Blaising and Bock 1993:57-105, especially 90-96). We should be cautious about predictions of Jesus' return that are too precise. This discourse and the other New Testament apocalyptic texts indicate a general pattern of events, but since Jesus will return "like a thief in the night," the best we can do is keep watching and be prepared for his return. Jesus has told the church to be ready, so every generation should keep watch. But we should be suspicious of anyone who is certain of the exact timing, for even Jesus said only the Father knows that (Mk 13:31-32). In the meantime the church is called to serve him faithfully, share the gospel and grow in grace.

Jesus assures the disciples that these signs will be so. *"Heaven and earth will pass away, but my words will never pass away."* The things

Jesus has taught are true, more firm than creation itself.

In the midst of this note of assurance is one of the most-discussed passages in Luke. For Jesus also says, *"This generation will certainly not pass away until all these things have happened."* The prediction is made emphatically, using the strong Greek phrase *ou mē.* This generation *will not (!)* pass away.

On the surface it looks as if Jesus is predicting the end within his generation, especially since Luke normally uses the term *generation (genea)* to mean the current generation (7:31; 9:41; 11:29-32, 51; 17:25; Acts 2:40; 8:33). Often the term also has a negative implication, meaning this current generation is evil. Against applying this interpretation to 21:32, however, is the reality of the delay. The generation of Jesus' utterance was passing away even as Luke wrote, and Luke had described numerous intervening events. Jesus had spoken in the thirties, but Luke was writing, in all likelihood, in the sixties. A reference to the current generation is unlikely.

Neither is it likely that Luke refers to the Jews as this generation. According to this view, the promise is that "the generation of Jews" will not pass away. Though this approach removes any problem for the meaning, it is unlikely because *genea* is not used in this general, nontemporal, ethnic sense elsewhere.

Two other options are possible. If the term has no temporal force, then it could mean "the evil generation of humankind." Using the term with this descriptive, ethical force would mean Jesus is speaking of a *quality* of human being: evil persons will not escape the judgment when it comes. This evil generation will not pass away before God deals with them. There will be judgment and vindication.

Finally, the term might refer to the generation of the end. In other words, once the beginning of the end arrives with the cosmic signs of verses 25-26, the Son of Man will return before *that* generation passes away. Such a meaning honors the term's temporal force and reads it as somewhat contextually limited by Luke's clear distinction between near and far events. This view has been rejected by some as too obvious a sense—the last generation will not pass away (Stein 1992:526). However, this misreads the view's force. It is arguing that the end will occur within one generation; the same group that sees the start of the end will see its end. This is the option I slightly prefer, though the previous sense is also possible.

However the phrase *this generation* is taken, Jesus' statements in verses 32-33 emphasize that Jerusalem's destruction and then the events of the end, including the Son of Man's return and the cosmic signs that accompany it, are more certain than creation's permanence. Be assured, Jesus says, these things will come to pass.

So Jesus calls for faithful living in the interim. *"Be careful, or your hearts will be weighed down with dissipation, drunkenness and the anxieties of life."* Harking back to the imagery of 8:12-15 and 12:42-48, Jesus warns that excessive concern for or indulgence in this life's affairs can leach away one's faithfulness. Such distractions "weigh down one's heart" *(mēpote barēthōsin hymōn hai kardiai).* The emotional load can grow into a snare that traps us in that day when our stewardship before God is revealed. However, to the one who is watching, the day will not come as a sudden, embarrassing surprise because of unpreparedness. Still, the day will impact all. No one will escape standing before the Son of Man. We are all subject to him.

So Jesus says, *"Be always on the watch, and pray that you may be able to escape all that is about to happen, and that you may be able to stand before the Son of Man."* Here is why Jesus has revealed the plan—to call disciples to be on the alert. Heeding, watching and praying lead to endurance. Heeding really means following in obedience. Watching means that our eyes are expectant and looking for the Lord's return, focused on the fact that he will bring us to himself. Praying means we are dependent, looking to him to give us the strength to walk in faithfulness. No matter how tough things get, we can know as we look to God that he cares for us.

Luke notes that Jesus continues to teach at the temple and to lodge at the Mount of Olives. He is still popular with the people, who rise early to hear him in the temple. But that popularity will not last long. The black cloud of rejection and the cross approaches.

Notes: 22:1-6 The parallels are Matthew 26:1-5 and Mark 14:1-2. Luke's short version is

A Betrayal and a Farewell (22:1-38) Luke 22 begins Luke's version of the passion. The story of the crucifixion extends through chapters 22—23, while resurrection is the topic of chapter 24. The account begins with Judas's betrayal and Jesus' final meal with his disciples. Jesus is the exemplary righteous sufferer, even as Satan again works to foil God's plan (22:3). The brief mention of the archdemon makes it clear that the battle over Jesus is not merely a human conflict. Cosmic forces are concerned about the outcome.

Jesus' final moments with his disciples involve a farewell meal. As he celebrates the Passover and adds his own new elements to it, Jesus reveals that his work is modeled after that sacrifice. His humility is to mark the disciples' own efforts to serve others. Their service will occur in the face of rejection, but service is still the disciple's calling.

Judas's Plan to Betray Jesus (22:1-6) The solution to the leaders' desire to get Jesus is Judas, one of the disciples. Enlisting him in their scheme clears the way for Jesus' arrest.

Jesus probably suffered no greater personal disappointment than Judas's betrayal. Sometimes rejection and failure come from within the ranks of those who minister. Success is not guaranteed for those associated with Jesus. Yet such failure is always tragic.

The final act begins on the feast of Passover, also known as the Feast of Unleavened Bread (Ex 12:1-20; Deut 16:1-8; Jeremias 1967:898-904; Josephus *Antiquities* 14.2.1 §21; 17.9.3 §213; Jewish Wars 2.1.3 §10). Actually the two names represent different feasts that come right after one another, so often a reference to one really meant both. Passover came on Nisan 14-15, while the Feast of Unleavened Bread came on Nisan 15-21. Passover celebrated the night of Israel's exodus from Egypt (Ex 12), while the Feast of Unleavened Bread commemorated the exodus journey as well as the beginning of harvest season (Lev 23:5-8). During this time pilgrims from all over the region flocked into Jerusalem for a national celebration, rather like a combination of the Independence Day and Thanksgiving holidays in the United States. The combined Jewish feast celebrated salvation.

---

more like Mark than Matthew. Unlike both the parallels, Luke lacks an anointing of Jesus after the account of Judas's betrayal.

Yet the leadership is plotting to execute the one who claimed to be the fulfillment of all the exodus deliverance represented. The irony is not to be missed. Luke intends to show the distortion of perspective that accompanies sin, especially when it is the sin of rejecting Jesus.

The only obstacle to the leaders' desire to get Jesus is the people. Their fear of a popular backlash makes them cautious. It does not look as if anything will happen in this holiday period.

But things change rapidly once *Satan entered Judas, called Iscariot.* Luke's statement reveals a behind-the-scene actor in this drama. Judas does not act alone. Deception has infiltrated the camp. The passage does not explain how this happened or what may have led to it. What is important is that the subsequent events occur because Satan has his way with Judas. No matter what the devil promises, Satan's entry into one's life is destructive; Luke has already offered the illustration of the Gerasene man (8:26-39). For when Satan enters a life, he leads the person in sinister directions.

So Judas goes to confer with the leadership, *the chief priests and the officers.* Religious officials and temple guards are in view here. Since someone from the inside is willing to betray Jesus, the leaders can now plan to intercept him in a more private setting than the crowd-filled temple region. They must be rubbing their hands together with anticipation: at last Jesus can be stopped. A sum of money is exchanged. The amount is not given here, but the mere mention of money makes the act look even more underhanded. This is not an act of honor for Judas, for the betrayer makes sure he has more to gain than merely the removal of a messianic movement's leader.

22:7-38 The parallels should be covered in subunits. The parallels to obtaining the site of the meal are Mark 14:12-16 and Matthew 26:17-19. Again, Luke's version is more like Mark, though Luke tells which two disciples were sent. The parallels of the Last Supper itself are very complex. Here Matthew 26:20, 26-29 and Mark 14:17, 22-25 stand closer to one another. Luke mentions an extra cup that the parallels lack. Paul is aware of the Lukan version of the supper, as 1 Corinthians 11:23-26 shows. In the discourse after the supper, 23:35-38 is unique to Luke. The prediction of Judas's betrayal and Peter's denials appears also in Matthew 26:21-25, 30-35 and Mark 14:18-21, 26-31, though Luke 22:31-32 has no parallel. The discussion of leadership and the thrones occurs in Matthew 19:28 and 20:24-28, as well as in Mark 10:41-45. There the same topics are treated in different settings; thus they are distinct events, not true parallels.

22:7-20 Whether this was a Passover meal is much debated. Whereas the Synoptics all seem clear that it was a Passover celebration, John 18:28 and 19:14 give the impression that

Judas's involvement is doubly fortunate for the leadership. First, they can now seek Jesus away from the crowds and take him in private. Second, if trouble arises and their plans go disastrously wrong, they can make the case that one of Jesus' own has been the cause of his downfall. Judas can be blamed for whatever follows. The leaders can say they have just done their duty in dealing with Jesus. So Judas's offer simplifies matters greatly.

With the agreement in place, the leaders only need a good opportunity. Double-dealing has led to betrayal. The Jewish celebration of national salvation becomes the occasion for a plot to arrest and convict Jesus. Once again, irony abounds. The leadership steers a course of murder in the name of righteousness. Sin always distorts reality. In addition, a cosmic chess match comes to its crucial moment. Satan will put Jesus in check, but Jesus will make the final move that means checkmate.

The Last Supper and Jesus' Final Teaching (22:7-38) Luke loves meals. This is his seventh meal scene; it is also one of his most dramatic (see 5:29-32; 7:36-50; 9:12-17; 10:38-42; 11:37-54; 14:1-24; two more remain, 24:28-32, 36-43). At the dinner table friends can enjoy fellowship and reflect on events. Such an intimate occasion is the setting for Jesus' final words to his disciples. Added to the intimacy of the scene is its timing. A Passover meal is being celebrated (vv. 7-9). During the celebration of God's saving of Israel, Jesus will discuss his sacrifice on behalf of his disciples. It will be a meal to remember, not only because this event forms the basis of the Lord's Supper but also because Jesus predicts a betrayal, defines true leadership, promises authority to the eleven, predicts Peter's failure and warns of coming rejection. Even as he faces

---

Passover had not yet been celebrated. Some regard the problem as yet unsolved (Stein 1992:539-40). Others see it as a clear error on the part of at least one of the evangelists (Fitzmyer 1985:1381-82; L. T. Johnson 1991:341, who also disputes whether the details of a first-century Passover meal can be determined).

The issues are complex. A solution may emerge when one realizes that many meals required ritual cleanliness during the feast week, so John 18:28 need not refer to a Passover meal. In addition, various worship calendars were in use at the time for different streams of Judaism, so meals may have spanned a thirty-six-hour period. For the calendrical details, see Hoehner 1977:85-90; for the debate, see Marshall 1980:30-75, Carson 1984:531-32 and Bock 1995: exegesis of these verses; for the issue of Jewish practice, see Jeremias 1966:15-84. Despite Johnson's objections, it is likely the outlines of the ancient meal are known. The Mishnaic *Pesaḥim* and the more complete ninth-century *Seder Rav Amri Gaon* are close enough in outline to afford a general sense of the meal's progression, though its order is

death, Jesus serves by preparing others for their task.

The passion did not catch Jesus by surprise. In fact, many of the Passion events reveal that Jesus is in control; and the Passover meal preparation is no exception. The Passover meal launched the celebration of both Passover and the Feast of Unleavened Bread, which ran in the week following Passover. So Luke's introduction makes a combined reference to the two. Jesus directs Peter and John to prepare the meal and tells them where to find the room for it. It was a legal requirement that the meal be celebrated within Jerusalem, which meant that a suitable location was necessary (2 Chron 35:18; *Jubilees* 49:15-16 even held the temple was the desirable locale). The preparation would involve organizing the sacrifice of lambs in the temple, cooking them, preparing the place, assembling the side dishes and utensils, and serving the wine.

Jesus tells Peter and John that *"a man carrying a jar of water"* will show them *"a large upper room, all furnished."* Peter and John find things just *as Jesus had told them.* So they prepare the meal. The room would have been filled with cushions on which to recline. So Jesus directs the disciples, and they are faithful in following him. They see that he is aware of the events that are unfolding. They can trust him.

The meal itself is fraught with emotion. Jesus expresses how much he has longed to eat this meal with the disciples. He uses a Hebrew idiom, "I have desired with desire," to make the point emphatically (NIV: *I have eagerly desired;* compare Gen 31:30; Num 11:4). Before Jesus suffers, he has this last meal with them. The meal serves literarily for Luke as a "last testament," Jesus' parting words to his own. Like an ill person on his deathbed, Jesus leaves his last impressions on those who have ministered with him. We can only imagine how he felt knowing what was ahead and realizing, *"I will not eat [this meal] again until it finds ful-*

---

not certain in all the details. It seems likely that this was a Passover meal.

If the meal followed the normal pattern, it would have had a preliminary course with a blessing, a cup of wine, green and bitter herbs, a meal serving and then preparation of the second cup. With the second cup of wine came the Passover liturgy. The main meal followed with a prayer said over the bread. Here is where Jesus would have spoken of his broken body. The main meal consisted of lamb, unleavened bread and herbs. Then came the third cup of wine, known as the cup of blessing. Here is where Jesus would have discussed his shed blood. Finally, the meal closed with the singing of the Hallel psalms (Ps 114—18), another prayer and a fourth cup of wine, which on this occasion Jesus refused. The first of Luke's two cups of wine would have been either the first or the second cup.

fillment in the kingdom of God." Jesus knows that his earthly ministry is drawing to a close and only the future great messianic banquet table will permanently and physically unite these special men to him again. He knows that the Passover will not touch his lips again until the promise is fulfilled with the consummation of the kingdom of God, just as he had discussed in 21:25-28.

Some see the fulfillment of these words in Acts and in the Lord's Supper, but Jesus does not eat that meal himself, he only is present. Also, the Lord's Supper is not a Passover meal, which is what he alludes to here. Jesus has in mind the great consummation of promise, when he returns to earth and directly and visibly rules with his saints. (I prefer a premillennial approach to the end times. Amillennialists will see this return as involving the setting up of the new heavens and new earth.) With Jesus' return, redemption will draw near and the kingdom will come in its decisive, most fulfilling form.

Like the meal, the cup is a final sharing of fellowship with his disciples. Only Luke mentions this first cup. The moment clearly is bittersweet for Jesus. His destiny requires separation from those he loves. When the kingdom comes, they will resume celebration.

The sequence of bread and cup follows. They form the basis of our Lord's Table. It is likely that Jesus is lifting the third cup of the Passover here. This cup followed the eating of the Passover lamb, the unleavened bread and the bitter herbs. It have followed the explanation of why the meal was being celebrated, a review of the exodus. Thus Jesus' words mirror earlier salvation events and resonate with all the imagery of that linkage. As he reinterprets the symbols, he fills them with fresh meaning.

So the bread is *"my body given for you; do this in remembrance of me."* Jesus is not arguing that the bread becomes his body, the view

22:19-20 These verses involve one of Luke's most famous textual problems. Were these verses originally in Luke's text? The long text is supported by numerous key witnesses, including Aleph, A, B, p⁷⁵ and the Byzantine tradition. Uncial D and some itala manuscripts have the shorter reading. Internally some of the subsequent verses assume the longer reading (Schürmann 1951:364-92, 522-41). In addition, the tradition as reflected in 1 Corinthians 11:23-26 assumes its presence. If a scribe were trying to fill in a suspected gap in the Gospel text, would he pick a Pauline letter over Matthew or Mark to do it? Would he add it, especially since the result would be the presence of multiple cups? It is more likely that the long text is original. For an attempt to argue for the shorter text, see Ehrman 1991:576-91.

called transubstantiation. Nor is he arguing that he surrounds and enters the bread with his presence, a view known as consubstantiation. Like the Passover, the bread pictures his death and represents his self-sacrifice as his body is broken for the disciples on the cross. The Lord is present, but the elements serve to remind and proclaim; the elements are not transformed (1 Cor 10:15-18).

The call to remember shows the symbolic nature of the meal. "Keep in mind my sacrifice" recalls the Hebrew concept of *zikrôn,* where something is to grip the memory (Ex 2:24; Lev 24:7; Num 5:15; 10:9-10; Ps 20:3; Ezek 21:23). When the church takes this meal looking back to this event, it becomes a statement of solidarity with Jesus, a public covenant renewal—which is why taking the meal is such serious business for Paul in 1 Corinthians 11:17-34.

In the same way, after the supper he took the cup, saying, "This cup is the new covenant in my blood, which is poured out for you." The new covenant is a major theme of the New Testament (see Jer 31:31; Mt 26:28; Lk 24:49, the Father's promise; Acts 2:14-39; 2 Cor 3—4; Heb 8—10). Jesus' blood is shed for his followers. By it he purchases the church (Acts 20:28). The foundation for a new era is laid. A new sacrifice brings an era of fresh fulfillment. That new era starts with Jesus' death and the distribution of the Spirit.

Two features are key to this understanding of the sacrifice of Jesus as pictured by the cup. First, his death takes our place in paying for sin. Paul says this most explicitly in Romans 3:20-26. Luke's language only leaves it implied, though he is aware of the teaching, as Acts 20:28 shows. Second, Jesus notes that his death is inseparably connected to the establishment of the new covenant. A covenant is always inaugurated with the shedding of blood. By far the most eloquent explanation of this new covenant idea is found in Hebrews 8—10.

Jesus sits at the table and reveals why he is going away: to provide a new sacrifice for forgiveness that will open the way for the coming of God's Spirit (24:44-49). In order to give the Spirit, he must give himself. John 14—16 discusses this point in detail in a text unique to that Gospel. Jesus will sit again at the table one day. But then he will do so having offered himself so that others might sit with him. That is the story of God's grace.

There is great pathos here. Even as Jesus gives himself for those he loves, one of them is giving Jesus over in betrayal. The table fellowship is not pure. One sits at the table who longs for Jesus to be removed. So *"the Son of Man will go as it has been decreed, but woe to that man who betrays him."* Jesus reveals that his death is no surprise. His passing away is not a sign of a plan disappointed or of salvation gone awry. Still, the betrayer is responsible to God for his betrayal. Judas may have met the leadership in private, but God was not fooled. As with all secretly plotted sin, God was there. Luke has placed this remark in a different order from the parallels, where Jesus reveals his knowledge before the meal. The effect is to magnify the note of irony. As Jesus dies to secure forgiveness for others, he himself meets with betrayal. Even one of his own betrays him (Ps 41:9). Woe will befall Jesus' rejecter. It is a fearful thing to reject the One who gives his life to secure our forgiveness.

The disciples do not know who the betrayer might be. So they speculate with one another: "Who would do this?" Sometimes those allied to Jesus are near him for a time before they reveal that their heart truly lies elsewhere. As John 6:70 puts it, Judas was "a devil" even though for more than three years he looked like Jesus' devoted follower. Those who know the Son cling to him; those who do not know him depart from him through denial (Col 1:21-23).

So what makes for greatness? Faithfulness, yes, but even more the service that reveals faithfulness. Amazing as it seems, in the midst of Jesus' revelation about his coming suffering the disciples are fighting over who is number one among them. The text speaks of a "rivalry" (NIV: *dispute*) breaking out among them. Using the comparative "greater" with a superlative force, the disciples want to know who God puts at the top of the Best Disciple list.

In response, Jesus contrasts leadership in the world with leadership in the kingdom. In the world leadership involves the bald exercise of authority—people *lord it over* others. In the ancient world when men exercised such power, people publicly recognized their authority and called them *benefactors.* A benefactor in the ancient world had clients who were to appreciate their lower position (Josephus *Jewish Wars* 3.9.8 §459; 4.2.5 §113). Glory and honor came to the leader.

In contrast stands greatness in the kingdom. The disciple-leader should serve with youthful deference. The greatest among the disciples will be the one who is *like the youngest* and *like the one who serves.* Jesus points to his own example, not that of the culture. In the ancient world the greater person sits at table while the lesser person serves the meal (see 17:7-10). The Greek interrogative particle *ouchi* expects a positive reply to the question whether the one at the table is considered greater than the servant. But Jesus notes that he is among the disciples *as one who serves.* The offering of his life for them is service. He has taught them in service. John 13 tells us that before this meal, Jesus washed the disciples' feet in humble service. Greatness is defined not by position nor résumé, but by one's attitude and service.

As Jesus calls them to service, he also gives them a promise. He notes their constancy; unlike the betrayer, they have continued with Jesus in his trials. In the face of pressure, like exemplary disciples, they have stood firm with God's chosen one. So they will share in something he already possesses. The Father has assigned to Jesus a kingdom. Authority has become his (Mt 28:18-20). So he will assign them a role with him. They are to share in his rule. The rule in the future involves table fellowship with Jesus and authority over God's people, Israel. They will celebrate with him at the messianic banquet table, and they will administer justice over Israel. Their union with Jesus means that they share in the benefits of his rule.

Jesus' words about greatness and rule are especially important, since they come in the shadow of his death. He wants to remind his followers that no matter how bad the suffering, rejection and persecution get, a day will come when vindication and authority will reign. We can suffer now if we remember not only what Jesus did but also what he will do. Though the authority given to the eleven is unique, all disciples share the promise of reward and a place at the table of messianic fellowship.

Not all of Jesus' news is good. The cosmic battle is not just between

---

22:30 Though many argue that Jesus refers to reconstituted Israel here and therefore describes the church, such a reading ignores the contextual point. Jesus is about to suffer at the hands of the nation's leaders. As he has said before, such rejection will lead to the judgment of those leaders by some of their other sons (11:19). Such vindication is what Jesus alludes to here. The remarks are not simply ethnically symbolic of the church. When Jesus says *"the twelve tribes of Israel,"* it is best to see the Jewish nation as the referent. The disciples never gave up hope that God would deal with and restore the nation (Acts

Jesus and Satan. Anyone associated with Jesus is subject to satanic attack. Nothing makes this clearer than the section where Peter is warned about his coming denials. Jesus' awareness of events continues as he predicts Peter's temporary unfaithfulness. Verses 31-32 are unique to Luke and follow his stress on prayer. Satan has put in a request *to sift* all the disciples like *wheat.* Though Peter is discussed individually in verse 32, the use of *hymas,* the plural "you all," in verse 31 shows that he is only part of the coming battle. "Sifted like wheat" is an idiom that in our culture would parallel "take someone apart" (Amos 9:9 has the image). Perhaps Satan believes that if Peter is shamed, others will be disheartened.

Jesus' prayer has dealt with the threat through a request not that the failure be prevented but that any permanent damage be averted. His request is that Peter's *faith may not fail.* Here is our advocate stepping to our defense through a ministry of prayer. Peter will make no total renunciation of Jesus. The disciple's failure of nerve will not come because of a failure of heart, nor will it be permanent. There will be restoration. In fact, Peter will turn from his denial. His call then will be to strengthen his fellow disciples. What he will be able to teach them may well be revealed by his response. Having learned that failure is possible and the flesh is weak, Peter will be able to strengthen the saints. Though failure is regrettable, sometimes our best lessons come in reflection on failure.

Peter is sure that he is ready to serve in prison, even to die, for Jesus. He is perceptive in that he understands that Jesus' suffering will envelop his followers. Yet he is confident that he can face whatever comes. Though such self-assurance might seem commendable, one's own strength is not sufficient to resist severe temptation (1 Cor 10:12-13). Peter is brave in the privacy of a quiet meal, and when the soldiers show up, he will initially take up arms to defend Jesus. But what will he do when those hostile to Jesus ask him where his allegiance lies? Jesus' prediction of a triple denial *before the rooster* crows shows that he knows Peter better than Peter

1:6-8; 3:18-22; Campbell and Townsend 1992:187-91).

22:34 Luke's wording of this prediction is distinct from that of Matthew 26:34, Mark 14:30 or John 13:38. The difference with Mark is the clearest, since Mark speaks of the cock's crowing twice before three denials come. Most scholars argue that Matthew, Luke and John are summarizing, simply making the point that before the morning crowing begins, the threefold denial will come.

does. When we try to stand up to pressure in our own strength, we may wilt. Self-confidence when we are not relying on Jesus is deceptive.

Peter will be able to strengthen fellow believers after his fall because he will understand how easy it is to fall. He can call on them to embrace God's mercy, be prepared to suffer and be ready to give a defense because he will have experienced all of these opportunities himself—some with failure and others with success.

Jesus teaches God's grace in this warning to Peter: Do not trust in your own strength, but realize that after failure there will be opportunity for restoration. Jesus intercedes for his own even when he knows they will fail him. Intercession evidences the Savior's love (1 Jn 2:2). Even disciples who fail in a moment of weakness can experience the success of God's work. The lesson is an important one not only for Peter but also for all the disciples he represents. Though Satan will come after all of them, Jesus will be praying for them all.

Jesus' final words make it clear that circumstances are changing. Opposition to the disciples is rising. Where before Jesus had sent them out empty-handed yet they were provided for (9:1-6; 10:3-4), now they will have to take provisions and protection for their travel. They will have to procure *a sword*. Scripture such as Isaiah 53:12 is finding its fulfillment in Jesus. Jesus is rejected; he is *numbered with the transgressors*.

The disciples take Jesus' remarks literally and incorrectly. They note that they have two swords, but Jesus cuts off the discussion. Something is not right, but it is too late to discuss it. As the arrest will show, they have misunderstood. They draw swords then, but Jesus stops their defense in its tracks. He is not telling them to buy swords to wield in physical battle. They will have to provide for themselves and fend for themselves, but not through the shedding of blood. They are being

---

22:36 The syntax of this verse is notoriously difficult. Several options for reading the verse exist (Stein 1992:555 n. 49). The issue revolves around whether the verse's two halves, one dealing with the *bag* and *purse* and the other with the *sword,* are parallel or distinct situations. Does the one who has a bag and purse and the one who does not have either item go and sell their cloak to buy a sword? Does the one who has a bag and purse now also take a sword? Or does the one without a bag and purse now take a sword, while the person who lacks a sword sells his cloak to obtain one? Of these three options, the last one is syntactically most likely. The point is the same regardless: the disciples should now take full provisions; they will have to fend for themselves. That defense will involve their own

drawn into a great cosmic struggle, and they must fight with spiritual swords and resources. The purchase of swords serves only to picture this coming battle. This fight requires special weapons (Eph 6:10-18).

Humility, dependence, promise of authority and reward, warnings about opposition and the pursuit of faithfulness are the topics of Jesus' final testament meal. Luke assumes that disciples will engage the larger world and face a great cosmic battle. But they are not to withdraw or be afraid. Rather, with humility and looking to God, they can face suffering and the world bravely and effectively. Jesus is about to exemplify the walk of the innocent before a hostile world. His success is not indicated by his withdrawal or even his survival; it is indicated by his faithfulness (1 Pet 2:21-25).

The Trial and Death of Jesus (22:39—23:56) The overriding theme of this section is that Jesus suffers innocently. His death is not just. Nonetheless, even as he hangs on the cross, Jesus ministers salvation to those who cry out to him, as he promises the thief on the cross a place in paradise. In fact, the section begins with Jesus agreeing to follow God's will unto death. He ministers to his enemies, as he heals the severed ear of one of those who come to arrest him (see 6:27-36). Though Jesus suffers unjustly, it is God's will that he continue to minister for the sake of those he came to save.

The world's view of Jesus does not change, as he is taken through a series of trials that lead to his death without a clear cause. Yet up to the end, Jesus looks for opportunities to reveal why he has come. He shows God's love by dying for the ungodly (Rom 5:1-11).

Preparation Through Prayer (22:39-46) Like a terminally ill patient, Jesus knows that death is around the corner. God has mapped out a path and written a ticket reading "End of Earthly Life." Our mortality

---

physical provision of food and even more: spiritual provision as symbolized by the purchase of a sword.

22:37 This is one of the few places Luke draws from Isaiah 52:13—53:12. Acts 8:32-33 quotes from the middle portion of this suffering servant song. Interestingly, when Luke speaks of Jesus as a servant, he quotes Isaiah's words about suffering, not the substitutionary imagery. This shows Luke's emphasis on Jesus' suffering as an innocent, an example for others. The servant imagery in Luke 2:28-32 highlights the servant's exaltation (see also Acts 3:13-26).

is a frightening thing. Jesus faces it by doing what he always did: he took his concerns to God in prayer. While warning the disciples throughout this scene of the danger of temptation, Jesus walks into his valley of the shadow of death through the heavenly courts of God's presence. Unlike some who face death, he is not angry; nor is he stoic. He is not withdrawn, he is not bereft of hope. He simply is honest with God: *"Father, if you are willing, take this cup from me."* If there is any way I can avoid experiencing your cup of wrath for others, he prays, then remove it (on cup as wrath, Ps 11:6; 75:7-8; Is 51:17, 19, 22; Jer 25:15-16; 49:12; 51:57; Ezek 23:31-34). Like many who face death, Jesus would like to avoid dying now. If he were considering only his personal preference, he would rather not experience the pain of mortality and the horror of paying for sin.

But Jesus has a more fundamental concern: *"Yet not my will, but yours be done."* Here Jesus submits to God's plan and will. If it is time and this is the way to accomplish your desire, he says, then, Lord, take me. Jesus is committed to God's will, even above his own desires. If that means suffering, so be it. If that means death, so be it. By relying on prayer and communion with God, Jesus faces his dark hour as a shining light.

Almost as if in answer to the prayer, an angel ministers to Jesus. Its ministering presence strengthens him. Details about how this happens are not noted. What is clear is that Jesus does not face this moment alone.

Already committed to God's will, Jesus continues to pray with even more intense emotion. He prays *more earnestly* and is laboring so hard in his prayer that *his sweat* is *like drops of blood falling to the ground.* Such sweating indicates the intensity of Jesus' feelings and condition. In

---

Notes: 22:39-46 The parallels are Mark 14:32-42 and Matthew 26:36-46, though Luke's version is the most concise. Luke lacks several of the details of the other versions (for a full list, Bock 1995: introduction to this passage). Another issue is whether verses 43-44 were originally a part of Luke. This textual problem is much discussed, and many omit the text. Fitzmyer (1985:1443-44) is but one outstanding example (also Stein [1992:559], who correctly explains in n. 55 why talking about such omissions is not heretical but is simply a discussion of the nature of the original text). External evidence does slightly favor omission, since p[69], p[75], corrected Aleph, B, A, T and W exclude the text, while original Aleph, D and the Byzantine tradition include it. Following the shorter reading rule would also suggest omission. But other internal features make inclusion more likely (Neyrey 1985:59-62). Does the "shorter reading" guideline apply when whole verses are being discussed? Justin Martyr

a literary sense, the shedding of blood is already beginning. A deep dependence on the Father sometimes comes with great pain.

While Jesus is laboring hard in prayer, the disciples are asleep from *sorrow*. The rapidly spiraling succession of events has worn them down. Again, Jesus makes a spiritual picture of it all, asking them, *"Why are you sleeping? . . . Get up and pray so that you will not fall into temptation."* Surviving the pressure of suffering and rejection, overcoming the harrowing prospect of persecution and facing mortality require being on constant alert. Like the military guarding a country, disciples must maintain preparedness and communication with those in charge if they are to prevent defeat.

The Betrayal and Arrest (22:47-53) Jesus' arrest is full of pathos. The many persons involved reflect the full array of responses to Jesus. The event itself is told in three quick movements. First, the exchange with Judas provides its note of betrayal and hypocrisy. The arrest occurs as this "friend" draws near to give the teacher a customary kiss of greeting. Second comes the disciples' attempt to defend Jesus with the sword, an approach Jesus explicitly rejects. Third, Jesus rebukes his captors while he acts to heal the severed ear of one of his arresters. Jesus shows his love for his enemies to the end (see 6:27-35). Even at his arrest, he controls the flow of events. As the hour of the power of darkness comes (v. 53), Jesus faces it directly and in love.

Among the reactions to Jesus, Judas represents one in close proximity to Jesus who turns on him with vengeance. Jesus questions his attitude with a simple question, *"Are you betraying the Son of Man with a kiss?"* Judas's abandonment of God's servant has led to an ironic act of betrayal. Sometimes the strongest enemies of Jesus are those who grow up in his

---

is aware of this text (*Dialogues* 103.8). More important, Luke speaks of angelic aid here, where in 4:13 he omitted a reference to such angelic help that the other Synoptics have. In addition, the absence of parallels to the angelic presence and the sweatlike blood in the Synoptics and the tension of the portrait of Jesus' humanity needing aid from an angel in the verse make it a more difficult reading. The verses are likely to have been a part of the original Luke.

22:47-53 The parallels are John 18:2-11, Matthew 26:47-56 and Mark 14:43-52. Luke's version is most concise. He does not note why Judas kissed Jesus nor why the servant was attacked. He does not mention the servant's flight upon the arrest. Jesus is the central character here more than in the other parallels. The healing of the ear (v. 51) and Jesus' remark to Judas (v. 48) are unique to Luke's version. He may have had access to additional sources.

shadow. The irony is not only obvious but tragic.

The disciples represent those in panic who try to take matters into their own hands. They fight to avoid the path of suffering God has laid out for his messenger and those who follow him. While one asks, *"Lord, should we strike with our swords?"* another one answers on his own, wielding the sword and cutting off the right ear of the high priest's servant. Sometimes disciples believe they must take matters into their own hands to defend Jesus. But here Jesus stops the attempt to defend him with violence. His path takes a different direction.

The healed servant pictures the opportunity that exists to experience God's grace. Here is a man who rejects Jesus and participates in the arrest leading to Jesus' death. Yet the avowed enemy is not beyond Jesus' healing touch. A severed ear can always be restored, if one will listen to him.

Those who arrest Jesus represent those who remain defiant against him. Despite his grace and gentleness, they react with hostility to the one who came to give them life. The question Jesus poses to them is, *"Am I leading a rebellion, that you have come with swords and clubs?"* This rendering in the NIV, though possible, may be too specific. The term Jesus uses means "robber" *(lēstēs)* and is also used of the thieves in the parable of the good Samaritan. So we need not assume Jesus is contrasting himself with a revolutionary.

The arrest is marked not only by hostility but also by cowardice and hypocrisy. They could have arrested him in the temple but chose not to lay hands on him in public. What they would not do openly among the public, they gladly do in a more private setting. Luke has already told us why: they fear the people. So they have worked behind the scenes to oppose Jesus. It is their hour. Sin loves to work in secret.

But behind them stands a more desperate character. The drama is not merely a human one. The power of darkness lies behind this human

---

22:54-71 Some argue for only two trials, with the high priest's examination involving Caiaphas only. Though John speaks of the home of Annas, the two priests shared the same house so that complicates making a decision (Liefeld 1984:8:1035-38). This is quite possible, since the account of the inquiry before Annas is so brief that it may well have been an initial phase of a larger, single meeting. John may have named Annas because he was the elder of the family. (For this distinction, see Carson 1984:552-53, who also discusses the relationship between Caiaphas and Annas on p. 524.)

activity. The battle is of cosmic proportions, with the people on stage mere players in a larger game. The domain of evil is present. Jesus fights this battle not with weapons of war but with armaments of character (4:1-13; Eph 6:12-18; Col 1:12-14). Darkness must fall before a new day can come. It is a time *when darkness reigns.*

The Trials and the Denials (22:54-71) After Jesus' arrest, Luke narrates three events that occur in quick succession: the denials by Peter (vv. 54-62), the mocking of Jesus (vv. 63-65) and the trial of Jesus (vv. 66-71). It seems likely that Jesus is examined at the high priest's home during the evening and then is reexamined by the Sanhedrin in the early morning (vv. 54, 66). When all the Gospel accounts are considered, it appears that there is one quick inquiry before Annas, at which nothing is decided (Jn 18:13), followed by two trials—one in the evening (Mt 26:57-68; Mk 14:53-65) and another, more official meeting in the morning (Lk 22:66-71). The evening and morning trials are very similar because the morning trial simply confirms what had taken place the previous evening. Three more examinations follow these first three meetings, since encounters with Pilate, Herod and then the entire pilgrim crowd follow in Luke 23:1-25.

As interesting as the historical sequence is, more significant is the way Luke narrates these events. The various responses to Jesus are highlighted. Events are swirling around Jesus rapidly, but he is still in control. He utters the words that send him to his death, leaving no need for outside witnesses. Though all his close disciples abandon him, including the formerly confident Peter, he stills walks the path of God's will. Though the soldiers insult and taunt him, he still goes to the cross for them. Jesus is mocked as a prophet who does not know what is happening, but he is quite aware of what he is doing and why. The scene drips with the tragic irony of humankind's hostility to God's plan and the tenacity of God's Son to rectify what is awry with us all.

How one interprets the order of the trials influences whether one sees the trial scene in Luke as truly parallel to Matthew and Mark. Since I argue for a morning trial in Luke, I do not see it as strictly parallel to Matthew and Mark; the distinction is a fine one, however, since the morning trial simply replicates the evening examination or may just be an extension of it.

There is much debate about the historicity of the trials tradition. For the most comprehensive studies, all of which evidence a bit more skepticism than I do about all the historical details of this event, see Blinzler 1969, Winter 1961 and Catchpole 1971.

Seized under official arrest, Jesus is led to the high priest's house. *Syllambanō* in verse 54 is the Greek technical term for arrest (compare Jn 18:12; Acts 12:3; 23:27; 26:21). Since Matthew 26:57 names Caiaphas's house here and John 18:13 mentions Annas's residence, there is a question whether the same locale or a different locale is intended (see note on 22:54-71). If two locales are in view, then the first meeting leads very quickly into a second.

It is during this time that Peter has his public oral exam on his faithfulness and relationship to Jesus, just as Jesus had predicted (22:31-34). Having failed, Peter learns that resisting peer pressure can be tougher than he had imagined. It is easy to fall when one is surrounded by hostility and fails to look to the Lord for strength.

The test itself takes over an hour (v. 59). Peter has followed at a distance. John 18:15-16 mentions that "another disciple," probably John, is also present in the courtyard. In the chill of the late evening air, a fire is kindled to keep the gathering warm. The *courtyard (aulē)* where the servants are gathered could be a yard or an area around an open hallway. When Peter's face becomes visible, a servant girl stares at him, recognizing him as one of the disciples. She announces the surprising guest to the crowd with the simple words *"This man was with him."*

Probably aware that Jesus' fate is in doubt and that guilt by association is a genuine risk, Peter denies any knowledge of Jesus. The astute observation has been made that Peter in this way does not deny Jesus as much as deny *knowing* him (Stanley 1980:195; Stein 1992:565). His lie is like the "end around" maneuver in American football; Peter takes an indirect route to avoid the question. He does not attack Jesus, but neither does he assert his association with him. In baseball terms, Peter has taken strike one.

Afterward another person takes up the accusation. Luke identifies the second challenger as a man, while Mark 14:69 and Matthew 26:71 mention a woman. It is likely that the woman's initial effort received wide attention. Emphatically comes the charge: *"You also are one of them."* The second-person pronoun *you (su)* is spoken with *ex autōn,* "from among them," so Peter's association with Jesus is emphasized. The charge is "You are one of them!" Once again, Peter tries to parry the thrust: *"Man, I am not!"* Peter has taken strike two. Or as cricketers say, he is in danger of being run out.

A third person identifies Peter. Luke leaves him nameless, but John 18:26 says he is a relative of the priest's servant Malcus, who had his ear severed and healed earlier. John notes that this questioner is positive that Peter's face is familiar, since he saw him in the garden. Since he had been at the scene, his testimony is significant. Luke simply narrates his confidence: *"Certainly this fellow was with him, for he is a Galilean."* Like American Southerners or people from the north of Scotland, Galileans had a distinctive accent (Mt 26:73).

Peter again denies the connection: *"Man, I don't know what you're talking about!"* Luke is kind to Peter, for he does not refer to the cursing and swearing that accompany this denial. The mighty, confident Peter has struck out; he has given up his wicket.

But the rooster's crowing and Jesus' glance rock Peter's memory. *Peter remembered the word the Lord had spoken to him.* Luke's wording reminds us of Jesus' prophetic awareness of what is taking place—that even his closest allies will leave him to face his death alone.

Peter's failure prompts his departure and painful tears. It is easy to claim Jesus in the solitude of one's living room among like-minded friends, but it can be hard to do so in public. Peter will learn the lesson and return to be a courageous voice for Jesus in Acts 2. But here he is a total disappointment. He has failed to pray and rest in the Lord's provision (Lk 12:11-12; 22:40, 46). His nerve has failed, and the failure has stabbed his heart. He knows he has let Jesus down.

But Jesus knows his heart and will soon restore him (Jn 21:1-14), a restoration he had prepared him for earlier (Lk 22:32). Failure, though painful, can be a means of growth; by God's grace we can learn from our mistakes.

After his friend's withdrawal, Jesus is mocked by enemies. Things are going from bad to worse. Luke strains to relate this account, calling the action of those who hold Jesus in custody blasphemous (v. 65). They mock him and beat him, as others had reviled a prophet earlier (1 Kings 22:24). Here the soldiers play an ancient version of blindman's buff (Stählin 1972:264-65; Is 53:3-5). They think Jesus should name his tormenters. If he is the prophet the public claims, this should be an easy task (Lk 7:16; 9:7-9; 24:19). The opponents' reviling of Jesus is full of scorn and insult. When the world turns from indifference to hostility against Jesus, this is how their reaction to him looks. It is easy to mock what is not appreciated.

From injury and insult, Luke turns to inquiry. What will the officials of Judaism do with Jesus? Luke does not mention at all the effort to charge Jesus with claiming to destroy and raise up the temple. Luke's trial scene stays focused on one issue, Christology. Who is Jesus? That is the key question for this Gospel.

Much historical information is available on trials of the time, especially in the Mishnaic tractate *Sanhedrin.* Made up of seventy-one members, with the high priest serving as its leader, this council sat in a semicircle when investigating matters of importance (*m. Sanhedrin* 1:6; 4:3). It seems likely that such a procedure took place here. The council consisted of Sadducees, Pharisees and leading middle-class laymen, known as the elders (Josephus *Antiquities* 12.3.3 §142). So priests, scribes and the wealthy dominated this ruling group, which had authority over internal Jewish matters except where the death penalty was involved (Josephus *Antiquities* 20.9.1 §§197-203 on the illegal slaying of James the brother of Jesus; *t. Šabbat* 15a).

Though Luke clearly makes the leadership responsible for Jesus' death both here and in Luke 23:13-25, there is no reason to call him anti-Semitic. His appeal is for Jews to complete their salvation by coming to their Messiah. Their refusal to do so is seen as blindness and ignorance (Acts 2:22-24; 3:17-26; 26:12-23). But he continually pleads for them to enter into God's promise and blessing.

Luke moves right into the questioning. The Sanhedrin requests, *"If you are the Christ . . . tell us."* In an echo of his earlier discussion with them about himself and John the Baptist (20:1-8), Jesus replies that if he answers positively they will not believe, and if he asks them they will not answer.

But Jesus does not stop there. What he says next is the key to his claims

---

22:66 Some have challenged the historicity of this text because Mishnaic rules for trials were not followed. Whether the trial rules of the tractate *Sanhedrin* applied in the first century is debated, given that the *Mishna* dates from the late second century A.D. In addition, in some cases where unusual circumstances existed, the rules were sometimes not followed (Josephus *Antiquities* 20 §§197-207; *Jewish Wars* 6 §§300-309). The Jews were sensitive to

and his guilty verdict at this trial: *"But from now on the Son of Man will be seated at the right hand of the mighty God."* The Greek refers to the "right hand of the power of God." Both the translation and the Greek emphasize God's sovereign might. The claim here is extensive. It was not a crime in ancient Judaism to claim to be Messiah, as the Bar Kochba revolt in A.D. 132 showed. But Jesus is saying more than this. He is claiming to be able to go directly into God's presence and rule at the divinity's side from heaven. This is worse than claiming that he could march into the Holy of Holies in the temple and reside there (Bock 1994c:186-91). The Jews fought the Maccabean War over the holiness of the temple's inner sanctum; but they held the holiness of heaven itself in an even higher regard. Jesus' statement offends their sense of God's holiness.

In addition, it implies an even more significant claim. The Sanhedrin has Jesus on trial. Its members are his judges. His fate is in their hands. But if Jesus is to rule from God's side in heaven, then they cannot judge him, since he is their judge. The use of *Son of Man* recalls the picture of authority given from God to "one like a son of man" in Daniel 7. The implication does not slip by the theologians in the crowd. The scene's irony in terms of who holds God's power cannot be greater. Jesus argues that *from now on* whatever happens at the trial is irrelevant. His rule from God's side will follow. People may think they have the right to make a judgment about Jesus, but the judgment that counts is the one made by the resurrected Son of God.

In sum, Jesus makes himself and his authority the issue. The leaders are astute enough to see the claim. So they ask, *"Are you then the Son of God?"* They sense the depth of what Jesus is claiming—that Jesus uniquely shares God's rule and power.

Jesus' answer is both a positive reply and a type of circumlocution; in effect, he says, "I will not deny it, but I would mean it a little differently from the way you mean it." So Jesus says, "You say that I am" (Blass and

---

Roman concerns as well (Josephus *Jewish Wars* 7 §§412-13). Nonetheless, some have noted various "violations" of these later rules, such as holding a capital trial at night (*m. Sanhedrin* 4:2), not waiting a day to confirm the guilty verdict (*m. Sanhedrin* 4:2; 5:5) and insisting that witnesses' testimony agree to gain a guilty verdict (*m. Sanhedrin* 5:2). Of course, on this last point Jesus' own remarks, not that of the witnesses, came to be decisive.

Debrunner 1961:par. 441.3; Catchpole 1970:226; Stein 1992:571). The NIV gives the force of this indirect reply: *"You are right in saying I am."*

So the judgment is rendered against Jesus. *"Why do we need any more testimony? We have heard it from his own lips."* The judgment's irony is that Jesus will be crucified for being who he is. The trial pictures the world's rejection of him and his claims. His own have received him not. Sin's blindness leads to Jesus' dying for being who he is. Confirmation of this understanding of the trial as picturing humanity's rejection will come when the people add their voices to call for Jesus' death, opting to free a murderer in the place of this innocent one (23:13-25; Acts 4:24-31). Jesus utters his own death sentence by speaking what Luke would regard as the truth.

So this account is really the story of two courtrooms. One is run by the Sanhedrin, the other by Jesus at the Father's side. One utters blasphemy against the Son, because they have taken his words as blasphemous. The other will receive the Son as an equal. The division of opinion could not be greater. No relativism can bring the two views together. Either Jesus is right or the Jewish court is right. Jesus' claim is either blasphemy or deadly serious truth. For if he sits at God's side, then he does exercise divine authority. There is no appeal higher than the Supreme Court of heaven.

The Trial Before Pilate (23:1-5) With Jesus in hand and a guilty verdict in place, there is only one more hurdle to Jesus' removal. The leadership needs the Roman government's support. A plan that has long been in the works now requires a deft political touch (6:11; 11:53-54). A death penalty could not be executed unless Rome issued it (Josephus *Jewish Wars* 2.8.1 §117; Jn 18:31). So the leadership takes Jesus to Pilate. The charges must be formulated in a way that causes Pilate, as procurator and protector of Roman regional concerns, to be worried about his future as governor if he does not stop Jesus. Such capital crime rulings were often made when Pilate would make assize judgments as Roman governor (Kinman 1991).

The trial before Pilate was not unusual in its style. Luke's account

_____

23:1-5 The parallels to this event appear in Mark 15:1-5, Matthew 27:2, 11-14 and John

reflects the threefold structure of Roman trial procedure: charges, *cognito* (examination) and verdict (Neyrey 1985:77). Intrigue surrounds the rejection of Jesus. The leaders' maneuvering reaches its high point here.

The three charges are stated in verse 2. Only one of them is even partially true: *"We have found this man subverting our nation."* The Greek speaks of "perverting our customs," a charge slightly broader than the political tone of the NIV. Issues of Jewish law and politics are in view. This charge reflects two realities. First, the leaders are uncomfortable with Jesus and regard him with contempt. That is why they do not name him but refer to him as "this one" instead (22:56, 59). These words are a far cry from their public affirmations of respect to Jesus in 20:21. Second, they regard him as a threat to their nation's tradition. He misleads the people. This statement reverses Jesus' charge in 9:41. Such unrest would be of concern to Pilate, because anyone who stirred up Jewish religious sensibilities could be a source of political upheaval.

"He opposes payment of taxes to Caesar." This charge concerning the poll tax is patently false, as 20:25 has already shown. But the charge is clever, because Pilate's major political responsibility is the collection of taxes for Rome. A second element in the charge is also a source of concern. The taxes go to Caesar, raising the issue of Pilate's personal loyalty or disloyalty. Failure to act against one who opposes Caesar would mean one is not a friend of Caesar either. Servants of Rome unfaithful to Caesar are not servants for long!

The third charge is that he *"claims to be Christ, a king."* Here the threat of an opposing ruler is made explicit. Is Pilate being careless on his watch, allowing revolution to foment under his very nose? Jesus is painted as a dangerous revolutionary. It is Pilate's obligation to Caesar to stop him.

Seen in light of Pilate's responsibilities, these charges are serious, especially since the Jewish leadership portrays itself as sensitive to Roman concerns here. Politically and personally, these charges push all the right buttons. So Pilate moves to examine Jesus.

Luke has a very abbreviated version of this encounter, in which Pilate focuses only on Jesus' claim to kingship. The first charge is not really

---

18:29-38. Luke's version is closest to Mark's, but some of the details suggest that Luke had access to additional information.

central to Pilate, since he is not a Jew. The second can be handled by going directly to the third question about kingship. Does Caesar have a rival or not? John 18:33-38 shows a longer questioning in which Jesus responds to the kingship charge by stating that his kingdom is not of this world. Luke in contrast has Jesus answer Pilate's question whether he is *king of the Jews* with a qualified affirmation, "You have said so." As before, the NIV renders the force of the indirect reply, *"Yes, it is as you say."* Though there is truth in the charge, it is not the direct threat that the Jews imply.

Pilate seems not terribly concerned after his examination. His judgment is that he finds *no basis for a charge against this man.* Pilate will declare Jesus innocent several times in this chapter (vv. 14-15, 22). This should bring the trial's end and Jesus' release, but Luke is proving that Jesus was an innocent sacrifice. If justice had prevailed, the arrest would have ended here and Jesus' ministry would have resumed. But the Son of Man is not treated with justice. Sinful humanity rejects him and overrides any concern for justice. Though Rome is not without blame, the real responsibility lies with the Jewish leadership. Insistently they keep noting that *he stirs up the people.* Luke uses an imperfect tense here *(epischyon)* to show that they press their case with continual pleading. Pilate needs to understand that law and order, not to mention his own job, are at stake.

Under such pressure, Pilate does what many politicians do: he passes the buck and lets someone else make the tough call. When Pilate discovers that Jesus is Galilean, he sends Jesus over to Herod. Let the Jewish ruler decide the matter; let him take the heat. If any political mistakes are to be made, they will be made in consultation with the region's ethnic political leaders. If Pilate has problems later, he can always say, "Herod made me do it."

So political and social forces are swirling like a tornado around Jesus. Despite his innocence, the trial proceeds. Sin has a way of ignoring or

23:6-12 This passage is unique to Luke. Justin also describes this scene (*Dialogues with Trypho* 103). Some have challenged its historicity, but without cause. For a defense of its historical character, see Sherwin-White 1963:28-32 and Hoehner's study in Bammel 1970:84-90. In fact, it is likely that this event allowed Pilate and Herod to patch up a strained relationship after the fall of Sejanus, Tiberius's ruthless, anti-Semitic righthand man. For

deferring Jesus' claims. Political expediency will make Jesus a sacrificial lamb.

The Examination Before Herod (23:6-12) The sending of Jesus to Herod excuses Pilate from responsibility and shows political skill. No one can accuse Pilate of demagoguery on the touchy issue of Jesus.

Because of the holiday season, Herod himself is also in Jerusalem— a coincidence of divine proportions—staying at a beautiful palace west of the temple (Josephus *Jewish Wars* 2.16.3 §344; 5.4.4 §§176-83; on debate over Herod's authority, see *Antiquities* 14.15.2 §403). When Jesus is brought before him, Herod hopes for a show, for he has been longing to see Jesus work miracles. But Jesus is not an entertainer given to fulfilling curiosity.

With his innocence established in the previous examination, Jesus takes a new defense tactic. He remains silent. No longer will he answer any questions. Justice should have dictated his release. He has defended himself with brief statements of truth. Now that justice is silent, he responds with his own silence. The events recall Isaiah 53:7, which Luke cites in Acts 8:32.

The silence deeply disappoints Herod. In the face of Jesus' silence, the chief priests and scribes press their case, *vehemently accusing him.* Once they formed their opinion of Jesus, their accusations have never stopped (Lk 6:7; 23:2, 14). The leadership is turning up the pressure.

Herod takes advantage of the occasion to mock Jesus, arraying him in bright, regal apparel and sending him back to Pilate. The contempt that Herod shows to Jesus was predicted in Luke 18:32. Herod's verdict is not noted here but is mentioned in verse 15. Herod's comical antics show that he sees no threat in Jesus.

Pilate's move reaps the dividend of Herod's appreciation. Where there had been enmity, now there is friendship, for Pilate has shown respect for Herod's position.

Thus Jesus has become a political pawn. Since he has been declared

---

information on his fall, see Dio Cassius *Roman History* 58.4.1—58.11.7. If this scenario is correct, then the date of the crucifixion is likely to be A.D. 33.

23:11 It is debated whether *elegant robe* refers to white regal garb or purple. There is no way to choose. More important than the particular color is the soldiers' flippancy. Herod senses no threat from Jesus and his silence.

innocent by two leaders, justice would say that Jesus should be released, but injustice and destiny are at work. Ironically, his presence has brought reconciliation between two old opponents. Their reconciliation is another step on the way to his unjust death.

The Examination Before the People (23:13-25) In many ways the passion account's real turning point occurs here. Until this point, the common people have been strongly supportive of Jesus. On a few occasions the leadership had found it prudent not to carry out its threats against Jesus because of the people (20:19; 22:2). But now the people react against Jesus, stopping Pilate's attempt to release him.

Pilate regards Jesus as not worthy of death but still does not grant him freedom. Two leaders have acquitted Jesus, but that is not enough. The Jewish teacher has become a political football. In a crazy game, a murderer is released and a deliverer is slain.

The scene begins with Pilate's attempt to release Jesus. He addresses everyone—*the chief priests, the rulers and the people.* Pilate is clear that he regards the Jews as having *"no basis for your charges against him."* Herod has taken the same position: there is nothing deserving death in Jesus. Pilate proposes a compromise: he will beat Jesus and then release him. The beating would be either the less severe *fustigata* or the dreaded *verberatio,* which would leave one on the edge of death. In either case, the whip used possessed short teeth that would cut the skin and lead to bleeding. Pilate supposes that punishment would deter the teacher and calm the leadership.

But no compromise can be found. When the decision comes for Jesus to be crucified, he receives the heavier beating, the *verberatio,* since it prepares the victim for crucifixion and makes death come more quickly.

In an astounding act of popular judgment, all call out for Barabbas's

23:13-25 This account mixes unique Lukan elements with traditional ones. Verses 13-16 are unique to Luke, while verses 18-25 appear to be a mixture of unique material and tradition like that in Mark 15:6-15 and Matthew 27:15-26. Elements unique to Luke include the repeated mention of Jesus' innocence. Such details indicate that Luke likely drew on a special source for his account. Some have questioned the account because of the inconsistency between Pilate's declaration of Jesus' innocence and the flogging. But Jesus is said to be innocent only of a crime that would *deserve death,* and those who are skeptical underestimate the political pressure Pilate faced here.

23:17 The oldest and better manuscripts of Luke lack this verse. It is omitted by p75, A, B and the itala. It states what Mark 15:6-8 also notes, namely that Pilate often released a

release. They choose a violent insurrectionist and murderer over Jesus. A shocked Pilate tries to persuade them otherwise. Luke explicitly states that Pilate wants *to release Jesus*. But the crowd insists on Jesus' execution.

For a fourth time, and for the third time publicly, Pilate tries to halt the momentum (vv. 4, 14, 20, 22). Asking the crowd to name the evil Jesus has done, he repeats his verdict that Jesus has done nothing meriting a death sentence. Pilate still wishes only to "discipline" *(paideuō)* Jesus with the whip. But *they kept shouting,* and later *they insistently demanded.* Again the imperfect tenses stress the ongoing cry for Jesus' demise. They want him crucified.

In the face of such a public outcry, Pilate crumbles. *Their shouts prevailed.* Pilate grants their demand: Barabbas will go free, while Jesus is *surrendered . . . to their will.* Acts 3:13-14 will allude to this verdict, while Jesus' prediction recorded in Luke 22:37 comes to pass. Jesus is reckoned among the criminals, even though he is innocent. He is suffering as a servant. Though the suffering is unjust and intense, exaltation will follow (Is 52:13-15). He also has been "handed over" to the Gentiles (Luke 18:32), only to be handed back to the Jews.

There is both tragedy and a lesson in this event. The tragedy is that justice has not prevailed. Sin's blindness has caused the nation to reject its Savior. The decision to miss the opportunity for deliverance is a grave mistake. Luke tells the story of the turnaround in the people's attitude to show the fickleness with which Jesus is treated. In a way he was trivialized by the people. Such trivializing has often been Jesus' lot in history. For Luke, the loser is the one who reduces Jesus to a trivial pursuit.

The lesson has to do with why the trivializing is tragic. Jesus is the substitute for the sinner. Barabbas's release and Jesus' death make up a portrait of the exchange God engages in to save sinners from the penalty

---

prisoner during the feast.

23:21 Crucifixion was viewed as a horrible way to die. On the ancient practice, see Schneider 1971:573-81, Hengel 1977 and Fitzmyer 1978:493-513. Ancient descriptions include Josephus *Antiquities* 2.5.4 §77; 17.10.10 §295; 11.6.11 §261, 266-67; 13.14.2 §380; *Jewish Wars* 1.4.5-6 §§93-98; 5.11.1 §§449-51; and 7.6.4 §203, where he calls it the worst of deaths. Crucifixion came in four steps: (1) the trip to the cross with the criminal bearing the cross beam, (2) the criminal bound to the cross by nails or by rope, (3) the beam fastened to an upright pole, and (4) a tablet specifying the crime hung to indicate the offense to the public. Of course, these four steps would be preceded by a severe flogging, the *verberatio,* which I describe in the commentary text.

of their ways (Rom 5:5-9). This sacrifice at the altar of injustice is the ultimate expression of God's love. Amazingly, in the midst of a monstrous injustice God can design a means of victory. Jesus' death means the possibility of life for another. No matter how severe the sin, release is made possible through Jesus' death.

The people think they have stopped Jesus. But in fact their action both exposes sin and shows how God will deal with it. The offer of the Savior became the better sacrifice. Eternal life can now be offered to those who recognize who he is and who they are before him (Heb 8—10). Sinners need to see their sin as a blot before God, producing a chasm between him and them. Those who come to this realization can now experience forgiveness through the shed blood of Jesus, the One sacrificed on their behalf. In this way Jesus has "purchased" the church through his own blood (Acts 20:28). In death has come the opportunity for life. Just ask Barabbas.

Jesus will die as an innocent martyr, one of the many saints who have suffered unjust rejection. Numerous Old Testament quotes develop this Lukan theme of rejection. In the story of the crucifixion to follow, lament psalms are quoted that detail how saints of old suffered unjustly. The earlier use of Psalm 118 in Luke 13:34-35 and 19:38 has the same background. Psalm 2 is quoted in Acts 4:24-28 to make a similar point. Speeches in Acts 2 and 3 will say explicitly that Jesus died unjustly. The just one dies unjustly for the unjust to make them just! The ways and wisdom of God are beyond our figuring out; we cannot understand them until he gives us revelation.

The Crucifixion (23:26-49) The central issue of Jesus' crucifixion is his character and work. From the creation to watching bystanders, everything and everyone have opinions about the death of this king-prophet. This passage consists of many subunits: the journey (vv. 26-32), the crucifixion (vv. 33-38), the discussion with the two thieves (vv. 39-42) and

---

23:26-49 For this passage I note parallels a subunit at a time. Luke 23:26-32 has partial parallels in Matthew 27:31-32 and Mark 15:20-21. But the presence of the mourning women is unique to Luke, part of his special material. When it comes to describing the crucifixion, the two thieves and Jesus' death, points of contact among the Synoptics, unique Lukan details and omissions of detail are all mixed together. Verses 33-34 are like Matthew 27:33, 35 and Mark 15:22, 24. Verses 35-38 parallel Matthew 27:39, 41-42, as well as Mark 15:29, 31-32. Verses 44-45 match with Matthew 27:45 and Mark 15:33. Verse 46b is similar to Matthew 27:50 and Mark 15:37. Verse 47 is close to Matthew 27:54 and Mark 15:39. These

the cosmic signs along with human reactions to Jesus' death (vv. 43-49).

Jesus dies as an innocent sufferer, yet even to the end he is saving those who look to him. In fact, he even continues requesting forgiveness for those who kill him. As the hymnwriter says, "Amazing love, how can it be?" Around him reactions run the entire spectrum, from cruel mocking to painful mourning. The division of opinion Jesus causes is evident in this key event. Neutrality is not really permitted by Jesus' life and claims, if one understands who Jesus saw himself to be. His death as described here is attested by several ancient historians, though often very briefly (Josephus *Antiquities* 18.3.3 §§63-64; Tacitus *Annals* 15.44; *t. Sanhedrin* 43a; see F. F. Bruce 1974). Each of us must face up to the claims of both his person and his death, deciding either for him or against him.

Jesus' journey to his death is halted temporarily when the cross becomes too heavy for him to bear. Such cross bearing was customary, but the day had been a long one. Romans did not bear the cross, which was considered a symbol of great shame. Someone was chosen from the crowd—Simon from Cyrene, a major North African center of Judaism, was conscripted to bear the cross (Mt 27:31-32; Mk 15:20-21; on Cyrene, Acts 6:9; 11:20; 13:1; 1 Maccabees 15:23; Josephus *Antiquities* 14.7.2 §114; 16.1.5 §169; 16.6.1 §160; *Jewish Wars* 7.11.1-3 §§437-50). Cyrene is located near the modern area of Tripoli.

Many suggest that Simon pictures the disciple following in the way of Jesus, but this seems unlikely. The description of his following with the cross does not echo the wording of Luke 9:23 and 14:27, and Simon suffers nothing during the process. At best what is pictured involves Jesus' sharing the shame of his death march with another who accompanies him. But such shame is less than a picture of discipleship with its accompanying rejection by the world.

---

points of contact suggest a unified tradition behind the Synoptics' description of Jesus' death. Luke has unique elements in verses 33, 34a, 35a, 36, 37 and 39-43. Among the outstanding Lukan features are the rending of the veil, the dialogue with the two thieves and the use of Psalm 31, not Psalm 22. So Luke's portrayal is both traditional and fresh.

23:26 On the custom of the victim's bearing his own cross, see Plutarch *The Divine Vengeance* 554 A-B. The cross is described by many of the church fathers: Justin *Trypho* 91; *Apology* 55; Irenaeus *Against Heresies* 2.24.4; and Tertullian *Against the Jews* 10.

Though exhausted and needing aid, Jesus still interacts with the crowd, especially a group of women mourning over his coming demise. Luke singles them out from the *large number of people*. The great multitude appears to be caught up in the curiosity of the event, but the *women* who trail behind are not merely curious. They beat their breasts and wail for him (Mic 1:8; Zech 12:10-14). It is debated whether these mourning women are merely the standard Jewish mourners present at any death, those who gave the victims drugged drink to soothe their painful end (*t. Sanhedrin* 43a) or genuine in their grief. Whatever option is intended, the text appears to treat their lament as entirely sincere. Jesus explains to them that the real tragedy is not his but the nation's.

In prophetic-sounding words, Jesus addresses the women as representative of the nation: *"daughters of Jerusalem"* (Is 37:22; Mic 1:8; Zeph 3:14; Zech 9:9). Jesus notes that they weep for the wrong thing: *"weep for yourselves and for your children."* Jesus' rejection means judgment for the nation (Lk 13:34; 19:41-44; 21:20-21). In fact, that judgment represents the price for anyone who rejects Jesus. A key period of divine activity will come, as Jesus notes: *"The time will come"* (5:35; 17:22; 21:6, 23; Schneider 1964b:671). All blessings and curses will be reversed, for in those bitter days of judgment it will be better to be barren than to bear and nurture a child. As Jesus had told the Sanhedrin, he is the real judge, and to reject him is to come under God's judgment. So Jesus warns these women of the nation's coming pain for slaying its promised one. It will be better in those days to ask the creation, both mountains and hills, to collapse on top of one than to experience the misery of this judgment.

Jesus closes with a parabolic question: *"If men do these things when the tree is green, what will happen when it is dry?"* The basic point is clear enough. The green wood is Jesus, while the dry wood is Jerusalem in judgment. If this situation is bad, it is nothing compared to what is to come. But there is debate as to who "they" are that treat the live (or green) wood this way: Rome, the Jews, humanity or God? One of two options is best. Most likely is that the word is a circumlocution for God.

23:34 There is some dispute whether verse 34a is part of Luke's original text. Many good witnesses omit it (p⁷⁵, B, Aleph^c, D*), but others include it (Aleph, C, D^c, families 1 and 13, most itala). But internal factors suggest that it should be included: (1) The parallel with Acts 7:60 and Stephen suggests a conscious parallel like those Luke is fond of making

If God does this in judging his own Son for the sake of forgiveness, what will his judgment look like on those who reject his offer (Schneider 1967:38 n. 7; Stein 1992:586)? A similar indirect reference to God appears in 12:20. The point is that if it is possible to consume live wood, think how easy it will be to consume wood that is dry (Is 10:16-19; Ezek 20:47).

If this reading is not right, then "they" would be the nation itself, since that is the natural historical referent (L. T. Johnson 1991:373). The tragedy, Jesus says, is not his death but the nation's failure to choose deliverance, life and forgiveness. The failure to choose correctly about Jesus has grave consequences.

So on this note the journey to the cross continues. Jesus and two criminals head to their fate. The Greek term describing the other offenders, *kakourgos,* is a generic one for "lawbreaker" (Prov 21:15). Mark 15:27 and Matthew 27:38 describe the men with the term *lēstēs,* which can mean "bandit" or "revolutionary." This is the word Jesus used to question his arrest in Luke 22:52.

At "the place of the skull" *(kranion),* Jesus is crucified. The hill had this name because it protruded from the ground much as a head does from a body. Here Jesus is nailed to the cross beam (Jn 20:25; Col 2:14). The beam was placed on the upright piece of wood, and the whole structure was then lifted up and dropped into the ground. Jesus would hang there unable to get support to breathe.

Even in this desperate situation, Jesus prays for those who will kill him. He asks that his executors be forgiven, since they have acted in ignorance. Jesus' intercession lays the basis for God's offer of forgiveness. National consequences will follow from Jesus' rejection, but God's love expressed here shows that the rejection need not be permanent, neither for an individual nor for a nation.

Though Jesus pleads their ignorance, such ignorance does not remove culpability. They have chosen a course that reflects a lack of understanding, but they still need God's mercy. Jesus' lack of vindictiveness illustrates the very love he called for from his disciples (6:29, 35).

---

between Luke and Acts. (2) The absence of a parallel in the other Synoptics argues for its originality here. (3) The motif of ignorance is Lukan (Acts 3:17; 13:27; 17:30). (4) Sayings are found in each of the subunits of Luke's crucifixion account, but if this saying is omitted, the pattern is broken (for additional reasons, see L. T. Johnson 1991:376).

As the men hang, the soldiers cast lots for Jesus' clothes. This allusion to Psalm 22:18 portrays Jesus as a righteous sufferer (Mt 27:35; Mk 15:24; Jn 19:24). Unjustly afflicted, he dies with nothing on his back.

The scene produces various reactions. Some watch out of curiosity; others mourn. Still others treat the event with indifference, entertaining themselves on the leftovers of clothes. But the rulers sneer (Ps 22:7). They contest Jesus' ability to save, even as he prays to call for their forgiveness. The irony is amazing. Vindictiveness is face to face with compassion. Certain of their victory, they challenge Jesus to step down from the cross: *"He saved others; let him save himself."* This is the first of three taunts in the Lukan account (the others are in vv. 37, 39), all dealing with the issue of Jesus' saving activity. Ironically, by accepting the way of the cross, saving is exactly what Jesus is doing. But these rejecters never see it. The taunters make the issue Jesus' person: *If he is the Christ of God, the Chosen One,* then Jesus should be a deliverer (contrast 9:35). In their view a Messiah does not hang on a cross and suffer. What the taunters do not realize is that the servant of God does suffer for his own (Is 52:13—53:12). Suffering precedes exaltation.

Soldiers join the taunt: *"If you are the king of the Jews, save yourself."* These taunts are ironic, unconscious testimonies. Though intended to make fun of Jesus, they speak truth about which the utterers are unaware.

In fulfillment of Psalm 68:21, they offer him sour wine, what the text calls vinegar, to relieve his thirst. But the taunt and action together show that compassion is not the motive. The rapid repetition of the titles, a detail unique to Luke, keeps Jesus' person the issue. Is he who he claimed to be? That is the question Luke wishes his readers to ponder. Even the placard describing the charge says simply, "THIS IS THE KING OF THE JEWS." Such an inscription was common at a crucifixion (Suetonius *Caligula* 32; *Domitian* 10; Eusebius *Ecclesiastical History* 5.1.44). It was called the *titulus.* All the Gospels note that such an inscription hung over Jesus, but with some variation in the wording (Mt 27:37; Mk 15:26; Jn 19:19). The inscription itself is filled with ironic testimony. Even in hatred and rejection, there is testimony to Jesus.

The reactions to Jesus vary in intensity. Perhaps no incident sums up the range of responses more than the discussion among the thieves and Jesus. The other Synoptics mention these thieves, but they only note that they reviled Jesus (Mt 27:44; Mk 15:32). Apparently one of them has a change of heart, however, as he hears Jesus intercede for others and watches him tolerate the taunts. The final taunt comes from one of the thieves: *"Aren't you the Christ? Save yourself and us."* When the criminal chimes in against Jesus, it is too much for the other lawbreaker.

It is often said that the thief on the cross does not evidence his faith, for he has the equivalent of a deathbed conversion. But the testimony he gives for Jesus in his last moments is one of the most eloquent evidences of faith in the Bible. The faith in his heart is expressed by his lips. He addresses his colleague first and then Jesus. He expresses his rejection of the taunt by exclaiming, *"Don't you fear God, . . . since you are under the same sentence? We are punished justly, for we are getting what our deeds deserve. But this man has done nothing wrong."* It could be said that the injustice of the entire crucifixion is summed up in this short commentary. Other men die justly, but Jesus hangs on the cross as a matter of injustice. To mock Jesus is to support injustice at its worst. Those who fear God had better realize what it means to taunt him.

Then in words full of faith, the thief turns to Jesus: *"Jesus, remember me when you come into your kingdom."* The criminal anticipates the restoration and resurrection. He asks to be included. His depth of perception stands in contrast to the blindness of those who taunt. This man, despite a life full of sin, comes to Jesus and seeks forgiveness in his last mortal moments. He confesses his guilt and casts himself on Jesus' mercy and saving power. Luke could not have painted a clearer portrait of God's grace.

Jesus' reply gives the man more than he bargained for in terms of acceptance. The thief hopes that one day in the future he will share in Jesus' rule. Instead, Jesus promises him paradise from the moment of his death: *"I tell you the truth, today you will be with me in paradise."* The "truly I say to you" formula represents Jesus' most solemn way to reassure his neighbor. Faith's confession and request have been heard. From this day the man will be in the abode of the righteous—the Jews' longed-for paradise, the restored creation in which the righteous dwell (Is 51:3; Ezek 31:8-9, Assyria pictured like the garden of Eden; *Testament of Levi* 18:10-14; *Psalms of Solomon* 14:2-3; *1 Enoch* 60:8; 61:12). Jesus does not explain how this will work, but the assurance he gives to the thief is clear. Ironically, though dying amidst mocking, Jesus has saved while on the cross. The request of the taunts has been granted to one who learned to believe.

Next the heavens join the discussion, issuing their own commentary on events. In Scripture, when God moves the creation to speak, events are marked as having a high significance. Creation speaks with darkness and through a sign in the temple. At *the sixth hour* (midday), darkness descends on the earth. This suggests the presence of judgment (Joel 2:10, 30-31; Amos 8:9). God is aware of what is taking place. The sign lasts for three hours. The sun's failure pictures creation awry.

Even at the place that signifies God's presence all is not right. *The curtain of the temple was torn in two.* Two questions arise for readers here: Which curtain is in view? What does its tearing signify?

Two curtains are possible. Is it the curtain at the entrance to the Holy of Holies or the curtain that separated the outer court from the temple proper? The Greek term used by Luke, *katapetasma,* is itself ambiguous. There is no way to decide for certain. Either way, the basic symbolism of a disruption at the nation's place of worship is clear.

What does it mean? Numerous suggestions exist (Green 1991:543-57; Sylva 1986:239-50): (1) It shows that a time of judgment on the nation has come, as the darkness also indicates. (2) It reflects judgment on the temple. (3) It shows Jesus opening the way to paradise (23:43). (4) It pictures the end of the old covenant (Heb 8—10). (5) It shows that all have equal access to God. The text does not tell us specifically which of these is meant, though all are good candidates. Contextually, the first three options all make good literary sense. Canonically, all the views could apply, since Hebrews is an exposition of the significance of Jesus' death and Acts makes it clear how the gospel can be sent to all in light of who Jesus is and what he has done. Judgment and grace often appear side by side in God's plan.

Jesus dies uttering words from a psalm of confidence, Psalm 31:5. This psalm was often used in Jewish evening prayer as one commended oneself into God's care during the night's sleep. As Jesus enters the sleep of death, he takes a similar step of faith. His last words are a commentary not only on his death but also on his life: *"Father, into your hands I commit my spirit."* From first to last, Jesus has lived to serve God. His life's creed on his lips, he dies. The psalm comments on the trust that Jesus places in God as he passes away. The other Synoptics quote Psalm 22:1 and its lament, while noting that Jesus dies uttering a loud cry. Luke supplies the detail of this final confident cry to God. Lament has gone to trust and victory. The righteous sufferer has suffered and won by trusting God every step of the way. Stephen will die a similar death years later (Acts 7:54-60).

One more witness, a soldier, observes what takes place and in one sentence echoes the sentiments of the saved thief on the cross: *"Surely this was a righteous [innocent] man."* The ambiguity of the rendering reflects the ambiguity of *dikaios,* which can bear either meaning. In the context, where Jesus' innocence has been stressed from start to finish, "innocent man" fits. But such a verdict implies Jesus' purity of character (Acts 3:14; 7:52; 22:14). Here is the final verbal testimony at the cross. A soldier witnessing the traumatic events of the day has come to his own conclusion: Jesus was who he claimed to be. The other Gospels make this same point though they summarize it differently: "Surely this man was the Son of God!" There is no contradiction here, since to call Jesus innocent is to accept the claim of who he is.

The event's mood emerges in the closing description. It was sad and wrong for Jesus to have died. The multitudes return home in mourning and *beat their breasts.* Some of them have been forced to pause and consider what has taken place. Maybe Jesus' condemnation was a serious mistake. Perhaps his death was a deep tragedy. Apparently events have helped some change their minds about Jesus. Sometimes a closer look at Jesus does change a person's mind.

The Galileans and women who had followed him from Galilee (see 8:1-3) stood at a distance. They have watched it all. They have seen the jeering and taunting. They have seen the casting of lots and the soldiers mocking. They have seen Jesus die between two very different thieves. They have seen the lights of the world's stage fall dim as the sleep of death came. They have seen it all. People do react to Jesus in a variety of ways. They assume that Jesus' story has ended here. But a few days hence they will be amazed to discover that it has all just begun. God's testimony to Jesus in exaltation still remains.

The One who came to seek and save the lost has saved by dying. To take the opportunity of gaining life, there remains only for each one to respond to him.

The Burial of Jesus (23:50-56) Though Jesus has been assaulted by rejection, a few have remained faithful. Jesus' burial reveals a few who stood beside him. Joseph of Arimathea is a Sanhedrin member who did not agree with Jesus' conviction by the official council. His presence is interesting because it reveals a small responding remnant within the Jewish leadership. The text describes him as *a good and upright man,* one who *was waiting for the kingdom of God.* His character description recalls the great saints whose stories Luke told to open his account (1:6-7; 2:25-27, 36-38). Devout figures surround Jesus at his birth and death. Those who are righteous and seek God respond to Jesus and look forward to what he will bring.

Joseph asks permission to give Jesus a decent burial. Burial will need to come quickly, since the sabbath is approaching, and Jews did not believe in letting a corpse linger (see discussion of 7:11-17). The detail here makes it clear that Jesus had died. Wrapping the body in fine linen *(sindōn),* Joseph places it in *a tomb cut in the rock, one in which no one had yet been laid.* Joseph's kind act fulfills Deuteronomy 21:22-23: Jesus is not buried among thieves in dishonor.

The Day of Preparation is Friday, and that means the sabbath is drawing near. The women who had watched the scene at the crucifixion (v. 49) also watch as Jesus is buried. They see where he is laid to rest. But they resolve to return after the sabbath and anoint his body with spices to preserve it. Jews did not embalm corpses, so spices served to mitigate the stench. But these women are faithful Jews, so on the sabbath they rest according to the commandments.

Jesus has been laid to rest in honor. But things will not remain quiet for long.

23:50-56 The parallels to this event are Mark 15:42-47 and Matthew 27:57-61. Unique to Luke is the note that these women were from Galilee. He lacks any mention of guards at the tomb.

24:1-53 Though much of verses 13-53 is unique to Luke, verses 1-12 are similar to Matthew 28:1-20, Mark 16:1-8 (assuming an original shorter ending for Mark) and John 20:1-29. Each Gospel tells these final events in its own way. Some details differ, and attempts to harmonize them abound. Detailed studies of these and other literary issues have been

The Resurrection of Jesus (24:1-53) Jesus' vindication involves the exercise of God's power bringing him to life in a new, glorified state. After the discovery of the empty tomb (vv. 1-12), Luke narrates the conversation with the Emmaus-bound disciples, an account unique to him (vv. 13-35). Then follows the Gospel's closing scene, where Jesus visits the disciples (vv. 36-53). This final visit also is unique to Luke. Here Jesus appears to them (vv. 36-43) before giving them final instructions and departing (vv. 44-53).

A key feature of this section is the note of surprise among the disciples that Jesus is raised. Among the women, the disciples and the Emmaus travelers there is no hint that resurrection was anticipated. Such surprise is important, because it shows that even Jesus' own followers had to be convinced of his resurrection. They were not a gullible group that simply took resurrection as a given. Their surprise itself might seem strange, given Jesus' predictions of his resurrection as early as 9:22. But as late as 18:34, it is clear that the disciples never grasped the point of what Jesus was promising.

God's power underlies Jesus' resurrection. In addition, Scripture's claim (24:44-47), Jesus' promise (24:5-7), the angelic messengers' testimony (24:3-5, 23) and the testimony of disciples, both men and women, make up an impressive range of witnesses to this event (24:1-35). God's power stands behind the resurrection, because a passive verbal idea points to God's being responsible for it. This event is part of the reassurance Luke promised Theophilus in 1:1-4. The resurrection leads to the ascension and the events that grow from it.

As we come to the end of the Gospel, it is important to recall that Luke is only half finished with his story. The sequel comes in Acts. The resurrection-ascension is the link between the two volumes. That Luke regards the ascension as crucial is clear from Peter's speech in Acts 2. Now that Jesus is raised and seated at God's right hand, the mediating

produced by John W. Wenham (1984) and Grant R. Osborne (1984). By far the most difficult problem is the sequence of events tied to Mary Magdelene. I have argued elsewhere that resolution comes at a literary level in John, who first tells the story of how he came to see that Jesus was raised before going back and picking up Mary's temporally earlier story in detail (Bock 1995: see introduction to the pericope and 24:1-12). These attempts at resolution are not foolproof, but neither are the accounts irreconcilable.

Ruler at the Father's side can pour out the blessing of God's Spirit (Acts 2:30-36). As the first ten chapters of Acts will make clear, the gospel can go to all because Jesus is Lord of all. The apostle Paul becomes the supreme example of a mission to all of humanity.

The Resurrection Discovered (24:1-12) First thing in the morning, the women come to the tomb with their spices, fully expecting to find Jesus' remains. All the accounts agree that it was early morning. Matthew 28:1 and Mark 16:2 refer to the dawn or early morning, while John 20:1 notes that it was still dark when they started their journey.

The following point cannot be stressed too strongly: these women did not go believing in resurrection. They did not go to check and see if the tomb was empty. The fact that they took spices along to anoint the decaying body shows what they expected to find, and this despite six resurrection predictions in Luke. So the first people who had to be convinced of the resurrection were the disciples themselves. They may have belonged to the era of the ancients, but they did not think as a matter of course that resurrection would occur. In a real sense they were the first skeptics to become convinced that Jesus was raised!

The first hint that something had happened was the rolled-away stone. This stone, as was typical of ancient tombs, had covered the entrance. It was laid in a channel that had been carved out for it. While Mark 16:3 shows that the women had debated how they would get the heavy stone moved, Luke simply presents what confronts them on their arrival: *They found the stone rolled away from the tomb, but when they entered, they did not find the body of the Lord Jesus.*

The women are at a loss, stymied, filled with perplexity. Their quandary is broken by the appearance of *two men in clothes that gleamed,* a description that suggests Luke means angels. Heavenly appearances are often bright (9:29; 10:18; Acts 9:3; 22:6). Any doubt that Luke means they are angels is removed in verse 23. The presence of the pair may invoke the "two witnesses" theme of the Old Testament (Deut 19:15). Luke's noting of two angels corresponds with John 20:12, while Matthew 28:2-4 and Mark 16:5 mention only one figure. The angelic appearance

_____

24:3 I opt for a reading here that calls the body the Lord's. Too many manuscripts read this text to accept the shorter D text as an original "Western noninterpolation" of Luke. For

frightens the women, who bow to the ground in reverence. They know heaven is visiting the earth (Dillon 1978:26-27). The reason becomes clear in the angels' response.

It begins with a mild rebuke that is also an explanation: *"Why do you look for the living among the dead?"* Put simply, Jesus is alive, so do not expect to find him in a tomb. Then the angels ask them to recall the promise he made to them in Galilee. *"Remember how he told you, . . . 'The Son of Man must be delivered into the hands of sinful men, be crucified and on the third day be raised again' "* (9:22; 18:32-33). God is not surprised at Jesus' resurrection, and neither should they be surprised. Jesus' authority is summarized in the crucial Son of Man title. Here is a man who bears the authority of deity, through judgment given over to him by the Ancient of Days (Dan 7:13-14). Luke 22:69 is coming to pass. In fact, the key term *dei* ("it is necessary") is used here to express the idea of divine design. God, the great cosmic director, has orchestrated what took place here (compare Acts 2:22-24). From the arrest through the death to the resurrection, Jesus walked in God's will. The women need not have wasted their money on the spices to preserve Jesus' body; God has taken care of it and has been in control all along.

The angels' words bring Jesus' words back to mind. The women cannot keep to themselves what has just happened—they return to tell the eleven and those with them. The entourage had included a large group of women, but Luke only names Mary Magdalene (8:2), Joanna (8:3) and Mary the mother of James (Mk 16:1).

Though the women are convinced, the rest are not. They come to belief slowly. Many of the disciples are originally skeptics about resurrection. At first they regard the women as hysterical, telling an idle tale. *Lēros* (NIV *nonsense*), used here for "idle tale," was used in everyday Greek to refer to the delirious stories told by the very sick as they suffer in great pain or to tales told by those who fail to perceive reality (4 Maccabees 5:11; Josephus *Jewish Wars* 3.8.9 §405). The other disciples think these women must be dreaming. Luke notes most of them do not believe their story, except for perhaps one or two present.

its inclusion are p[75], Aleph, A, B, C and families 1 and 13, along with Byzantine witnesses.

Yet Luke 24:12, if a part of the original document, indicates that Peter cannot sit still upon hearing the report. He has learned to trust what Jesus predicts. So he gets up and runs to the tomb, sees the linen clothes by themselves and departs. He wonders, or marvels, about what has come to pass. There is a little debate among interpreters whether Peter believes at this point. In fact, most doubt it, arguing that the term "marveling" (*thaumazō;* NIV *wondering*) is ambiguous (see 4:22; 11:38; Acts 13:41). But surely it is hard to call Peter doubting here, and the term can be positive (as in Lk 1:21, 63; 2:18, 33; 7:9; 8:25; 11:14; 20:26; 24:41; Stein 1992:607). Something stirs him to check out the story when others are incredulous. In addition, his recent experience with his denials has surely taught him to trust what Jesus says.

Peter walks away from the tomb simply contemplating what may be ahead. Something is happening, and its reality is slow to sink in with Jesus' followers. Just how much they struggle to understand the reality of Jesus' exaltation is indicated in the Emmaus incident that follows.

Though the church proclaims the resurrection confidently today, the original witnesses had to be convinced that it had occurred. Resurrection had been promised by Scripture and by Jesus, but only slowly, grudgingly and methodically did the disciples come to see that it had come to pass.

The Emmaus Dialogue (24:13-35) This resurrection account is one of the most dramatic stories in the Bible. Part of what makes it such an enjoyable story is that the reader knows more about what is taking place than the two disciples who unknowingly encounter Jesus. The British would call such a story "cheeky," because it pokes fun boldly at the doubting of resurrection. The reversal of emotion within the account shows how powerful a truth resurrection is. If God has power over Jesus' life and death, he also has power over all life and death. God is the Creator of life and is sovereign over death. If he points an endorsing finger at Jesus, how can humanity doubt him?

This meeting occurs as two disciples journey to Emmaus. They are

---

24:12 There is debate whether this verse was originally in Luke. But the external evidence for its inclusion is exceedingly strong. Including it are p⁷⁵, Aleph, A, B, K, L and the Byzantine manuscripts. D and the itala lack the verse. It is one of the several "Western noninterpolations" in chapter 24. Those who support the rule of the shorter text's being original argue

sixty stadia, or *about seven miles,* from Jerusalem (the exact location of ancient Emmaus is not known today). The recent events have given them plenty to discuss, just as a major political event does among us today. In fact, the text portrays their discussion as rather intense, since *syzēteō* can refer to debating (Mk 8:11; Lk 22:23; Acts 6:9).

As they journey, a man joins them. Now Luke cleverly notes that it is Jesus, but he also mentions that the men cannot recognize him as Jesus. For once the joke is not on the reader but on the participants. Jesus is not being cruel here, but his gradual revelation of himself allows them to learn certain lessons about trusting God's promises. The disciples had been told about these events many times, but they cannot conceive how they could come to pass. The gradual revelation drives the point home vividly and calls on them to remember God's Word while trusting that what he says will come to pass. As we remember God's promise, we should rest in it (vv. 5-7). Luke's detailed account gives the reader an inside glimpse at how events were understood by disciples before they became aware that Jesus had risen from the dead. In all of these encounters, God shows himself to be in total control (note also v. 31).

So Jesus asks the two men about their conversation. Their countenance says it all: *they stood still, their faces downcast.* For these disciples, hope had been buried in the tomb provided by Joseph. In fact, one of them, Cleopas, is shocked that their new companion is unaware of recent events. His question's irony can hardly be overstated: "Are you the only visitor to Jerusalem who does not know the things that have happened there in these days?" (so correctly RSV). If anyone knows, it is the One they are speaking to! But to draw them out, he asks them about their discussion.

Reviewing the story of Jesus of Nazareth, they refer to him as a prophet, a popular conception of who Jesus was (4:16-30; 7:16; 9:7-9, 18; 13:31-35). In fact, this view of Jesus, when comparing him to a prophet like Moses, correctly reflects an aspect of his ministry (Acts 3:14-26; 10:38-39). This Jesus was *powerful in word and deed before God and all the*

---

for its exclusion, but I wonder whether the rule should apply at all to whole verses. The inclusion fits with verses 24 and 34, though the latter verse notes an appearance to Peter as well.

---

people. But the leadership, chief priests and rulers, *handed him over to be sentenced to death, and they crucified him* (23:13). The disciples' hope had been different: *"We had hoped that he was the one who was going to redeem Israel."* For them, Jesus' death had spelled a seeming end to that hope. The leaders had handed the promise over to Rome, and their persistence had extinguished its flame. Where these disciples place responsibility for Jesus' death is clear, and so is their disappointment.

But the story is not over. Three days have passed, and new events have caused a stir. Some of the female disciples journeyed to the tomb, only to find no body inside. They claimed to have seen *a vision of angels.* They claimed that he was alive. Still others went to the tomb and found it empty, but they did not see Jesus. This empirical note seems to be key for the two, since it seems they are not yet convinced that Jesus has been raised from the dead. Thomas gets all the contemporary press as a doubter of the resurrection, but Luke 24 makes it clear that he was merely one of a crowd, including these two followers. Like modern people in their skepticism, they will be persuaded only if they actually see Jesus. As readers we almost want to yell at the two, "Take a close look!"

Here is the major lesson of the Emmaus Road experience. Though resurrection is hard to believe, be assured that it took place. Its reality means that Jesus' claims are true. He was more than a teacher and more than a prophet. He was the promised, anointed one of God. A host of skeptics saw that this was so, and they believed. Do not be skeptical as these men were. Remember what God required of his Messiah: suffering, then vindication in exaltation.

Jesus starts to break their misconceptions with a rebuke: *"How foolish you are, and how slow of heart to believe all that the prophets have spoken! Did not the Christ have to suffer these things and then enter his glory?"* For the second time in the chapter, Luke notes how these events were necessary (*dei;* compare v. 7). Jesus reviews the rest of the story from the book that reveals it. Events and Scripture together raise the issue of faith in God's promises. The disciples have been slow to believe. They have not read Isaiah 52—53 or Psalm 16 with understanding, not to mention Deuteronomy 18:15, Psalm 2:7, Psalm 110:1, Psalm 118 or Daniel 7:13-14. No doubt when *beginning with Moses and all the Prophets, he explained to them what was said in all the Scriptures concerning himself,* Jesus used many of the texts that show up in other places in Luke and Acts. By taking them back to the Scripture, Jesus is noting that what took place was part of God's plan and promise. Luke highlights the point by speaking about *all* the Prophets and interpreting *all* the Scripture. Scripture's promise centers on Jesus. This text is a primary witness to Jesus. We can rest assured that Jesus is who he claims to be.

The lesson has not ended, but it is getting late. So as they draw near to Emmaus, Jesus pretends (NIV *acted as if;* Greek *prosepoiēsato*) he would journey on, but the men prevail upon him to stay with them. Since he has revealed the plan, now it is time to reveal the person.

It is in the intimacy of fellowship that Jesus is recognized. This setting is no mistake; it is a major Lukan theme. Many of the resurrection appearances he describes are associated with table fellowship (Lk 24:41-43; Acts 1:4; 10:41; also Jn 21:9-15). As Jesus sits at the table, takes the bread, blesses it, breaks it and gives it to them, *their eyes were opened.* In a situation that recalls the feeding of the five thousand and the Last Supper, the disciples realize that they have been talking with the Lord himself (Lk 9:22; 22:19). Though not a reenactment of the Last Supper, this meal does show that Jesus is present and is known when his disciples remain close to him. The lack of recognition of verse 16 is reversed. Their perplexity over recent events is removed. It is through sitting with Jesus and listening to him that we get to know him.

After his recognition by the disciples, Jesus disappears. That Jesus is alive is all the disciples need to understand. They can now appreciate that he is with them. All of a sudden the entire discussion on the road makes sense. Like a lost key found or a huge mystery solved, the direction of recent events becomes clear and the way to understand life anew is opened up. Because of this new awareness, the disciples recall their recent scriptural review in a new light: *"Were not our hearts burning within us while he talked with us on the road and opened the Scriptures to us?"* Their words point to how emotional the exposition had been for them, like a message being sown into the soul.

With a flame relit in their hearts, they return to the gathering of disciples in Jerusalem. The news is too good to keep to themselves. To know Jesus is to be thrilled at the prospect of sharing news of him with others.

Good news travels fast, and news of the verification of the resurrection was no exception. Jesus has, in effect, been everywhere. The two returning disciples are greeted with a report like their own: *"The Lord has risen and has appeared to Simon!"* This is a new detail in chapter 24, since earlier all Luke had reported was the empty tomb Peter saw (v. 12). So the message of the Emmaus disciples is preempted. Jesus is among all of them. It is becoming clear to all in the community that the women were right after all. Jesus is alive, and their hope remains as firmly in place as ever. The Emmaus report follows. Luke stresses that Jesus revealed himself to the two disciples during the breaking of the bread. In the quietness of the table Jesus is especially revealed.

We can imagine the flood of emotion in the room as these stories of Jesus' appearances flowed in. It must have been like a newsroom full of reporters collecting facts on a breaking story. The room was probably abuzz.

What is more, though it is late and much has already happened, Jesus' appearances are not over quite yet. Despite his "physical" absence, he has actually been with all of them all along through resurrection—a very crucial message for the disciples to learn about how Jesus will be with them in the future. To say Jesus is risen is to say that he is with us.

Jesus' Commission, Promise and Ascension (24:36-53) Though Luke is concluding his Gospel, the real story is just beginning. Ahead is the disciples' empowerment through the bestowal of the Spirit so they can carry out their call on behalf of God. Beyond that is the mission to proclaim to the world what they have experienced and understood. Jesus had ministered to them to prepare them for this time. Now it is nearly time to go. Training camp is just about over; a long season of ministry lies ahead.

This account is unique to Luke and allows him to link the Gospel with Acts, given that the ascension ends and begins each volume. This final Gospel unit has a few similarities to the Emmaus account. Both include a resurrection appearance, a meal and scriptural exposition. Jesus is present with his disciples and is present in the Word. The union of the two reflects what life is designed to be.

24:33 Given the nature and timing of this meeting, it is possible that this scene and John

Though I have separated these final verses from the Emmaus account, Luke has effectively woven the two stories together. As the room is buzzing with reports of Jesus' self-manifestations, he appears and says, *"Peace be with you."*

The disciples are still trying to take it all in, so peace is hardly their reaction. Rather, they are *startled and frightened.* They think for sure it is a spirit *(pneuma;* NIV *a ghost).* Even with the numerous reports of appearances, the idea that Jesus is alive and present is hard to accept. Empirical modernists are not the only skeptics: for the first disciples Jesus' resurrection was a difficult truth to swallow. Only a rapid-fire succession of demonstrations convinced the community it was so.

Jesus deals with their shock by challenging them. *"Why are you troubled, and why do doubts rise in your minds? Look at my hands and my feet. It is I myself! Touch me and see; a [spirit] does not have flesh and bones, as you see I have."* Jesus invites them to determine once and for all that what has been reported is true. Offering himself to be handled, Jesus wants to lay to rest for all time any doubt about his resurrection's truthfulness. *He showed them his hands and feet.* This is no phantom. There is no hallucination. The disciples have not fabricated the stories that they heard. Psychosis has not created an account to fill an emotional hole. This is no immaterial Jesus, as the Gnostics later claimed had come, a Jesus who walked but left no footprints. No, this is the crucified Jesus with the marks of nails in his hands to prove he had gone the limit to overcome sin. It is Jesus raised from the dead, pure and simple.

It is all too much. The disciples still fight unbelief, but it is mixed with joy as the truth is slowly but surely dawning like morning light. Amazement is the dominant emotion. To prove the point, Jesus asks for food: *"Do you have anything here to eat?"* He accepts the broiled fish, probably obtained in the city, and eats it. The meal's consumption destroys the disciples' now short-lived "spirit" hypothesis. Jesus is really in their midst. He has come to have a final word on this momentous day.

Jesus reminds them that everything that had occurred had been discussed by him. His life has been a fulfillment of Scripture. *"Everything*

20:19-24 are the same.

must be fulfilled that is written about me in the Law of Moses, the Prophets and the Psalms." Once again Luke highlights the divine design by using the term *dei,* "it is necessary." The Bible is an open book on Jesus' life and mission.

Then Jesus explains the Scriptures. Like a prophet-teacher, *he opened their minds so they could understand the Scriptures.* A careful look at the syntax shows that three themes dominate his exposition, since verses 46-47 are governed by three Greek infinitives *(pathein, anastēnai, kērychthēnai).* It is crucial to appreciate that fulfillment centers on the person of the Christ. It is in the promised Son of David that these events are fulfilled. Old Testament hope is being realized here (though at the time Jesus spoke the scriptural texts were not known as the Old Testament, but simply as the revered writings of the Jewish faith, the Scriptures). Jesus says he is the completion and fulfillment of scriptural promise and hope: What God promises, he brings to pass. In fact, you are experiencing the center of his plan right now. To know Jesus is to be in the will of God.

First, the Christ had to suffer. Jesus had predicted this all along (9:22, 44; 17:25; 18:31-33; 22:37). His death was anticipated by Scripture. Luke has quoted Psalm 118 in describing Jesus' rejection, along with portions of Isaiah 53 in relation to his suffering. In addition he alluded to Psalm 22, Psalm 31:5 and Psalm 69 in the passion account.

Second, Messiah was to be raised. In this concept are bound up Psalm 16:10, Psalm 110:1 and Psalm 118:22-26. The disciples are experiencing this truth even as Jesus speaks.

Third is what remains to be accomplished. Five elements dominate this mission statement.

1. The disciples will be called to preach. They began to fulfill this call in Acts 2, and ever since the church has been proclaiming Jesus through the preached word. Preaching the gospel is an honorable ministry with the most ancient of roots.

2. Their message is a call to repentance. Since Jesus draws attention to the Old Testament roots of this concept, he is not merely discussing

---

24:44 The threefold division of the ancient Hebrew Bible (the Law of Moses, the Prophets and the Psalms) is similar to a threefold division described in 4QMMT from Qumran and

the "change of mind" that the Greek term *metanoia* suggests but the "turning" that is bound up in the Hebrew concept of repentance. Those who need a relationship with God are called to turn to God in faith. Coming to God involves the awareness that the road one was traveling was the wrong one. To come to know him is to change one's direction in life.

3. What is offered is forgiveness of sins. There need no longer be an obstacle between humankind and God because of sin. As we turn to God through Jesus, the offer of forgiveness manifests God's willingness to be gracious and to cancel the debt of sin that Jesus paid (Rom 1—8, especially 3:21-31).

4. The authority for it all resides in Jesus' name. Here is a major theme in Acts. Events are tied to his personal presence and his regal authority. Baptism, healing and forgiveness are especially noted in Acts (Acts 2:38; 3:6; 4:7; 8:16; 9:15-16; 10:43, 48; 15:14). As the Risen Lord and Christ, Jesus himself carries out these things.

5. The message is for all nations, and the preaching will start in Jerusalem. It took the church until Acts 10 to get this point. They initially thought Jesus had meant preaching in all nations to Jews of the diaspora. But God's vision to Peter showed that the message was for all humanity. Jesus is Lord of all, so the message can go to all (Acts 10:34-43).

The Old Testament elements behind the preaching seem to be the promises of the various covenants. The Abrahamic covenant included the promise that through Abraham's seed all the nations would be blessed (Gen 12:3; Gal 3). The Davidic covenant had promised a ruler who would be a son to God and a source of blessing to Israel and the nations (2 Sam 7:5-16; Ps 2; 45; 89; 110; 118; 132; Is 2:2-4; especially Is 9—11; Ezek 34 on the Davidic son as shepherd). The new covenant promised a new heart, which Joel 2 tells us comes by the pouring out of God's Spirit. Luke calls this the *what my Father has promised* in verse 49, and John the Baptist had said the bestowal of the Spirit was the evidence of Messiah's arrival in Luke 3:15-17. The arrival is proclaimed in Acts 2, and Gentiles are seen as included in Acts 11:15-18.

the prologue to Sirach. For more details on this and the history of the Old Testament canon, see Ellis 1992:3-50.

With the mission set forth, Jesus calls all present his *witnesses* (compare Acts 1:8, 22; 3:15; 5:32; 10:39, 41; 13:31; 22:15; 26:16). They have seen with their eyes and held in their hands the truth that Jesus is alive. So he calls them to this preaching task. They have experienced truth into which angels, kings and prophets had longed to look (Lk 10:23-24; 1 Pet 1:10-12).

The task's scope and difficulty mean that they are not simply to launch out, but they must wait until God has given them authority from above, what Jesus calls being *clothed with power from on high.* First Chronicles 12:18 shows the Old Testament roots of this image. The Lukan reference to God's promise describes the coming of the Spirit's enabling power. In this brief statement is the Synoptic equivalent of the great Paraclete address of Jesus in John 14—16. The church's task will be difficult; special ability will be needed to accomplish it. It is not to be carried out in mere human strength. Just as Jesus' presence at the table has shown, God's intimate, indwelling presence is necessary to make it work.

It is also significant that it is Jesus who sends this promise *(I am going to send).* He is now the mediator of blessing from God. Acts 2:33 makes a similar point. To experience the Father's goodness, one must pass through the Son.

Luke describes Jesus' departure very briefly. The conciseness of this account is probably because Luke also spends time narrating a departure in Acts 1. It is much discussed whether this event is the same as the one in Acts 1 or is a distinct event. If it equals Acts 1, then Luke has simply summarized quickly here what took place forty days later to establish a literary tie to Acts. The possibility of literary compression makes a choice very difficult to establish (for one event, see Parsons 1987:193-94; for the options, Osborne 1984:137-38 and especially 266-70; Osborne opts for two perspectives on the one event: Lk 24 as theological and Acts 1 as historical).

The Gospel's final scene closes with a note of blessing and worship. Such an ending is perfectly appropriate, for Jesus came to offer hope. From the opening words of the infancy material to the end of the Gospel, Luke has sounded the trumpet that Jesus brings God's promise and blessing in fulfillment of God's design. What he did was necessary. What he did brought a new era, as God moved from a time of promise to the beginning of realized promise. Jesus is to bring more, as Acts 3 makes especially clear, but the corner has been turned in God's plan. Blessing is available in a way only dreamed of before Jesus.

Many people wish that they had lived in the Old Testament times of great miracles. To see Moses or Elijah at work would have been inspiring. But Luke's perspective is that these Old Testament saints would have seen our era as the blessed one. What they had worked toward met its realization in Jesus. So the Gospel's closing note of blessing is very appropriate. To experience Jesus' presence is to be blessed. The disciples head to Jerusalem with hearts filled with joy, gratitude and worship—attitudes that we too should experience as we learn to appreciate God's grace.

The disciples' response is to await the blessing. They journey to Jerusalem, obeying the Lord's command to wait for the Spirit there. But more than their obedience is the attitude that accompanies it. They are filled with *great joy. And they stayed continually at the temple, praising God.* There was not just obedience, there was joy, praise and thanksgiving, along with a commitment to be constantly present with the Lord. The resurrection has strengthened these disciples' relationship with God. Their sense of privilege at being involved in God's plan did not waver even years later, when persecution and rejection of their message became strong. They loved their enemy and took the message of the living and ascended Christ to the world. They challenged the world to receive blessing from Jesus and, without shrillness, warned of the judgment to come (Acts 2:36-41; 10:42-43; 13:23-41; 1 Pet 3:15-16). But their mission was not a task or a business to them. It was a joy, an act of worship to experience Jesus' presence and do his will.

The Gospel of Luke has an open-ended conclusion. In a real sense it ends at a beginning. No longer is the story about what Jesus did during his earthly ministry. Now it is the saga of what he continued to do through God's people, whom he equipped to perform a task and carry a message. That message is not one of words alone but of life, love and light. The message is both proclaimed and lived out before a world covered with darkness.

As the Gospel closes, it is important not to forget the words that came early in this Gospel when both John the Baptist and Jesus were introduced:

And you, my child, will be called a prophet of the Most High;
> for you will go on before the Lord to prepare the way for him,
to give his people the knowledge of salvation
> through the forgiveness of their sins,
because of the tender mercy of our God,
> by which the rising sun will come to us from heaven
to shine on those living in darkness and in the shadow of death,
to guide our feet into the path of peace.

Jesus departed into the heaven from which he came. He did so not to leave us but to guide us, not to disappoint us but to intercede for us. He departed with a blessing. He departed to equip us. For those who know him, his blessing is always with us. So we worship him with joy and serve him with gladness, continually blessing God for the gift of his Son.

Great is God's faithfulness. That is the understanding, desire and assurance Luke longed to leave in the heart of his reader Theophilus. That is the precious legacy Luke left to the church.

Bibliography

Alexander, Loveday
 1992   "Sisters in Adversity: Retelling the Martha Story." In *Women in the Biblical Tradition*. Edited by George Brooke. Lewiston, N.Y.: Edwin Mellen Press.

Bahnsen, Gary L.,
 Walter C.
 Kaiser Jr.,
 Douglas J. Moo,
 Wayne G.
 Strickland and
 Willem A.
 VanGemeren
 1993   *The Law, the Gospel and the Modern Christian: Five Views*. Grand Rapids, Mich.: Zondervan.

Bammel, Ernst
 1968   "πτωχός." In *Theological Dictionary of the New Testament*, 6:888-915. Edited by Gerhard Kittel and Gerhard Friedrich. 10 vols. Grand Rapids, Mich.: Eerdmans.

 1970   *The Trial of Jesus*. Studies in Biblical Theology 13. London: SCM Press.

Banks, Robert
 1975   *Jesus and the Law in the Synoptic Tradition*. Society of New Testament Monograph Series 28. Cambridge: Cambridge University Press.

Barclay, William
 1975   *The Gospel of Luke*. Daily Bible Study Series. Philadelphia: Westminster Press.

Barr, James
1988   "Abbā Isn't Daddy." *Journal of Theological Studies* n.s.
                       39:28-47.

Bauer, Walter
1979   *A Greek-English Lexicon of the New Testament and Other
                       Early Christian Literature.* Translated by William Arndt, F.
                       Wilbur Gingrich and Frederick Danker. 2nd ed. Chicago:
                       University of Chicago Press.

Bauernfeind, Otto
1967   "πανουργία, πανοῦργος." In *Theological Dictionary of
                       the New Testament,* 5:722-27. Edited by Gerhard Kittel
                       and Gerhard Friedrich. 10 vols. Grand Rapids, Mich.:
                       Eerdmans.

Bayer, Hans
1986   *Jesus' Predictions of Vindication and Suffering.* Wissen-
                       schaftliche Untersuchungen zum Neuen Testament, Band 2,
                       20. Tübingen: J. C. B. Mohr/Paul Siebeck.

Beasley-Murray,
George R.
1954   *Jesus and the Future: An Examination of the Criticism of
                       the Eschatological Discourse, Mark 13, with Special
                       Reference to the Little Apocalypse Theory.* London:
                       Macmillan.

1986   *Jesus and the Kingdom of God.* Grand Rapids, Mich.:
                       Eerdmans.

Behm, Johannes
1964   "ἄρτος." In *Theological Dictionary of the New Testament,*
                       1:477-78. Edited by Gerhard Kittel. 10 vols. Grand Rapids,
                       Mich.: Eerdmans.

1967a   "νῆστις κτλ." In *Theological Dictionary of the New
                       Testament,* 4:924-35. Edited by Gerhard Kittel. 10 vols.
                       Grand Rapids, Mich.: Eerdmans.

1967b   "νοέω κτλ." In *Theological Dictionary of the New
                       Testament,* 4:948-80. Edited by Gerhard Kittel. 10 vols.
                       Grand Rapids, Mich.: Eerdmans.

Bertram, Georg
1972   "ὕβρις κτλ." In *Theological Dictionary of the New
                       Testament,* 8:295-307. Edited by Gerhard Kittel and Gerhard
                       Friedrich. 10 vols. Grand Rapids, Mich.: Eerdmans.

1974   "φρήν κτλ." In *Theological Dictionary of the New Testament,* 9:220-35. Edited by Gerhard Kittel and Gerhard Friedrich. 10 vols. Grand Rapids, Mich.: Eerdmans.

Betz, Otto
1964   "The Dichotomized Servant and the End of Judas Iscariot." *Revue de Qumrân* 5:43-58.

1974   "φωνή κτλ." In *Theological Dictionary of the New Testament,* 9:278-309. Edited by Gerhard Kittel and Gerhard Friedrich. 10 vols. Grand Rapids, Mich.: Eerdmans.

Blaising, Craig A.,
and Darrell L.
Bock
1992   *Dispensationalism, Israel and the Church: The Search for Definition.* Grand Rapids, Mich.: Zondervan.

1993   *Progressive Dispensationalism.* Wheaton, Ill.: Victor Books.

Blass, F., and
A. Debrunner
1961   *A Greek Grammar of the New Testament.* Translated by R. W. Funk. Chicago: University of Chicago Press.

Blinzler, Josef
1969   *Der Process Jesu.* 4th ed. Regensburg, Germany: Pustet.

Blomberg, Craig L.
1984   "The Law in Luke-Acts." *Journal for the Study of the New Testament* 22:53-80.

1990   *Interpreting the Parables.* Downers Grove, Ill.: InterVarsity Press.

Bock, Darrell L.
1987   *Proclamation from Prophecy and Pattern: Lucan Old Testament Christology.* Journal for the Study of the New Testament Supplement Series 12. Sheffield, U.K.: Sheffield Academic Press.

1991   "The Son of Man in Luke 5:24." *Bulletin for Biblical Research* 1:109-21.

1992   "Luke, Gospel of." In *Dictionary of Jesus and the Gospels.* Edited by Joel B. Green, Scot McKnight and I. Howard Marshall. Downers Grove, Ill.: InterVarsity Press.

1993 "The Son of David and the Saints' Task: The Hermeneutics of Initial Fulfillment." *Bibliotheca Sacra* 150:440-57.

1994a "Current Messianic Activity and Old Testament Davidic Promise: Dispensationalism, Hermeneutics and New Testament Fulfillment." *Trinity Journal* n.s., 15:55-87.

1994b *The Gospel of Luke: 1:1—9:50.* Baker Exegetical Commentary of the New Testament. Grand Rapids, Mich.: Baker Book House.

1994c "The Son of Man Seated at God's Right Hand and the Debate over Jesus' 'Blasphemy.' " In *Jesus of Nazareth, Lord and Christ: Essays on the Historical Jesus and New Testament Christology,* pp. 181-91. Edited by Joel Green and M. Max Turner. Grand Rapids, Mich.: Eerdmans.

1994d "A Theology of Luke-Acts." In *A Theology of the New Testament.* Edited by Roy B. Zuck and Darrell L. Bock. Chicago: Moody Press.

1995 *The Gospel of Luke: 9:51—24:53.* Baker Exegetical Commentary of the New Testament. Grand Rapids, Mich.: Baker Book House.

Booth, Roger P.

1987 *Jesus and the Laws of Purity: Tradition History and Legal History in Mark 7.* Journal for the Study of the New Testament Supplement Series 13. Sheffield, U.K.: Sheffield Academic Press.

Bornkamm, Günther

1967 "μυστήριον, μυέω." In *Theological Dictionary of the New Testament,* 4:802-28. Edited by Gerhard Kittel. 10 vols. Grand Rapids, Mich.: Eerdmans.

1968 "πρέσβυς κτλ." In *Theological Dictionary of the New Testament,* 6:651-83. Edited by Gerhard Kittel and Gerhard Friedrich. 10 vols. Grand Rapids, Mich.: Eerdmans.

Bovon, François

1989 *Das Evangelium nach Lukas.* Evangelisch-katholischer Kommentar zum Neuen Testament 3/1. Köln and Neukirchen-Vluyn: Benzinger Verlag and Neukirchener Verlag.

Brown, Raymond E.
1977   *The Birth of the Messiah: A Commentary on the Infancy Narratives in Matthew and Luke.* London: Geoffrey Chapman.

Bruce, F. F.
1974   *Jesus and Christian Origins Outside the New Testament.* Grand Rapids, Mich.: Eerdmans.
1975-1976   "Is the Paul of Acts the Real Paul?" *Bulletin of the John Rylands University Library of Manchester* 58:282-305.

Bultmann, Rudolf
1964a   "ἔλεος κτλ." In *Theological Dictionary of the New Testament,* 2:477-87. Edited by Gerhard Kittel. 10 vols. Grand Rapids, Mich.: Eerdmans.

1964b   "ζάω κτλ." In *Theological Dictionary of the New Testament,* 2:855-75. Edited by Gerhard Kittel. 10 vols. Grand Rapids, Mich.: Eerdmans.

Campbell, Donald K., and Jeffrey Townsend, eds.
1992   *The Case for Premillennialism: A New Consensus.* Chicago: Moody Press.

Caragounis, Chrys C.
1974   "*ΟΨΩΝΙΟΝ*: A Reconsideration of Its Meaning." *Novum Testamentum* 16:35-57.

Carson, Donald A.
1984   *Matthew.* Expositor's Bible Commentary 8. Grand Rapids, Mich.: Zondervan.

Catchpole, David R.
1970   "The Answer of Jesus to Caiaphas [Matt xxvi.64]." *New Testament Studies* 17:213-26.

1971   *The Trial of Jesus: A Study in the Gospels and in Jewish Historiography from 1770 to the Present.* Studia Postbiblica. Leiden: E. J. Brill.

1977   "The Son of Man's Search for Faith (Luke XVIII 8b)." *Novum Testamentum* 19:81-104.

Charlesworth, James, ed.
1992   *The Messiah: Developments in Earliest Judaism and Christianity.* Philadelphia: Fortress.

Cohen, Shaye J. D.
1989   "Crossing the Boundary and Becoming a Jew." *Harvard Theological Review* 82:13-33.

Colpe, Carsten
1972   "ὁ υἱὸς τοῦ ἀνθρώπου." In *Theological Dictionary of the New Testament*, 8:400-477. Edited by Gerhard Kittel and Gerhard Friedrich. 10 vols. Grand Rapids, Mich.: Eerdmans.

Conzelmann, Hans
1961   *The Theology of Saint Luke.* Translated by G. Buswell. Philadelphia: Fortress.

Cortés, J. M., and
F. M. Gatti
1987   "On the Meaning of Luke 16:16." *Journal of Biblical Literature* 106:247-59.

Craddock, Fred B.
1990   *Luke.* Interpretation. Atlanta: John Knox Press.

Cullmann, Oscar
1959   *The Christology of the New Testament.* Translated by Shirley Guthrie and Charles A. M. Hall. Philadelphia: Westminster Press.

Dahl, Nils A.
1966   "The Story of Abraham in Luke-Acts." In *Studies in Luke-Acts.* Edited by L. Keck and J. Martyn. London: SPCK.

Danker,
 Frederick W.
1988   *Jesus and the New Age.* 2nd ed. Philadelphia: Fortress.

Darr, John
1992   *On Character Building: The Reader and the Rhetoric of Characterization in Luke-Acts.* Literary Currents in Biblical Intepretation. Louisville, Ky.: Westminster/John Knox Press.

de Jonge, Marinus
1965-1966   "The Use of the Word 'Anointed' in the Time of Jesus." *Novum Testamentum* 8:132-48.

Derrett, J. D. M.
1970   *Law in the New Testament.* London: Dartman, Longman and Todd.

1971   "Law in the New Testament: The Palm Sunday Colt." *Novum Testamentum* 13:241-58.

Dillon, Richard J.
1978   *From Eye-Witnesses to Minsters of the Word.* Analecta Biblica 82. Rome: Pontifical Institute Press.

Donahue, J. R.
 1971   "Tax Collectors and Sinners." *Catholic Biblical Quarterly*
                33:39-61.

Duling, Dennis C.
 1975   "Solomon, Exorcism and the Son of David." *Harvard
                Theological Review* 68:235-52.

Dunn, James D. G.
 1970a   *Baptism in the Holy Spirit.* London: SCM Press.

 1970b   "The Messianic Secret in Mark." *Tyndale Bulletin* 21:92-117.

 1975   *Jesus and the Spirit: A Study of the Religious and Charismat-
                ic Experience of Jesus and the First Christians as Reflected
                in the New Testament.* London: SCM Press.

Ehrman, Bart D.
 1991   "The Cup, the Bread and the Salvific Effect of Jesus' Death
                in Luke-Acts." In *1991 SBL Seminar Papers,* pp. 576-91.
                Edited by E. Lovering. Atlanta: Scholars Press.

Ellis, E. Earle
 1972   *Eschatology in Luke.* Philadelphia: Fortress.

 1974   *The Gospel of Luke.* Rev. ed. New Century Bible
                Commentary. Grand Rapids, Mich.: Eerdmans.

 1992   *The Old Testament in Early Christianity: Canon and
                Intepretation in Light of Modern Research.* Grand Rapids,
                Mich.: Baker Book House.

Eppstein, V.
 1964   "The Historicity of the Gospel Account of the Cleansing of
                the Temple." *Zeitschrift für die neutestamentliche
                Wissenschaft* 55:42-56.

Evans, C. F.
 1990   *Saint Luke.* London: SCM Press.

Evans, Craig A.
 1989   "Jesus' Action in the Temple: Cleansing or Portent of De-
                struction?" *Catholic Biblical Quarterly* 51:237-70.

 1990   *Luke.* New International Biblical Commentary. Peabody,
                Mass.: Hendrickson.

Fitzmyer, Joseph A.
 1973-1974   "The Contribution of Qumran Aramaic to the Study of the
                New Testament." *New Testament Studies* 20:382-407.

1978   "Crucifixion in Ancient Palestine, Qumran Literature and the
                   New Testament." *Catholic Biblical Quarterly* 40:492-513.

1981   *The Gospel According to Luke.* Anchor Bible. Garden City,
                   N.Y.: Doubleday.

1985   *The Gospel According to Luke.* Anchor Bible 28A. Garden
                   City, N.Y.: Doubleday.

Foerster, Werner
1964a   "βδελύσσομαι κτλ." In *Theological Dictionary of the New
                   Testament,* 1:598-600. Edited by Gerhard Kittel. 10 vols.
                   Grand Rapids, Mich.: Eerdmans.

1964b   "εἰρήνη κτλ." In *Theological Dictionary of the New
                   Testament,* 2:406-20. Edited by Gerhard Kittel. 10 vols.
                   Grand Rapids, Mich.: Eerdmans.

1964c   "ἐπιούσιος." In *Theological Dictionary of the New
                   Testament,* 2:590-99. Edited by Gerhard Kittel. 10 vols.
                   Grand Rapids, Mich.: Eerdmans.

1964d   "ἐχθρός, ἔχθρα." In *Theological Dictionary of the New
                   Testament,* 2:811-15. Edited by Gerhard Kittel. 10 vols.
                   Grand Rapids, Mich.: Eerdmans.

1967   "ὄφις." In *Theological Dictionary of the New Testament,*
                   5:576-82. Edited by Gerhard Kittel and Gerhard Friedrich. 10
                   vols. Grand Rapids, Mich.: Eerdmans.

Frerichs, E., William
   Green and Jacob
   Neusner, eds.
1987   *Judaisms and Their Messiahs at the Turn of the Christian
                   Era.* Cambridge: Cambridge University Press.

Geldenhuys, Norval
1951   *Commentary on the Gospel of Luke.* New International
                   Commentary. Grand Rapids, Mich.: Eerdmans.

Gooding, David
1987   *According to Luke: A New Exposition of the Third Gospel.*
                   Grand Rapids, Mich.: Eerdmans.

Goppelt, Leonhard
1968a   "πεινάω." In *Theological Dictionary of the New Testament,*
                   6:12-22. Edited by Gerhard Kittel and Gerhard Friedrich. 10
                   vols. Grand Rapids, Mich.: Eerdmans.

1968b   "πίνω κτλ." In *Theological Dictionary of the New Testament*, 6:135-60. Edited by Gerhard Kittel and Gerhard Friedrich. 10 vols. Grand Rapids, Mich.: Eerdmans.

1972   "ὕδωρ." In *Theological Dictionary of the New Testament*, 8:314-33. Edited by Gerhard Kittel and Gerhard Friedrich. 10 vols. Grand Rapids, Mich.: Eerdmans.

Green, Joel B.
1991   "The Death of Jesus and the Rending of the Temple Veil (Luke 23:44-49): A Window into Luke's Understanding of Jesus and the Temple." In *SBL 1991 Seminar Papers*, pp. 543-57. Edited by Ernest Lovering. Atlanta: Scholars Press.

Greeven, Heinrich
1968   "περιστερά, τρυγών." In *Theological Dictionary of the New Testament*, 6:63-72. Edited by Gerhard Kittel and Gerhard Friedrich. 10 vols. Grand Rapids, Mich.: Eerdmans.

Grundmann, Walter
1964   "δύναμαι κτλ." In *Theological Dictionary of the New Testament*, 2:284-317. Edited by Gerhard Kittel. 10 vols. Grand Rapids, Mich.: Eerdmans.

1965   "ἰσχύω κτλ." In *Theological Dictionary of the New Testament*, 3:397-402. Edited by Gerhard Kittel. 10 vols. Grand Rapids, Mich.: Eerdmans.

Guelich, Robert
1982   *The Sermon on the Mount*. Waco, Tex.: Word.

Hauck, F.
1967   "μαμωνᾶς." In *Theological Dictionary of the New Testament*, 4:388-90. Edited by Gerhard Kittel. 10 vols. Grand Rapids, Mich.: Eerdmans.

Hendriksen, William
1978   *Exposition of the Gospel According to Luke*. New Testament Commentaries. Grand Rapids, Mich.: Baker Book House.

Hengel, Martin
1968   "Das Gleichnis von den Weingärtnern Mc 12,1-12 im Lichte der Zenonpapyri und der rabbinischen Gleichnisse." *Zeitschrift für die neutestamentliche Wissenschaft* 59:1-39.

1974   "φάτην." In *Theological Dictionary of the New Testament*, 9:49-55. Edited by Gerhard Kittel and Gerhard Friedrich. 10 vols. Grand Rapids, Mich.: Eerdmans.

1977   *Crucifixion in the Ancient World and the Folly of the Message of the Cross.* London: SCM Press.

1981   *The Charismatic Leader and His Followers.* Translated by J. Creig. New York: Crossroad.

1989   *The Zealots: Investigations into the Jewish Freedom Movement in the Period from Herod I Until 70 A.D.* Translated by D. Smith. (Original German edition 1961.) Edinburgh: T & T Clark.

Heth, William A., and Gordon Wenham

1984   *Jesus and Divorce: The Problem with the Evangelical Consensus.* London: Hodder & Stoughton.

Hoehner, Harold W.

1972   *Herod Antipas: A Contemporary of Jesus Christ.* Society for New Testament Studies Monograph Series 17. Cambridge: Cambridge University Press.

1977   *The Chronological Aspects of the Life of Jesus.* Grand Rapids, Mich.: Zondervan.

House, H. Wayne, ed.

1990   *Divorce and Remarriage: Four Views.* Downers Grove, Ill.: InterVarsity Press.

Hunzinger, Claus-Hunno

1971   "συκῆ κτλ." In *Theological Dictionary of the New Testament,* 7:751-59. Edited by Gerhard Kittel and Gerhard Friedrich. 10 vols. Grand Rapids, Mich.: Eerdmans.

Ireland, Dennis J.

1992   *Stewardship and the Kingdom of God: An Historical, Exegetical and Contextual Study of the Parable of the Unjust Steward in Luke 16:1-13.* Supplements to *Novum Testamentum* 70. Leiden: E. J. Brill.

Jeremias, Joachim

1964a   "ἄβυσσος." In *Theological Dictionary of the New Testament,* 1:9-10. Edited by Gerhard Kittel. 10 vols. Grand Rapids, Mich.: Eerdmans.

1964b   "ἄνθρωπος, ἀνθρώπινος." In *Theological Dictionary of the New Testament,* 1:364-67. Edited by Gerhard Kittel. 10 vols. Grand Rapids, Mich.: Eerdmans.

1964c   "γραμματεύς." In *Theological Dictionary of the New Testament,* 1:740-42. Edited by Gerhard Kittel. 10 vols. Grand Rapids, Mich.: Eerdmans.

1966   *The Eucharistic Words of Jesus.* Translated by Norman Perrin. London: SCM Press.

1967   "πάσχα." In *Theological Dictionary of the New Testament,* 5:896-904. Edited by Gerhard Kittel and Gerhard Friedrich. 10 vols. Grand Rapids, Mich.: Eerdmans.

1971   *The Proclamation of Jesus Christ.* Vol. 1 of *New Testament Theology.* Translated by John Bowden. London: SCM Press.

1972   *The Parables of Jesus.* Translated by S. Hooke. London: SCM Press.

Johnson, Luke T.
1991   *Luke.* Sacra Pagina. Wilmington, Del.: Michael Glazier.

Johnson, M. D.
1969   *The Purpose of the Biblical Genealogies.* Society of New Testament Studies Monograph Series 8. Cambridge: Cambridge University Press.

Keener, Craig S.
1991   *. . . And Marries Another: Divorce and Remarriage in the Teaching of the New Testament.* Peabody, Mass.: Hendrickson.

1993   *The IVP Bible Background Commentary: New Testament.* Downers Grove, Ill.: InterVarsity Press.

Kinman, Brent
1991   "Pilate's Assize and the Timing of Jesus' Trial." *Tyndale Bulletin* 42:282-95.

Kümmel, Werner G.
1957   *Promise and Fulfillment: The Eschatological Message of Jesus.* Studies in Biblical Theology 1/23. Translated by D. Barton. London: SCM Press.

Liefeld, Walter L.
1984   *Luke.* Expositor's Bible Commentary 9. Grand Rapids, Mich.: Zondervan.

Linnemann, Eta
1966   *Parables of Jesus: Introduction and Exposition.* London: SPCK.

Lohse, Eduard
   1968   "πρόσωπον κτλ." In *Theological Dictionary of the New Testament*, 6:778-80. Edited by Gerhard Kittel and Gerhard Friedrich. 10 vols. Grand Rapids, Mich.: Eerdmans.

   1971   "σάββατον κτλ." In *Theological Dictionary of the New Testament*, 7:1-35. Edited by Gerhard Kittel and Gerhard Friedrich. 10 vols. Grand Rapids, Mich.: Eerdmans.

Longenecker,
Richard N.
   1970   *The Christology of Early Jewish Christianity.* Twin Books Series. Grand Rapids, Mich.: Baker Book House.

Machen, J. Gresham
   1930   *The Virgin Birth.* Grand Rapids, Mich.: Baker Book House.

McKnight, Scot
   1991   *A Light Among the Gentiles: Jewish Missionary Activity in the Second Temple Period.* Philadelphia: Fortress.

Manson, T. W.
   1957   *The Sayings of Jesus.* London: SCM Press.

Marshall, I. Howard
   1969   "The Son of God or Servant of Yahweh? A Reconsideration of Mark 1:11." *New Testament Studies* 15:336-46.

   1970   *Luke: Historian and Theologian.* Grand Rapids, Mich.: Zondervan.

   1978   *Commentary on Luke.* New International Greek New Testament. Grand Rapids, Mich.: Eerdmans.

   1980   *Last Supper and Lord's Supper.* Grand Rapids, Mich.: Eerdmans.

Mattill, A. J., Jr.
   1979   *Luke and the Last Things: A Perspective for the Understanding of Lucan Thought.* Dillsboro, N.C.: Western North Carolina Press.

Maurer, Christian
   1968   "πράσσω κτλ." In *Theological Dictionary of the New Testament*, 6:632-44. Edited by Gerhard Kittel and Gerhard Friedrich. 10 vols. Grand Rapids, Mich.: Eerdmans.

Metzger, Bruce
   1958-1959   "Seventy or Seventy-two Disciples?" *New Testament Studies* 5:299-306.

Meyer, Rudolf
1971   "Σαδδουκαῖος." In *Theological Dictionary of the New Testament*, 7:35-54. Edited by Gerhard Kittel and Gerhard Friedrich. 10 vols. Grand Rapids, Mich.: Eerdmans.

1974   "Φαρισαῖος." In *Theological Dictionary of the New Testament*, 9:11-35. Edited by Gerhard Kittel and Gerhard Friedrich. 10 vols. Grand Rapids, Mich.: Eerdmans.

Michaelis, Wilhelm
1967a   "λέπρα λεπρός." In *Theological Dictionary of the New Testament*, 4:233-34. Edited by Gerhard Kittel. 10 vols. Grand Rapids, Mich.: Eerdmans.

1967b   "λύχνος, λυχνία." In *Theological Dictionary of the New Testament*, 4:324-27. Edited by Gerhard Kittel. 10 vols. Grand Rapids, Mich.: Eerdmans.

1967c   "ὁδός κτλ." In *Theological Dictionary of the New Testament*, 5:42-114. Edited by Gerhard Kittel and Gerhard Friedrich. 10 vols. Grand Rapids, Mich.: Eerdmans.

1971   "σκηνή κτλ." In *Theological Dictionary of the New Testament*, 7:368-94. Edited by Gerhard Kittel and Gerhard Friedrich. 10 vols. Grand Rapids, Mich.: Eerdmans.

Michel, Otto
1965a   "κόκκος, κόκκινος." In *Theological Dictionary of the New Testament*, 3:810-14. Edited by Gerhard Kittel. 10 vols. Grand Rapids, Mich.: Eerdmans.

1965b   "κύων, κυνάριον." In *Theological Dictionary of the New Testament*, 3:1101-4. Edited by Gerhard Kittel. 10 vols. Grand Rapids, Mich.: Eerdmans.

1967   "οἶκος κτλ." In *Theological Dictionary of the New Testament*, 5:119-59. Edited by Gerhard Kittel and Gerhard Friedrich. 10 vols. Grand Rapids, Mich.: Eerdmans.

1972   "τελώνης." In *Theological Dictionary of the New Testament*, 8:88-105. Edited by Gerhard Kittel and Gerhard Friedrich. 10 vols. Grand Rapids, Mich.: Eerdmans.

Moessner, David P.
1989   *The Lord of the Banquet*. Philadelphia: Fortress.

Moulton, James H.,
and George
Milligan
1930   *The Vocabulary of the Greek Testament.* London: Hodder.

Neyrey, Jerome H.
1985   *The Passion According to Luke.* New York: Paulist.

Nolland, John
1990   *Luke 1—9:20.* Word Biblical Commentary 35A. Dallas:
                      Word.

1993   *Luke 9:21—18:43.* Word Biblical Commentary 35B. Dallas:
                      Word.
Oepke, Albrecht
1964a   "βάπτω κτλ." In *Theological Dictionary of the New
                      Testament,* 1:529-46. Edited by Gerhard Kittel. 10 vols.
                      Grand Rapids, Mich.: Eerdmans.

1964b   "γυνή." In *Theological Dictionary of the New Testament,*
                      1:776-89. Edited by Gerhard Kittel. 10 vols. Grand Rapids,
                      Mich.: Eerdmans.

1965   "ἰάομαι κτλ." In *Theological Dictionary of the New
                      Testament,* 3:194-215. Edited by Gerhard Kittel. 10 vols.
                      Grand Rapids, Mich.: Eerdmans.

1967   "νεφέλη, νέφος." In *Theological Dictionary of the New
                      Testament,* 4:902-10. Edited by Gerhard Kittel. 10 vols.
                      Grand Rapids, Mich.: Eerdmans.
Osborne, Grant R.
1984   *The Resurrection Narratives: A Redactional Study.* Grand
                      Rapids, Mich.: Baker Book House.
Parsons, Mikeal C.
1987   *The Departure of Jesus in Luke-Acts: The Ascension
                      Narratives in Context.* Journal for the Study of the New
                      Testament Supplement Series 21. Sheffield, U.K.: Sheffield
                      Academic Press.
Plummer, Alfred
1922   *The Gospel According to St. Luke.* 5th ed. International
                      Critical Commentary. Edinburgh: T & T Clark.

Porter, Stanley E.
1992   "In the Vicinity of Jericho: Luke 18:35." *Bulletin for Biblical Research* 2:91-104.

Preisigke, F.
1922   *Sammelbuch griechischer Urkunden aus Ägypten.* Vol. 2. Strassburg: K. J. Trübner.

Preisker, Herbert
1964   "ἔθος." In *Theological Dictionary of the New Testament,* 2:372-73. Edited by Gerhard Kittel. 10 vols. Grand Rapids, Mich.: Eerdmans.

1967a   "μισθός κτλ." In *Theological Dictionary of the New Testament,* 4:695-706. Edited by Gerhard Kittel. 10 vols. Grand Rapids, Mich.: Eerdmans.

1967b   "μυκτηρίζω, ἐκμυκτηρίζω." In *Theological Dictionary of the New Testament,* 4:796. Edited by Gerhard Kittel. 10 vols. Grand Rapids, Mich.: Eerdmans.

Reicke, Bo
1986   *The Roots of the Synoptic Gospels.* Philadelphia: Fortress.

Rengstorf, Karl   "διδακτός, διδακτικός." In *Theological Dictionary of the*
Heinrich   *New Testament,* 2:135-65. Edited by Gerhard Kittel. 10 vols.
1964   Grand Rapids, Mich.: Eerdmans.

1965   "κλαίω, κλαυθμός." In *Theological Dictionary of the New Testament,* 3:722-26. Edited by Gerhard Kittel. 10 vols. Grand Rapids, Mich.: Eerdmans.

1972   "ὑπηρέτης, ὑπηρετέω." In *Theological Dictionary of the New Testament,* 8:530-44. Edited by Gerhard Kittel and Gerhard Friedrich. 10 vols. Grand Rapids, Mich.: Eerdmans.

Riesenfeld, Harald
1949   "Ἐμβολεύειν-ἐντος." *Nuntius* 2:11-12.

1972   "τηρέω κτλ." In *Theological Dictionary of the New Testament,* 8:140-51. Edited by Gerhard Kittel and Gerhard Friedrich. 10 vols. Grand Rapids, Mich.: Eerdmans.

Safrai, S., and
M. Stern, eds.
1974   *The Jewish People in the First Century: Historical Geography, Political History, Social, Cultural and Religious Life and Institutions.* 2 vols. Philadelphia: Fortress.

Sanders, E. P.
   1985   *Jesus and Judaism.* Philadelphia: Fortress.

Sasse, Hermann
   1965   "κοσμέω κτλ." In *Theological Dictionary of the New Testament,* 3:867-98. Edited by Gerhard Kittel. 10 vols. Grand Rapids, Mich.: Eerdmans.

Schmitz, Otto,
  and Gustav Stählin
   1967   "παρακαλέω, παράκλησις." In *Theological Dictionary of the New Testament,* 5:788-93. Edited by Gerhard Kittel and Gerhard Friedrich. 10 vols. Grand Rapids, Mich.: Eerdmans.

Schneider, Gerhard
   1977   *Das Evangelium nach Lukas.* 2 vols. Ökumenischer Taschenbuch-Kommentar zum Neuen Testament 3. Gütersloh, Germany: Gütersloher Verlags haus.

Schneider,
  Johannes
   1964a   "βάσανος κτλ." In *Theological Dictionary of the New Testament,* 1:561-63. Edited by Gerhard Kittel. 10 vols. Grand Rapids, Mich.: Eerdmans.

   1964b   "ἔρχομαι κτλ." In *Theological Dictionary of the New Testament,* 2:666-84. Edited by Gerhard Kittel. 10 vols. Grand Rapids, Mich.: Eerdmans.

   1967   "ζύλον." In *Theological Dictionary of the New Testament,* 5:37-41. Edited by Gerhard Kittel and Gerhard Friedrich. 10 vols. Grand Rapids, Mich.: Eerdmans.

   1971   "σταυρός κτλ." In *Theological Dictionary of the New Testament,* 7:572-84. Edited by Gerhard Kittel and Gerhard Friedrich. 10 vols. Grand Rapids, Mich.: Eerdmans.

Schoedel,
  William R.
   1972   "Parables in the Gospel of Thomas: Oral Tradition or Gnostic Exegesis?" *Concordia Theological Monthly* 43:548-60.

Schrenk, Gottlob
   1964a   "βίβλος, βιβλίον." In *Theological Dictionary of the New Testament,* 1:615-20. Edited by Gerhard Kittel. 10 vols. Grand Rapids, Mich.: Eerdmans.

1964b	"εὐδοκέω, εὐδοκία." In *Theological Dictionary of the New Testament*, 2:738-51. Edited by Gerhard Kittel. 10 vols. Grand Rapids, Mich.: Eerdmans.

Schürer, Emil
1973	*The History of the Jewish People in the Age of Jesus Christ (175 B.C.-A.D. 135)*. Rev. ed. Edited by Geza Vermes, Fergis Millar and Matthew Black. Edinburgh: T & T Clark.

Schürmann, Heinz
1951	"Lk 22,19b-20 als ursprüngliche Textüberlieferung." *Biblica* 32:364-92, 522-41.

1969	*Das Lukasevangelium*. Herders theologischer Kommentar zum Neuen Testament 3. Erster Teil. Freiberg, Germany: Herder.

Schweizer, Eduard
1974	"ψυχή κτλ." In *Theological Dictionary of the New Testament*, 9:637-56. Edited by Gerhard Kittel and Gerhard Friedrich. 10 vols. Grand Rapids, Mich.: Eerdmans.

1984	*The Good News According to Luke*. Translated by David E. Greer. Atlanta: John Knox.

Sherwin-White, A. N.
1963	*Roman Society and Roman Law in the New Testament*. Grand Rapids, Mich.: Baker Book House.

Sloan, Robert B., Jr.
1977	*The Favorable Year of the Lord: A Study of Jubilee Theology in the Gospel of Luke*. Austin, Tex.: Schola.

Smith, M.
1971	"Zealots and Sicarii: Their Origin and Relation." *Harvard Theological Review* 64:1-19.

Snodgrass, Klyne
1974	"The Parable of the Wicked Husbandmen: Is the Gospel of Thomas Version the Original?" *New Testament Studies* 21:142-44.

Stählin, Gustav
1965	"κοπετός κτλ." In *Theological Dictionary of the New Testament*, 3:830-60. Edited by Gerhard Kittel. 10 vols. Grand Rapids, Mich.: Eerdmans.

1967	"ξένος κτλ." In *Theological Dictionary of the New Testament*, 5:1-36. Edited by Gerhard Kittel and Gerhard Friedrich. 10 vols. Grand Rapids, Mich.: Eerdmans.

1971   "σκάνδαλον, σκανδαλίζω." In *Theological Dictionary of the
               New Testament,* 7:339-58. Edited by Gerhard Kittel and
               Gerhard Friedrich. 10 vols. Grand Rapids, Mich.: Eerdmans.

1972   "τύπτω." In *Theological Dictionary of the New Testament,*
               8:260-69. Edited by Gerhard Kittel and Gerhard Friedrich. 10
               vols. Grand Rapids, Mich.: Eerdmans.

1974a   "φιλέω κτλ." In *Theological Dictionary of the New
               Testament,* 9:113-71. Edited by Gerhard Kittel and Gerhard
               Friedrich. 10 vols. Grand Rapids, Mich.: Eerdmans.

1974b   "χήρα." In *Theological Dictionary of the New Testament,*
               9:440-65. Edited by Gerhard Kittel and Gerhard Friedrich. 10
               vols. Grand Rapids, Mich.: Eerdmans.

Stanley, David M.
1980   *Jesus in Gethsemene.* New York: Paulist.

Stein, Robert H.
1992   *Luke.* New American Commentary 24. Nashville: Broadman.

Sterling, Gregory
1991   *Historiography and Self-Definition: Josephos, Luke-Acts and
               Apologetic Historiography.* Supplements to *Novum
               Testamentum* 64. Leiden: E. J. Brill.

Strack, Hermann L.,
and Paul Billerbeck
1926   *Kommentar zum Neuen Testament aus Talmud und
               Midrasch.* 6 vols. Munich: C. H. Beck.

Strathmann, H.
1967   "μάρτυς κτλ." In *Theological Dictionary of the New
               Testament,* 4:474-514. Edited by Gerhard Kittel. 10 vols.
               Grand Rapids, Mich.: Eerdmans.

Sylva, Dennis D.
1986   "The Temple Curtain and Jesus' Death in the Gospel of
               Luke." *Journal of Biblical Literature* 105:239-50.

Tannehill, Robert C.
1986   *The Narrative Unity of Luke-Acts: A Literary Interpretation.*
               Vol. 1. Foundations and Facets: New Testament. Philadel-
               phia: Fortress.

Theissen, Gerd
1991   *The Gospels in Context: Social and Political History in the
               Synoptic Tradition.* Translated by L. Maloney. Minneapolis:
               Fortress.

Thrall, Margaret
1970   "Elijah and Moses in Mark's Account of the Transfiguration."
            New Testament Studies 16:305-17.

Tiede, David L.
1980   *Prophecy and History in Luke-Acts.* Philadelphia: Fortress.

1988   *Luke.* Augsburg Commentary on the New Testament.
            Minneapolis: Augsburg.

Traub, Helmut
1967   "οὐρανός κτλ." In *Theological Dictionary of the New
            Testament,* 5:509-43. Edited by Gerhard Kittel and Gerhard
            Friedrich. 10 vols. Grand Rapids, Mich.: Eerdmans.

Tuckett,
  Christopher M.
1983   *The Messianic Secret.* Issues in Religion and Theology 1.
            Philadelphia: Fortress.

Tyson, Joseph B.
1992   *Images of Judaism in Luke-Acts.* Columbia: University of
            South Carolina Press.

van der Loos,
  Hendrik
1965   *The Miracles of Jesus.* Supplements to *Novum Testamentum*
            9. Leiden: E. J. Brill.

Vielhauer, Philipp
1966   "On the 'Paulinism' of Acts." *Studies in Luke-Acts.* Edited by
            L. Keck and J. Martyn. London: SPCK.

von Rad, Gerhard
1964   "εἰρήνη." In *Theological Dictionary of the New Testament,*
            2:402-6. Edited by Gerhard Kittel. 10 vols. Grand Rapids,
            Mich.: Eerdmans.

Wachsmann, S.
1988   "The Galilee Boat: 2,000 Year Old Hull Recovered Intact."
            Biblical Archaeology Review 14:18-33.

Wall, Robert
1989   "Martha and Mary (Luke 10:38-42) in the Context of a Chris-
            tian Deuteronomy." *Journal for the Study of the New
            Testament* 39:19-35.

Weiss, Hans-
  Friedrich
1974   "Φαρισαῖος." In *Theological Dictionary of the New Testa-
            ment,* 9:35-48. Edited by Gerhard Kittel and Gerhard Fried-
            rich. 10 vols. Grand Rapids, Mich.: Eerdmans.

Wenham, David
1984   *The Rediscovery of Jesus' Eschatological Discourse.* Gospel
              Perspectives 4. Sheffield, U.K.: JSOT Press.

Wenham, John W.
1984   *Easter Enigma.* Grand Rapids, Mich.: Zondervan.

Wikgren, A.
1950   "*ΕΝΤΟΣ.*" *Nuntius* 4:27-28.

Wilkinson, J.
1977   "The Case of the Bent Woman in Luke 13:10-17."
              Evangelical Quarterly 49:195-205.

Windisch, Hans
1964   "ἀσπάζομαι κτλ." In *Theological Dictionary of the New
              Testament,* 1:496-502. Edited by Gerhard Kittel. 10 vols.
              Grand Rapids, Mich.: Eerdmans.

Winter, Paul
1961   *On the Trial of Jesus.* Studia Judaica, Forschungen zur
              Wissenschaft des Judentums 1. Berlin: Walter de Gruyter.

Witherington,
  Ben, III
1990   *The Christology of Jesus.* Philadelphia: Fortress.